CANADIAN LAW

AN INTRODUCTION

SIXTH EDITION

NEIL BOYD

SIMON FRASER UNIVERSITY

NELSON

NELSON

Canadian Law: An Introduction, Sixth Edition

by Neil Boyd

**Vice President, Editorial
Higher Education:**
Anne Williams

Publisher:
Maya Castle

Marketing Manager:
Terry Fedorkiw

Developmental Editor:
Jessica Freedman

Permissions Researcher:
Melody Tolson

Production Project Manager:
Christine Gilbert

Production Service:
Cenveo Publisher Services

Copy Editor:
Kelli Howey

Proofreader:
Pushpa

Indexer:
BIM Indexing Services

Design Director:
Ken Phipps

Managing Designer:
Franca Amore

Interior Design:
Jennifer Stimson

Cover Design:
Jennifer Stimson

Cover Image:
© Olaf Hirschberg/Corbis

Compositor:
Cenveo Publisher Services

**Library and Archives Canada
Cataloguing in Publication Data**

Boyd, Neil, 1951-, author
   Canadian law: an introduction /
Neil Boyd. — Sixth edition.

Includes bibliographical references
and index.
ISBN 978-0-17-653169-0 (pbk.)

1. Law—Canada—Textbooks. I. Title.

KE444.B69 2014   349.71
C2014-903362-1
KF385.ZA4B69 2014

ISBN-13: 978-0-17-653169-0
ISBN-10: 0-17-653169-6

To all my students, past, present, and future

Brief Contents

CONTENTS

PREFACE

This text has been in development through 15 years and now six editions. Originally, after teaching a university-level introductory law course for 20 years, I found that I was uncomfortable with the existing learning materials. No text seemed to combine the basic building blocks of Canada's system of public law with a relatively broad social analysis of that system, giving the reader competing perspectives on the role of law, sources of law, the significance of the *Canadian Charter of Rights and Freedoms,* the value of statutory interpretation, criminal law, family law, administrative law, and torts.

The purpose of this book in its sixth edition remains consistent with the goals of the first edition: to introduce Canadian public law to college and university students, using specific case law to prompt debate and discussion. Law is a changing human construction, and it is my hope to interest students in the principles, powers, and privileges that law conveys. In its idealized form, law can be conceptualized either as the instrument of democracy or as a force to be employed, in axiomatic fashion, against those without the power to resist. In practical terms, law is both a democratic institution and an instrument of control or oppression, depending on the specific historical context and the lens that one adopts in the study of law. And that mix of critical values, changing culture, and conflict is what makes this enterprise both interesting and worth the effort.

This text is designed to introduce students to Canadian law: first, to its role and origins; second, to the building blocks of the system: statutory interpretation, the Constitution, the courts, and the legal profession; and third, to areas of substantive law and their fundamental principles: tort law, family law, administrative law, and criminal law.

Each chapter concludes with Web links, discussion questions, and a listing of references and further readings, all of which are also available on the Student Companion site at http://www.nelson.com/canadianlaw6e. Case law is used to highlight competing perspectives, as well as to provide teachers and students with a focus for further analysis and debate. This sixth edition contains an appendix, with the full text of the *Canadian Charter of Rights and Freedoms,* and a glossary. Terms defined in the glossary are in bold at their first relevant occurrence in the text. In teaching introductory law, I have found that ancillary material comprising both current judicial decisions and critical analyses, updated each semester, is a useful addition to any course text.

Part 1, Role and Origin, comprises three chapters. Chapter 1 sketches the different perspectives on the role of law in society, and explores the strengths and weaknesses of each perspective. Chapter 2 considers legal history and the question of how to understand sources of law in both specific and general contexts. Chapter 3 introduces what may be the primary task of the lawyer: statutory interpretation. The rules of interpretation and construction are canvassed and questioned, and then applied to specific sets of facts.

Part 2, Building Blocks of the Canadian Legal System, also contains three chapters. Chapter 4 presents the most critical building blocks of Canadian law: the *Constitution Act, 1982* and its fusion of the *British North America Act, 1867* and the *Canadian Charter of Rights and Freedoms*. Chapter 5 is concerned with the Canadian court structure, its reform over time, and the functions and purposes of the different levels of courts. Chapter 6 focuses on the legal profession and the task of legal education: What is the essence of education about law? What are the priorities of the law school curriculum, and how does law school relate to the legal profession? What standards of conduct do we expect from lawyers, prosecutors, and judges?

Part 3, Substantive Law, consists of four chapters. Chapter 7 sets out the key principles of tort law, the legal mechanism for the remedy of private wrongs. Intentional torts and torts of negligence are described, with excerpts from case law highlighting relevant principles and issues in dispute. Chapter 8 examines family law, focusing on the significant changes to the *Divorce Act* and to related provincial legislation over the past 40 plus years. The social meanings of these changes are explored, and the major provisions of the *Divorce Act* are set out; legal provisions relating to same-sex marriage, matrimonial property, spousal support, and child custody are also discussed. Chapter 9 sets out the key principles of administrative law, charting the onus that the state has placed upon itself in relation to the conduct of its affairs. Finally, Chapter 10 surveys the often-discussed terrain of criminal law: the principles of *mens rea* and *actus reus,* the possible defences to criminal charges, and the principles to be employed in sentencing a guilty person.

Law is, in most important respects, a site of political, economic, and social conflict and debate. At the end of the day, this book will have accomplished its purpose if students see law as entirely human, changeable, and deserving of both institutional respect and continual criticism—as something in which we all have a stake and which we can influence.

New to the Sixth Edition

Throughout the sixth edition you will find that the text has been updated to reflect critical changes in legislation and judicial decision making. In some chapters I have changed a number of examples, so as to make them more current. For example, in the chapter on the legal profession, in discussing matters of discipline of lawyers I have taken cases decided within the past few years, replacing decisions from almost a decade ago. In every chapter I have also made some changes to the questions for discussion that flow from the chapter's content. What follows are the most critical and significant changes from each of the 10 chapters.

CHAPTER 1

- Incorporation of the recent 2013 Supreme Court decision *Canada v. Bedford* (re: prostitution) as the key example in explaining different perspectives on law
- Addition of a provision from the *Safe Streets and Communities Act* of 2012, again with relevance to the existing range of perspectives on law

CHAPTER 2

- Replaced and updated introductory quotes
- Revised case example (replacing the 2008 judgment in *Beatty* with the 2012 judgment of the Supreme Court in *Ipeelee* and *Ladue*)
- Updated current state of the law in the section dealing with the history of the *Narcotic Control Act* and the *Controlled Drugs and Substances Act*

CHAPTER 3

- Replacement of introductory case on statutory interpretation, *New Brunswick Human Rights Commission,* with a more contemporary 2012 decision of the Supreme Court of Canada, *R. v. Boudreault*

CHAPTER 4

- Updated throughout where necessary, using 2013 and 2014 figures, and some changes in relevant case law

CHAPTER 5

- Updated throughout where necessary, using 2013 and 2014 figures, and noting jurisdictional changes where relevant

CHAPTER 6

- Updated chapter introduction and updated 2013–2014 content throughout, notably in relation to the discipline of lawyers by provincial Law Societies

CHAPTER 7

- Replaced the 1986 decision in *John Deere* with a 2011 decision, *More v. Bauer Nike Hockey Inc.*
- Updated the readings to reflect more contemporary texts

CHAPTER 8

- New opening to the chapter for discussion of issues within family law
- Updates to relevant case law, replacement of older cases with more recent decisions

CHAPTER 9

- New opening extract
- Replacement of the *St. Catharines* case with two significant Supreme Court decisions dealing with the nature of judicial review

CHAPTER 10

- Updated the introduction to juxtapose the views of Winston Churchill and Stephen Harper
- Updated 2013–2014 content throughout
- New cases regarding the defences of intoxication and mistake of fact

SUPPLEMENTARY MATERIAL

ABOUT THE NELSON EDUCATION TEACHING ADVANTAGE (NETA)

The **Nelson Education Teaching Advantage (NETA)** program delivers research-based instructor resources that promote student engagement and higher-order thinking to enable the success of Canadian students and educators. To ensure the high quality of these materials, all Nelson ancillaries have been professionally copy-edited.

Be sure to visit Nelson Education's **Inspired Instruction** website at http://www.nelson.com/inspired/ to find out more about NETA. Don't miss the testimonials of instructors who have used NETA supplements and seen student engagement increase!

Assessing Your Students: *NETA Assessment* relates to testing materials. NETA Test Bank authors create multiple-choice questions that reflect research-based best practices for constructing effective questions and testing not just recall but also higher-order thinking. Our guidelines were developed by David DiBattista, psychology professor at Brock University and 3M National Teaching Fellow, whose research has focused on multiple-choice testing. All Test Bank authors receive training at workshops conducted by Prof. DiBattista, as do the copy-editors assigned to each Test Bank. A copy of *Multiple Choice Tests: Getting Beyond Remembering,* Prof. DiBattista's guide to writing effective tests, is included with every Nelson Test Bank.

INSTRUCTOR RESOURCES

NETA Test Bank: This resource was written by Paul Wintemute, Niagara College. It includes approximately 200 multiple-choice questions written according to NETA guidelines for effective construction and development of higher-order questions. Also included are approximately 200 true and false questions and 70 essay questions.

The testbank can be found on the Instructor Companion Site at http://www.nelson.com/canadianlaw6e.

Acknowledgments

I would like to thank my publishers for their continuing support and enthusiasm for this project. I would particularly like to thank my editor, Jessica Freedman, for her work on this edition, Maya Castle, the publisher of Nelson Education, Terry Fedorkiw, Marketing Manager, and Christine Gilbert, Production Project Manager.

My legal colleagues at Simon Fraser University have also been generous in their insights and contributions: thanks go particularly to David MacAlister and Simon Verdun-Jones. I would also like to thank my wife, Isabel Otter, for her continuing support of this and other projects.

ABOUT THE AUTHOR

Carol Thorbes

Neil Boyd is a Professor and Director of the School of Criminology at Simon Fraser University, educated in psychology and law. He is the author of seven books, many government and agency reports, and academic articles. He is a frequent media commentator on subjects related to criminology and has received numerous awards, including Honorary Director, B.C. Civil Liberties Association; the President's Award for Contributions to the Media and Public Relations, Simon Fraser University; and the George Ryga Award for Social Awareness in Literature.

PART 1
Role and Origin

CHAPTER 1

THE ROLE OF LAW: WHAT IS THE RELEVANCE AND PURPOSE OF OUR LEGAL SYSTEM?

The life of the law has not been logic; it has been experience.... The law embodies the story of a nation's development through many centuries and it cannot be dealt with as if it contained only the axioms and corollaries of a book of mathematics.

(Oliver Wendell Holmes, *The Common Law*, 1881)

So the conflict between natural law and positivism tends to become a dispute as to whether the authority of a legal system as a whole can only be understood and judged in relation to some specific moral purpose (such as promoting the common good) for which all legal systems exist. In general, the answer of natural lawyers is yes, and of positivists, no.

(Roger Cotterrell, *Comparative Jurisprudence*)

The positivist thesis does not say that law's merits are unintelligible, unimportant, or peripheral to the philosophy of law. It says that they do not determine whether laws or legal systems exist. Whether a society has a legal system depends on the presence of certain structures of governance, not on the extent to which it satisfies ideals of justice, democracy, or the rule of law.

(*Stanford Encyclopedia of Philosophy*)

What are these terms—positivism and natural law? And what of Oliver Wendell Holmes' famous quote above, introducing the notion of legal realism, a concept now described by the distinguished legal scholar Brian Leiter as "the correct descriptive account of appellate decision-making"?[1] Have the practical and reality-based advantages of a legal realist perspective simply eclipsed long-standing debates between positivist and natural law perspectives?

And, perhaps more important for you as a student, how do these apparently abstract notions allow you to understand the relevance and purpose of our legal system? In large measure, my task in this first chapter is to try to give meaning to these abstract terms and others—to give you a sense of the intellectual excitement embedded within competing perspectives on law, to explain to you why these apparently dry concepts are not only important, but also quite interesting and relevant to everyday life.

During the past decade Canadian courts and legislatures have had to respond to a number of morally and politically contentious issues; we will examine two particularly notable instances of response, one a decision of the Supreme Court of Canada in December of 2013, and the other, recent federal legislation—the *Safe Streets and Communities Act*—passed by the federal government in March of 2012.[2]

In *Canada (Attorney General) v. Bedford,* the Supreme Court of Canada was asked to rule on the legitimacy of Canadian criminal laws that prohibit solicitations for sex, the keeping of a "common bawdy house," and "living on the avails" of prostitution. Three women, former sex workers, with their cases bolstered by a significant amount of empirical evidence, argued that these laws violate their right to security of the person under section 7 of the *Charter of Rights and Freedoms* by making an already risky activity—street prostitution—considerably more dangerous. The laws prevent sex workers from using indoor locations and from setting up working relationships with individuals such as drivers, receptionists, and bodyguards, all of whom could help to reduce the risk of violence. Put differently, criminalization of the sex trade negatively impacts street prostitutes, the most vulnerable of sex trade workers, exposing them to physical and sexual abuse and a significant risk of culpable homicide.

The Supreme Court of Canada, in its unanimous decision in December of 2013, gave the federal government one year to fix the weaknesses identified within the law—to address, through legislation or otherwise, the harms that these laws impose on those involved in the industry. The Chief Justice noted in her decision, "Parliament has the power to regulate against nuisances, but not at the cost of the health, safety and lives of prostitutes." Reactions were mixed, with Michelle Rempel, a Minister of State within the federal government, noting, "Can't help but feel our judiciary struck a blow to women's safety and equality this morning. We aren't a commodity to be bought or sold."[3] At the same time, University of Ottawa law professor Carissima Mathen wrote in an op-ed, "For performing its duty, the Court deserves our thanks. But it is deeply unfortunate that this moment has taken 30 years to manifest, at an incalculable human cost, because the state chose to do nothing. Parliament now has the opportunity to craft a humane law to deal with the legitimate social problems caused by the sex trade. In doing so, it must keep those who are most marginalized front and centre."[4]

In March of 2012 the federal government passed the *Safe Streets and Communities Act,* legislation that focused on a substantial range of changes to existing criminal law—most notably, introducing mandatory minimum terms of imprisonment for child exploitation and for the production and distribution of various illegal drugs; enshrining victim participation in the process of releasing offenders; and eliminating the possibility of pardons for certain offenders.

The most contentious of these changes was probably the mandatory minimum term of imprisonment to be applied to individuals who grow more than five marijuana plants—six months in jail, irrespective of whether the grower was simply producing his or her own supply, and irrespective of whether the marijuana was actually commercially distributed. The Conservative government of Stephen Harper argued that the legislation was critical, targeting organized crime by imposing tougher sentences for the production and distribution of illegal drugs. The Canadian Bar Association argued against the legislation, noting that it would "add complexity to existing sentencing principles and increase court time required for sentencing hearings ... (it) would often conflict with existing common law and statutory principles of sentencing, and sentences could become excessive, harsh and unfair in some cases."[5] Others noted a series of polls indicating that almost two-thirds of Canadians are supportive of either decriminalization or taxation and regulation of marijuana; they argued that the government was imposing its own relatively extreme and narrow views on the majority of Canadians.

In this chapter we will examine various perspectives or theories—grand designs for the role of law in Canadian society. And we shall then see how these various perspectives can be linked to such pragmatic issues as those noted above: analysis of the value and utility of criminal prohibitions against offences related to prostitution, and consideration of the value and utility of mandatory minimum sentences for the production of cannabis.

INDIVIDUAL PERSPECTIVES ON THE LAW

Law is a vitally important force; it is the skeleton that structures our economic, social, and political lives. It is also a barometer of the nation's view of human relations, whether in the realm of criminal law, taxation, or constitutional law. It is as difficult to conceive of complex societies without law as it is to conceive of human beings without communication. Our attitudes toward law—and the laws that we create—define us as citizens of our society, politically, economically, and morally.

If, for example, we turn to Canada's *Income Tax Act,* the *Criminal Code,* and the *Canadian Charter of Rights and Freedoms,* we find legal structures that have, over time, defined and re-defined, among other things, the fair taxation of earned income, the moral legitimacy of physician-assisted suicide, and the political legitimacy of preferential treatment for people who are said to be disadvantaged.

Now let us consider three questions with roots in these economic, moral, and political realms: (1) Should high-income earners be more highly taxed than low-income earners? (2) Should physicians be able to assist in suicide without criminal sanction? (3) Should persons with mental disabilities be given preferential treatment in certain kinds of employment?

All of us will have opinions on these questions as well as justifications for our responses. For the law is a malleable human creation, which both reflects the movements of political actors and changing social mores, and influences those actors and mores. Our individual perceptions of **justice** and **injustice** define our relationship as citizens to the state. We see ourselves as more and less oriented to protection of individual liberty within each of these realms--and we may define what we mean by individual liberty quite differently in each of these circumstances.

THEORETICAL PERSPECTIVES ON THE LAW

Theoreticians of law have staked out territories according to their perceptions of the law; there are positivists, natural lawyers, legal realists, Marxists, critical legalists, feminists, anarchists, and libertarians, among others. We will examine the most dominant, or perhaps the more traditional, of these perspectives first, using the three questions about income taxation, assisted suicide, and preferential treatment in employment to highlight the central ideas of each perspective.

But first, consider the following five definitions of the meaning of law within our culture. The perspectives that are outlined following these definitions—the positivist, natural law, legal realist, Marxist, critical legalist, feminist, anarchist, and libertarian points of view—go beyond this first task of description to make normative arguments about the moral, economic, and political objectives of the legal process. But note, as well, that the definitions that follow also have points of view embedded within them. Consider, for example, Cheffins and Tucker's point that law is simply a subdivision of a larger political process, or Waddam's quite sensible suggestion that the law exists to maintain a delicate balance between the rights of the individual and the rights of the society. Is this not a helpful way of understanding the dilemmas posed above, in relation to either controlling prostitution or cannabis use and distribution?

> "Law is a set of rules which are generally obeyed and enforced within a politically organized society." (Professor Philip James, *Introduction to English Law*)
>
> "Law is a rule established in a community by authority or custom; a body of such rules; the controlling influence of or obedience to this; the subject or study of such rules."* (*The Oxford Reference Dictionary*)
>
> "Law ... is that part of the overall process of political decision making which has achieved somewhat more technical, more obvious, and more clearly defined ground rules than other aspects of politics. It is still, however, an integral subdivision of the overall political process." (Cheffins and Tucker, *The Constitutional Process in Canada*)
>
> "Law in any society is the society's attempt to resolve the most basic of human tensions, that between the needs of the person as an individual, and her needs as a member of a community. The law is the knife edge on which the delicate balance is maintained between the individual on the one hand, and the society on the other." (Professor S.M. Waddams, *Introduction to the Study of Law*)

The Oxford Reference Dictionary, edited by Joyce M. Hawkins, Clarendon Press, Oxford, 1986, Pg. 467.

"Law is one of the devices by means of which men can reconcile their actual activities and behaviour with the ideal principles that they have come to accept, and can do it in a way that is not too painful or revolting to their sensibilities and in a way which allows ordered (which is to say predictable) social life to continue." (Paul Bohannan, "Law and Legal Institutions," in *The Sociology of Law* edited by William Evan)

TRADITIONAL THEORIES OF THE ROLE OF LAW

POSITIVISM AND THE POSITIVIST RESPONSE

Positivism is defined by *The Oxford Reference Dictionary* as "the theory that laws are to be understood as social rules, valid because they are enacted by 'the **sovereign**' or derive logically from existing decisions, and that ideal or moral considerations (e.g., that a rule is unjust) should not limit the scope or operation of the law."

Accordingly, positivism is a systematization of the law, seeking precision by what is apparently an almost mechanical analysis of law as a matter of logic and interpretation; the values that lie behind the law can only muddy a clear vision of the legal process. In studying the scope or operation of the law, positivists seek quantitative and qualitative facts—to explain how the "machine" works.

Hence, for legal positivists, the answers to the three questions above regarding taxation, assisted suicide, and preferential treatment in employment are straightforward: yes, supportable if this is the law; no, not supportable if it is not the law. The first question is, for example, defined by analyzing the *Income Tax Act*. As students and practitioners of the law, positivists are not concerned with its moral content. As citizens, they may have strong feelings about the direction that further amendments to law should take, but these concerns do not—and, they would argue, should not—enter legal analysis or legal practice.

Positivism essentially states that adherence to a just legal process is more important than the specifics of law, for these specifics will necessarily vary across time and space. The student of law should not be misled into thinking that those who espouse support for a positivist framework are inherently amoral or motivated by a desire to defer to the status quo. To the contrary, positivists argue passionately for a legal process that protects liberty and democratic institutions and prevents the abuse of political power. Consider, for example, the danger posed by those ideologues who would disband courts, legislatures, and burdens of proof without recourse to legal process, all in the name of their own version of social justice. Simply put, the process of law is seen as more important than the specific content of law.

Positivists draw a firm line between the practice of law and the practice of politics. They regard the House of Commons and the legislative assemblies of the provinces as the proper places for debate—in the case above, about appropriate levels of taxation, physician-assisted suicide, or differential treatment for those with mental disabilities.

In this world-view, the task of lawyers, judges, or students of the law is technical and, accordingly, much more circumscribed. The advantage of creating this dichotomy between the content of law and the content of politics is said to be increased certainty, stability, and predictability. Law is the outcome of the political process, not a part of it. For example, if individual views of the morality of economic relations were to dominate, there would be no consistent application of the law, only an anarchic distribution of economic resources.

Positivism is rooted in the British doctrine of parliamentary supremacy. This doctrine, described by constitutional scholars Dicey and Wade, dictates that Parliament is supreme: Parliament can make or unmake any law, and no person or body shall override or set aside its legislation. Parliamentary supremacy originated as a response to the arbitrary edicts of Britain's monarchical system of government; it reserves the practice of lawmaking—and the resolution of disputes about the content of those laws—to the political process. The task of the legalist is, at its most expansive, to interpret the intentions of lawmakers, not to make moral choices. Law is a valid set of rules, enforced through a system of economic and social sanctions. It is vital that the rules be applied correctly, but the morality of the law need not be subjected to scrutiny—that is the role of the legislature. This is a good point to pause and ask about the *Charter of Rights and Freedoms* and its avowedly moral content. Is it not the point of the *Charter* to subject law to timeless moral values, hence subverting positivism?

Positivism is also rooted in the notion of a **social contract**—that is, law ties individuals to the collective through a binding, democratically constructed agreement. Democratic elections are expressions of the will of the people, and those who are successful in these elections are given the power to create laws. These laws then become binding and enforceable, for they flow from the will of the people. According to this view, the state, or the government of the day, is an expression of the sovereignty of the people who live within it.

For the nineteenth-century legal philosopher John Austin, all human laws had to conform to God-given laws, an assertion that twentieth-century legal philosopher H.L.A. Hart rejected as a "confusion." Hart suggested that this claim confuses law as it is and "law as morality would require it to be." "For him," Hart writes of Austin, "it must be remembered, the fundamental principles of morality were God's commands."[6]

H.L.A. Hart viewed law as a secular construction, although, like Austin, he believed that law and morality must be severed for purposes of legal practice and legal analysis. He was not, however, blind to its injustices:

> The step from the simple form of society, where primary rules of obligation are the only means of social control, into the legal world with its centrally organized legislature, courts, officials, and sanctions brings its solid gains at a certain cost. The gains are those of adaptability to change, certainty, and efficiency, and these are immense; the cost is the risk that the centrally organized power may well be used for the oppression of numbers with whose support it can dispense.[7]

In his best-known book, *The Concept of Law,* Hart argued that equating the validity of law with its morality will blind us to critical moral principles. What of the law that should now apply to German informers during the Nazi occupation, he asked. Hart conceded that the laws applying at the time were monstrous and immoral, but argued that "morality may also demand that the state should punish only those who, in doing evil, did what the state at the time forbade. This is the principle of **nulla poena sine lege**."[8]

The Latin maxim quoted by Hart dictates that "there shall be no penalty without a valid law," a principled limitation on the power of the state to punish. In Hart's view, should the law's validity be analytically synonymous with the law's morality, retroactive punishment will be disguised as ordinary punishment. For Hart, while in the simple positivist doctrine "morally iniquitous rules may still be law," positivism also "offers no disguise for the choice between evils which, in extreme circumstances, may have to be made."[9] The principle of "no penalty without a valid law" does not allow for repressive, retroactive law. However, this principle can comprehend retroactive law that benefits those touched by its imposition. For example, the Supreme Court of Germany ruled that Nazi law is not valid for those who suffered under its racist oppression. At the same time, however, those enforcing Nazi law in good faith (with a few exceptions) cannot be punished, because of the principle "no penalty without a valid law."

Positivists are conservative in the sense that they view law as a valid set of rules. However, this does not mean that positivists adhere to conservative positions on economic, moral, or political issues, for the content of the law may be premised on "radical," "liberal," or "conservative" moral values. For example, the positivist response to the question of the legitimacy of physician-assisted suicide posed at the start of this discussion mirrors that of the question of legitimacy in taxation. The existing law is a valid set of rules. Since there is a prohibition of physician-assisted suicide, the practice is not legally valid; that is, it is criminally prohibited. Similarly, positivists will answer the question about persons with mental disabilities on the basis of existing law. If an employer decides to give preference to such candidates in a hiring competition, this decision will be valid as long as the employer has, in terms of its process, the legal power to insist upon such a preference.

NATURAL LAW AND THE NATURAL LAW RESPONSE

The natural law perspective is diametrically opposed to positivism. While positivists insist upon a strict separation of law and morality, the adherents of natural law insist on a clear link between law and morality. The essence of the natural law perspective is **lex iniusta non est lex**: an unjust law is no law at all.

Natural law has a longer history than positivism; it can be traced through more than 2500 years of Western development, from Plato, Socrates, and Aristotle to Hobbes,

Spinoza, and Rousseau. Until the twentieth century, natural law theory was generally conceived to be based upon Christian theology or Judeo-Christian values. Those who believed in this necessary coincidence of morality and law argued that there are God-given moral values that must inform the operation and study of law and legality. Unlike Austin and the positivists, however, the natural lawyers could not be sure that God-given moral values would always find expression in law. There are also many variations of this kind of natural law: Christian law, Islamic law, Sikh law, and so on.

In this century, the secular basis of natural law has become more dominant, but the emphasis on determining moral values and principles remains. Philosopher David Lloyd explains, "We have a feeling of discontent with justice based on positive law alone, and strenuously desire to demonstrate that there are objective moral values which can be given a positive content."[10] However, the lack of clarity in such a perspective on law was well captured by the late law professor Gerald Gall: "The problem, of course, with natural law is defining the particular nature of the natural law to which [to] conform. The danger is that anyone can invoke his version of the natural law in order to suit his purposes."[11]

If law and morality are always to be coincident, which law and which morality are to prevail? In a largely secular society such as contemporary Canada, it is no answer to assert that "God's will must prevail." Even organized religions do not agree on important social issues. Muslims, Seventh-day Adventists, Jehovah's Witnesses, Hindus, Anglicans, Catholics, Jews, and Unitarians will provide different responses to the question of the morality of a given law—and there will often be additional differences of opinion, even within these categories of belief. And for those whose beliefs are based on foundations other than religion, or for non-religious citizens, the proper coincidence of law and morality is a purely secular matter.

Legal theorist Roger Cotterrell has suggested that, as a perspective on law, natural law is virtually dead, eclipsed first by positivism and later by realist and Marxist conceptions. His argument is that the utility of a natural law approach has been limited because legal doctrine has become increasingly a compromise among diverse interests within the population of a given nation-state. It is difficult to discern a moral soul within such a product of conflict and compromise. Moreover, law is used, within specific geographic and temporal contexts, to create a certain kind of social order. What guides the operation of the law are not timeless moral principles, but time-specific pragmatism. The issue for lawmakers is less "what is moral" than "what works" in a specific time and place. According to Cotterrell,

> The problem is that even if there *are* universal principles of natural law, they may not offer a convincing guide or grounding for complex, highly technical and ever-changing modern law. After all, legal positivism does not deny that the substance of law can be subject to moral criticism. The issue is not whether law can be morally evaluated, but whether its essential character must be explained in moral terms.[12]

Nonetheless, there are many senses in which natural law remains very much alive. Both the U.S. Constitution and the *Canadian Charter of Rights and Freedoms* are statements of natural law ideals. In the latter, for instance, there is a guarantee of freedom from cruel and unusual punishment, and freedoms of conscience, religion, expression, and association. These are essentially moral precepts, having their roots in "some higher system to which mere positive law should conform."[13]

The problem for natural lawyers is to identify how natural law will be determined. For example, is the 25-year minimum sentence for first degree murder cruel and unusual punishment? If we subscribe to the tenets of natural law, do we look to the deterrent impact of the penalty, or to its inherent "justness" (i.e., the extent to which it adequately reflects community denunciation of such a crime)? Or do we seek answers in the often contradictory writings of religious or moral thinkers? Since there is no single, clear morality to guide the operation of legality, an attempt to determine natural law can be compared to the futile task of trying to nail Jell-O to the wall.

So, then, how would the adherent of the natural law perspective answer the questions on taxation, assisted suicide, and persons with disabilities, which are, after all, clearly moral questions? If resources are seen to be morally distributed, if assisted suicide is felt to be morally repugnant, if equality of treatment is considered a moral value to which all others should be subservient, then high-income earners should not be more highly taxed, physicians should never assist with suicide, and persons with disabilities should not be given preferential treatment in matters of employment. On the other hand, if resources are seen to be unfairly distributed, if assistance with suicide is seen as sometimes fair and just, if persons with disabilities are considered deserving of differential assistance, then high-income earners should be more highly taxed, assisted suicide should not be criminally sanctioned, and persons with disabilities should be given preferential treatment in employment.

In these opposing answers, we find the Achilles' heel of the natural law perspective. There is no doubt that morality is at the heart of the legal process. However, a perspective that demands a linkage between law and morality must specify the moral premises that will be operative at any specific time and place.

LEGAL REALISM AND THE REALIST RESPONSE

The legal realist movement began in the United States in the early twentieth century, primarily as a reaction to the ongoing failure of legal doctrine to predict legal outcomes in specific instances. Legal realists are often referred to as skeptics; they argue that, in order to understand the legal process, one must be aware of the political, economic, and social contexts in which law arises, changes, and persists.

Legal realists see the personality and political orientation of individual judges, community sentiments, specific economic realities, and political imperatives as all contributing to the growth of statutory law and judicial decisions. Karl Llewellyn, perhaps the most prominent of American legal realists, has noted that realism is less a philosophy of law than a method or technology for achieving a more grounded understanding of law and legal process. "There is no school of realists," Llewellyn declared in 1931. "There is no group with an official or accepted, or even with an emerging creed.... There is, however, a movement in thought and work about law."[14]

The essence of this "movement in thought and work about law" is its rejection of the idea that a specific "correct" solution will inevitably emerge from the application of formal legal doctrine and formal logic to a particular legal problem. Indeed, the realist argues that legal doctrine cannot be understood without a serious empirical study of the social, economic, and political context in which that doctrine takes shape. Legal realists may be conservative, liberal, or radical in political, economic, or moral orientation, but all advocate the view that legal doctrine alone cannot explain legal decision making. There are many senses in which **legal realism** can be seen as the natural consequence of positivism. Legal realism provides the tools for a more nuanced interpretation of the content of law, one that positivism alone appears not to speak to or easily comprehend—or incorporate within its logic.

In answering the question whether higher-income earners should be more highly taxed, realists would respond that they would need to know more about the social environment before making any decision. What social circumstances led to different forms of taxation (e.g., income, sales, corporate, capital gains) and, more specifically, to the most recent amendments to taxation law and regulation? What are the moral, political, and economic issues surrounding these amendments? In empirical terms, how are resources taxed, and why? Similarly, in responding to the questions on assisted suicide and the treatment of persons with disabilities, there will be empirical inquiry into the social, economic, and political conditions that gave rise to the current state of the law. That is, legal realists share an epistemology—a method or grounds for obtaining knowledge—but it does not follow that there is or need be a realist consensus on moral, economic, and political issues. Realists might ultimately be divided on all three questions, but they are likely to be better informed about the issues underlying the law than those who take either a positivist or a natural law perspective.

At the heart of the realist enterprise is a skeptical empiricism that creates an understanding of the law that is arguably distinct from both positivism and natural law. Llewellyn described the realist style of legal decision making as "grand style judging." He contrasted it with "the orthodox ideology," in which judicial precedents are seen as binding. In grand style judging, precedents are persuasive, but much more is involved: the reputation and approach of the judge writing the opinion, the general conceptual sense of the argument, and, most important, the possible consequences of the law under consideration. By contrast, the orthodox ideology is essentially a more limited, positivist position. It holds that difficult cases are to be decided by the rules of law alone. Policy is something to be debated by legislatures, not courts. The job of the court, as Llewellyn notes, is "to prune away those 'anomalous' cases or rules which do not fit."[15] In this process of pruning anomalies, judges are not creating new law, but discovering the meaning of existing law and clarifying the intent of the legislature.

At the time of its inception in the United States, legal realism presented a major challenge to established thinking and writing about law. Legal realists could point to the limits of the explanatory power of positivism and to the natural law perspective's poorly contoured definitions of morality. But critics of the realist school could, in turn, point to the lack of a coherent vision or morality within its regimen of skeptical empiricism. The Marxist view offered a new holy grail: a fusion of morality and science.

A MARXIST THEORY OF LAW AND THE MARXIST RESPONSE

The Oxford Reference Dictionary defines **Marxism** as "the political and economic theories of Karl Marx, especially that, as labour is basic to wealth, historical development, following scientific laws determined by **dialectical materialism**, must lead to the violent overthrow of the capitalist class.... Events would then progress toward the ideal of a classless society."*

In most important senses, it is almost absurd to speak of a Marxist analysis of law and legal order; Marxists have traditionally urged "the withering away of the state" (and hence of law and legal order). They have also typically urged what must now be seen as the hopelessly naïve notion of the "dictatorship of the proletariat."

It is difficult to define a single Marxist approach to law. Are we referring to the writings and teachings of Karl Marx? Law as practised within self-described communist states? Indeed, is a Marxist approach ultimately reducible to a basic core? There appears to be no simple or universally agreed-upon answer to these questions.

Moreover, there are those who work within a Marxist tradition, yet reject some of Marx's claims and analyses—his call for violence, the possibility or desirability of an end to contradiction, his omission of gender from his analysis, his insistence that economic power determines law, his failure to recognize the environmental need to limit production, and his lack of insight into the flexibility that capitalism would have to change itself—to counter and, at least in some ways, surmount the challenges of Marxist claims.

Marx argued that the relationship between material circumstances and human beings is dialectical in form. The economic organization of capitalism carries the seeds of its destruction. Being inherently oppressive, the distributive character of capitalism will be resisted by those who labour; it will therefore change, producing new contradictions that will require further remedy. The final result of these struggles, Marx believed, would be the "withering away" of the law; human beings would live in equality and harmony in a utopian communist state.

Capitalism has changed since Marx wrote of the contradictions of economic life in Europe and czarist Russia. Although inequality in the distributive structure of economic relations is still very much with us in Western industrialized democracies, child labour laws, trade union legitimacy, universal social assistance, and universal health care have changed the social order in Europe, and, to a more limited extent, in North America.

The Oxford Reference Dictionary, edited by Joyce M. Hawkins, Clarendon Press, Oxford, 1986, Pg. 515.

How, then, are we to assess the Marxist analysis of law? Obviously, a literal adherence to the writings of Karl Marx has limited appeal. The problems that an avowedly communist Soviet Union faced during its last years were problems that Marx could not foresee: environmental limits to production, inefficiencies of state ownership, and the apparently ceaseless continuation of enormous inequality and privilege—despite 1917 and the violent overthrow of the capitalist class.

Still, this does not mean that all elements of the Marxist view of law should be cast aside, and the perspective rejected as irrelevant. Robert Heilbroner has eloquently argued for its continued usefulness:

> A dialectical view of reality, enlarging our view of things with a tension and contradictoriness that is lacking in other philosophic perspectives, should help clarify our knowledge of the world. A materialist view of history will enrich our understanding of the past and of the present, as long as the processes of production play a powerful role in human affairs and exert such enormous influences over the stratification of society.... And socialism—the grail of Marxism—must continue to exert its influence as long as humanity suffers the unnecessary bondages imposed by its own social organization, a condition that is certain to persist for generations.[16]

How, then, would a Marxist perspective view our three questions? First, should high-income earners be more highly taxed than low-income earners? Absolutely: the labour of certain citizens is disproportionately rewarded; increased taxation of the wealthy is a mechanism to ensure that those who expend similar amounts of labour are similarly rewarded. From the Marxist perspective, the sheer magnitude of current discrepancies in financial rewards cannot be justified, even given a different time and effort typically expended in labour by the richer and poorer in American (or Canadian) society.

Critics of the Marxist insistence upon economic equality argue that there are substantive differences in individual contributions to society. In the lowest-income quintile of the population, one typically finds large numbers of people unable or unwilling to labour productively. Moreover, economic rewards have historically created incentives for inventive contributions to the common good, such as new medicines and vaccines, computers, mass transit, and global systems of communication and transportation.

Perhaps the future of resource distribution is neither nineteenth-century **laissez-faire capitalism** nor Marxist economic equality. The New England ice cream corporation Ben and Jerry's initially set out a provocative 5 to 1 ratio for the salaries of its employees. No employee of this self-avowed socially and environmentally conscious company could make more than five times the salary of any other employee. Among American families, however, there is a ratio of more than 73 to 1 between the top 1 percent of earners and the lowest 20 percent.[17]

The second question, that of physician-assisted suicide, falls outside the Marxist perspective, since the theory is economically rather than morally based. (In fairness, Marx could not easily have contemplated such a dilemma.)

Finally, the question about preferential treatment in employment for those with disabilities might well be answered positively, given the Marxist emphasis on economic equality. Although the issue arose after the time of Marx, it might be argued that while Marxist theory would ultimately produce legal remedies that give preference to disempowered minorities, it is not clear that such programs are particularly Marxist in their derivation.

CONTEMPORARY THEORIES OF THE ROLE OF LAW

THE CRITICAL LEGAL PERSPECTIVE

The critical legal studies movement arose in U.S. law schools during the late 1970s. Like the legal realist movement of the 1920s, it attracted law teachers and social scientists who had become increasingly disenchanted with current forms of legal analysis. Those first attracted to the so-called CLS movement

> were simply seeking to locate those people working either at law schools or in closely related academic settings with a certain vaguely perceived, general political or cultural predisposition ... people on the left at least relatively sceptical of the State Socialist regimes ... egalitarian, in a more far-reaching sense than those committed to tax-and-transfer-based income redistribution ... those appalled by the routine Socratic discussions of appellate court decisions, repelled by their sterility, and thorough disconnection from actual social life ... repelled by the supposition that neutral and apolitical legal reasoning could resolve charged controversies ... put off by the hierarchical classroom style in which phony priests first crush and then bless each new group of initiates.[18]

The critical legal studies movement has not always been well received by the academic mainstream. Law professor Gerald Gall suggested that critical legal studies is "an amalgam of traditional legal realism and modern cynicism." He argues that, while realists are often content to examine extra-legal factors influencing the operation of the law, critical theorists look to the purposes, values, and assumptions of the legal system, challenging their contemporary relevance, rationales, and validity. Gall has asserted that the critical legalists argue not from a sound philosophical basis but from personal and political values.[19]

Critical legal studies is clearly an assault on a positivist understanding of law and legal process, but its precise nature is not easy to discover. Law professor Mark Kelman has argued that it is more than simply a continuation of the realist critique; it also seeks to strip away the illusory certainty upon which the language of the law is based:

> We think in prepackaged categories, clusters, reified systems. We forget the degree to which we invent the social world. We come to think that rules make us act impersonally; we often forget that we must continually choose to act impersonally....

> [S]oon we think that the rules make us do good rather than that we sometimes collectively choose to do the good things we do when applying rules.... [L]egalist practice ... makes us passive by making us confused.[20]

There are elements not only of legal realism within this critique of law, but also of dialectical materialism and Marxist analysis. Kelman suggested that the aim of critical legal studies is to uncover illusion or delusion in the legal form, not to remedy simple ignorance. And while Kelman and other proponents of critical legal studies have recognized the limitations and weaknesses of the Marxist view of law, it is not clear that what they offer is either more than a combination of legal realism and Marxist analysis, or a variation in kind rather than substance. The critical legal studies movement has, unlike legal realism, typically conceptualized matters in normative terms and, like Marxism, has pointed consistently to issues of social disadvantage.

Nonetheless, it is not clear how practitioners of critical legal studies would respond to our three questions. Most likely, they would view high-income earners as deserving of greater taxation, assisted suicide as a matter of personal choice and dignity, and preferential employment for those with disabilities as advantageous. Yet none of these conclusions flow unequivocally from the critical legal studies perspective. Like legal realists, the adherents of this perspective speak to method, but like Marxists and natural lawyers, they often champion an understanding of law premised upon a specific vision of the role of law or the nature of morality in a specific society.

FEMINIST THEORIES OF LAW

A feminist theory of jurisprudence did not really begin to emerge until the 1960s, though its origins are appropriately traced to the **suffragette** movement of the early twentieth century. Feminists argue that history—and hence law—has been written from a male point of view and, as such, cannot adequately reflect the contributions that women have made to the structure of social life. A **feminist theory of law** holds that both the language and the logic of law reinforce male values—that prevailing conceptions of law serve to perpetuate male power and female subordination. Feminist analysts of the legal system have worked to identify the "gendered" nature of law, pointing to laws affecting divorce, reproductive rights, domestic violence, and employment as areas of concern.

Feminist theories of jurisprudence have had a particularly significant effect on legal scholarship and legal practice within the past few decades. Contemporary law journals almost universally reflect this focus and interest. Many involved in feminist theory point to a number of waves of feminist thought: first-wave feminism, and second- and third-wave feminism. First-wave feminism was preoccupied with the social and legal inequalities inflicted on women in the late nineteenth and early twentieth centuries: the lack of access to educational opportunities, the subordination of women embodied in the laws of marriage, and the denial of the right to vote.

First-wave feminists were, generally speaking, middle-class women whose challenge to legal order sprang from their own experiences of injustice.

Second-wave feminists emerged in the late 1960s and early 1970s in North America, Britain, and Europe. There were multiple concerns expressed with respect to the regulation and control of women: lack of access to birth control and the double standards of male and female sexual expression, the plight of working women, and discrimination against lesbians and women of colour. Unlike first-wave feminists, who voiced their displeasure with laws that reflected inequality, second-wave feminists went further, challenging the culture that was driving the subordination of women and urging changes not only in law but in the lived experiences of women in their private and domestic lives. In second-wave feminism, the institution of law itself was seen as problematic and contributing to the subordination of women; this was a more profound critique than that offered by first-wave feminists, who strove largely to address their own concerns with respect to equality.

Third-wave feminism is explicit in its endorsement of social activism, and it is this third wave that has spawned much recent feminist legal theory. The third wave of feminism has emerged from the political consciousness of second-wave feminism, but with a more explicitly radical analysis of the role of law, and a critique of long-established legal notions such as reasonableness, objectivity, and neutrality. The feminist legal theorist Catharine MacKinnon has argued, for example, that positivism or what might be called mainstream legal theory actually hides a very explicit partiality or point of view behind what she terms its "point-of-viewlessness."[21] In denouncing such notions as reasonableness, objectivity, and neutrality, this kind of radical feminism necessarily opens the door to alternative methods for constructing knowledge—to what theorists term an alternate epistemology. Feminist narratives—the storytelling of experiences of subordination by gender and their intersecting realms of class and race—are viewed as sound epistemology, more deserving of the mantle of legal scholarship than any dispassionate analysis of legal doctrine. There is, of course, a very contradictory logic in such an approach—an outright rejection of scientific method, and its corresponding dispassionate analysis of facts, claims, and issues is, in itself, a framework of analysis that is not likely to be either compelling or persuasive.

In many ways a feminist theory of law represents a more substantial challenge to contemporary theories of the role of law than does any other contemporary theoretical framework. There is, however, no uniform or singular feminist analysis of law. While all feminists share a commitment to the moral, political, and social equality of men and women, beyond this vision substantial disagreement exists, especially in the everyday practice of feminism. Pornography is seen by some radical feminists as worthy of censorship and criminalization—as the embodiment of the male abuse of women. Yet other self-described radical feminists reject this criminalization or censorship of pornography as critical to the feminist agenda, urging that protection of sex trade workers constitutes a more worthy struggle. Similarly, some feminists celebrate differences between men and women, asserting that women tend to emphasize different values and skill sets in their everyday life; other feminists reject this kind of analysis, its empirical merits notwithstanding. A rejection of biological relevance leads these self-described radical feminists to suggest that the only sex differences of any consequence are largely socially constructed—those that emanate from the realm of power.

A useful summary of the origins of a feminist theory of law and the range of definitions within it is offered by Obiora and Perry in the *International Encyclopedia of the Social Sciences.* Their analysis differs slightly from that set out above, but is offered as another lens through which to observe the continuing emergence of a feminist theory of law. It is perhaps most useful for documenting a lengthy history of the legal oppression of women:

> Although it was only as recently as the 1970s that feminist legal theory or feminist jurisprudence were first heard as names for the diversity of gender-focused currents in legal scholarship and argumentation, these strands of contemporary thought have their roots in the "rights revolution" that took place in the political thought of seventeenth and eighteenth century Europe and the Americas. The foundations of early feminist thought can be traced to explicit efforts to appropriate the emancipatory liberal ideals for women.
>
> The extension of the right to vote was central to the nineteenth century feminist legal agenda. Informed by the social contract theory, early feminists believed that women's political enfranchisement would facilitate their emancipation from historical oppression. The women's rights movement was closely linked to the struggle for the abolition of slavery. In the United States, the campaign for women's vote is associated with the 1848 Seneca Falls convention and the Declaration of Sentiments that emerged from the meeting. It was at Seneca Falls that the former slave, Sojourner Truth, gave her celebrated "Ain't I a woman?" speech, which questioned the parallel that is often drawn between the legal status of white women and that of slaves in the rhetoric of early nineteenth century feminism.
>
> Despite the significance of voting as the emblematic act of citizenship and of full participation in the *polis,* gender-based discrimination was no less pervasive in other spheres of life. Under the common law doctrine of coverture, a woman lived under the tutelage of her father or other male guardian, until through the sacramental covenant of marriage, her civil legal identity was subsumed by that of her husband under whose cover she derived protection. A woman was typically incapable of making contracts or testamentary dispositions, owning and alienating real property, testifying as a witness in court against her husband, suing or being sued in her own name, or controlling her earnings. She could not even protect her own physical integrity—her husband had the right to chastise her, although only with a switch no thicker than his thumb.
>
> The legal fiction of the unity of spouses as well as the rise of separate spheres ideology exempted the private sphere of the family from state intervention, and rendered women vulnerable to an array of abuses, including rape by their husbands.

Beginning in the middle of the nineteenth century, a series of statutes—generically called the Married Women's Property Acts—removed some of the most severe civil disabilities pertaining to women, and acknowledged their personhood for the purposes of the law. Ultimately, struggles for the right to vote, for property rights, for protective labor legislation, for access to education and professional careers, and for related entitlements helped transform the legal landscape. Over the past few decades, feminist strategies have continued to effect change in consciousness and in laws. Legal efforts have focused, *inter alia*, on expanding reproductive freedom, deterring sexual violence, and eliminating sex-based discrimination in employment, education, family, welfare, and related contexts.

Feminist legal theory is a legacy both of the nineteenth century campaigns for women's emancipation and of the renaissance of feminist activism in the United States and elsewhere since the 1960s. Although there is much debate about its definition, feminist legal theory can be understood as the manifestation in the legal academy of a range of efforts to understand the nature of women's subordination—especially the ways in which it is rationalized and naturalized—and to propose remedies for this subordinate condition. Drawing upon cross-cutting academic and activist traditions, feminist inquiry approaches law both as an ensemble of potential tactics for reform and, more generally, as a site of struggle for a more general political transformation. Most strands of contemporary feminist legal theory have conceptualized law as a historically and socially constructed artifact embedded in particular social relations. Feminist legal theory elucidates the ways in which law facilitates patriarchal dominance and control. Explicating how the doctrines, discourses, institutions, and culture of law perpetuate gender hierarchy, feminist legal theory has provided the impetus for reconceptualizing tightly bonded concepts and premises of legal thought.[22]

THE ANARCHIST AND LIBERTARIAN PERSPECTIVES: CRITICAL DIFFERENCES

There have been many other grand designs for understanding law besides those examined to date. The **anarchist perspective on law** and society is suspicious of all forms of state control, but anarchists also endorse a communitarian ethic that is quite distinct from contemporary libertarian perspectives. In nineteenth-century Europe, libertarianism—freedom of the individual from state control—was generally thought of as synonymous with anarchism. Anarchism of this kind holds, even today, that all forms of government are unnecessary and oppressive—the state is seen as the mechanism responsible for the murder of more than 100 million human beings, for concentration camps, and for widespread famine. In this view, the economic system would ideally be organized on the basis of cooperatives and communal ownership. Unlike twentieth-century libertarians, anarchists are committed to a principle of egalitarianism; they argue that inequalities of wealth and power are obstacles to overcome—that these inequalities will necessarily give rise to the abuse of power by the state.

Libertarians, in contrast, celebrate the rights of the individual and reject the notions of social security that are often at the heart of the anarchist tradition. David Friedman, in his book *The Machinery of Freedom,* summarizes libertarian beliefs about the role of the state—and hence, the role of law:

> The central idea of libertarianism is that people should be permitted to run their own lives as they wish. We totally reject the idea that people must be forcibly protected from themselves. A libertarian society would have no laws against drugs, gambling, pornography—and no compulsory seat belts in cars. We also reject the idea that people have an enforceable claim on others, for anything more than being left alone. A libertarian society would have no welfare, no social security system. People who wished to aid others would do so voluntarily through private charity, instead of using money collected by force from the taxpayers. People who wished to provide for their old age would do so through private insurance.[23]

CANADA (ATTORNEY GENERAL) V. BEDFORD AND THE *SAFE STREETS AND COMMUNITIES ACT*: TESTING PERSPECTIVES ON LAW

Let us now return to the cases raised at the beginning of this chapter—first, the issue of whether criminal prohibitions against solicitation, keeping a common bawdy house, and living on the avails of prostitution are violations of the right to life, liberty, and security of the person guaranteed by section 7 of the *Canadian Charter of Rights and Freedoms*; and second, the *Safe Streets and Communities Act* and its mandate of a minimum term of six months' imprisonment for any individual who grows more than five marijuana plants.

THE POSITIVIST PERSPECTIVE

The legal positivist might well be inclined to support the interpretation of the Supreme Court in *Canada v. Bedford,* as the *Charter of Rights and Freedoms* is a part of Canada's *Constitution Act* and validly enacted law. The Supreme Court is simply doing what the law requires: testing legislation against the section 7 *Charter* protection of the right to life, liberty, and the security of the person. But some positivists also might be skeptical of the role of the *Canadian Charter of Rights and Freedoms* in this case, arguing that judicial decisions that can override legislation are undemocratic, substituting the judgment of non-elected individuals for the democratic will of representative government. Ultimately, however, there is a positivist logic of support for the *Charter*. The *Charter* is, after all, a part of the Constitution, validly enacted law, and, as such, deserving of support; the law mandates judicial overview to protect what are considered to be timeless human rights. The manner in which section 7 of the *Charter* was interpreted, however, would probably be applauded by most, but not all, positivists. Stability, certainty, and predictability of law are arguably not enhanced when the Supreme Court rules that the federal government has one year to either amend laws relating to prostitution, or decide to accept the ruling without any further legislative intervention.

The legal positivist would have little to say about the passage of the *Safe Streets and Communities Act* and its imposition of a mandatory minimum term of imprisonment for those who produce more than five marijuana plants. The law was validly enacted by the federal government, consistent with its powers under section 91 of the *Constitution Act.* Irrespective of one's personal views on the utility or wisdom of imposing a mandatory term of six months' imprisonment in such circumstances, the law is certainly within the purview of Parliament; more specifically, the law flows from the federal jurisdiction under section 91(27) of the *Constitution Act*: the federal government's exclusive right to legislate in relation to criminal law and procedure.

THE NATURAL LAW PERSPECTIVE

The natural lawyer is as likely to applaud the decision in *Canada v. Bedford* as to condemn it. It is difficult to know what particular morality would be supported—that which saw merit in undertaking all legitimate means to rid Canadians of the possible harms that flow from prostitution, or that which suggests that the law deprives street prostitutes of their rights to life, liberty, and security, thereby jeopardizing their personal safety. If the scientific method is to be employed, it seems reasonable to conclude that it is the latter position that would be endorsed. However, as noted above, the use of the scientific method is not a critical feature of the natural law position. If we look to the historical record of natural law, however, and its insistence upon a religious basis for the construction of law, it might be that rejection of the Supreme Court's position would be more probable than support. Again, however, there are many religious viewpoints on prostitution, some supportive of enhancing the rights of prostitutes and others unalterably opposed to any form of tolerance of the practice of prostitution.

With the *Safe Streets and Communities Act,* the advocate of natural law would again not easily fall into a camp of being for or against, given the fluid character of morality and moral judgments. If violation of the law by growing marijuana plants is seen as morally repugnant, the natural lawyer would be likely to applaud the stern approach within the Act. If, on the other hand, the natural lawyer's view was that growing marijuana plants should be thought of as analogous to the making of beer or wine, irrespective of the state of current law, this provision within the Act might well be seen to be immoral—in essence, an unjust law.

THE LEGAL REALIST AND CRITICAL LEGALIST PERSPECTIVES

The legal realist and the critical legalist would want more information about the social and political context in which the *Canada v. Bedford* decision was made—the public perceptions and changing conditions of street prostitution over time, the specific nature of the empirical evidence provided to the trial court, and the intentions and consequences of punishments for these kinds of crimes. As analysts of law, legal realists will, like positivists, be less concerned about the "justness" of the verdict than about the internal logic of the decisions. Legal realists will cast their analytic nets more widely than positivists, employing more than doctrinal analysis. But their task will ultimately be quite similar: to understand how and why this case takes issue with the existing law relating to prostitution. Critical legalists, on the other hand, will be more inclined to fuse their analysis with moral judgment, and, consequently, more likely to be either critical or supportive of the judgment of the court. For those who identify themselves as critical legal scholars, this case might well be quite divisive. Those who are critical of orthodoxy in law may be inclined to view tolerance of prostitution as regressive, failing to uphold the rights of women. Alternatively, however, perhaps most critical legal scholars would be supportive of the decision, as it might ultimately work to enhance the safety and protection of highly marginalized citizens.

With the provision in the *Safe Streets and Communities Act* both legal realists and critical legalists would want to understand the political, social, and historical backdrop to the legislation. And, again, the critical legalists would be more likely than the legal realists to either applaud or condemn its passage. In this particular instance it seems likely that most critical legal scholars would be highly skeptical of the need for the legislation, noting that it provides a harsh penalty that could be highly inappropriate and arbitrary in many circumstances, given the often trivial nature of the action of growing more than five marijuana plants.

THE MARXIST PERSPECTIVE

Those who work within a Marxist framework might well see Bedford and her colleagues as victims of a form of class repression—the state has arguably used criminal law to disenfranchise those who labour in the trade in sexual services. On the other hand, self-described Marxist regimes have, to date, often endorsed punitive state responses to those who violate criminal law. While it is possible that those involved in the sex trade could be seen as victims of class repression, it is also realistic to note that these self-described Marxist regimes have, historically, been quite punitive in their responses to women who engage in prostitution.

Similar sentiments arise with the provision in the *Safe Streets and Communities Act*. While those who labour in production of cannabis might be viewed as potential victims of state and class oppression, they might also be seen as individuals who are participating in an industry that is not socially productive, and might serve to diminish possibilities for productive labour. Again, as with the control of prostitution, it is fair to observe that most self-described Marxist regimes have been rather punitive in responding to those who violate the criminal law, irrespective of the utility or logic of such law.

THE FEMINIST PERSPECTIVE

The feminist theory of law does not appear to have a singular response to the issues raised by the *Canada v. Bedford* decision, as feminists are very divided on the issue of whether the trade in sexual services should be subject to criminal prohibitions. As noted earlier in the chapter, some women who consider themselves to be advocates for women's rights applauded the Supreme Court's decision, while others within the feminist camp were highly critical. Prostitution, as discussed and considered in *Canada v. Bedford,* is an occupation that endangers women's lives, and all feminists take issue with this reality. They remain divided, however, on the appropriate remedy for the problem.

With the provision in the *Safe Streets and Communities Act,* there is, again, no singular feminist position. One might argue that the feminist perspective on law would likely be critical of the mandatory minimum term of imprisonment, noting that equality in the realm of psychoactive drug use has parallels to gender equality. It might be said that those who produce marijuana, like the early suffragettes, are simply seeking equal treatment—a kind of level playing field with those who produce other mind-active (and arguably more dangerous) legal drugs, such as alcohol and tobacco.

THE ANARCHIST AND LIBERTARIAN PERSPECTIVES

Finally, anarchists and libertarians, with their skeptical view of state power, might well view the possibility of a mandatory term of imprisonment for marijuana production as a state abuse of power. This is especially true of laissez-faire libertarians, who are particularly suspicious of a potential tyranny of the collective. In their view marijuana producers are the victims of a Big Brother mentality on the part of the Canadian state. However, at least some anarchists, who adopt a more communitarian ethic, might well argue that this kind of criminal conduct violates a shared common code and, as such, deserves a common punishment. With *Canada v. Bedford,* both libertarians and anarchists likely would be supportive of the Supreme Court's decision—libertarians happy to confront the power of the state, and anarchists skeptical of the state, but also specifically supportive of this community of marginalized women, now potentially able to emerge from a dangerous set of circumstances.

CONCLUSION: THE IMPORTANCE OF COMPETING PERSPECTIVES

Our views of law can be somewhat simplistically condensed into two opposing camps: those who view law and its transactions as morally neutral exercises of logic and interpretation, and those who view law and legal practice as a terrain for moral, political, and economic debate. The proponents of the first analysis embrace positivism, the dominant view among legal practitioners and, to a lesser extent, among legal academics. Those who embrace a natural law, realist, Marxist, critical legalist, feminist, anarchist, or libertarian perspective argue that such a view is insufficient: to study and practise law is, they say, to engage the moral, political, and economic issues that infuse the legal process.

Yet we should be mindful of the limitations of these somewhat artificial categories. When Canadians speak of their views of law, these are not typically abstract, but concrete. Canadians do not identify themselves as positivists, realists, or Marxists, but speak either in favour of or against specific statutes and judicial decisions. Canadians are for and against mandatory minimum terms of imprisonment for marijuana producers, for and against current criminal controls on prostitution, for and against income surtax of the wealthy. The categories of positivism, natural law, realism, Marxism, and critical legal studies are more properly conceptualized as heuristic aids to understanding a range of perspectives or theories about law. It may also be that these categories are slowly being eclipsed by a more fundamental tension—the state's complex task of finding a workable middle ground between the interests of the individual (individualism) and the interests of the collective (collectivism).

And, of course, there are other perspectives than these. One can claim, for example, that law is best understood as an instrument of social engineering, the will of God as revealed to human beings, or an implicit or explicit instrument of economic, gender, and racial oppression.

All these definitions of law will have merit for some Canadians in some circumstances. There is a sense in which law is an instrument of social engineering. But is this definition all-encompassing and ultimately definitive of an understanding of law? Or is it another conception of positivism, restated in different form? Then, for those who believe in an invisible deity ordering human affairs, law may well be formulated as the will of God. But can this perspective fully define the continuing amendment of law? Is it a conception of natural law, perhaps stated in its original form?

Finally, those who believe that law is an instrument of oppression distance themselves from both the natural law and the positivist perspectives, and show interest in some amalgam of the Marxist, legal realist, anarchist, libertarian, feminist, and critical legal studies perspectives. But, once again, can this definition fully inform an understanding of the law? The late British historian E.P. Thompson noted that although law can be an instrument of oppression, it can also be a tool for liberation.[24] Laws that serve to assist the disadvantaged—the granting of universal health care, compensation for disability, and the provision of a basic level of economic support—are not easily viewed as inherently oppressive.

For the typical Canadian citizen, however, the legal form may not be, as Thompson suggested, "an unqualified human good." Remarks and sentiments about law and legal process may be more likely to run in the direction of Shakespeare's exhortation (in *Henry VI, Part 2*), "The first thing we do, let's kill all the lawyers." Lawyers are often perceived as advocates for affluence and amorality, corrupted by privilege and motivated by material gain. Nevertheless, lawyers are also indispensable to the processes of dispute settlement in representative democracies, developing arguments, and creating effective advocacy. For how should disputes within societies be ordered, if not by law, and therefore by those expert in it? In its ideal form, law is the outcome of an informed verbal argument in which the interests of all relevant parties are adequately represented.

The various perspectives or theories about law suggest that the task of understanding cannot be too limited in focus. There is a need, as the positivists assert, to understand the form and structure of specific statutes and attendant judicial decisions. But the student of law and legal process must also seek to understand the political, economic, and moral values represented in statute law and judicial decisions—the very issues that necessitate verbal argument and law.

WEB LINKS

The Internet Encyclopedia of Philosophy
http://www.iep.utm.edu/law-phil/
This page, part of a larger site encompassing the Encyclopedia, is devoted to the philosophy of law. The Encyclopedia is prepared by two philosophy professors and maintained at the University of Tennessee at Martin. It is an excellent resource for background material and definitions on philosophy.

JURIST: The Legal Education Network
http://jurist.law.pitt.edu/
This ambitious Internet project is designed to provide links to most legal resource materials available on the Internet. The main website is located at the University of Pittsburgh School of Law and has an international advisory board of legal academics. It links to the Canadian section at http://jurist.law.utoronto.ca/, which is hosted by the University of Toronto, Faculty of Law. The website is jointly maintained in other common-law jurisdictions, including Canada, Australia, and the U.K. Links are especially good for law journals and online legal publications.

Judgments of the Supreme Court of Canada

http://scc-csc.lexum.com/scc-csc/en/nav.do

This site posts Supreme Court of Canada decisions and news. Cases on the site date back to 1876, accessible without a subscription. A search engine is located at the top of the page, which makes searching for cases very simple.

Criminal Code of Canada

http://laws.justice.gc.ca/en/C-46/index.html

This site is accessed through the Department of Justice's laws page and provides the entire *Criminal Code* with all amendments. Searches can be conducted for specific information in the *Code* from the first page of the site.

QUESTIONS FOR DISCUSSION

1. The Supreme Court's judgment in *Canada (Attorney General) v. Bedford* and the passage of law regarding mandatory minimum terms of imprisonment for cannabis production are closely related legal and moral issues. It is very difficult to support the Supreme Court's argument and at the same time support the government's approach in the *Safe Streets and Communities Act*. Discuss.

2. The categories of positivism, natural law, Marxism, and critical legal studies are more properly conceptualized as categories that help us to understand a range of perspectives or theories about law. It may also be that these categories are slowly being eclipsed by a more fundamental understanding: that legal realism best describes the processes of both legislative and judicial decision making. Discuss.

3. The British historian E.P. Thompson observed that a system of law represents "an unqualified human good." Do you agree or disagree? Why?

FURTHER READING

Baer, J.A. *Our Lives Before the Law: Constructing a Feminist Jurisprudence.* Princeton: Princeton University Press, 1999.

> This book has been described by one reviewer as a "clear and broad-based introduction" to feminist theories of jurisprudence. Baer's writing is quite accessible and critical, and allows students to understand a range of viewpoints within feminist scholarship.

Donovan, J. *Feminist Theory: The Intellectual Traditions.* 3rd ed. New York: Continuum, 2000.

> This book has a useful compilation of the history and range of the traditions of feminist theory, considering liberal, Marxist, existential, and radical conceptions of feminist thought.

Green, L., and Leiter, B. *Oxford Studies in Philosophy of Law, Volumes 1 and 11*. Oxford University Press, 2011 and 2013.

> These volumes provide a forum for much new philosophical work on law. As the editors note, the work ranges from issues in general jurisprudence to specific areas of law, the history of legal philosophy and topics that illuminate problems in legal theory.

Hart, H.L.A. *The Concept of Law*. Oxford: Clarendon Press, 1961.

> This book is a complex examination of positivist views of law. Hart's analysis allows the reader to see the moral judgments that underlie a positivist analysis.

Heilbroner, R. *Marxism: For and Against*. New York: Norton and Company, 1980.

> This is a relatively accessible analysis of a Marxist view of society, one that explains both the strengths and the weaknesses of this framework for analysis.

Woodcock, G. *Anarchism: A History of Libertarian Ideas and Movements*. London, U.K.: Penguin, 1986.

> This history is a useful primer from a major scholar of anarchism. Often described as one of British Columbia's intellectual treasures, Woodcock was a theorist who managed to capture the interest of popular culture with his writings.

NOTES

1. Brian Leiter, *Leiter Reports: A Philosophy Blog*, at http://leiterreports.typepad.com/blog/2003/11/what_is_legal_r.html.
2. See *Canada (Attorney General) v. Bedford*, http://www.canlii.org/en/ca/scc/doc/2013/2013scc72/2013scc72.html, and *Safe Streets and Communities Act*, Statutes of Canada 2012, c.1.
3. Michelle Rempel, quoted in "A Blow to Equality: Tories Look to Defang Ruling after Court Strikes Down Prostitution Laws," *National Post*, December 20, 2013.
4. Carissima Mathen, "Op-Ed: In Bedford Case, the Supreme Court Says 'Do No Harm,'" *Ottawa Citizen*, December 20, 2013.
5. Canadian Bar Association, *Submission on Bill C-10, Safe Streets and Communities Act*, October 2011, at 5.
6. H.L.A. Hart, "Positivism and the Separation of Law and Morals," in *Philosophy of Law*, 2nd ed., edited by J. Feinberg and H. Gross (Belmont, CA: Wadsworth Publishing, 1980), 50. Reprinted from *Harvard Law Review* 71 (1958): 593H.
7. Hart, *The Concept of Law* (Oxford: Oxford University Press, 1961), 197–8.
8. Ibid, p. 207.
9. Ibid.
10. David Lloyd, *The Idea of Law* (Harmondsworth, U.K.: Penguin Books, 1973), 111.
11. G. Gall, *The Canadian Legal System*, 3rd ed. (Toronto: Carswell, 1990), 11.

12. R. Cotterrell, *The Politics of Jurisprudence: A Critical Introduction to Legal Philosophy* (London, U.K.: Butterworths, 1989), 124.
13. D. Lloyd and M.D.A. Freeman, *Introduction to Jurisprudence,* 5th ed. (London, U.K.: Stevens, 1985), 92.
14. K.N. Llewellyn, "Some Realism about Realism," in *Jurisprudence: Realism in Theory and Practice* (Chicago: University of Chicago Press, 1962), 42–76.
15. K. Llewellyn, *The Common Law Tradition: Deciding Appeals* (Boston: Little Brown, 1960), 510.
16. R. Heilbroner, *Marxism: For and Against* (New York: Norton and Company, 1980), 173.
17. See P. Carlin, "Pure Profit," *Los Angeles Times*, February 5, 1995.
18. M. Kelman, *A Guide to Critical Legal Studies* (Harvard University Press, 1990), 294–5.
19. Gall, *The Canadian Legal System,* above, 17.
20. Kelman, *A Guide to Critical Legal Studies,* above, 294–5.
21. C. MacKinnon, *Feminism Unqualified: Discourses on Life and Law* (1987), 16.
22. L.A. Obiara and R. Perry, "Feminist Legal Theory," *International Encyclopedia of the Social Sciences*, Vol. 8 (Oxford: Elsevier, 2001), 5464–9.
23. D. Friedman, *The Machinery of Freedom,* 2nd ed. (Lasalle, IL: Open Court, 1989).
24. See E.P. Thompson, *Whigs and Hunters: The Origin of the Black Act* (New York: Pantheon Books, 1975). Thompson writes, on page 265, of law as a "human good": "To deny or belittle this good," he suggests, is "a desperate error of intellectual abstraction. More than this, it is a self-fulfilling error, which encourages us to give up the struggle against bad laws and class-bound procedures, and to disarm ourselves before power. It is to throw away a whole inheritance of struggle about law, and within the forms of law, whose continuity can never be fractured without bringing men and women into immediate danger."

REFERENCES

Becker, H. *Outsiders.* New York: Free Press, 1973.
Boyd, N. *The Last Dance: Murder in Canada.* Scarborough: Prentice-Hall, 1988.
———. *The Social Dimensions of Law.* Scarborough: Prentice-Hall, 1986.
Cain, M., and A. Hunt. *Marx and Engels on Law.* London, U.K.: Academic Press, 1979.
Chambliss, W., and R. Seidman. *Law, Order and Power.* 2nd ed. Reading, MA: Addison-Wesley, 1982.
Cheffins, R., and R. Tucker. *The Constitutional Process in Canada.* Toronto: McGraw-Hill Ryerson, 1986.
Claydon, J., and D. Galloway. *Law and Legality.* Toronto: Butterworths, 1979.

Coral, S.C., and J.C. Smith. *Law and Its Presuppositions: Actions, Agents and Rules.* Boston: Routledge and Kegan Paul, 1986.

Cotterrell, R. *The Politics of Jurisprudence: A Critical Introduction to Legal Philosophy.* London, U.K.: Butterworths, 1989.

Dworkin, R.M. *Law's Empire.* Cambridge, MA: Harvard University Press, Belknap Press, 1986.

Evan, W., ed. *The Sociology of Law.* New York: Free Press, 1980.

Feinberg, J., and H. Gross. *Philosophy of Law.* 2nd ed. Belmont, CA: Wadsworth, 1980.

Gall, G. *The Canadian Legal System.* 3rd ed. Toronto: Carswell, 1990.

Hart, H.L.A. *The Concept of Law.* Oxford: Oxford University Press, 1961.

Heilbroner, R. *Marxism: For and Against.* New York: Norton and Company, 1980.

James, P.S. *Introduction to English Law.* 11th ed. London, U.K.: Butterworths, 1985.

Kelman, M. *A Guide to Critical Legal Studies.* Cambridge, MA: Harvard University Press, 1987.

Kolmar, W.K., and F. Bartkowski. *Feminist Theory, Second Edition: A Reader.* Boston: McGraw Hill, 2005.

Kramer, M. *In Defense of Legal Positivism,* Oxford, Oxford University Press, 1999.

Leiter, B. *Naturalizing Jurisprudence: Essays on American Legal Realism and Naturalism in Legal Philosophy,* Oxford, Oxford University Press, 2007.

Llewellyn, K. *The Common Law Tradition. Deciding Appeals.* Boston: Little, Brown, 1960.

———. *Jurisprudence: Realism in Theory and Practice.* Chicago: University of Chicago Press, 1962.

Lloyd, D. *The Idea of Law.* Harmondsworth, U.K.: Penguin Books, 1973.

Lloyd, D., and M.D.A. Freeman. *Introduction to Jurisprudence.* 5th ed. London, U.K.: Stevens, 1985.

MacKinnon, C. *Feminism Unmodified: Discourses on Life and Law.* Cambridge, MA: Harvard University Press, 1987.

Pfohl, S.J. *Images of Deviance and Social Control.* New York: McGraw-Hill, 1985.

Phillips, O.H. *A First Book of English Law.* 8th ed. London, U.K.: Sweet and Maxwell, 1988.

Pound, R. *Social Control Through Law.* New Haven: Yale University Press, 1942.

Rawls, J. *A Theory of Justice.* Cambridge, MA: Harvard University Press, Belknap Press, 1971.

Salmond, Sir J.W. *Salmond on Jurisprudence.* 12th ed. London, U.K.: Sweet and Maxwell, 1966.

Thompson, E.P. *The Poverty of Theory and Other Essays.* London, U.K.: Monthly Review Press, 1978.

———. *Whigs and Hunters: The Origin of the Black Act.* New York: Pantheon Books, 1975.

Twining, W.L. *Legal Theory and Common Law*. New York: Basil Blackwell, 1986.

Unger, R.M. *The Critical Legal Studies Movement*. Cambridge, MA: Harvard University Press, 1986.

Waddams, S.M. *Introduction to the Study of Law*. 4th ed. Scarborough: Carswell, 1992.

Walker, R.J., and M.G. Walker. *The English Legal System*. 6th ed. London, U.K.: Butterworths, 1985.

THE SOURCES OF CANADIAN LAW: FROM THE PLAINS OF ABRAHAM TO STATUTES AND JUDICIAL DECISIONS

The only direct utility of legal history ... lies in the lesson that each generation has an enormous power of shaping its own law. I don't think that the study of legal history would make men fatalists; I doubt that it would make them conservatives. I am sure that it would free them from superstitions and teach them that they have free hands.

(Frederic Maitland, 1896)

It is hard to write a history about something that is still happening—like a biography of a person still alive or a history of a people still existing. The problem is not that the historian cannot know those parts of the story that have yet to take place. Rather, the problem is that the historian's interpretation of the story so far may be influenced—consciously or unconsciously—by a sense of how the story might (or should) turn out and by an appreciation that the way in which the story is presented can become part of the story, influencing the way it does turn out. Moral evaluations of past actions are particularly problematic in this respect. Condemning a people of the ancient past as wicked will have only indirect practical implications today, but to condemn the past acts of a living nation as wicked is to identify possibilities of redemption, reparation, and reconciliation. The writer of a history about something that is still happening therefore has a special responsibility to appreciate that choices about how to portray the past may affect the ways in which moral discourse unfolds today.

(Mark Walters, *University of Toronto Law Journal*, 2007)

EARLY SOURCES: RETHINKING THE PLAINS OF ABRAHAM

The **Magna Carta** of 1215 is significant for bringing the English their first true shift from monarchy to democracy. In clauses 60 to 63 of the *Magna Carta*, King John provided an important political—and legal—concession by ceding to a council of 25 barons the opportunity to change certain of his decisions. Royal powers were no longer absolute. As legal historian Margaret Ogilvie noted, however, the *Magna Carta* was far from a statement of democratic nationhood:

> *Magna Carta* was a feudal charter, a restatement of classical feudalism, and as such, benefited primarily the baronial interests. Those few clauses relating to freemen or

villeins (feudal tenants), or merchants, reflected the status of those social segments; no magnanimous grants of important liberties were made. That the barons sought a written guarantee of established feudal usages was significant in itself; the Great Charter was a description of the past, not a prescription for the future.[1]

It was not until 1666 that **feudalism**—the political and economic system that granted nobility and land in exchange for the labour and military service of serfs or vassals on the land—was abolished in England. By this time, both the French and the British had established themselves in what were to become, respectively, Quebec and Ontario.

In 1627, Cardinal Richelieu established in law, at arm's length from France, the Company of New France, granting the land in part of what is now Quebec in perpetuity on the basis of a system of feudal tenure. By 1660, there was a governor and an elected council. In the 1670s, when the Company of New France was unable to defend itself against the Native peoples of the area, it surrendered its charter to France's King Louis XIV. From this time until the Battle of the Plains of Abraham in 1759, Canada became, in legal terms, the territory of two competing nations: Britain and France. Aboriginal claims were in the process of being restructured and extinguished.

The Battle of the Plains of Abraham took place on September 13, 1759. It would be the wellspring of significant future legal pronouncements: the **Royal Proclamation of 1763**, the *British North America Act, 1867*, and, ultimately, the *Constitution Act, 1982*. The battle was one event of the Seven Years' War (1756–1763), which ended with Britain establishing itself as the dominant naval and colonial power within Europe. British General James Wolfe and his 4,500 men surprised General Louis-Joseph Montcalm and his equally large French contingent by sailing past the fortified settlement of Quebec and climbing up the cliffs several kilometres above the city. Hundreds of men died in a bloody exchange of rifle power, and the better-trained and organized English ultimately prevailed. The French retreated up the St. Lawrence River. In 1760, they tried to recapture the city but failed, and in 1761, the British were able to capture Montreal.

The British Parliament set out a legal structure for its new colony in the Royal Proclamation of 1763. The proclamation provided for a governor and council to administer Quebec until conditions permitted an elected assembly; the introduction of English laws and courts; and a guarantee of Aboriginal self-government. It was hoped that American settlers would flood into Quebec, ultimately assimilating the French. This vision of cultural conquest did not materialize, however, and in 1774 the British Parliament passed the *Quebec Act*, providing, among other things, for the right of Roman Catholics to participate in government and for the use of French civil law.

The *Constitution Act of 1791* divided Quebec into Upper and Lower Canada. While ultimate legislative authority was retained by the British Parliament, the 1791 act created legislative and executive branches of government in each of the Canadas, modelled to some extent on the emerging British parliamentary form. The executive branch of government, to mirror the Cabinet, was composed of a lieutenant governor and a council appointed by him. The legislative branch of government had two houses: a Legislative Council, not unlike the House of Lords, appointed by the British Parliament; and a Legislative Assembly, to which landowners in Upper or Lower Canada could be elected.

The 1791 *Constitution Act* was, again, far from a model of representative democracy. The executive branch of government was not responsible to the Legislative Assembly of either Upper or Lower Canada, but to Britain and British interests. In Lower Canada, the Executive Council was dominated by the English-speaking minority, and dubbed the "Château Clique" by Louis-Joseph Papineau and his *patriotes.* Papineau argued for the economic independence of Quebec and its annexation by the United States. The control of Quebec's commerce by appointed British interests ultimately led to armed rebellion in Quebec.

In Upper Canada, too, rebellions broke out against the legality of British rule, specifically against the Family Compact, which represented British interests. William Lyon Mackenzie and a group of 800 rebels seeking independence from Britain marched south on Toronto's Yonge Street in 1837, armed with rifles, staves, and pitchforks. Like the rebels of Lower Canada, they were easily defeated by British troops. The rebellions led to the appointment of Lord Durham, whose task was to propose some resolution for the disputes in the colonies. Durham's 1839 report advocated union and self-government for Upper and Lower Canada, with Britain continuing to be responsible for the management of public lands and the emerging country's foreign interests. The 1840 *Act of Union* created the United Province of Canada, with Kingston as the capital. Both Upper and Lower Canada were granted an elected assembly and an appointed Upper House. By the 1850s, the Province of Canada was essentially a self-governing nation-state.

During the next 20 years, there was a series of political discussions about the integration of all British colonies north of the United States. The British in North America feared American expansion, and could also envision the economic advantages of sharing regional resources. Canada, in legal terms, was conceived in this period, emerging on July 1, 1867, as a result of the union of Upper and Lower Canada, Nova Scotia, and New Brunswick. Other provinces soon joined Confederation: Manitoba in 1870, British Columbia in 1871, and Prince Edward Island in 1873. Alberta and Saskatchewan joined in 1905, and Newfoundland in 1949.

The form of union sought by participants in the conception of Canada was a federal, rather than unitary, system of government. The distinctiveness of each province was a central aspect of the original legal design. Legal historian Ogilvie has noted the following of Canada's original form:

> A legislative union and unitary form of government was impossible, and a federation at least permitted some local self-government which would hopefully guarantee the continuation of regional identities. Even so, the compromise was not adopted without a fight in each province.[2]

The *British North America Act, 1867* is Canada's original and defining source of law, setting out in sections 91 and 92 the respective powers of federal and provincial governments, and, more generally, a strategy for legal governance of the country (see Chapter 4). From 1867 to the present, provincial and federal governments have enacted thousands of statutes regulating family organization, labour relations, income taxation, contracts, behaviour defined as deviant (criminal law), and acts of negligence, among other matters. And the monarchy, though no longer retaining decision-making power of any kind, remains a part of the Canadian legal tradition for better or worse, embodied in the office of the Governor General of Canada.

The Conceptual Divisions of Law

In the contemporary Canadian state, we can make two conceptual classifications of law: **domestic law**, the law of a single nation-state, and **international law**, law that is, ideally, common to all nation-states. International law is typically mediated by the United Nations and involves the governance or accommodation of nations in relation to global treaties, conventions, and customs. All forms of Canadian domestic law can be further classified as public or private, and as **substantive** or **procedural**. For example, the section of the *Criminal Code* that prohibits first degree murder (section 231) is substantive law. Sections 645 and 646 of the *Code*, dealing with trial procedures and the taking of evidence at trial, are, on the other hand, procedural law.

The distinctions commonly made between private and public law and substantive and procedural law do have limitations. Procedural law is also substantive in that the procedural mechanism is often set out within specific statutes, as noted above with the example of the *Criminal Code*. Additionally, private agreements have public-interest issues embedded within them; private law affects the public interest, and public law affects private interests. The late law professor Gerald Gall suggested the following classification:

Public Law	Private Law	
Constitutional law	Contracts	Torts
Criminal law	Real estate	Company law
Administrative law	Property	The law of agency
Taxation law	Family law	Patent law
	Wills and trusts	

Source: Gerald Gall. *The Canadian Legal System*, 5th ed. 2004. Adapted by permission of Carswell, a division of Thomson Reuters Canada Limited.

As Gall noted, the classification of **private** or **public law** is dependent on the issue of public as opposed to private interest. If the area of law is primarily concerned with the definition and regulation of individual matters, the law will be classified as private. If the area of law is primarily of collective interest, it is appropriately classified as public law. Constitutional and criminal law are therefore defined as public law, the former concerned with the construction and regulation of political life, the latter concerned with the collective definition of intolerable behaviours. On the other hand, the law of contract between individuals or corporations and the law of tort (the remedy of individual or corporate wrongs or wrongdoing) are defined as matters of essentially private interest, theoretically regulating not so much the economic interests of the collective but economic relations between individuals and their legal creations.

In the case of family law, Gall's classification as private law appears more problematic. There is a strong collective interest in the legal definition of "family" relationships and in the responsibilities that flow from these relationships, particularly when children are involved. Likewise, in the case of the law of wills and trusts and the law of property, it is not clear that we are primarily concerned with private interests. The rules governing the passage of wealth from one generation to the next and both personal and real property and their acquisition define the collective character of a nation—economically, socially, and politically.

All classifications or divisions of law are to some degree arbitrary: "[O]ne must appreciate the integrated nature of the law and the legal system, and thus not fall prey to an element of artificiality which befalls an attempt at categorization."[3] We must add a corollary here. The classifications of law into domestic and international, substantive and procedural, private and public do have some meaning, even if the meaning, like law itself, is subject to some degree of disagreements, qualifications, and caveats.

CANADA'S LEGAL HISTORY: THE SOCIAL, POLITICAL, AND ECONOMIC CONTEXT

The enactment of all forms of law in Canada spans a little more than 140 years, but the history of law spans over 4,000 years. In the seventeenth century B.C.E., Hammurabi, the sixth king of the first dynasty of Babylonia, constructed a code of 282 case laws and had it inscribed on a slab of rock in the temple of the god Marduk. Hammurabi's Code dealt with economic issues and family, criminal, and civil law in Babylon. Confucius, writing in China some 2,600 years ago, developed a system of philosophical and ethical teachings that substantially influenced the development of Chinese law. Confucius stressed decorum, virtue, and love for one's fellow human beings. Muhammad, born in Mecca over 1,000 years later, was inspired to develop the Islamic faith, which influenced and continues to influence the law in Muslim nations.

THE SOURCES OF CANADIAN LAW

If we are to speak and write of the sources of Canadian law, we need to be sensitive to this lengthy global history and to the many religious and ideological constructions of law that have emerged during the past 4,000 years. Some, such as Confucianism and Islam, have had relatively little direct effect on the development of Canada's legal system. Others, such as Christianity and Judaism, have had profound influence. In nation-specific terms, Canadian law has been most substantially influenced by the British, French, and U.S. legal systems.

British law professor Philip James has proposed that, in order to understand the sources of law in society, we need to think of these influences as either principal or subsidiary.[4] He cites two sources as principal: legislation and case law (written judicial decisions), and two influences as subsidiary: custom and books of authority. These four sources of law will be discussed in detail later in this chapter.

Historically, law has also been distinguished as either written or unwritten, with legislation defined as written law, and case law, custom, and books of authority as unwritten law. As James has noted, the distinction between written and unwritten law is not particularly helpful. Judicial decisions really do amount to written law, but because they do not take the form of a statute, they have typically been classified as unwritten. Custom, particularly in commerce, may also have the essential structure and importance of written law, and yet be classified as unwritten law.

The sources of Canadian law are to be found in both legislation and judicial decisions from 1867 to the present, as well as in the great body of British common law that was in existence before 1867 and was received into Canadian law upon Confederation. Specifically, Canada is given its legal identity by the *British North America Act, 1867* and the *Constitution Act, 1982*, with its entrenched Canadian *Charter of Rights and Freedoms*. (See Chapter 4.) Debate about the essential structure of Canadian law continues in the early decades of the twenty-first century, with the separatist Bloc Québécois currently holding the majority of federal seats from the Province of Quebec, and with the propositions of the Meech Lake and Charlottetown Accords unable to win political support during the 1990s.

At the heart of the continuing disputes about Canada's legal identity is the centrality of Quebec and Québécois culture within Canada, and the political and legal reality of both French and English as the founding cultures of the country. But there is more to the dispute: an argument for recognition of the Aboriginal peoples of Canada, men and women displaced during the past 300 years by the aggressive policies of French and English colonization, but the first founders of the nation. There is also the 1982 *Charter*, a moral covenant of the country's values, which for more than 30 years has been adjudicated by a politically appointed judiciary.

STATUTE LAW

Statutory or enacted law is generally accorded dominance as a source of the legal form because of the long-standing tradition of British parliamentary supremacy. Parliament is said to be supreme in that it represents the will of the people, after democratic debate and resolution. The other sources of law   judicial decisions, custom, and books of authority—cannot have the same direct accountability to a democratic system of representative government.

But there is also a sense in which Parliament cannot be supreme. All statutes must be applied, and in the process they must often be interpreted, giving judicial decision makers a measure of control over the meaning and operation of law. Philip James has provided an illustration of the power exerted by the judiciary over the operation of **statute law**: Suppose that Old King Cole, who is an absolute despot, commands that all "dogs" in his kingdom are to be killed. Suppose that Jack Sprat has an Alsatian wolfhound, and applies to the court for a decree that it shall be spared, alleging that it is a "hound" and the royal command is concerned only with "dogs." The court will have to decide whether the word "dogs" is to be taken to embrace "hounds"; whichever way it decides, it will influence the practical application of the King's command.[5] In all circumstances, such judicial interventions provide a sharper focus for the understanding of statute law, and in some circumstances they may serve to reconstruct the operation and meaning of the statute in question.

The sources of statute law in Canada are the House of Commons and the legislative assemblies of the provinces and territories. These parliaments collectively produce hundreds of statutes every year, often with regulations attached. In the early twenty-first century, the average Canadian citizen can be aware of only the most basic operations of the law, and in complex matters of either public or private law must purchase specialized legal advice.

The legislative process for the creation of a statute is similar for the federal, provincial, and territorial governments. The government of the day introduces a bill into either the House of Commons or the Legislative Assembly and gives it what is called its "first reading." It is then passed to second reading without debate. At this point, many bills simply die on the order paper. The government often decides not to proceed, often for reasons related to Cabinet and caucus priorities.

If there *is* a second reading of the legislation, the minister responsible for the proposed law sets out the purpose of the legislation. This is followed by a full debate. After debate, the bill is typically sent to a committee of the House or Assembly composed of both government and Opposition members.

Next comes further debate and, possibly, public hearings. For example, in making changes to criminal law, a committee of the House of Commons will often travel across Canada in order to receive public input from a wide range of Canadians. When the bill comes back to the House or Assembly for its third reading, it may contain one or several proposed amendments. At third reading, if the government still wishes to proceed and has sufficient support, the bill is passed. For federal legislation, this process must be repeated in the Senate before the bill is submitted to the governor general for approval. Provincial or territorial legislation passed on third reading is submitted to the lieutenant governor of the province or territory for approval. The submission for approval to the governor general or lieutenant governor is simply a formality, a monarchical remnant dating to the time when English barons had to submit their legislation for the approval of the king or queen. The governor general and the lieutenant governors are the monarch's representatives in Canada.

Statutes of the various governments are published every year, and can be found in the libraries of Canada's courts and most other libraries. This annual legislative production is typically cited in reference catalogues as *Statutes of Canada, 2000*; *Statutes of Ontario, 2000*; and so on. There are also occasional compilations of all federal and provincial statutes, to a given date. The most recent compilation of all federal statutes is *Revised Statutes of Canada, 1985*, a set of more than 15 volumes of legislation. In our increasingly electronic age, these statutes can now be found online, in addition to tens of thousands of case law decisions from various levels of courts.

CASE LAW

Case law is the law established by decisions in specific court cases. Subsequent courts will turn to these decisions, known as judicial precedents, when attempting to make judgments about similar issues. The importance of a judicial precedent depends upon the hierarchical placement of the court issuing the decision. If, for example, the Supreme Court of Canada issues a judgment defining obscenity, pursuant to section 163(8) of the *Criminal Code,* the decision will potentially affect all Canadian courts. If the same decision emanates from a provincial court judge, it will have no determinative influence on the prosecution of obscenity in the province, or in other jurisdictions. (See Chapter 5.)

The continuing interpretation of statute law by the courts renders the legal system dynamic, with new cases permitting and requiring new rules. An open system of interpretation is, in theory, a kind of legislative democracy, adjudicated by the courts in concert with legislators. Ideally, the rules come to reflect the litigants' realities, not the more abstract designs of a legislator.

There are at least two problems with judicial precedents as sources of law. First is the danger that, in trying to mesh current situations with pre-existing case law, the courts and counsel may make illogical distinctions. Judicial decisions must be set against a complex backdrop of precedents; in trying to fit the current case into this framework, both lawyers and the judiciary may lose contact with the intention of the legislators (see Chapter 3, How Do Judges Interpret Ambiguous Statutes?). For litigator and advocate alike, the object of statutory interpretation is to distinguish one's case from damaging precedents, from facts that would seem to bind the court to make a finding contrary to the interest of one's client.

The second problem has to do with the ability of a court, particularly the Supreme Court of Canada, to reverse itself. The logic of a system of binding precedent is that the court of last resort binds itself and all other courts in the country by its decisions. Yet the Supreme Court must occasionally depart from its past decisions, weighing the value of new evidence or responding to new conceptions of a problem. The need to reverse earlier judgments presents a difficulty for those who argue that judges do not make law, but only interpret statutes. In reversing previous decisions, the judiciary is exercising, at the least, a quasi-legislative power; it cannot be said simply to be building a binding system of precedent.

Reporting Case Law

The decisions of the judiciary are published or "reported" in a variety of sources. However, not all judicial decisions are reported. *Supreme Court Reports* carries all important judgments from the Supreme Court of Canada. *Dominion Law Reports* carries significant judgments from the Supreme Court of Canada, provincial courts of appeal, and some county courts. There are also reporting services for specific regions of the country: *Ontario Reports* and *Western Weekly Reports* are two prominent examples. Finally, some reporting services cater to specific areas of legal practice; examples include *Canadian Criminal Cases* and *Reports of Family Law.*

The editors of these reporters (as they are called) make decisions about which cases to report, typically selecting judicial decisions made in superior courts—those with the power to bind other courts to their findings. They then write what is called a headnote, and place it before each judicial decision. A headnote is a summary of the facts of the case, the issues in dispute, and the reason for the court's decision. The reason for the decision is termed the *ratio decidendi*—the judge's determination of law, in relation to the particular set of facts. The court may also issue what are termed *obiter dicta*—literally, "statements, by the way"—legal pronouncements on issues not directly relevant to the present case. *Obiter dicta* may, nonetheless, carry substantial weight in future cases that are at least somewhat related to the present case.

When searching for judicial decisions, you might attempt to locate various reporting services: *Supreme Court Reports, Canadian Criminal Cases,* and so on. Judicial decisions are cited in a manner allowing for easy access. For example, the citation *R. v. Gunn and Ponak* (1971), 5 C.C.C. (2d) 503 (B.C.C.A.) tells you that this was a criminal case against the accused Gunn and Ponak, decided in 1971; it can be found in Volume 5 of *Canadian Criminal Cases,* 2nd edition; and it was a decision of the British Columbia Court of Appeal. In criminal cases, the abbreviation "R." refers to *Rex* or *Regina*—the king or queen of England. This designation is, again, a remnant from the British system of prosecution, in which the monarch is said to be acting in the interest of the state against the criminal accused. In the United States, criminal prosecutions are commenced in the name of "the people," as in *People v. Aguilar,* 35 Cal. Rptr. 516 (1963).

But what is much more likely today is that you will search for and find most judicial decisions online—and most of these reporting services will be available to you through your university's electronic library services. Here are excerpts from a relatively recent Supreme Court decision in 2012 as set out in CanLII, the online product of the Canadian Legal Information Institute. CanLII is a non-profit organization managed by the Federation of Law Societies of Canada. The goal of the organization is to make Canadian law accessible for free on the Internet. My comments, in bracketed italics and on a shaded background, describe the practical meaning of relevant portions of the judgment.

Citation: R. *v.* Ipeelee, 2012 SCC 13, [2012] 1 S.C.R. 433

Date: 20120323

Docket: 33650, 34245

(The citation indicates that the judgment can be found at 2012, Volume 1, Supreme Court Reports; the judgment was issued on March 23, 2012.)

BETWEEN:

Manasie Ipeelee

v.

Her Majesty the Queen Respondent, and Director of Public Prosecutions and Aboriginal Legal Services of Toronto Inc.

AND BETWEEN:

Her Majesty the Queen

v.

Frank Ralph Ladue, and British Columbia Civil Liberties Association and Canadian Civil Liberties Association

CORAM: McLachlin C.J. and Binnie, LeBel, Deschamps, Fish, Abella, and Rothstein JJ.

(The "Coram" is the court; in this case seven of the nine members of the court are sitting on Mr. Ipeelee's appeal from the decision of the Ontario Court of Appeal and the Crown's appeal from the decision of the B.C. Court of Appeal regarding Mr. Ladue.)

REASONS FOR JUDGMENT (paras. 1 to 98): LeBel J. (McLachlin C.J. and Binnie, Deschamps, Fish and Abella concurring)

REASONS DISSENTING IN PART (paras. 99 to 157): Rothstein J.

(The judgment is written by Justice LeBel, and concurred with by Chief Justice McLachlin and Binnie, Deschamps, Fish, and Abella; reasons for dissenting in part are provided by Justice Rothstein from paragraphs 99 to 157.)

File Nos.: 33650, 342456

Present: McLachlin C.J. and Binnie, LeBel, Deschamps, Fish, Abella and Rothstein JJ.

On appeal from the Courts of Appeal for Ontario and British Columbia.

Criminal law — Sentencing — Aboriginal offenders — Breach of condition of long-term supervision order — Principles governing sentencing of Aboriginal offenders — Whether principles outlined in R. v. Gladue apply to breach of long-term supervision order — Criminal Code, R.S.C. 1985, c. C-46, s. 718.2(e).

(This is a summary of the issues in the case—its focus is criminal law, and specifically, the principles governing sentencing of Aboriginal offenders. More specifically, the case is dealing with the issues of whether the principles outlined in *Gladue* apply to a breach of a long-term supervision order.)

These two appeals involve Aboriginal offenders with long criminal records. Both Aboriginal offenders were declared long-term offenders and had long-term supervision orders ("LTSOs") imposed. The offender I is an alcoholic with a history of committing violent offences when intoxicated. He was sentenced to six years' imprisonment followed by an LTSO after being designated a long-term offender. After his release from prison, I committed an offence while intoxicated thereby breaching a condition of his LTSO. He was sentenced to three years' imprisonment, less six months of pre-sentence custody at a 1:1 credit rate. The Court of Appeal dismissed the appeal brought by I. The offender L is addicted to drugs and alcohol and has a history of committing sexual assaults when intoxicated. L was sentenced to three years' imprisonment followed by an LTSO after being designated a long-term offender. After his release from prison, he failed a urinalysis test; thereby breaching a condition of his LTSO. L was sentenced to three years' imprisonment, less five months of pre-sentence custody at a 1.5:1 rate. A majority of the Court of Appeal allowed L's appeal and reduced the sentence to one year's imprisonment.

(This is a summary of the history of the case before it appeared in the Supreme Court of Canada, and sets out the key issues in dispute.)

Held (Rothstein J. dissenting in part): The appeal should be allowed in *Ipeelee*. The appeal should be dismissed in *Ladue*.

(This is the finding of the case; Ipeelee's appeal against sentence from the Ontario Court of Appeal is allowed, and the Crown's appeal against the one-year sentence given to Ladue by the B.C. Court of Appeal is dismissed by the Supreme Court of Canada; it is noted that Justice Rothstein dissented in part from the majority judgment.)

Per McLachlin C.J. and Binnie, LeBel, Deschamps, Fish and Abella JJ.: The central issue in these appeals is how to determine a fit sentence for a breach of an LTSO in the case of an Aboriginal offender in particular. Trial judges enjoy a broad discretion in the sentencing process. A sentencing judge has a duty to apply all of the principles mandated by ss. 718.1 and 718.2 of the *Criminal Code* in order to devise a fit and proper sentence which respects the well-established principles and objectives of sentencing set out in Part XXIII of the *Criminal Code*. Proportionality is the *sine qua non* of a just sanction. Proportionality, the fundamental principle of sentencing, is intimately tied to the fundamental purpose of sentencing—the maintenance of a just, peaceful and safe society through the imposition of just sanctions. An appellate court must be satisfied that the sentence under review is proportionate to both the gravity of the offence and the degree of responsibility of the offender.

The purpose of an LTSO is two-fold: to protect the public and to rehabilitate offenders and reintegrate them into the community. It is the sentencing judge's duty, adopting a contextual approach, to determine which sentencing options will be proportionate to both the gravity of the offence and the degree of responsibility of the offender. Sentencing is an individual process. The severity of a given breach will ultimately depend on all of the circumstances, including the nature of the condition breached, how that condition is tied to managing the particular offender's risk of reoffence, and the circumstances of the breach.

Section 718.2(e) of the *Criminal Code* is a remedial provision designed to ameliorate the serious problem of overrepresentation of Aboriginal people in Canadian prisons, and to encourage sentencing judges to have recourse to a restorative approach to sentencing. Courts must ensure that a formalistic approach to parity in sentencing does not undermine the remedial purpose of s. 718.2(e). Section 718.2(e) does more than affirm existing principles of sentencing; it calls upon judges to use a different method of analysis in determining a fit sentence for Aboriginal offenders. The enactment of s. 718.2(e) is a specific direction by Parliament to pay particular attention to the circumstances of Aboriginal offenders during the sentencing process because those circumstances are unique and different from those of non-Aboriginal offenders. To the extent that current sentencing practices do not further the objectives of deterring criminality and rehabilitating offenders, those practices must change so as to meet the needs of Aboriginal offenders and their communities. Sentencing judges, as front-line workers in the criminal justice system, are in the best position to re-evaluate these criteria to ensure that they are not contributing to ongoing systemic racial discrimination. Just sanctions are those that do not operate in a discriminatory manner.

When sentencing an Aboriginal offender, a judge must consider the factors outlined in *R. v. Gladue*, 1999 CanLII 679 (SCC), [1999] 1 S.C.R. 688: (a) the unique systemic or background factors which may have played a part in bringing the particular Aboriginal offender before the courts; and (b) the types of sentencing procedures and sanctions which may be appropriate in the circumstances for the offender because of his or her particular Aboriginal heritage or connection. Systemic and background factors may bear on the culpability of the offender, to the extent that they shed light on his or her level of moral blameworthiness. Failing to take these circumstances into account would violate the fundamental principle of sentencing—that the sentence must be proportionate to the gravity of the offence and the degree of responsibility of the offender. The *Gladue* principles direct sentencing judges to abandon the presumption that all offenders and all communities share the same values when it comes to sentencing and to recognize that, given these fundamentally different world views, different or alternative sanctions may more effectively achieve the objectives of sentencing in a particular community. The principles from *Gladue* are entirely consistent with the requirement that sentencing judges engage in an individualized assessment of all of the relevant factors and circumstances, including the status and life experiences, of the person standing before them. *Gladue* affirms this requirement and recognizes that, up to this point, Canadian courts have failed to take into account the unique circumstances of Aboriginal offenders that bear on the sentencing process. Section 718.2(e) is intended to remedy this failure by directing judges to craft sentences in a manner that is meaningful to Aboriginal peoples.

When sentencing an Aboriginal offender, courts must take judicial notice of such matters as the history of colonialism, displacement, and residential schools and how that history continues to translate into lower educational attainment, lower incomes, higher unemployment, higher rates of substance abuse and suicide, and of course higher levels of incarceration for Aboriginal peoples. These matters provide the necessary context for understanding and evaluating the case-specific information presented by counsel. However, these matters, on their own, do not necessarily justify a different sentence for Aboriginal offenders. Furthermore, there is nothing in the *Gladue* decision which would indicate that background and systemic factors should not also be taken into account for other, non-Aboriginal offenders. The parity principle which is contained in s. 718.2(b) means that any disparity between sanctions for different offenders needs to be justified. To the extent that the application of the *Gladue* principles lead to different sanctions for Aboriginal offenders, those sanctions will be justified based on their unique circumstances—circumstances which are rationally related to the sentencing process. Counsel has a duty to bring individualized information before the court in every case, unless the offender expressly waives his right to have it considered. A *Gladue* report, which contains case-specific information, is tailored to the specific circumstances of the Aboriginal offender. A *Gladue* report is an indispensable sentencing tool to be provided at a sentencing hearing for an Aboriginal offender and it is also indispensable to a judge in fulfilling his duties under s. 718.2(*e*) of the *Criminal Code*.

The sentencing judge has a statutory duty, imposed by s. 718.2*(e)* of the *Criminal Code,* to consider the unique circumstances of Aboriginal offenders. If the sentencing judge fails to apply the *Gladue* principles in any case involving an Aboriginal offender this would run afoul of this statutory obligation. Furthermore, the failure to apply the *Gladue* principles in any case would also result in a sentence that is not fit and is not consistent with the fundamental principle of proportionality. Therefore, application of the *Gladue* principles is required in every case involving an Aboriginal offender, including the breach of an LTSO, and a failure to do so constitutes an error justifying appellate intervention.

In the instant case of I, the courts below made several errors in principle warranting appellate intervention. The courts below erred in concluding that rehabilitation was not a relevant sentencing objective. As a result of this error, the courts below gave only attenuated consideration to I's circumstances as an Aboriginal offender. A sentence of one year's imprisonment should be substituted. In the instant case of L, the decision of the majority of the Court of Appeal is well founded and adequately reflects the principles and objectives of sentencing. The appeal is dismissed and the sentence of one year's imprisonment is affirmed.

(This is properly referred to as a headnote, a synopsis of the reasons for judgment of six of the seven Justices of the Supreme Court of Canada who were sitting on this case; lazy law students sometimes are said to have simply read the headnote, rather than the full text of the decision.)

Per Rothstein J. (dissenting in part): In sentencing for the breach of a condition of an LTSO, which is central to the risk of the long-term offender violently reoffending, the protection of the public, more so than the rehabilitation or reintegration of the offender, must be the dominant consideration of the sentencing judge in the determination of a fit and proper sentence. The majority in this case does not specifically address the issue of the sentencing of Aboriginal offenders who have been found to be long-term offenders and have been found guilty of breaching a condition of an LTSO. They have not taken account of the difference between the objectives and requirements of LTSOs for long-term offenders who abide by the conditions of their LTSOs and the objectives and requirements of sentencing long-term offenders who have breached a condition of their LTSOs.

The breach of an LTSO raises serious concerns that rehabilitation and reintegration are not being achieved and calls into doubt whether, despite supervision, the long-term offender has demonstrated that the substantial risk of reoffending in a violent manner in the community by the long-term offender can be adequately managed. Section 753.3(1) of the *Criminal Code* provides that a breach of an LTSO constitutes an indictable offence, as opposed to a hybrid offence, with a maximum sentence of 10 years. The maximum term is for the breach of the LTSO exclusively and is not dependent on the long-term offender having been found guilty of another substantive offence, violent or otherwise. The necessary implication is that Parliament viewed breaches of LTSOs as posing such risk to the protection of society that long-term offenders may have to be separated from society for a significant period of time. Where a breach is central to the substantial risk of reoffending, such as where alcohol or substance consumption has been found to be the trigger for violent offences by the long-term offender, the breach must be considered to be very serious.

Section 718.2(e) of the *Criminal Code* requires a sentencing judge to consider background and systemic factors in crafting a sentence, and all available sanctions other than imprisonment that are reasonable in the circumstances for all offenders, with particular attention to Aboriginal offenders, including long-term Aboriginal offenders. As with all sentencing, this must be done with regard to the particular individual, the threat they pose, and their chances of rehabilitation and reintegration. Evaluating these options lies within the discretion of the sentencing judge. In the case of long-term offenders, the paramount consideration is the protection of society. This applies to all long-term offenders, including Aboriginal long-term offenders who have compromised the management of their risk of reoffending by breaching a condition of their LTSOs.

Once an Aboriginal individual is found to be a long-term offender, and the offender has breached one or more conditions of his or her LTSO, alternatives to a significant prison term will be limited. The alternatives to imprisonment must be viable and the sentencing judge must be satisfied that they are consistent with protection of society. Alternatives may include returning Aboriginal offenders to their communities. However, as in all cases, this must be done with protection of the public as the paramount concern; Aboriginal communities are not a separate category entitled to less protection because the offender is Aboriginal. Where the breach of an LTSO goes to the control of the Aboriginal offender in the community, rehabilitation and reintegration into society will have faltered, if not failed. In such case, the sentencing judge may have no alternative but to separate the Aboriginal long-term offender from society for a significant period of time. Nevertheless, during the period of incarceration, the Aboriginal status of the long-term offender should be taken into account for the purpose of providing appropriate programs that are intended to rehabilitate the offender so that upon release, the substantial risk of reoffending may be controlled.

In this case, it has not been shown that the sentence imposed on the offender I was demonstrably unfit and the appeal should be dismissed. The sentencing judge's findings demonstrate a thorough appreciation of the circumstances. He properly recognized that protection of the public was the paramount concern in breaches of LTSOs. As a long-term offender, I has been found to show a pattern of repetitive behaviour with a likelihood of causing death or physical or psychological injury or a likelihood of causing injury, pain or other evil to other persons in the future through failure to control his sexual impulses. His alcohol consumption is central to such behaviour.

With respect to the offender L, one year's imprisonment was a fit and proper sentence and the appeal should be dismissed. The sentencing judge did not err in focussing on protection of society as the paramount consideration in her sentencing decision. The sentencing judge found that the only way to protect the community, given L's high risk of reoffending sexually and moderate to high risk of reoffending violently, was to emphasize the objective of isolation. She noted that even if L did not commit a substantive offence, his breach was serious. But this was a case where there was a realistic opportunity for rehabilitation that was denied L because of a "bureaucratic error." The sentencing judge does not appear to have considered that it was this error that caused L to be sent to a residential halfway house, which apparently tolerates serious drug abusers and does not provide programs for Aboriginal offenders. This failure meant that L's moral blameworthiness was not properly assessed.

(This is, finally, a summary of the reasons of Justice Rothstein.)

APPEAL from a judgment of the Ontario Court of Appeal (Laskin, Sharpe and Cronk JJ.A.), 2009 ONCA 892 (CanLII), 2009 ONCA 892, 99 O.R. (3d) 419, 264 O.A.C. 392, [2009] O.J. No. 5402 (QL), 2009 CarswellOnt 7783, affirming a sentence imposed by Megginson J., [2009] O.J. No. 6413 (QL), 2009 CarswellOnt 7864. Appeal allowed, Rothstein J. dissenting.

APPEAL from a judgment of the British Columbia Court of Appeal (Levine, Chiasson and Bennett JJ.A.), 2011 BCCA 101 (CanLII), 2011 BCCA 101, 302 B.C.A.C. 93, 511 W.A.C. 93, 271 C.C.C. (3d) 90, [2011] 2 C.N.L.R. 277, [2011] B.C.J. No. 366 (QL), 2011 CarswellBC 428, varying a sentence imposed by Bagnall Prov. Ct. J., 2010 BCPC 410 (CanLII), 2010 BCPC 410 (CanLII), [2010] B.C.J. No. 2824 (QL), 2010 CarswellBC 3822. Appeal dismissed.

(This is an explanation of the history of these two cases heard by the Supreme Court: one was an appeal from the Ontario Court of Appeal and the other from the British Columbia Court of Appeal; the Ontario Court of Appeal had affirmed the sentence imposed by the trial judge, Megginson; the B.C. Court of Appeal had varied a sentence imposed by the trial judge, Bagnall. The Supreme Court of Canada disagreed with the judgment of the Ontario Court of Appeal, and agreed with the decision of the B.C. Court of Appeal, allowing the first appeal and dismissing the second.)

Fergus J. (Chip) O'Connor, for the appellant Manasie Ipeelee.
Gillian Roberts, for the respondent Her Majesty The Queen.
Susanne Boucher and *François Lacasse,* for the intervener the Director of Public Prosecutions.

Jonathan Rudin and *Amanda Driscoll,* for the intervener the Aboriginal Legal Services of Toronto Inc.

Mary T. Ainslie, for the appellant Her Majesty The Queen.

Hovan M. Patey, Lawrence D. Myers, Q.C., and *Kristy L. Neurauter,* for the respondent Frank Ralph Ladue.

Kelly Doctor, for the intervener the British Columbia Civil Liberties Association.

Written submissions only by *Clayton C. Ruby, Nader R. Hasan* and *Gerald J. Chan,* for the intervener the Canadian Civil Liberties Association.

(These are the lawyers appearing in the Court for the accused and the federal government, and for various interveners in the case, granted status by the court; the actual text of the Court's decision then follows.)

CUSTOM

Most forms of law originally derived from **custom**, the practices and patterns of behaviour through which society had come to order itself. As Philip James has observed, this was particularly true in Britain, where centuries of commercial practice, for example, were ultimately shaped into legislative form in the *Sale of Goods Act* of 1893. But in contemporary Canada, custom did not have as significant an effect as a form of law in most areas of conduct. Law was typically imported from Britain and had already incorporated custom, whether in the realm of commerce or in the designation of deviant behaviour.

One notable exception to the preeminence in Canada of law over custom is constitutional law, where Supreme Court decisions have typically given considerable prominence to the role of custom or "convention" in federal-provincial disputes over constitutional change. The Supreme Court's decision in 1981 on the patriation of the Canadian Constitution is probably the best example. In *Manitoba (A.G.) v. Canada (A.G.) (Patriation Reference)*,[6] the Supreme Court held that there was a constitutional convention requiring the federal government to have the consent of the provinces before amending the *British North America Act*. Although the Supreme Court indicated that the federal government required no such consent as a matter of law, its emphasis on convention served to push the constitutional reform initiative back into the political arena.

BOOKS OF AUTHORITY

From the time of Hammurabi to the present, there have been scholars of law who have written authoritative texts or commentaries summarizing various forms of law and applicable principles. Within the British parliamentary tradition, Coke and Blackstone are two prominent authors of books of authority. Coke wrote *Institutes* in the seventeenth century; Blackstone's *Commentaries* followed in the next century. Both works survive as useful documents for the present era.

During the past three decades, the application of books of authority to judicial decisions has increased in both breadth and volume. The courts seek guidance from the contributions of outstanding early scholars, as well as from living academics and writers of treatises who contribute to a developing legal and socio-legal literature. The courts also seek expertise from "expert witnesses" who give opinions in their specialized area of knowledge in court.

Consider, for example, the Supreme Court of Canada's decision in *Ipeelee*, in 2012, cited above. The justices referred, with approval, to Professor Michael Jackson's article "Locking Up Natives in Canada" from *UBC Law Review*, as well as to Professor Tim Quigley's article "Some Issues in Sentencing of Aboriginal Offenders." The Court also mentioned being helped by Professor Jonathan Rudin's articles, documenting increases in Aboriginal overrepresentation in Canadian prisons from 1999 to the present.

In other areas of law besides criminal—constitutional, family, and labour relations—courts are increasingly using books of authority to assist them in the construction of judicial precedent. The growth of interest in the social implications of law and the increasing complexity of statutory and regulatory law have led to the production of a wide array of treatises and articles. In turn, and for similar reasons, the judiciary has been prompted to consult these books of authority to a greater extent than at any other time in Canadian history.

This development seems likely to continue. Since the entrenchment of the *Charter* as a constitutional document, the courts have been looking for both empirical and theoretical guidance with respect to the meaning to be given to such complex rights as freedom of religion, freedom from cruel and unusual punishment, and freedom of expression. While books of authority have only subsidiary power as sources of law, they have become an important part of the process of lawmaking, providing the Canadian legal system with a more comprehensive knowledge of itself. Similarly, courts will continue to hear from experts in a wide range of disciplines: medicine, engineering, criminology, and anthropology, among others.

FURTHER SOURCES OF LAW

We have now considered four sources of law: the principal sources, statute law and case law; and the subsidiary sources, custom and books of authority. But there is more to law and to understanding its sources than these essentially written forms of law. They are typically the outcomes of the legal process; they cannot provide a full understanding of the process itself.

Consider, for example, the task of tracking the current provisions respecting culpable homicide in the *Criminal Code* retrospectively, in order to determine the source of such law in Canada. We find the statute law defining murder and manslaughter in the current *Code* and trace the statute back, noting the years of amendments. In the case of the murder provisions, we find a considerable number of amendments from 1961 to the present but very few between 1892, the date of Canada's first *Criminal Code*, and 1961. We see, in 1961, Canada's original legal definitions of "murder" and "manslaughter" transformed into legal definitions of "capital murder," "non-capital murder," and "manslaughter"; then, in 1976, into "first degree murder," "second degree murder," and "manslaughter."

This exercise provides us with a statutory "paper trail," a sequence of statute law over time. The exercise can be repeated with any form of law. It is a necessary part of understanding the growth of a particular kind of legislation from its inception to the present. At the same time, it is important to look to judicial decisions relating to these various statutes: to construct a historical weave of statute and case law, looking to the relationship between legislative amendments and judicial decisions.

The history of judicial decisions will also give us a history of books of authority as further sources of law; there may, in addition, be some circumstances when custom or convention becomes preeminent. What we ultimately arrive at is a history of law over time, with law and judicial decisions and books of authority often in conflict. We can see clearly enough the changes in statutes over time, and the various issues litigated by the judiciary in response to these statutes. We can see custom or convention in specific circumstances, and the occasional influence of books of authority. What we do not see, after engaging in this exercise, are critical connecting threads. We don't have an organizing description of events or sources, a narrative that attempts to make objective sense of the intentions and consequences of law in historical context.

For example, as an entirely technical task, it may be sufficient simply to cite the various sources of law that apply to first degree murder, second degree murder, and manslaughter, documenting statutory change, case law, and the relevance of custom and books of authority. But this analysis would not be sufficient; the debates of the House of Commons and many other sources (newspapers, commission hearings, polls of public opinion) reveal that legislation regarding homicide has virtually always been focused on the question of penalty for the crime, and, more specifically, on the appropriateness of capital punishment. The 1976 legislation abolishing capital punishment and simultaneously increasing minimum terms of imprisonment cannot be fully understood without a thorough documentation of social, political, and historical developments in Canada from the early years of the twentieth century to 1976. And, of course, debates continue with respect to the form and substance of existing legislation. For example, the so-called "faint hope clause" which permitted the possibility of early parole for some individuals convicted of first and second degree murder, was abolished by the Conservative government of Stephen Harper in 2011.[7] The question of appropriate penalties for crime continues as a subject of argument within the House of Commons.

In virtually any form of lawmaking, law represents power, but also, of course, political compromise: the power to compel certain kinds of conduct, to support certain world-views and simultaneously to reject others, the ability to create legislation that is crafted by compromise. Law is the prize that various political actors seek within a terrain of social, political, and economic conflict. In the face of social consensus, there would be little need for statutory enactments or judicial decisions, the enforcement of custom or the application of books of authority. Law is invariably constructed as a response to conflict or, specifically, to a given social problem; it is a mechanism that attempts to control certain kinds of activities or behaviours. Changes to the *Income Tax Act* may benefit certain taxpayers and disentitle others; they may even seem to be contradictory. Changes to the *Criminal Code* increase or decrease penalties, supporting certain interests and rejecting others. Changes to the constitutional law of Canada benefit certain provinces and constituencies, and correspondingly place limitations on the powers of other provinces and constituencies.

There is, however, considerable support for the idea that law reflects consensus, at least in certain contexts. In order to maintain law and legal order, it is necessary to build a consensus with respect to the moral and social legitimacy of law. A predominant ideology or at least clusters of predominant ideologies are constructed and maintained over time. Hegemony—the ongoing maintenance of a predominant ideology—is said to be the linchpin of legal control. In truth, the practice of lawmaking is much more messy and contradictory than this; clashing world-views sometimes find expression in the same piece of legislation.

Any organizing description of the sources of law must take into account this backdrop of conflict, compromise, and consensus. The legal formalist or legal positivist will argue that the morality, politics, or economics underlying the law is unimportant; what counts are the validity of the legal form and the ability to accurately document the contributing sources of law.

But the limitation of this technical conception of law and the sources of law is that it views law as separate from the social world from which it is created; it asserts that reference to statute law, judicial decisions, custom, and books of authority will provide a fully sufficient account of the legal sources of law. What follows is a more thorough accounting of the sources of law within one specific context, looking beyond statute law, judicial decisions, custom, and books of authority to gain a more complete understanding of the process of law's creation.

THE CRIMINALIZATION OF ILLEGAL DRUG USE AND DISTRIBUTION: TAKING ACCOUNT OF THE COMPLEXITIES OF SOURCES OF LAW

The history of Canada's criminalization of certain mind-active drugs, to take just one example, demonstrates that the sources of data noted above are *not* sufficient. Law can be fully comprehended only by documenting and analyzing the social, political, and economic contexts that gave it life and continue to influence its existence.

On June 6, 1998, a surprising letter was delivered to Kofi Annan, secretary general of the United Nations. "We believe," the letter declared, "that the global war on drugs is now causing more harm than drug abuse itself." The letter was signed by statesmen, politicians, academics, and other public figures. Former U.N. secretary general Javier Perez de Cuellar signed. So did George Shultz, the former American secretary of state, and Jocelyn Elders, the former American surgeon general. Nobel laureates such as Milton Friedman and Argentina's Adolfo Perez Esquivel added their names....

The drug policies the world has been following for decades are a destructive failure, they said. Trying to stamp out drug abuse by banning drugs has only created an illegal industry worth $400 billion U.S. ... The letter continued, "This industry has empowered organized criminals, corrupted governments at all levels, eroded internal security, stimulated violence, and distorted both economic markets and moral values." And it concluded that these were the consequences "not of drug use per se, but of decades of failed and futile drug war policies."*

The criminalization of certain drugs began in Canada in 1908, when *An Act to prohibit the importation, manufacture, and sale of opium for other than medicinal purposes* was passed by the federal government of Wilfrid Laurier. The act provided penalties of up to three years' imprisonment for the importation, manufacture, or sale of the drug, a fine of not less than $50, and a six months' grace period during which opium merchants could sell their remaining stocks.

What circumstances gave rise to narcotics law? Or, put differently, what are its sources? Canadian narcotics legislation is unusual in the realm of criminal law in that its genesis cannot be traced, at least entirely, to late-nineteenth-century England or to other jurisdictions of that era. It is a twentieth-century development, quite unlike laws relating to homicide or theft, originating in both Canada and other Western nations in the early years of that century.

---

*Dan Gardner, "Why the War on Drugs has failed," *Ottawa Citizen*, Sept. 5, 2000. Material reprinted with the express permission of: Ottawa Citizen, a division of Postmedia Network Inc.

THE ORIGINAL 1908 STATUTE

As noted above, the original statute was titled *An Act to prohibit the importation, manufacture and sale of opium for other than medicinal purposes*. The legislation was introduced into the House of Commons by the Minister of Labour, and was strongly supported by all parties in the House. But the statute itself gives no suggestion as to how and why it was introduced and quickly passed into law. Why was the legislation introduced by the Minister of Labour? Why was it strongly supported by all parties? We will need other information if we are to comprehend more fully the meaning to be attributed to legal sources: the intentions and consequences of lawmaking.

As noted above in our brief discussion of homicide, the first important information source is **Hansard**, the recorded proceedings of debates in the House of Commons. Hansard gives some idea of the intentions of legislators at the time a bill is introduced and debated; and though Hansard may not be used for the purpose of statutory interpretation (as you will learn in Chapter 3), it is, nonetheless, a valuable aid to understanding the sources of law. Many other kinds of information are also likely to be useful in this exercise: the archival papers of those involved in the passage of law, particularly the papers of government ministers; the newspapers of the day; the work of historians; the reports of relevant commissions; and other relevant government documents.

When we examine these sources to reach an understanding of the genesis of Canadian narcotics legislation, we find there does not seem to have been significant public clamour for this law. In fact, in British Columbia, the cities of Vancouver, Victoria, and New Westminster had licensed smoking-opium factories as legitimate businesses for almost 40 years. The major local newspapers, the *Vancouver Province* and the *Victoria Times-Colonist,* carried advertising for the sale of opium daily, and there were few expressions of concern about the distribution or use of the drug.

In 1885, when testifying before a commission on Chinese immigration, Sir Matthew Begbie, the chief justice of British Columbia, made the following comments, which were endorsed by other members of the court:

> I altogether disbelieve in any widespread mischief here from opium.... Opium, as generally used here, is probably as harmless as tobacco, which is also extensively used in British Columbia.... Neither opium nor tobacco extend in their evil effects beyond the individual. They are not nearly so dangerous to the public peace as whiskey.... All the evils arising from opium in British Columbia in a year do not, probably, equal the damage, trouble, and expense occasioned to individuals and to the state by whiskey in a single month, or perhaps in some single night.[8]

The opium factories sold a black-tar opium to whites and Chinese in about equal numbers; the opium users would smoke the drug, typically as a recreation. But this was not the only opium business in the province; opiated tonics, elixirs, and analgesics—the products of a white patent medicine industry—were sold to a predominantly white population. Other drugs were, of course, also in use in the province during this time. Alcohol was consumed at saloons and privately. Tobacco was smoked privately and publicly.

The smoking-opium businesses were owned and operated by Chinese. Asians had been encouraged to come to Canada in the 1870s to assist in building the Canadian Pacific Railway and the industrial infrastructure of western Canada. Some brought smoking-opium with them. By 1900, western Canada's labour shortage gave way to a labour surplus; and the Chinese, willing to work for half the wages of white workers, were vilified. The Asiatic Exclusion League was formed, and the local newspapers caricatured the recent immigrants in almost daily racist cartoons. On September 7, 1907, anti-Asian sentiment reached a fever pitch when a crowd of 10,000 angry white workers stormed through the Asian section of Vancouver, assaulting the inhabitants and damaging and destroying property.

In response to this racially and economically motivated violence, the federal government appointed a young federal civil servant, William Lyon Mackenzie King, the deputy minister of labour, to settle Chinese claims for damages resulting from the riot. In the course of the hearings, Mackenzie King received two claims from opium manufacturers. After also receiving a deputation from a local Chinese scholar, merchants, and clergy opposed to the drug, Mackenzie King told the assembled commission, "My own opinion is that it should be made impossible to manufacture this drug in any part of the Dominion. We will get some good out of this riot yet."[9]

In a report to Parliament, King spoke of the "dire" consequences of smoking-opium and urged the prohibition of its sale, importation, and manufacture. Opiated tonics, elixirs, analgesics, and cocaine-laced mixtures—the products of the white patent medicine industry—were not to be affected by the law; they would continue to be regulated by the *Patent or Proprietary Medicine Act*.

We can see from this history that the prohibition of opium originated in a racially motivated labour confrontation on the west coast of Canada. The legislation was intended to "get some good" out of an anti-Asian riot, and only secondarily to prevent the harms of opiate use and dependence. There was no presentation of any sound empirical analysis of harm caused by the distribution and use of the drug. Alcohol and tobacco were not to be considered drugs, in the political and economic sense that smoking-opium was a drug. Even the opiated tonic, containing the same product as smoking-opium, was not conceptualized as a drug, and, therefore, not subject to criminal prohibition.

Can we understand the statute law of 1908 without reference to this social history? Or, to put it more conservatively, does a consideration of the specifics of legislative history enrich or diminish our comprehension of the sources of law and legal process?

At the least, the original 1908 statute provides evidence of law as arising from political expediency: "We will get some good out of this riot yet." What is less clear is the intent of the legislation. Although the statute was designed to resolve a labour conflict, it was also premised on the harm that was said to flow from the use and distribution of smoking-opium. But it is not at all certain that Mackenzie King, the architect of the legislation, believed in this supposition of harm. His 1907 diaries contain the following comments about an upcoming visit to India, and the Indian trade in opium:

> I would learn the part that opium played in the life of the people. Some persons, for example, were of the opinion that opium was used by many of the Sikhs in the same way that Lord Morley was using the cigar which he smoked; that it did not appear to harm them in that climate when used in moderation; that if taken from them, it might lead to other drugs being used.... Lord Morley would give me the names of one or two gentlemen to whom I could speak freely.... [T]hey would give me a true statement of conditions, not to be given, for example, to the people in North Waterloo [King's constituency], but which I might impart privately to Sir Wilfrid. I would be informed on the real conditions so that the Government of Canada might be made fully aware of them.[10]

Mackenzie King's diary notations only complicate our understanding of the intentions of the 1908 statute: the people of Canada are to be given one view of a social problem and the purpose of the law, while the government of Canada (the prime minister and, presumably, his Cabinet) is to be provided with the "truth."

How are we to understand the legislation, in light of this admission? The legal positivist would respond that all the scrutiny is irrelevant. The law was validly enacted, and it continues to stand as a valid source of our current ***Controlled Drugs and Substances Act***, passed in 1997 as an update and relatively minor revision of the former *Narcotic Control Act*. Still, given this background knowledge, it is difficult to argue that a full understanding of the origins or sources of law can be obtained from relevant statutes, **case law** (cited legal decisions—i.e., judicially made law), customs over time, and **books of authority** (influential and comprehensive texts). As we continue to document other sources of Canadian narcotics legislation from 1908 to the present, this difficulty in limiting the scope of our inquiry does not disappear.

THE *OPIUM AND DRUG ACT* OF 1911

In 1911, two key changes were made to the 1908 legislation. One provided that cocaine be added to the list of prohibited drugs; the second made possession of either smoking-opium or cocaine an offence punishable by imprisonment. The new statute, the *Opium and Drug Act*, premised the possession offence on police experiences with the original legislation. When moving a second reading of the proposed law, Mackenzie King had noted, "The police have found that the present legislation is not drastic enough, or broad enough, to give them the powers of seizure and confiscation which they regard as necessary. One of the objects of the present Bill is to make more drastic the regulations in that regard."

King was speaking specifically of the new possession offence and another section of the Act that provided penalties for being in a "house, room, or place" where opium was smoked. These changes in law were a product of difficulties in police enforcement against consensual transactions of importation, manufacture, and sale. Hence, possession was criminalized, not because of informed debate about the possible evils of opiate or cocaine use, but because effective enforcement required this weapon in the statutory arsenal: evidence of distribution offences had proven to be difficult to obtain.

The House of Commons debate dealing with the 1911 legislation was highlighted by opposition to one section of the bill: a proposal that the federal Cabinet be given a procedural power to add prohibited drugs to the schedule to the Act without debate in Parliament. This prompted a significant exchange between Mackenzie King and the Opposition. "We might pass this Act just as it is," one member began, "and the Governor in Council will still be free to add tobacco to that schedule. The Governor in Council are taking a power without any limit." King shot back: "Cigarettes and tobacco have not yet been considered a drug. In naming the three drugs, cocaine, morphine, and opium, Parliament makes it plain that it is legislating against what are known as habit-forming drugs."

We know today that this view of tobacco as something different from a "habit-forming drug" is not defensible—another indication, perhaps, of the elusive and contradictory theoretical and empirical foundations on which both the 1908 and the 1911 statutes were premised.

THE *OPIUM AND NARCOTIC DRUG ACT* OF 1922

In 1922, amendments to the *Opium and Narcotic Drug Act* provided for a minimum term of six months' imprisonment upon conviction for possession; the amendments also provided for whipping of the convicted, at the discretion of the trial judge, and the deportation of immigrants convicted of drug offences. Section 7 of the 1922 legislation enabled a police officer "with reasonable cause to suspect, to search, without warrant, any premises other than a dwelling house."

The 1922 amendments were influenced by Judge Emily Murphy's book *The Black Candle*, serialized in *Maclean's* magazine in 1921. Murphy advocated increased penalties for both use and distribution, and expanded powers of search and seizure for police. Her book depicted a drug trade monopolized by Blacks and Asians, a conspiracy against the "bright-browed races of the world":

> [T]he Chinese pedlars taunted him with their superiority at being able to sell the dope without using it, and by telling him how the yellow race would rule the world. They were too wise, they urged, to attempt to win in battle, but would win by wits; would strike at the white race through "dope," and when the time was ripe, would command the world.... Some of the Negroes coming into Canada—and they are no fiddle-faddle fellows either—have similar ideas, and one of their greatest writers has boasted how ultimately they will control the white men.[11]

It is appropriate to consider *The Black Candle* a book of authority with respect to the development of Canadian narcotics legislation. Emily Murphy was a judge of the Family Court in Edmonton, and a leading suffragette; her views, though often racist and typically uninformed, had a profound impact on both statute and case law during the 1920s.

In 1923, marijuana was added to the schedule of prohibited drugs, with the consent of all parties and with no debate. By 1929, penalties for the distribution and sale of opiates, cocaine, or marijuana had risen from a maximum of six months to seven years imprisonment. Anti-narcotics police had also been given relatively sweeping powers of search and seizure through the legal mechanism of writs of assistance, which allowed the holder to enter any dwelling without a search warrant if the person believed that "narcotics" might be on the premises.

There was very little case law during the 1920s relating to the *Opium and Narcotic Drug Act*. The cases that were decided, however, strongly supported the thinking of Emily Murphy and the general philosophy of the statute law; the judiciary endorsed exceptional prosecutorial powers and increased penalties for those convicted. In *R. v. Venegratsky*, which was a Crown appeal against a six-month term for trafficking, the Manitoba Court of Appeal increased the sentence to three years, noting, "The narcotic problem in Canada is a very acute one.... The government is evidently alarmed and determined to stamp out this illegal traffic.... In an effort to effect such a laudable object, it is entitled to every assistance the Court can legitimately give it."[12]

In the case of *R. v. Sung Lung*,[13] a Quebec court indicated that, unlike for other *Criminal Code* offences, there was no **mens rea** requirement in cases of possession of opium. (See Chapter 10 for an in-depth discussion of the concept of *mens rea*.) In other words, in order for a criminal conviction to be valid, it was not necessary that there be any "evil intent." Specifically, the court decided that it was not necessary for the accused to be proven to have knowledge of possession of opium. "If such a defence could be admitted," the judge wrote, "it would be very easy to evade the law and as this law must be, in the public welfare and interest, strictly interpreted, I find the defendant guilty."[14]

From the 1930s until the early 1960s, there was very little legislation or case law in relation to narcotics in Canada. Any amendments substantially increased both the penalties for all offences and the powers of search and seizure provisions. Within both statute and case law, we find the gradual transformation of certain kinds of drug use "from a status of private indulgence to a status of public evil."[15] The "war on some drugs" was already in full flight.

THE *NARCOTIC CONTROL ACT* OF 1961

In 1961, the Conservative government of John Diefenbaker passed the *Narcotic Control Act*, a statute that remained for more than 35 years until May 1997, when it was replaced by the *Controlled Drugs and Substances Act*.[16] (The *Controlled Drugs* and Substances Act is essentially an amalgamation of the *Food and Drugs Act* and *Narcotic Control Act*, with a few revisions.) The *Narcotic Control Act* set terms of life imprisonment for importation or "trafficking" in "narcotics," principally the opiates, cocaine, and marijuana. But within a few years of its implementation, the number of Canadians using illegal drugs increased substantially. In the mid-1960s, there were about 1,000 narcotics convictions annually; by the mid-1970s, the figure had grown to more than 40,000. More than 90 percent of the increase could be tied to marijuana distribution and consumption.

In response to this increase, a significant change in the punitive direction of the law was made in 1969. The *Narcotic Control Act* was amended to provide for the possibility of summary conviction procedure in cases of narcotic possession. Prior to the amendment, prosecutors were required to proceed by indictment in all cases of possession; the move to a hybrid form of prosecution was a sign that the government was prepared to punish possessors less severely, particularly in marijuana cases.

Millions of Canadians, particularly the young, continued to challenge the legitimacy of the *Narcotic Control Act*. Illegal drugs were intrinsic to the counterculture advocacy of sex, drugs, and rock-and-roll; the peaceful practice of hedonistic pursuits; and they were said by some, likely naïvely, to represent a retreat from materialism and war. The response of the federal government to their challenge of authority was the LeDain Commission, an inquiry into the "non-medical" use of drugs, chaired by Osgoode Hall Law School dean Gerald LeDain. The commission was to gather research findings, hold public hearings, and interview medical and law enforcement experts in order to recommend how the law might be changed to respond more usefully to the growing use of illegal drugs.

In 1972 and 1973, the commission submitted its reports to the government. The five commissioners—prominent physicians, lawyers, and academics—advocated the abolition of the criminal offence of possession of marijuana, as well as a general philosophical shift on the drug problem from a strict model of criminal enforcement toward the "wise exercise of freedom of choice." However, its recommendations were never acted upon directly by the government.

Nevertheless, in 1973 some relevant amendments were made to the *Criminal Code,* providing for two new criminal sanctions: absolute and conditional discharges. The amendments provided that offenders convicted of a wide range of offences could now be granted "absolute" or "conditional" discharges rather than be fined, placed on probation, or imprisoned. Their significance lay in the fact that those convicted of these offences could now claim, for purposes of employment, that they had never been convicted of a criminal offence. An absolute discharge involves no penalty other than courtroom appearance and a finding of guilt. A conditional discharge involves the completion of a condition, typically probation or community service, prior to discharge. The amendments were immediately incorporated into the sentencing of those convicted of narcotic possession, most notably in marijuana cases. By the late 1970s, about 20 percent of those convicted of marijuana possession received a discharge.

The *Narcotic Control Act* of 1961 was not the subject of much legislative debate and statutory enactment. The primary source of law in relation to illegal drugs since 1961 has been the judiciary, setting new norms for sentence length, striking down procedural provisions in conflict with the *Charter,* and drawing distinctions between marijuana and other "narcotics." For the past 20 years, case or common law has been the predominant source of law controlling illegal drugs.

In 1986, in *R. v. Oakes,*[17] for example, the Supreme Court of Canada decided unanimously that the reverse onus provision in section 8 of the *Narcotic Control Act* was unconstitutional, a violation of section 11(d) of the *Charter* and its presumption of innocence. The reverse onus section of the Act dealt with procedure in cases of possession for the purpose of trafficking; it had required that an individual convicted of narcotic possession must then prove, on a balance of probabilities, that he or she was not trafficking the drug. The section's reversal of the presumption of innocence had been justified by the perceived need to take extraordinary statutory measures against the trade in narcotics.

The courts have also drawn relatively consistent distinctions between marijuana and other narcotics in matters of sentencing. As early as 1970, the Ontario Court of Appeal made the following remarks in the case of *R. v. Johnston and Tremayne,* a case of conspiracy to import marijuana: "The maximum sentence ... [in this case] is life imprisonment. Thus, the framers of the Act regarded, and presumably still do regard, both offences as very grave, although I must confess at once that the Court takes a different view of the use or importation of marijuana as compared with the more serious drugs embraced by the Act, such as heroin."[18] Other cases since that time have generally endorsed these sentiments. Similarly, the *Controlled Drugs and Substances Act* of 1997 now places marijuana in a separate category; it is a Schedule II drug.

Most significantly, perhaps, the penalties prescribed by the judiciary have changed over time, despite the absence of statutory change. In the late 1960s, about 50 percent of all convicted marijuana users were sent to jail for their crimes. Notwithstanding this judicial "get tough" policy, the numbers of Canadians charged with the offence continued to rise.[19] Between 1966 and 1975, in response to a 4,000-percent increase in convictions, the judiciary moderated penalties for marijuana, fining most users, imprisoning about 5 percent, and generally giving the remainder either absolute or conditional discharges. It was not only marijuana possession, however, that was affected by this shift in judicial perceptions of appropriate punishment. While almost 90 percent of heroin and cocaine users were jailed in the 1960s, by the mid-1970s, fewer than half were imprisoned. These patterns of sentencing continue to this day.

The sources of our current prohibition of certain drugs are a complex interplay of statutory change and case law. Judges have generally acted to moderate the philosophy and penalties of the 1961 and 1997 statutes, having had to adjust their conceptions of the drug problem in light of the cultural changes of the late 1960s and the greater medical and social knowledge on drug use and abuse now available. Today, Emily Murphy's *Black Candle* is no longer regarded as a book of authority; it has been displaced by texts offering technically and empirically based analysis.[20] And yet the heart of the law—a criminal prohibition of certain drugs—remains.

CONTROLLING CANNABIS CULTIVATION: THE *SAFE STREETS AND COMMUNITIES ACT*, 2011

Now about halfway through the second decade of the twenty-first century, we continue to face an evolving set of issues with respect to the use and distribution of cannabis (and other illegal drugs). Although marijuana distribution was originally an import–export business, with the product coming from Thailand, Colombia, Lebanon, and Mexico, it emerged during the late 1990s and in this century as a burgeoning industry of domestic production, not only in Canada, but globally. "Grow-ops," large-scale indoor cultivation projects, have become widespread, and the judiciary have often been reluctant to impose substantial terms of imprisonment in response, given both the greater social acceptance of such drug use by adults, and the need to limit the use of imprisonment to acts that have a clear and identifiable social harm. The Conservative government of Stephen Harper has been trying to reverse this trend, however, passing legislation in 2011, the *Safe Streets and Communities Act*, that provides for a minimum term of six months' imprisonment for growing five marijuana plants or more. At the same time, however, some of our neighbours to the south do not appear to be heading in the same direction. In 2013, as a consequence of voter initiatives, both the states of Colorado and Washington moved to tax and regulate the distribution and recreational use of cannabis.

In Canada cannabis growers belong to a very large, unregulated, untaxed, and often-lucrative industry. What will become of the trade in this drug? The *Safe Streets and Communities Act* represents a starkly different direction from that taken during the past 30 years in response to illegal drug use and distribution. Rather than gradually moving toward a view of illegal drug use as a public health problem, this legislation continues criminalization of users and now provides mandatory prison terms for even small-scale cultivators of cannabis. At the same time, however, polls indicates that a majority of Canadians support less severe penalties, perhaps even taxation and regulation—and recent developments in the United States do hint at the possibility that taxation and regulation may be where we are collectively heading. In any event, the future of drug policy—and hence the law relating to illegal drugs—remains uncertain.

CONCLUSION: THE EVOLUTION OF SUBSTANTIVE AND PROCEDURAL LAW

We are now close to a decade past the 100th anniversary of prohibition in Canada (in July 2008), and the contradictions that flow from the criminalization of certain drugs—and the simultaneous promotion of other arguably more harmful drugs (alcohol and tobacco)—have not disappeared from the political stage. And, more important for our purposes in this chapter, it remains clear that an understanding of the continuing evolution of substantive and procedural law depends upon more than even the most detailed examination of statute law, case law, custom, and books of authority.

WEB LINKS

Parliament of Canada
http://www.parl.gc.ca/
This is the home page of Canada's Parliament, which comprises the House of Commons and the Senate. This site contains the debates of both houses, information about senators and members of Parliament, as well as links to House committees and to other sites concerning the parliamentary process.

World History of Democracy
http://www.nipissingu.ca/department/history/muhlberger/histdem/index.htm
Hosted by Nipissing University, North Bay, Ontario, this website contains an impressive number of links to primary writings on the historical roots of democracy. The site also contains scholarly research, essays, and original works devoted to the world history of democracy.

The Avalon Project at the Yale Law School: Documents in Law, History and Diplomacy
http://avalon.law.yale.edu/default.asp
The Avalon Project mounts documents relevant to the fields of law, history, economics, politics, diplomacy, and government, as well as providing links from those documents to their supporting material. Documents are listed from pre–eighteenth century, such as the Code of Hammurabi and *Magna Carta*, through to the twenty-first century.

British History
http://britannia.com/history/
This website, which is part of the main Britannia site, is a portal to extensive information about Britain's history.

National Library of Canada
http://www.nlc-bnc.ca/
The National Library of Canada has developed a website containing interesting information on Canada's history. There are links to historical documents

QUESTIONS FOR DISCUSSION

1. Must judges necessarily make law when they interpret ambiguous statutes, or is their task merely one of interpretation? Discuss.
2. Consider the Supreme Court of Canada's 2012 decision in *R. v. Ipeelee*. Which of the two summaries of the reasons of the Supreme Court justices is most persuasive?
3. The prohibition of certain drugs appears to have been developed for reasons related to race, cultural difference, and a labour crisis within the North American economy. What are the justifications for such law today? Discuss.

FURTHER READING

Giffen, P.J. et al. *Panic and Indifference: The Politics of Canada's Drug Laws*. Ottawa: Canadian Centre on Substance Abuse, 1991.
    This book attempts an explanation of the social origins of Canadian drug legislation, complementing the analysis presented within this chapter and pointing to the complexity of a comprehensive understanding of the origins of law.
Ogilvie, M.H. *Historical Introduction to Legal Studies*. Toronto: Carswell, 1982.
    A comprehensive analysis of the historical sources of Canadian law, an indispensable resource for those interested in the origins of the Canadian legal system.
Thompson, E.P. *Whigs and Hunters: The Origins of the Black Act*. London, U.K.: Allen Lane, 1975.
    A masterful analysis of a specific instance of the origins and consequences of law, undertaken by the British historian E.P. Thompson. The book chronicles the complexity of law's sources; it also has much to say about the importance of law as a mechanism for both asserting and denying social, economic, and political justice.

NOTES

1. M.H. Ogilvie, *Historical Introduction to Legal Studies* (Toronto: Carswell, 1982).
2. Ibid., 362.
3. G. Gall, *The Canadian Legal System*. 3rd ed. (Toronto: Carswell, 1990), 28.

4. P.S. James, *Introduction to Law.* 11th ed. (London, U.K.: Butterworths, 1985).

5. James, *Introduction to Law,* 9.

6. [1981] 1 S.C.R. 753.

7. Bill S-6, given Royal Assent March 2011.

8. "Report of the Commissioners Appointed to Inquire into the Subject of Chinese Immigration into the Province of British Columbia," *Sessional Papers,* no. 54A, 1885: 74–5.

9. *Vancouver Province,* June 3, 1908, 1.

10. *King Diaries,* Mission to the Orient, 1907–1909. (Ottawa: National Archives of Canada), 85–6.

11. E. Murphy, *The Black Candle* (Toronto: Thomas Allen, 1922), 188–9.

12. *R. v. Venegratsky* (1928), 49 C.C.C. 298 (Man. C.A.).

13. (1923), 39 C.C.C. 187 (Que. Dist. Ct.).

14. Ibid., at 189.

15. M. Green, "A History of Canadian Narcotics Legislation: The Formative Years," *University of Toronto Faculty of Law Review* (1979): 42–79.

16. R.S.C. 1996, c. 19.

17. (1986), 24 C.C.C. (3d) 321, 50 C.R. (3d) 1, [1986] 1 S.C.R. 103.

18. *R. v. Johnston and Tremayne,* [1970] 4 C.C.C. 64 (Ont. C.A.).

19. See P.G. Erickson, *Cannabis Criminals* (Aurora, ON: Canada Law Book, 1980). This volume offers a most authoritative description of the legislation on narcotics.

20. B. MacFarlane, *Drug Offences in Canada.* 2nd ed. (Aurora, ON: Canada Law Book, 1986).

REFERENCES

Alexander, B. *The Globalisation of Addiction.* Toronto: University of Toronto Press, 2009.

Boyd, N. "The Origins of Canadian Narcotics Legislation: The Process of Criminalization in Historical Context." *Dalhousie Law Journal* 8 (1984): 102–36.

Erickson, P.G. *Cannabis Criminals.* Aurora, ON: Canada Law Book, 1980.

Gall, G. *The Canadian Legal System.* 3rd ed. Toronto: Carswell, 1990.

Green, M. "A History of Canadian Narcotics Legislation: The Formative Years." *University of Toronto Faculty of Law Review* (1979): 42–79.

James, P.S. *Introduction to English Law.* 11th ed. London, U.K.: Butterworths, 1985.

LeDain, G. *Final Report of the Commission of Inquiry into the Non-Medical Use of Drugs.* Ottawa: Information Canada, 1973.

MacFarlane, B. *Drug Offences in Canada.* 2nd ed. Aurora, ON: Canada Law Book, 1986.

Murphy, E. *The Black Candle*. Toronto: Thomas Allen, 1922.

Ogilvie, M.H. *Historical Introduction to Legal Studies*. Toronto: Carswell, 1982.

Phillips, O.H. *A First Book of English Law*. 8th ed. London, U.K.: Sweet and Maxwell, 1988.

Safe Streets and Communities Act, Statutes of Canada, 2012, c.1.

Sim, R.S., and D.M. Scott. *"A" Level English Law*. 3rd ed. London, U.K.: Butterworths, 1970.

Walker, R.J., and M.G. Walker. *The English Legal System*. 6th ed. London, U.K.: Butterworths, 1985.

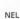

CHAPTER 3

HOW DO JUDGES INTERPRET AMBIGUOUS STATUTES? RULES AND PRINCIPLES AND THEIR APPLICATION

In 1983, University of Ottawa law professor Elmer Driedger wrote in the second edition of his text *The Construction of Statutes* that, "Today there is only one principle or approach, namely, the words of an Act are to be read in their entire context in their grammatical sense harmoniously with the scheme of the Act, the object of the Act and the intention of Parliament."[1] It is difficult to overstate the impact that this single sentence has had on judgments of the Supreme Court of Canada in the 30 years since 1984—and hence on the interpretation of statutes in Canada.

Consider, as an example, the 2012 decision of the Supreme Court in *R. v. Boudreault* 2012 SCC 56, [2012] 3 S.C.R. 157.

The Facts

The accused, Donald Boudreault, was inebriated and unfit to drive home after a night of drinking. A taxi was called for him, with his agreement, but the taxi was late and rather than waiting in the cold he got into his truck, started the engine, turned on the heat, and then fell asleep. When the taxi driver arrived on the scene, he called the police. The police arrested Boudreault and charged him with both impaired driving and driving with more than 80 mg of alcohol in 100 mL of his blood, contrary to sections 253 (1) (a) and (b) of the *Criminal Code*. He was acquitted of both these charges at trial, but the Court of Appeal allowed the Crown's appeal, set aside his acquittals, and entered convictions on both charges. The majority of the Supreme Court of Canada (six members of a seven-member bench) then restored the acquittals at trial.

The relevant section of the *Criminal Code*:

253. (1) Every one commits an offence who operates a motor vehicle or vessel or operates or assists in the operation of an aircraft or of railway equipment or has the care or control of a motor vehicle, vessel, aircraft or railway equipment, whether it is in motion or not,

    (a) while the person's ability to operate the vehicle, vessel, aircraft or railway equipment is impaired by alcohol or a drug; or

    (b) having consumed alcohol in such a quantity that the concentration in the person's blood exceeds eighty milligrams of alcohol in one hundred millilitres of blood.

(2) For greater certainty, the reference to impairment by alcohol or a drug in paragraph (1)(a) includes impairment by a combination of alcohol and a drug.

The central issue in the Boudreault case was that of the meaning to be given to the phrase, "the care or control of a motor vehicle." This is an issue of statutory interpretation. Justice Fish, writing for the majority of the Supreme Court of Canada, had this to say about care and control:

> For the reasons that follow, I have concluded that "care or control", within the meaning of s. 253(1) of the Criminal Code, signifies (1) an intentional course of conduct associated with a motor vehicle; (2) by a person whose ability to drive is impaired, or whose blood alcohol level exceeds the legal limit; (3) in circumstances that create a realistic risk, as opposed to a remote possibility, of danger to persons or property.

> Only the third element—realistic risk of danger—is in issue on this appeal. The Crown submits that risk of danger is not an element of "care or control" under s. 253(1) of the Code. The trial judge found that it is. With respect, I agree with the trial judge.

> The existence of a realistic risk of danger is a matter of fact. In this case, the trial judge, applying the correct legal test, found as a fact that there was no such risk.

> I recognize, as the trial judge did, that a conviction will normally ensue where the accused, as in this case, was found inebriated behind the wheel of a motor vehicle with nothing to stop the accused from setting it in motion, either intentionally or accidentally.

> Impaired judgment is no stranger to impaired driving, where both are induced by the consumption of alcohol or drugs. Absent evidence to the contrary, a present ability to drive while impaired, or with an excessive blood alcohol ratio, creates an inherent risk of danger. In practice, to avoid conviction, the accused will therefore face a tactical necessity of adducing evidence tending to prove that the inherent risk is not a realistic risk in the particular circumstances of the case.

> That is what happened here. The trial judge was satisfied that Mr. Boudreault would not, in fact, have set his vehicle in motion. And this was the only risk of danger in issue at trial.

But consider the dissent of Justice Cromwell, again focusing on the issue of care or control of a motor vehicle by Mr. Boudreault:

> The trial judge found that in order for the accused to be in "care or control" of a vehicle, his acts in relation to it must give rise to a risk of danger. In other words, creation of a risk of danger is an essential element of the offence. The judge also found that there was no such risk here because the appellant did not intend to drive. My colleague Fish J. would uphold these findings. I respectfully disagree.

> My view is that risk of danger is not an element of the offence. My colleague attempts to limit by means of statutory interpretation the potentially wide ambit of the care or control offence by reading in both this new essential element and a new evidentiary rule that operates against the accused. Respectfully, this result is not consistent with well-settled principles of statutory interpretation. In addition, this approach, in my respectful view, seriously undercuts the provision's preventive purpose. In any event, even if the creation of risk were an essential element of the offence, the trial judge erred in law in finding that it had not been proved. There is

no dispute that the absence of intent to set the vehicle in motion is not a defence. But the trial judge in effect made it so by basing his conclusion that there was no risk on evidence that the appellant did not intend to drive.

Further, Justice Cromwell goes on to say

> The question of what the expression "care or control" means in this section is of course an issue of statutory interpretation. The approach to the issue is not controversial: we are to read the words in their entire context, in their grammatical and ordinary sense harmoniously with the scheme of the Act, the object of the Act and the intention of Parliament....
>
> I begin with the text of the provision. "[C]are or control" are not technical legal words in this context. The ordinary sense of the word "care" denotes charge or protection while "control" denotes command and direction: see, e.g., R. v. Price (1978), 40 C.C.C. (2d) 378 (N.B.S.C., App. Div.), at pp. 383–84; R. v. Johal (1998), 124 C.C.C. (3d) 249 (Ont. Ct. (Gen. Div.)), at p. 253. It follows that if the ordinary meaning of these words applies, one is in care or control of a motor vehicle when one acts to assume the present ability to operate the vehicle or has its superintendence or management.
>
> The scheme and object of the provision suggest that Parliament intended the ordinary meaning to apply. The purpose of criminalizing having care or control of a vehicle while impaired (or over .08) is preventive. While the evil is the danger of impaired operation of a vehicle, a wider ambit of criminality has been created to prevent that evil from materializing. The unanimous Court, speaking through Fauteux J., commented on this preventive purpose in Saunders v. The Queen, [1967] S.C.R. 284, at pp. 289–90:
>
> *Obviously, every one agrees that the true object of the provisions ... is to cope with and protect the person and the property from the danger which is inherent in the driving, care or control of a motor vehicle by anyone who is intoxicated....*
>
> *....these and the other related provisions of the Code manifest the determination of Parliament to strike at the very root of the evil, to wit: the combination of alcohol and automobile, that normally breeds this element of danger which this preventive legislation is meant to anticipate. [Emphasis added; italics in original.]*
>
> In R. v. Whyte, [1988] 2 S.C.R. 3, when discussing the constitutionality of the presumption of care or control now found at s. 258 of the Code, Dickson C.J. held that "Parliament wished to discourage intoxicated people from even placing themselves in a position where they could set a vehicle in motion" (p. 26 (emphasis added); see also Ford v. The Queen, [1982] 1 S.C.R. 231, at p. 249; Toews, at p. 126).
>
> I conclude that the provision's preventive purpose supports giving the expression "care or control" in this context its ordinary meaning.

If we return to Elmer Driedger and his commentary regarding statutory interpretation, which of these interpretations of "care or control" is most compelling? To quote Driedger, what is the scheme of the Act, the object of the Act, and the intention of

Parliament? It seems fairly clear the case law cited by Justice Cromwell lends some support to his position—that Mr. Boudreault must be seen, as in *Whyte*, cited above, to have placed himself in a position where he could set a vehicle in motion.

But Justice Fish, in his decision, cites section 258 of the *Criminal Code*, which casts doubt on the arguments raised by Justice Cromwell. This section provides that an accused who is found in the driver's seat of a motor vehicle:

> ...shall be deemed to have had the care or control of the vehicle ... unless the accused establishes that the accused did not occupy that seat or position for the purpose of setting the vehicle ... in motion ....
>
> Accordingly, an accused found in the driver's seat will be presumed, as a matter of law, to have care or control of the vehicle, unless the accused satisfies the court that he or she had no intention to drive—an intention that, pursuant to Ford, is not an essential element of the offence!
>
> At a minimum, the wording of the presumption signifies that a person who was found drunk and behind the wheel cannot, for that reason alone, be convicted of care or control if that person satisfies the court that he or she had no intention to set the vehicle in motion. Dickson C.J. made this plain in R. v. Whyte, [1988] 2 S.C.R. 3, at p. 19: "It cannot be said that proof of occupancy of the driver's seat leads inexorably to the conclusion that the essential element of care or control exists...."
>
> Put differently, s. 258(1)(a) indicates that proof of voluntary inebriation and voluntary occupancy of the driver's seat do not by their coexistence alone conclusively establish "care or control" under s. 253(1) of the Criminal Code. Something more is required and, in my view, the "something more" is a realistic risk of danger to persons or property.

In other words, to return to Driedger, the strength of the majority judgment, authored by Justice Fish, is that when we read sections 253 and 258 of the *Code* together we begin to see that the intent of Parliament was to criminalize an impaired driver only when that driver occupies his seat or position for the purpose of setting the vehicle in motion. Does this mean that we can now conclude that the majority position better conforms to ascertaining the legislative intent of Parliament than does the minority judgement of Justice Cromwell?

Let's take a look at another relatively recent decision of the Supreme Court of Canada, again pointing to the importance of Driedger's approach to statutory interpretation, but also giving us a little more guidance as to particulars.

Castillo v. Castillo was a 2005 judgment of the Supreme Court of Canada focused on the issue of the limitation period for bringing an action in the province of Alberta. The Castillos had experienced an automobile accident in California in 1998, and the wife brought an action against the husband in an Alberta court just before the two-year limitation period (for filing such a claim in Alberta) had expired. The one-year limitation period for filing a claim in California—the jurisdiction in which the accident occurred—had already expired.

Consider the commentary of Justice Bastarache as it relates to the task of statutory interpretation:

This appeal concerns the proper interpretation and constitutional validity of s. 12 of the Alberta *Limitations Act,* R.S.A. 2000, c. L-12, which provides:

12 The limitations law of the Province shall be applied whenever a remedial order is sought in this Province, notwithstanding that, in accordance with conflict of law rules, the claim will be adjudicated under the substantive law of another jurisdiction.

The circumstances in which the question came to be presented to this Court are as follows.

While on a holiday, the parties were involved in a single car accident in or around Fresno, California, on May 10, 1998. The respondent was driving. The appellant and respondent are married and, at the time of the accident, were in the process of moving from British Columbia to Alberta. The vehicle they were driving was registered and insured in British Columbia. The parties have admitted that, for the purposes of this action, they were at all material times resident in Calgary, Alberta.

On May 9, 2000, the appellant filed a statement of claim in the Court of Queen's Bench of Alberta to recover compensation for the injuries and damages she sustained as a result of the accident. The respondent successfully sought an order for summary dismissal of the claim on the basis that the action was barred under California law, where the applicable limitation period is one year: (2002), 3 Alta. L.R. (4th) 84, 2002 ABQB 379. That decision was upheld by the Court of Appeal: (2004), 30 Alta. L.R. (4th) 07, 2004 ABCA 158. The appellant argues that the purpose and effect of s. 12 is to apply the two-year Alberta limitation period to the exclusion of the California one-year limitation period, thereby allowing the action to proceed.

The question before this Court is whether s. 12 effectively excludes the operation of the limitations law of the foreign jurisdiction whose laws otherwise govern the cause of action. Section 12 purports to apply Alberta limitations law "notwithstanding that, in accordance with conflict of law rules, the claim will be adjudicated under the substantive law of another jurisdiction". The difficulty in interpreting these words results in particular from the decision of this Court in *Tolofson v. Jensen,* [1994] 3 S.C.R. 1022, which recognized that limitation periods are substantive. As such, the reference to the substantive law of the foreign jurisdiction in s. 12 would normally include that jurisdiction's limitations law. The appellant argues here, however, that the use of the word "notwithstanding" serves to exclude the limitations law of the foreign jurisdiction (see section 12, above).

If, as the appellant suggests, s. 12 is interpreted as ousting the limitations law of the foreign jurisdiction, then Alberta limitations law applies exclusively in all cases where a remedial order is sought in Alberta. Where, as here, the relevant California limitation period is shorter than Alberta's, the longer Alberta limitation period applies and effectively recognizes a cause of action that California law would have extinguished. If the relevant California limitation period were longer than Alberta's, then the shorter Alberta limitation period would apply so as to bar the action in Alberta....

If, as the respondent suggests, s. 12 is interpreted so as not to oust the limitations law of the foreign jurisdiction, then the court must apply the California limitation period first, followed by the Alberta limitation period. This is because the Alberta limitation period applies notwithstanding the fact that the claim is adjudicated under the substantive law of the foreign jurisdiction, including its limitations law. Thus, where, as here, the substantive law of California bars the action, the Alberta limitations law does not apply. This is because there is no right upon which a remedial order can be sought in the Alberta courts, and the conditions of s. 12 are therefore not met....

The Proper Interpretation of Section 12 of the Limitations Act
The Plain Language of Section 12

The parties differ as to the meaning of the term "notwithstanding", specifically whether it ousts the limitations law of the foreign jurisdiction. According to P.-A. Côté, *The Interpretation of Legislation in Canada* (3rd ed. 2000), at p. 356:

Because the legislature is aware of possible inconsistencies, it sometimes adopts explicit rules establishing an order of priority between different enactments.

A variety of well-known terms is used. The statute will declare that it applies "notwithstanding" provisions to the contrary. If, on the other hand, precedence is to be given to another provision, the statute will operate "subject to" that enactment. Sometimes, a statute will contain a separate section decreeing that its provisions "prevail over any provision of any statute which may be inconsistent therewith".

Two types of difficulty arise with this kind of enactment. The more obvious is the problem of identifying the inconsistency. This is not always a simple matter. Deciding on the mere existence of inconsistency itself gives rise to major issues of interpretation. [Emphasis added; footnotes omitted.]...

Extrinsic Evidence of Legislative Intent

This Court has consistently held that

[t]oday there is only one principle or approach, namely, the words of an Act are to be read in their entire context and in their grammatical and ordinary sense harmoniously with the scheme of the Act, the object of the Act, and the intention of Parliament.

(Rizzo & Rizzo Shoes Ltd. (Re), [1998] 1 S.C.R. 27, at para. 21, quoting E. A. Driedger, The Construction of Statutes (2nd ed. 1983), at p. 87)

The appellant contends that where the plain language of a legislative provision is clear and unambiguous, extrinsic evidence of legislative intent should not be admissible. I do not find the ordinary meaning of s. 12 to be clear and unambiguous. I would also question whether statutory interpretation should ever proceed solely on the basis of the plain language of the legislation, without consideration of the entire context, including the purpose and the scheme of the Act. In approving of Professor Driedger's approach to statutory interpretation, Iacobucci J. recognized that "statutory interpretation cannot be founded on the wording of the legislation alone" *(Rizzo & Rizzo Shoes,* at para. 21; see also R. Sullivan, *Sullivan and Driedger on the Construction of Statutes* (4th ed. 2002), at pp. 9–18). It is now well accepted that legislative history, Parliamentary debates and similar material may be quite properly considered as long as they are relevant and reliable and not assigned undue weight: *Reference re Firearms Act (Can.),* [2000] 1 S.C.R. 783, 2000 SCC 31, at para. 17.

There is very little available extrinsic evidence of the legislative intent behind s. 12. The appellant relies on the Alberta Law Reform Institute, Report No. 55, *Limitations* (1989), which concluded that limitations law was properly classified as procedural and that courts should apply local procedural law. The recommendation in the Report to include s. 12 in the new Alberta *Limitations Act* was premised in part on the uncertainty resulting from the characterization of limitation periods as substantive or procedural, depending upon their particular wording. The Report predated the decision in *Tolofson* by five years. In *Tolofson,* La Forest J. recognized that all limitation periods, regardless of their particular wording, were substantive, thereby resolving the uncertainty that had motivated the Report and its recommendation.

More importantly, there is no evidence on the record that the legislature considered or debated *Tolofson* or the Report, which was not tabled at the time the Act was introduced and passed. The government of Alberta opted not to implement the Report's recommendation in 1989. In 1996, s. 12 was introduced by way of private member's bill. The only other extrinsic evidence upon which the appellant relies is a single sentence spoken by Mr. Herard, the member of the Legislature who introduced the bill.

What we can see in *Castillo v. Castillo* is the Supreme Court of Canada wrestling with the difficult question of statutory interpretation and using a variety of sources to determine legislative intent—parliamentary debates, legislative history, and relevant reports to government.

These two cases—*Boudreault* and *Castillo*—illustrate the complexity of statutory interpretation. Whom or what are we to consult about legislative meaning or intent? There are essentially two models of statutory interpretation: one derives from British traditions; the other, from European and U.S. traditions. In the former, a statute is interpreted literally; phrases and clauses are closely examined in order to extract their precise meanings. It is assumed that the law's intent has been fully formulated within the language of the statute, and, accordingly, there is usually no need to go beyond the wording. The European and U.S. traditions of statutory interpretation (and now the Canadian tradition) require a somewhat different focus for analysis. In order to determine the full intent of the legislature, any source that may assist in determining intent may be consulted: parliamentary or legislative debates, commission reports, and the statements of those responsible for the legislation. Within this latter framework of interpretation, there is an important difference in emphasis: it is assumed that the words of a statute are not always sufficient to allow the judiciary or the practising lawyer to understand the meaning that attaches to ambiguous language.

In many instances, statutory interpretation is aided by definition sections written into specific statutes. For example, section 2 of the *Criminal Code* of Canada provides definitions of dozens of words and expressions found within the *Code.* "Highway" is defined, for instance, as "a road to which the public has the right of access, and includes bridges over which or tunnels through which a road passes." "Motor vehicle" is defined as "a vehicle that is drawn, propelled, or driven by any means other than muscular power, but does not include railway equipment." And "weapon" is defined as "(a) anything used or intended for use in causing death or injury to persons, whether designed for that purpose or not, or (b) anything used or intended for use for the purpose of threatening or intimidating any person." The intention of such definitions is to limit ambiguity from the outset and to lessen the need for legal debate about the meaning to be ascribed to key words within the particular statute.

There also exist federal and provincial interpretation acts, which apply to all statutes within their respective sphere. They contain definitions of certain words that are to have the same meaning across federal or provincial legislation and regulation, together with general rules to be employed in the reading of statutes. For example, the preamble to a statute is always to be read as a part of that statute. (The preamble is designed to set out the purpose or gist of the legislation.) The use of the male gender within legislation is always to be read as including the female gender.

STATUTORY INTERPRETATION: RULES AND PRINCIPLES

Statutory interpretation in Canada historically rested on the British tradition of narrow interpretation of legislative intent, developed by the English judiciary from the sixteenth century forward. Irrespective of the breadth of legislative intent, however, three rules and three grammatical principles continue to exist to aid the construction of statutes. The rules have an elegant, albeit often elusive simplicity: (1) read the statute literally; (2) read it in context; and (3) read it in accordance with its intentions. The grammatical principles are still expressed in the traditional Latin: (1) **expressio unius est exclusio alterius**; (2) *ejusdem generis*; and (3) *noscitur a sociis*. Like the rules, they stress the importance of context and implication in the interpretation of ambiguous language. In most respects, statutory interpretation flows from a relatively straightforward and logical set of premises.

The rules and principles are simple but not simplistic, and provide a consistent method for analysis. As Ruth Sullivan has written in *The Canadian Bar Review*, "To resolve statutory interpretation disputes, judges must analyze and integrate a variety of factors, including textual meaning, legislative purpose, acceptable consequences, and presumptions of intent. The attention paid to the factors and the amount of emphasis each receives depend on the circumstances of the case—the type of legislation, the subject matter and audience, how precise the language is, the lapse of time since enactment, and the like. On this approach, judges have considerable discretion, but this discretion is structured and constrained by a principle-based practice of decision-making."[2] In other words, the principles are guidelines, to be used as dictated by the specifics of individual cases. The variables cited by Sullivan—the type of legislation, the lapse of time since enactment, and the audience to which the law applies—can all be relevant to the obviously multi-faceted task of statutory interpretation.

The Three Rules of Interpretation

THE PLAIN MEANING RULE: READ THE STATUTE LITERALLY

There is an appealing simplicity to the **plain meaning rule**, which demands that the words of a statute be read in accordance with their literal, grammatical sense. The courts are, as a consequence, not entitled to read a statute loosely or to impose their own construction upon the statute, even if a literal reading would appear to lead to an incorrect or incongruous result. The courts cannot assume that the legislature has made either errors or omissions. Consider, for example, a statute that prohibits dogs from a city park unless they are on a leash. It cannot be assumed or inferred that the statute was also designed, by implication, to apply to cats, or to any other animal, domesticated or not.

THE GOLDEN RULE: READ THE STATUTE IN CONTEXT

The second of the three rules is essentially a softening of the first. In 1857, in the case *Grey v. Pearson*, Lord Wensleydale wrote, "In construing statutes, the grammatical and ordinary sense of the words is to be adhered to ... [but if there is] some absurdity or some repugnancy or inconsistency with the rest [of the statute] ... the grammatical and ordinary sense of words may be modified so as to avoid that absurdity and inconsistency, but not further."[3] Thus, the **golden rule** proposes that words cannot always be read literally and that when inconsistency, absurdity, or repugnancy arises as a result of the wording of a statute, the inconsistency, absurdity, or repugnancy must be remedied. (A "repugnancy" within the law is not to be understood as something distasteful or horribly unpleasant, but as an anomaly or incompatibility.)

THE RULE IN HEYDON'S CASE: READ THE STATUTE IN ACCORDANCE WITH ITS INTENTIONS

The **rule in Heydon's case** has remained at the heart of statutory interpretation since it was first set out in England in 1584. "For the sure and true interpretation of all statutes," the court wrote, "four things are to be ... considered." The first is the state of the common law before the statute; the second, the mischief for which the common law did not provide; the third, the remedy that Parliament has used to address the problem; and the fourth, "the true reason of the remedy."[4]

The rule in Heydon's case, often referred to as the "mischief" rule, sets out a process for understanding legislative intent. (The word "mischief" is not meant here in its contemporary context of "troublesome but not malicious conduct." Rather, it refers to the defect or limitation in legal control that the statute was intended to correct.) The best-known application of this third rule is found in the Scottish case of *Gorris v. Scott* (1874). The plaintiff, Gorris, sued the defendant, Scott, to recover damages from the loss of his sheep. They were swept into the sea from Scott's boat during a storm. Scott had not provided pens for the animals, as required by law. However, the court held that Gorris was not entitled to recover damages for his loss because the law requiring pens was designed to prevent the spread of contagious disease, and not to prevent losses overboard. Since the law was not designed to control this form of mischief, the claim did not fall within the "mischief" of the act.

THE THREE GRAMMATICAL PRINCIPLES OF CONSTRUCTION

EXPRESSIO UNIUS EST EXCLUSIO ALTERIUS

This Latin maxim literally means "the expression of one is the exclusion of the other." It can be understood to mean that the expression of one thing or class of things excludes another thing or class of things. If an act of Parliament imposes a new property tax on the owners of "houses, outbuildings, apartments, and condominiums," it is to be assumed that the owners of land with no buildings on it are not to be taxed. The express mention of structures that sit on land and the corresponding omission of land itself suggest that the tax is meant to apply to building structures, not land. That is, the express mention of one category (in this case, buildings) excludes some other category (in this case, land).

Another example of *expressio unius est exclusio alterius* might be found in an invitation posted in a university residence inviting all graduates to attend a reception at the home of the university president. At the bottom of the invitation is the statement: YOUR THESIS MUST BE PRESENTED AT THE DOOR. Initially, the invitation appears a little ambiguous. Are all graduates of university programs welcome at the president's home—all those who have received diplomas, B.A. degrees, B.Sc. degrees, or postgraduate degrees? Or is the invitation extended only to those who have completed theses as part of their academic programs, typically master's and doctoral graduates?

The answer here appears to be that the express mention of the thesis excludes certain graduates. "Graduate" is to be defined in this context only as the graduate of a program with a thesis requirement. Hence, diploma and baccalaureate students are to be excluded.

EJUSDEM GENERIS

This Latin expression is literally translated as "of the same kind." It again emphasizes the importance of context in statutory interpretation. The **ejusdem generis** principle dictates that ambiguous phrases or clauses will derive their meanings from the specific context in which they appear.

Suppose, for example, that a statute prohibited citizens from carrying "knives, rifles, pistols, clubs, brass knuckles, or any other such implements on their person." If an individual was found to be carrying a machine gun, it seems likely that it would be interpreted to be a prohibited "implement." If, on the other hand, an individual was found to be carrying a garden spade, it seems unlikely that it would be covered by the statute. In ordinary English usage, a garden spade is an implement, as is a machine gun. But given the specific words and context of this statute, carrying a machine gun appears to be a prohibited act; carrying a garden spade would not fall within the same category. Hence, a garden spade could not be defined as "any other such implement."

NOSCITUR A SOCIIS

Noscitur a sociis means "it is to be known by its associates." This principle is a variation on *ejusdem generis*. It states that a general word followed by specific words will be defined by the context of those specific words. Thus, *noscitur a sociis* is essentially the mirror image of *ejusdem generis*. Instead of an ambiguous phrase taking its meaning from a series of specific words, an ambiguous word takes its meaning from the specific phrases that follow it.

For example, if a statute requires that citizens obtain a licence to operate any "vehicle, automobile, motorcycle, truck, or machinery of a similar kind," the general word "vehicle" is interpreted in light of the specific words that follow. An automobile, motorcycle, and truck all share the characteristic of being driven by an engine rather than muscular power. It therefore seems likely that a bicycle would not be defined as a vehicle, within the meaning of this particular section of the statute.

The *noscitur a sociis* and *ejusdem generis* principles are functionally equivalent; both require general, ambiguous language to take its meaning from the specific descriptive context in which it appears. Whether the ambiguous language follows or precedes more specific language is ultimately of no consequence.

ILLUSTRATIONS OF STATUTORY INTERPRETATION: APPLYING THE RULES AND PRINCIPLES

The three rules and grammatical principles are intended to facilitate the task of statutory interpretation. When judges encounter an ambiguous word or phrase, they, at least in theory, first resort to the plain meaning rule, then the golden rule, and finally the rule in Heydon's case. When interpreting grammatical or verbal context, they turn to the three principles couched in the Latin phrases: *expressio unius est exclusio alterius*, *ejusdem generis*, and *noscitur a sociis*. But it is also appropriate to note that the ultimate task of statutory interpretation is to determine the intention of the legislature in circumstances that are, by definition, ambiguous. In this context the skillful practitioner of statutory interpretation will not proceed in a strictly linear fashion, but will analyze the text of the statute, will look to its purpose, and will examine how different consequences might flow from different interpretive choices—the interpreter will be examining the policies that underlie different analyses, and looking at the various impacts of these policy choices. Or, put differently, in the Canadian context the arbiter will follow the path set out by Elmer Driedger, described above and referenced in both the *Boudreault* and *Castillo* cases.

It is important to recognize that there are times when the common-sense meanings of language are displaced by the language of a given statute. If, for example, the law says that marijuana is a narcotic (as it did under the *Narcotic Control Act* until 1997), it is not a legally useful response to say that science rejects such a classification. In law, words ultimately mean only what the law decides they mean. While a legal system cannot jettison everyday meanings of language and continue to be seen as legitimate, there is nonetheless something of a Humpty-Dumpty character to statutory interpretation, at least at times.

The Persons Case of 1927

Consider the famous Persons case of 1927.[5] In the late summer of that year, five women requested that the federal Cabinet refer section 24 of the *British North America Act, 1867* to Canada's Supreme Court for interpretation. The section reads:

> 24.   The Governor General shall from time to time, in the Queen's name, by instrument under the Great Seal of Canada, summon qualified persons to the Senate; and, subject to the provisions of this Act, every person so summoned shall become and be a member of the Senate and a senator.

Specifically, the women asked the Court to determine whether women were "qualified persons" and, hence, appropriate for appointment to the Senate.

The Supreme Court concluded that women were not "persons" and hence were not eligible for such appointment. The British Privy Council, on appeal from the five women, overturned the Supreme Court of Canada and declared that women were indeed persons and therefore eligible. From our vantage point, this all seems slightly absurd: women are clearly persons. In 1927, however, the word "person," in the context of political representation, meant men.

If the political and social context of law is placed to one side, there is ultimately little magic or mystery in the rules and principles of statutory interpretation. The rules state that we are to read statutes literally; to adjust their literal meanings if—and only if—absolutely necessary; and to determine the purpose or the "mischief" at which a given statute is directed: to determine legislative intention. The principles of grammatical context hold that we are to assume that each word has a meaning; that in setting out inclusive categories, statutes can simultaneously be exclusive; and that ambiguous words can be made unambiguous by relating them to a specific context.

There used to be limitations on the kinds of information that Canadian courts may use in determining legislative intent. Until a few decades ago, the major difference between the Canadian and U.S. methods of interpretation was to be found in the way in which certain kinds of legislative history were incorporated into legal decision making. In Canada, as in Britain, the political process that created the legislation was not subject to scrutiny. Hansard, the record of the House of Commons debates, could not be cited in support of understanding legislative intent. Additionally, it was not always acceptable to introduce the transcript of a minister's speech, the report of a parliamentary committee, or the transcript of a royal commission. It was argued that no certainty or clarity in understanding can be derived from consulting such documents, given their range of arguments. The conflicting social history that gives life to law was taken to be irrelevant as well—or at least confusing. At the same time, however, the evolution of the law itself—the history of amendment and of other legal sources—was admissible as an aid to interpretation. In our current era, however, these various records can be used to help understand legislative intent, fairly enough regarded as potentially valuable sources of information, as noted in the *Castillo* case above.

The accepted primary means of establishing legislative history are, first, tracing amendments to their source, and, second, consulting relevant case law. (A preamble to a statute may also be consulted, since it is read as part of the statute.) There were signs during the 1980s that we were moving away from a narrow conception of the role of legislative history in the determination of legislative intent. The *Charter,* in place since April 1982, has required a greater awareness of the social, political, and economic contexts in which law is constructed and mediated. The terminology — "freedom of expression," "fair hearing," "cruel and unusual punishment," and so on—requires theoretical and empirical analysis of the law's intentions and consequences if it is to be applied in a meaningful way.

In the context of the *Charter,* the rules and principles of interpretation become less significant, though a consideration of relevant case law and legislative intent remain as critical issues. The task of the judiciary is not only to reconcile ambiguities in language, but also to determine whether legislation is consistent with the broad general principles stated in the *Charter*—the putative values of the nation. In this respect, Canada is moving closer to the U.S. model of what is said to be an "activist" judiciary; the acceptability of federal and provincial legislation is assessed against a history of judicially constructed benchmarks of rights and freedoms.

The *Regina v. Ojibway* Case, or When Is a Horse a Bird?

At this point, you may be developing a feel for the application of the rules and principles of statutory interpretation. What meaning can you derive from the decision in *Regina v. Ojibway*,[6] a fictitious case involving a breach of the fictitious *Small Birds Act*?

Blue, J.: This is an appeal by the Crown by way of a stated case from a decision of the magistrate, acquitting the accused of a charge under the *Small Birds Act*, R.S.O., 1960, c. 724, s. 2. The facts are not in dispute. John Ojibway was riding his pony through Queen's Park on January 2, 1965. Being impoverished, and having been forced to pledge his saddle, he substituted a downy pillow in lieu of the said saddle. On this particular day, the accused's misfortune was further heightened by the circumstance of his pony breaking its right foreleg. In accord with veterinary practice, the accused then shot the pony to relieve it of its awkwardness.

The accused was thereupon charged with having breached the *Small Birds Act*, section 2 of which states:

2. *Anyone maiming, injuring, or killing small birds is guilty of an offence and subject to a fine not in excess of two hundred dollars.*

The learned magistrate acquitted the accused, holding, in fact, that he had killed his horse and not a small bird. With respect, I cannot agree.

In light of the definition section, my course is quite clear. Section 1 defines "bird" as "a two-legged animal covered with feathers." There can be no doubt that this case is covered by this section.

Counsel for the accused made several ingenious arguments to which, in fairness, I must address myself. He submitted that the evidence of the expert clearly concluded that the animal in question was a pony and not a bird, but this is not the issue. We are not interested in whether the animal in question is a bird or not in fact, but whether it is one in law....

Counsel also contended that the neighing noise emitted by the animal could not possibly be produced by a bird. With respect, the sounds emitted by an animal are irrelevant to its nature, for a bird is no less a bird because it is silent.

Counsel for the accused also argued that since there was evidence that the accused had ridden the animal, this pointed to the fact that it could not be a bird but was actually a pony. Obviously, this avoids the issue. The issue is not whether the animal was ridden or not, but whether it was shot or not, for to ride a pony or a bird is no offence at all. I believe counsel now sees his mistake.

Counsel contends that the iron shoes found on the animal decisively disqualify it from being a bird. I must inform counsel, however, that how an animal dresses is of no concern to this court.

Counsel relied on the decision in *Re Chickadee*, where he contends that in similar circumstances, the accused was acquitted. However, this is a horse of a different colour. A close reading of that case indicates that the animal in question there was not a small bird, but, in fact, a midget of a much larger species. Therefore, that case is inapplicable to our facts.... It remains then to state my reason for judgment which, simply, is as follows: Different things may take on the same meaning for different purposes. For the purpose of the *Small Birds Act*, all two-legged feather-covered animals are birds. This, of course, does not imply that only two-legged animals qualify, for the legislative intent is to make two legs merely the minimum requirement. That statute therefore contemplated multi-legged animals with feathers as well. Counsel submits that having regard to the purpose of the statute, only small animals "naturally covered" with feathers could have been contemplated. However, had this been the intention of the legislature, I am certain that the phrase "naturally covered" would have been expressly inserted just as "Long" was inserted in the *Longshoreman's Act*.

Therefore, a horse with feathers on its back must be deemed for the purposes of this act to be a bird, and, *a fortiori*, a pony with feathers on its back is a small bird.

Counsel posed the following rhetorical question: If the pillow had been removed prior to the shooting, would the animal still have been a bird? To this, let me answer rhetorically: Is a bird any less of a bird without its feathers?

(H. Pomerantz & S. Breslin, "Regina v. Ojibway," *Criminal Law Quarterly*, 137. Reproduced by permission of Canada Law Book, a division of Thomson Reuters Canada Limited.)

The case *Regina v. Ojibway* is, of course, a parody of statutory interpretation. But the satirical decision makes some useful points and raises questions about wresting certainty from the ambiguity of legal language. Note, for example, the court's comment, "We are not interested in whether the animal in question is a bird or not in fact, but whether it is one in law."

Let us apply the rules and principles of statutory interpretation to *Regina v. Ojibway*. The key issue in dispute is whether a pony with a downy pillow saddle can be properly defined as a "small bird," pursuant to the *Small Birds Act*. The relevant section is that which defines a bird as "a two-legged animal covered with feathers."

If we apply the plain meaning, or literal, rule, the pony in question would not appear to be a target of this definition. The pony, although it may have been covered with feathers, is not a two-legged animal. And the legislation does not provide for other possibilities: a one-legged animal or an animal with more than two legs. Counsel's argument in response is that the definition "does not imply that only two-legged animals qualify, for the legislative intent is to make two legs merely the minimum requirement." But can this argument be successful? If the intent was to make two legs the minimum requirement for defining small birds, would this not have been spelled out within the legislation? In this instance, the act would define a small bird as "an animal with two or more legs, covered with feathers." An application of the literal rule suggests that if the pony covered with feathers had two legs, it might well be defined as a small bird. But given the animal's four legs, it is difficult to argue that it would fall within this category.

The golden rule does not appear to apply to the case because there is no inconsistency or repugnancy within the words of the statute. Application of the rule in Heydon's case suggests that the mischief intended to be corrected by the legislation is the killing of small birds, and since the pony covered with feathers cannot be defined as a small bird, the intent of the legislation is not consistent with controlling the shooting of this pony, albeit a pony covered with feathers.

The grammatical principles of interpretation also suggest that the pony covered with feathers cannot be considered to be a small bird. While the *ejusdem generis* and *noscitur a sociis* maxims do not apply to the facts of the case, the principle of *expressio unius est exclusio alterius* does have relevance. In expressly mentioning two-legged animals in the definition of small birds, the legislators exclude all other possibilities, whether with fewer or more than two legs.

What of Blue, J.'s parting comment: Is a bird any less of a bird without its feathers? The answer is, of course, that a bird without feathers is not a bird at all, at least as defined by the *Small Birds Act*. Without the downy pillow saddle on the pony's back, this legal conundrum would never have arisen. But consider the effect on statutory interpretation if the *Small Birds Act* defined "bird" as "an animal with one or more legs, covered with feathers." Would Ojibway have been properly convicted of killing a small bird? And what of the argument that if one looks to the mischief targeted by the legislation, "only small animals 'naturally covered' with feathers could have been contemplated"? The court rebutted it by pointing out that if this had been the intention of the legislature, the words "naturally covered" would have been used in the statute.

In difficult cases, where legislative intention is a matter of debate, competing values are the focus of the court's attention. Which is more important, as debated within *R. v. Boudreault*—to convict all those who are impaired and simultaneously have the care or control of an automobile, or to restrict conviction to those who also pose a realistic risk of harm? In an albeit fictional context, how expansive should the legal definition of "small bird" be? Should we limit the definition, thereby prosecuting a smaller number of animal killers, or should we protect more animals by seeking the most logically permissible expansion of the term?

At this point, the interpretation of law is no longer a technical task, but a matter of the provision of relevant empirical information fused with moral and political debate. This is the heart of the task of statutory interpretation, most notably when there is substantial ambiguity within a statutory provision.

The Case of *Leskun v. Leskun*, 2006

At times a court has to take account of statutory history in arriving at an appropriate decision—in confronting ambiguity within a statute. Consider the case of *Leskun v.*

Leskun, a divorce proceeding in which the relevance of spousal misconduct was fused with the task of statutory interpretation and statutory history. The facts of the case are set out by Justice Binnie, writing for a unanimous Supreme Court of Canada:

The parties were married in 1978. They had one daughter who has a child. Both the daughter and the grandchild reside with the respondent wife, who is currently 59 years old. She and the appellant husband, who is about ten years younger, met while both were working at the Toronto-Dominion Bank. The respondent had two children from her first marriage. The appellant helped to raise them. The respondent continued to work at the bank for most of the marriage except for interruptions from time to time to help the appellant advance his education. He obtained an MBA from the University of Western Ontario and worked towards qualification as a Certified General Accountant. These educational qualifications substantially boosted his income earning capacity. To meet the family's needs while the appellant was studying, the respondent cashed in her RRSPs and obtained the return of her pension contributions, both of which in the long run contributed to her present financial problems.

In 1993, the appellant left the bank and joined Motorola, which in April 1998 moved him to Chicago as its local Director of Program Management. It was expected that the respondent would move to Chicago to join him. In September of that year, however, the appellant returned to Vancouver to inform her that he wanted a divorce, which was obtained in 1999. Pending resolution of a number of issues, the appellant agreed to pay the respondent $2,250 per month as interim support.

When the issue of permanent spousal support eventually went to trial, Collver J. was confronted with serious uncertainty about the wife's financial prospects: [2000] B.C.J. No. 1085 (QL), 2000 BCSC 1912. Firstly, as mentioned, the respondent had injured her back in 1995 (when she and the appellant were lifting a generator at their home). This required surgery. Her recovery was incomplete. Secondly, the month prior to the marital break-up, the respondent learned that her position at the TD Bank was about to be eliminated. Shortly thereafter she applied for long-term disability benefits arising out of her back injury. The benefits were granted but then discontinued in the fall of 1999. (Subsequent to the trial, the respondent received a severance award from the TD Bank of $83,000.)

In his decision, the trial judge held that the respondent had been disadvantaged by the marriage. The interruption in her career did not enhance her position at the bank and, as stated, she had cashed in her RRSPs and pension contributions to meet the family needs. Further, following the marital breakdown, the combined incomes of the appellant and his new wife enabled them to enjoy a standard of living that the respondent could not possibly maintain on her own. The respondent's ability to attain economic self-sufficiency was in some doubt. Collver J. held that she needed, and was entitled to, support until she had resolved outstanding issues with the TD Bank. He therefore ruled that: "Spousal support of $2,250 per month will continue until Sherry Leskun returns to full employment, when both entitlement and quantum will be reviewed" (para. 25b). However, the formal order issued over a year later did not put the condition so specifically and simply provided as follows:

The Plaintiff shall pay spousal support to the Defendant in the sum of $2,250.00 per month … until further Order of this Honourable Court, and the Plaintiff shall be at liberty to apply for an Order reviewing both entitlement to and quantum of spousal support. [Emphasis added; para. 2.]

At both the B.C. Supreme Court and the B.C. Court of Appeal the award of support to the wife was upheld, and at the Supreme Court of Canada Mr. Leskun argued that spousal misconduct—his spousal misconduct had been wrongly taken into account in determining his ability to pay support. This is what Justice Binnie had to say about the relevance of spousal misconduct, and the relevance of statutory interpretation—in this instance, a section of the Divorce Act. The two critical paragraphs of his text are italicized.

The appellant objects that the majority decision of the Court of Appeal wrongly relied on his alleged misconduct to exonerate his former wife from the consequences of her failure to achieve economic self-sufficiency. The appellant did not challenge the finding that the respondent was not self-sufficient. His point is that in the five years that elapsed between the marital break-up and the hearing before Morrison J. she *ought* to have moved on emotionally and become self-sufficient financially.

There is some merit in his complaint that his self-represented wife failed to put on the record documentary support corroborating her alleged job hunting efforts or to file medical evidence to support a finding of continued inability to achieve self-sufficiency. She filed considerable documentary evidence on lesser matters. Nevertheless the chambers judge heard the respondent and after reading the record was satisfied on that point. The finding of fact was upheld on appeal.

Self-sufficiency is one of the goals set out in s. 15.2(6) of the *Divorce Act* which provides that spousal support orders should

    (a)   recognize any economic advantages or disadvantages to the spouses arising from the marriage or its breakdown;

    (b)   apportion between the spouses any financial consequences arising from the care of any child of the marriage over and above any obligation for the support of any child of the marriage;

    (c)   relieve any economic hardship of the spouses arising from the breakdown of the marriage; and

    (d)   in so far as practicable, promote the economic self-sufficiency of each spouse within a reasonable period of time.

In forceful submissions, counsel for the appellant says that the court should not encourage unemployment self-induced by a spouse's "scorched earth" policy and warns that if the court is to permit "a claim that a spous[e]'s adulterous conduct has left the non-offending spouse so bitter and emotionally traumatized as to be unable to return to work", the court will not only be "opening the floodgates" but create a "legal tsunami" of review or variation applications which would not only "be the return to fault in the *Divorce Act*" but lead to a "weakening, I guess, of the Canadian economy".

I believe that stripped of the rhetoric, the appellant has a valid point of statutory interpretation. Prior to the 1985 Act, s. 11 of the Divorce Act, S.C. 1967–68, c. 24, directed the court to have "regard to the conduct of the parties and the condition, means and other circumstances of each of them" in exercising its discretion in making an award of spousal support. The 1985 Act sought to eliminate misconduct, as such, as a relevant consideration. Section 15.2(5) of the Divorce Act now provides that in making an interim or final order for spousal support, "the court shall not take into consideration any misconduct of a spouse in relation to the marriage". In addition, s. 17(6) instructs the court not to consider any conduct in a variation application that could not be considered in the making of the initial order. These provisions make it clear that misconduct should not creep back into the court's deliberation as a relevant "condition" or "other circumstance" which the court is to consider in making or varying a spousal support order (s. 15.2(4)). Misconduct, as such, is off the table as a relevant consideration.

There is, of course, a distinction between the emotional consequences of misconduct and the misconduct itself. The consequences are not rendered irrelevant because of their genesis in the other spouse's misconduct. If, for example, spousal abuse triggered a depression so serious as to make a claimant spouse unemployable, the consequences of the misconduct would be highly relevant (as here) to the factors which must be considered in determining the right to support, its duration and its amount. The policy of the 1985 Act however, is to focus on the consequences of the spousal misconduct not the attribution of fault.

Section 15.2(4) states that in making a spousal support order the court shall take into consideration the condition, means, needs and other circumstances of each spouse, including

    (a)   the length of time the spouses cohabited;

    (b)   the functions performed by each spouse during cohabitation; and

    (c)   any order, agreement or arrangement relating to support of either spouse.

Certainly, the "condition ... needs and other circumstances" includes the capacity of the respondent to be self-sufficient for whatever reason. Whether or not the claimed inability or incapacity of the claimant spouse is credible is for the trial judge to determine. It is not helpful to cast about to assign blame.

A break-up in the circumstances found here will perhaps inevitably precipitate a period of shock and emotional trauma for the jilted spouse, but Parliament has concluded that the attempt to get to the bottom of all the rights and wrongs that contributed to the break-up is likely impossible and in any event irrelevant to the task of sorting out the financial consequences. As to the "legal tsunami", I agree with the *amicus curiae* that for the most part parties will realize "that the only way out [of the financial difficulties consequent on the break-up] is if they pull themselves up by their own bootstraps".

If the misconduct point were to be viewed in isolation, the appellant is correct, but the point cannot be viewed in isolation. The fact is that both the chambers judge and Newbury J.A., who differed from her colleagues on the relevance of the misconduct, cited numerous other factors (also referenced by the majority judgment) to reject the appellant's attempt to extricate himself from any further financial responsibility for his former wife. Newbury J.A. observed that

> *Mrs. Leskun is now 57 years of age and her affidavit evidence points to various family dif-*
> *ficulties and to her medical problems and those of her family. A court cannot ignore these*
> *difficulties, which have been exacerbated by the breakdown of the Leskuns' marriage. For*
> *this reason, and not because of any self-imposed disability, I would reluctantly uphold the*
> *order of the Court below and dismiss the appeal. [para. 63]*
>
> I agree. I would add the point made by the chambers judge about the narrowness of the
> respondent's work experience, and underline the difficulty of someone now approaching 60
> years of age to re-enter the labour force after a lengthy absence and with few marketable
> skills outside the limits of her former job at the bank, now eliminated.

In sum, the Supreme Court of Canada underlines the importance of distinguishing between spousal misconduct and the consequences of spousal misconduct in granting spousal support—a perhaps subtle but critical distinction.

THE *R. V. LUXTON* CASE

In cases in which one argument can be as compelling as another, how are we to decide? Consider the Supreme Court of Canada's decision in *R. v. Luxton.*[7] In this case, counsel for Luxton asked the Court to rule that the current penalty for first degree murder, a minimum of 25 years' imprisonment before parole eligibility, constitutes cruel and unusual punishment as defined by the *Charter*. Section 12 of the *Charter* reads as follows:

    12.   Everyone has the right not to be subjected to any cruel and unusual treatment
    or punishment.

The relevant part of the *Luxton* judgment, written by Chief Justice Lamer and supported by a unanimous Court, states:

> In my view, the combination of ss. 214(5)(e) and 669 [the first degree murder provisions] does
> not constitute cruel and unusual punishment. These sections provide for punishment of the
> most serious crime in our criminal law, that of first-degree murder. This is a crime that car-
> ries with it the most serious level of moral blameworthiness, namely, subjective foresight of
> death. The penalty is severe and deservedly so. The minimum 25 years to be served before
> eligibility for parole reflects society's condemnation of a person who has exploited a position
> of power and dominance to the gravest extent possible by murdering the person that he or
> she is forcibly confining [as in the *Luxton* case]. The punishment is not excessive and clearly
> does not outrage our standards of decency. In my view, it is within the purview of Parliament,
> in order to meet the objectives of a rational system of sentencing, to treat our most serious
> crime with an appropriate degree of certainty and severity. I reiterate that, even in the case
> of first-degree murder, Parliament has been sensitive to the particular circumstances of each
> offender through various provisions, allowing for the royal prerogative of mercy, the availability

of escorted absences from custody for humanitarian and rehabilitative purposes, and for early parole: see s. 672 (now s. 745), 674 (now s. 747) and 686 (now s. 751) of the *Criminal Code. In Smith, supra,* at p.137, quoted with approval the following statement by Borins, District Court Judge, in *R. v. Guiller* (1985) 48 C.R. (3d) 226 (Ontario District Court):

> It is not for the Court to pass on the wisdom of Parliament with respect to the gravity of various offences and the range of penalties which may be imposed upon those found guilty of committing the offences. Parliament has broad discretion in proscribing conduct as criminal and in determining proper punishment. While the final judgement as to whether a punishment exceeds constitutional limits set by the Charter is properly a judicial function, the Court should be reluctant to interfere with the considered views of Parliament and then only in the clearest cases where the punishment prescribed is so excessive when compared with the punishment prescribed for other offences as to outrage standards of decency.

> Therefore, I conclude that in the case at bar, the impugned provisions in combination do not represent cruel and unusual punishment within the meaning of s. 12 of the *Charter*.[8]

How, then, are to we to define the expression, "cruel and unusual treatment or punishment"? If we apply the plain meaning rule or the golden rule, we encounter some difficulties. First, a literal reading suggests that treatment or punishment must be both cruel and unusual in order to be objectionable. This interpretation is strengthened by the grammatical principle of *expressio unius est exclusio alterius*, inasmuch as the express use of the word "and" within the definition implies the exclusion of "or." But the ultimate difficulty is that there is no literal or easily reconcilable understanding of the wording. There is, instead, an inherent subjectivity in defining the boundaries of acceptable treatment or punishment: one person's remedy may be another person's torment. If we look to the rule in Heydon's case, we find that the purpose of the *Charter* and its protective and liberating terminology was both to set out and to protect the rights that all Canadians are to enjoy.

The Supreme Court, writing in *Luxton,* clearly indicated reluctance to be activist in interpreting section 12. The Court quoted Ontario County Court Judge Borins with approval:

> It is not for the Court to pass on the wisdom of Parliament with respect to the gravity of various offences and the range of penalties which may be imposed upon those found guilty of committing ... offences.... [T]he Court should be reluctant to interfere ... only in the clearest cases where the punishment prescribed is so excessive ... as to outrage standards of decency.[9]

It may seem surprising that the Court is saying that a judicial definition of cruel and unusual punishment can stem only from a perceived outrage of decency, in response to the actions of the state. This interpretation is also consistent with a requirement that treatment or punishment must be not only cruel but also unusual in order to be a violation of human rights. The precise meaning that flows from the prohibition in section 12 of the *Charter* is the subject of a number of precedents, attempts to determine the validity of allegations about penalties or treatments that "outrage standards of decency." They include *Smith v. R.*,[10] *Steele v. Mountain Institution*,[11] and *Olson v. R.*[12]

CONCLUSION: PRECEDENT—THE GUIDING HAND OF STATUTORY INTERPRETATION

Mention of precedents brings us to a final element of concern in statutory interpretation. To this point in the chapter, we have been considering the rules and principles of statutory interpretation and their application to examples from various fields of law. We have seen that while the rules and principles can be extremely helpful in clarifying ambiguity, they can also conflict, and they offer no easy resolution of difficult cases. Rather, members of the judiciary are required to create law from among competing claims. Remember the importance of **precedent** in giving a real-world application to the sometimes obtuse rhetoric of statutes. Decisions of the Supreme Court of Canada bind all courts in the country to their interpretation of a specific configuration of fact and law; decisions of provincial or territorial Courts of Appeal bind all courts within the given province.

The hierarchical development of case law over time is what takes statute law from a statement of general principles to an endpoint of negotiated realities. The Latin term *stare decisis* is applied to the development of case law within a context of hierarchy. Literally translated, **stare decisis** means "to stand by decided things"; specifically, to stand by the decisions of higher courts. (Refer to Figure 3.1.)

As sections and subsections of statutes are continually litigated, the room for alternative explanations of ambiguity decreases. The advantage of the system of *stare decisis*, of building on precedent, is that it provides greater predictability of outcome and greater certainty concerning the application of law. A disadvantage of rigid adherence to precedent is that illogical distinctions will be made in order to stay within pronouncements from the Courts of Appeal and the Supreme Court of Canada. Another drawback is that the law may take on an absurdly tautological character over time. Cruel and unusual punishment, for example, is whatever it is said to be—within a specific historical context. Finally, the system of precedent, taken to its logical conclusion, raises the question of whether the Supreme Court of Canada—the nine men and women who bind all other courts to their decisions—can reverse itself. Are the justices bound by their own decisions, able to change their interpretation of law only after the House of Commons has amended the statute in question? The best answer to this question is that reversals of previous decisions must be rare if the country's court of last resort is to have legitimacy. But such reversals are permissible in rare circumstances.[13]

The late Bora Laskin once noted during his tenure as chief justice:

> It is worth remembering that for a final court, consistency in decisions is merely a convenience and not a necessity. No one expects the Supreme Court to break out in a rash of reversals of previous decisions, even if it should formally dissociate itself from *stare decisis*.... In my view, such dissociation, whether formally expressed or not, is imperative if the Court is to develop a personality of its own.[14]

Figure 3.1

The Operation of *Stare Decisis* in Canadian Courts

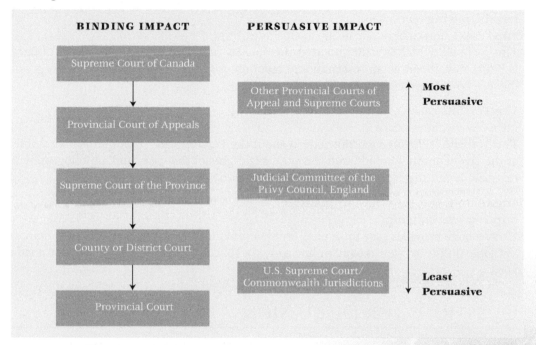

And so it is with statutory interpretation, and with all lawyers and all courts. In complex cases, where the rules and principles are contradictory or not clearly applicable, lawyers and judges must wrestle with their own beliefs and values in the process of construction of the law. In those brief moments, law is transformed from a technical task into an essentially political, economic, and social exercise, focused on data, relevant empirical study, and a choice between or among competing alternatives. In the process, the law is necessarily reconstructed, outside of the realm of the legislature, for better or for worse.

Web Links

Ontario e-Laws: Ontario Statutes and Regulations
http://www.e-laws.gov.on.ca/
Maintained by the Ontario government, this site provides a search engine to locate and read the statutes of Ontario, such as the *Family Law Act.*

Supreme Court of Canada Decisions
http://scc-csc.lexum.com/scc-csc/scc-csc/en/nav_date.do
Decisions of the Supreme Court of Canada are provided on this website.

Legal Drafting
http://aix1.uottawa.ca/ ~ resulliv/legdr/index.html
This website, which is maintained at the Faculty of Law at the University of Ottawa, is being developed as an international resource for legal and legislative drafters and those who interpret legal texts.

The Persons case
http://www.famous5.ca
This website is devoted to information about the Persons case. It contains biographies of the five women who initiated the case, highlights of the case, and a bibliography of material about the women's struggle for legal personality.

Canadian Legal Information Institute
http://www.canlii.org/
This website provides easy links to all federal, provincial, and territorial statutes that are available online, as well as to all online case law released directly from courts in Canada.

Questions for Discussion

1. What are the greatest strengths and the greatest limitations of Driedger's summary of the modern approach to statutory interpretation? Does it carry the power to predict outcomes in individual cases?
2. Does the Supreme Court's decision in *Leskun* appropriately assess the relevance of spousal misconduct for awards of spousal support?
3. How would you try to balance the tensions described in *R. v. Boudreault,* 2012— those of preventing impaired driving, but convicting only those who have a realistic risk of driving while impaired? Discuss.

FURTHER READING

Beaulac, S., and P.-A. Côté. "Driedger's 'Modern Principle' at the Supreme Court of Canada: Interpretation, Justification, Legitimization." *Revue Juridique Themis* 40 (2006): 131–172.

> A compelling analysis of the impact that Driedger's espousal of the modern principle of statutory interpretation has had on Supreme Court decision making from the early 1980s to the present, analysis that is both empirically and theoretically based.

Dworkin, R. "Hard Cases." *Harvard Law Review* 88 (1975): 1057.

> A very interesting legal and philosophical analysis of the hard cases that the judiciary is called upon to determine—an article that meshes nicely with the more legalistic interpretation of Willis in his 1938 article in the *Canadian Bar Review*.

R. v. Seaboyer; R. v. Gayme, [1991] 2 S.C.R. 577, 7 C.R. (4th) 117, 66 C.C.C. (3d) 321.

> This Supreme Court of Canada decision provides direction to legislatures as to the way a statute could be rewritten; see the comments of McLachlin, J. (as she then was). The Supreme Court's decision provides insight into the interpretation of ambiguous statutes.

Sullivan, R. "Statutory Interpretation in a New Nutshell." *Canadian Bar Review* 51 (2003): 82.

> This is a very useful and likely groundbreaking reworking of the classic *Canadian Bar Review* article by Willis. Sullivan restores lustre to the task of statutory interpretation by going beyond questions of text and legislative intent, and into the domain of a thoughtfully articulated "pragmatism." She develops a conceptual model of three quite different variants of statutory interpretation: textualism, intentionalism, and pragmatism. See also R. Sullivan, *Statutory Interpretation,* 2nd ed. Toronto: Irwin Law, 2007.

Willis, J. "Statute Interpretation in a Nutshell." *Canadian Bar Review* 16 (1938).

> This is a classic article on the subject of statutory interpretation. Through the use of very straightforward examples, Willis helps students to understand the operation of the rules and principles of statutory interpretation.

NOTES

1. Driedger, E.A. *The Construction of Statutes.* 2nd ed. Toronto: Butterworths, 1983.
2. R. Sullivan, "Statutory Interpretation in a New Nutshell," *Canadian Bar Review,* Vol. 82, Pg. 51, 2003.
3. *Grey v. Pearson* (1857), 6 H.L.C. 61.
4. *Heydon's Case* (1584) 76 ER 637, Pasch 26 Eliz, plea began 20 Eliz Rot 140.
5. *Edwards v. Canada (A.G.)* (The Persons Case), [1930] A.C. 124, [1929] 3 W.W.R. 479, [1930] 1 D.L.R. 98 (P.C.).

6. *Regina v. Ojibway* was written by H. Pomerantz and S. Breslin. It has been modified and edited for the purposes of illustration.
7. [1990] 2 S.C.R. 711, 58 C.C.C. (3d) 449.
8. Ibid., at 724–5.
9. Ibid., at 725.
10. (1987), 34 C.C.C. (3d) 97, [1987] 1 S.C.R. 1045, 58 C.R. (3d) 193.
11. (1990), 60 C.C.C. (3d) 1, 80 C.R. (3d) 257, [1990] 6 W.W.R. 673 (S.C.C.).
12. (1987), 38 C.C.C. (3d) 534, 62 O.R. (2d) 321, 32 O.A.C. 287 (C.A.), affd 47 C.C.C. (3d) 491, [1989] 1 S.C.R. 296, 68 O.R. (2d) 256.
13. See, for example, *Bell v. R.*, [1979] 2 S.C.R., 212, 9 M.P.L.R. 103, or *Paquette v. R.*, [1977] 2 S.C.R. 189, 39 C.R.N.S. 257, 30 C.C.C. (2d) 417, 70 D.L.R. (3d) 129, 11 N.R. 451.
14. *R. v. Gwillen* (1985), 48 C.R. (3d) 226.

REFERENCES

Allen, C.K. *Law in the Making*. 4th ed. Oxford: Clarendon Press, 1946.

Beaupré, M. *Interpreting Bilingual Legislation*. 2nd ed. Toronto: Carswell, 1946.

Bennion, F.A.R. *Statutory Interpretation*. London, U.K.: Butterworths, 1984.

Cross, R. *Statutory Interpretation*. 2nd ed. London, U.K.: Butterworths, 1987.

Driedger, E.A. *The Composition of Legislation, Legislative Forms and Precedents*. 2nd ed. Ottawa: Department of Justice, 1976.

_____. *The Construction of Statutes*. 2nd ed. Toronto: Butterworths, 1983.

_____. "Statutes: The Mischievous Literal Golden Rule." *Canadian Bar Review* 59 (1981): 780.

Dworkin, R. "Hard Cases." *Harvard Law Review* 88 (1975): 1057.

Edwards v. Canada (A.G.) (The Persons Case), [1930] A.C. 124, [1929] 3 W.W.R. 479, [1930] 1 D.L.R. 98 (P.C.).

Fisher v. Bell (1960), 3 All E.R. 731, [1961] 1 Q.B. 394.

Frankfurter, F. "Some Reflections on the Reading of Statutes." *Colorado Law Review* 47 (1947): 527.

Gall, G. *The Canadian Legal System*. 3rd ed. Toronto: Carswell, 1990, Chapters 10 and 11.

MacAdam, A.I., and T.M. Smith. *Statutes: Rules and Examples*. Sydney, Aus.: Butterworths, 1985.

Pearce, D.C. *Statutory Interpretation in Australia*. 2nd ed. Sydney, Aus.: Butterworths, 1981.

Pigeon, L.P. *Redaction et Interpretation des Lois/Drafting and Interpreting Legislation*. Toronto: Carswell, 1988.

Russell, P.H. "Overcoming Legal Formalism: The Treatment of the Constitution, the Courts and Judicial Behaviour in Canadian Political Science." *Canadian Journal of Law and Society* 1 (1986): 5–33.

Smith, J.A.C. "The Interpretation of Statutes." *Manitoba Law Journal* 4 (1970): 212.

Statsky, W.P. *Legislative Analysis and Drafting*. 2nd ed. New York: West Publishing, 1984.

Sullivan, R. "Statutory Interpretation in a New Nutshell." *Canadian Bar Review* 51, 82 (2003).

Vaughn, F. "The Canadian Courts and Policy Making: The Case of Justice Emmett Hall." *Saskatchewan Law Review* (1974): 357.

Willis, J. "Statute Interpretation in a Nutshell." *Canadian Bar Review* 16 (1938): 1.

Wittgenstein, L. *Philosophical Investigations*. London, U.K.: Academic Press, 1958.

PART 2
Building Blocks of the Canadian Legal System

THE CONSTITUTION OF CANADA: THE *BRITISH NORTH AMERICA ACT, 1867*, THE *CONSTITUTION ACT, 1982*, THE FUTURE OF FEDERALISM, AND THE *CHARTER OF RIGHTS AND FREEDOMS*

We shall like to remember, when Confederation has stood the test of time, how beautiful was the day when it began.

(Editorial, *Le Journal des Trois-Rivières*, 1867)

The Canadian Charter of Rights and Freedoms is not a perfect document. As with all such documents, it is a product of compromise and pragmatism. And certainly the courts have much work to do to fully avail themselves and the Canadian people of its potential and to implement and safeguard its content and purpose. In undertaking this work in the years to come, the courts should perhaps be guided by the words of Reverend King, "Injustice anywhere is a threat to justice everywhere. We are caught in an inescapable network of mutuality, tied in a single garment of destiny. Whatever affects one directly, affects all indirectly."

(Marc Rosenberg, Justice, Ontario Court of Appeal, 2009)

In 2006, the Supreme Court of Canada issued its judgment—a 4–3 verdict—in *R. v. Morris*, a case focused upon a matter of constitutional law. At stake were the treaty rights of the Tsartlip Indian Band, in direct conflict with provincial wildlife legislation. Section 27 of the *Wildlife Act of British Columbia* prohibits hunting wildlife during prohibited hours, hunting with the aid of a light or illuminating device, and hunting "without reasonable consideration for the lives, safety or property of other persons." The Tsartlip Indian Band argues that its right to hunt at night with illuminating devices is protected by treaty rights, specifically the North Saanich Treaty of 1852. The summary of the case[1] makes clear the markedly different points of view of the majority and minority positions:

The History

The accused, both members of the Tsartlip Indian Band of the Saanich Nation, were hunting at night when they shot at a decoy deer set up by provincial conservation officers to trap illegal hunters. They were arrested and charged with several

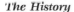

offences under British Columbia's Wildlife Act, including: (1) hunting wildlife with a firearm during prohibited hours (s. 27(1)(d)); (2) hunting by the use or with the aid of a light or illuminating device (s. 27(1)(e)); and (3) hunting without reasonable consideration for the lives, safety or property of other persons (s. 29). At trial, as a defence to the charges under s. 27(1), the accused raised their right "to hunt over the unoccupied lands ... as formerly" under the North Saanich Treaty of 1852. They also introduced evidence that the particular night hunt for which they were charged was not dangerous. The trial judge found that "night hunting with illumination was one of the various methods employed by the Tsartlip [people] from time immemorial". However, despite the evidence that night hunting by Tsartlip hunters had yet to result in an accident, he nonetheless concluded that the accused did not have a treaty right to hunt at night because hunting at night with an illuminating device was "inherently unsafe". The trial judge entered convictions on count 1, conditionally stayed count 2 because of the rule against multiple convictions arising from the same delict, and entered acquittals on count 3. Both the summary conviction appeal judge and the majority of the Court of Appeal upheld the convictions based on the prohibition of night hunting (s. 27(1)(d)).

The Majority View

The Tsartlip's right to hunt at night with the aid of illuminating devices is protected by the North Saanich Treaty. The historical context indicates that the parties intended the treaty to include the full panoply of hunting practices in which the Tsartlip people had engaged before they agreed to relinquish control over their lands. One of those practices was night hunting and, as the trial judge acknowledged, night hunting by the Tsartlip includes, and always has included, night hunting with the aid of illuminating devices. Even on a literal construction, the language of the treaty supports the view that the right to hunt "as formerly" means the right to hunt according to the methods used by the Tsartlip at the time of and before the treaty. The right of the Tsartlip to hunt at night with illuminating devices has of necessity evolved from its pre-treaty tools to its current implements, and the use of guns, spotlights, and motor vehicles reflects the current state of the evolution of the Tsartlip's historic hunting practices. However, it is acknowledged that it could not have been within the common intention of the parties that the Tsartlip would be granted a right to hunt dangerously, since no treaty confers on its beneficiaries a right to put human lives in danger. This is confirmed by the language of the treaty itself, which restricts hunting to "unoccupied lands", away from any town or settlement. Since British Columbia is a very large province, it cannot plausibly be said that a night hunt with illumination is unsafe everywhere and in all circumstances, even within the treaty area at issue in this case. Accordingly, while s. 29 of the Wildlife Act, which prohibits hunting or trapping "without reasonable consideration for the lives, safety or property of other persons", is a limit that does not impair the treaty rights of aboriginal hunters and trappers, paras. (d) and (e) of s. 27(1), which apply without exception to the whole province, are overbroad and infringe the treaty right to hunt. Something less than an absolute prohibition on night hunting can address the concern for safety.

The relevant provisions of the Wildlife Act are valid provincial legislation under s. 92(13) of the Constitution Act, 1867. Since treaty rights to hunt lie squarely within federal jurisdiction, provincial laws of general application that are inapplicable because they impair "Indianness" may nonetheless be found to be applicable by incorporation under s. 88 of the Indian Act. While, on its face, s. 88 cannot be used to incorporate into federal law provincial laws that conflict with the terms of any treaty, the provinces may regulate treaty rights under certain circumstances. Provincial legislation of general application that interferes in an insignificant way with the exercise of that right do not infringe the right; but where, as in the case of s. 27(1)(d) and (e), such legislation is found to conflict with a treaty in a way that constitutes a prima facie infringement, the protection of treaty rights prevails and the provincial law cannot be incorporated under s. 88 of the Indian Act.

The Minority View

The impugned ban on night hunting with a firearm (s. 27(1)(d)) is valid provincial legislation that applies to the accused.

The Wildlife Act falls in pith and substance within the province's powers. It is not directed at a federal head, like Indians, but more generally at safety, a matter within provincial power. The ban on night hunting is an integrated part of a broader provincial scheme applicable to all British Columbians and aimed at assuring the safety of the province's hunters and residents. Since this provision does not conflict with federal legislation, the doctrine of paramountcy has no application. Finally, where a provincial law of general application does not affect a treaty right, and does not otherwise touch upon core Indianness, that law applies ex proprio vigore, without recourse to s. 88 of the Indian Act. Provincial legislation that falls outside the internal limits on the treaty right that the parties to the treaty would have understood and intended does not encroach on the treaty right.

A treaty must be interpreted in a manner that best reconciles the interests of the parties to it. The right to hunt protected by the treaty is subject to an internal limit: it does not include the right to hunt in an inherently hazardous manner Rather, the right to hunt must be exercised reasonably. Although, at the time the treaty was signed, the practice of hunting at night did not pose the same dangers as it does today, the parties to the treaty must have understood that the right to hunt did not carry with it a right to hunt dangerously. Furthermore, just as the methods and means of exercising the right should not be frozen in time; neither should the government's legitimate safety concerns. Adapting the exercise of treaty rights to modern weaponry without adapting the corollary legitimate safety concerns would lead to unacceptable results.

Here, s. 27(1)(d) of the Wildlife Act regulates the internal safety limit on the treaty right of the accused. A ban on night hunting with a firearm is a reasonable exercise of the Province's regulatory power in defining this internal limit. Since the regulation of dangerous hunting falls outside the scope of the treaty right to hunt, no treaty right is engaged. Accordingly, as no aboriginal right is asserted, and as the provincial law does not otherwise go to Indianness, the law applies....

For as long as Canada has been a nation, Canadians have debated the utility and value of our legal structure. This particular case (*R. v. Morris*) demonstrates the historical tension between treaty rights and current legislation. How are we to balance claims of Aboriginal rights with provincial or federal law? Or, in another context, do the provinces have too much or too little power relative to the federal government? Should the Senate be reformed or abolished? What should be the process for constitutional amendment? Should judges have the power to determine whether law has violated individual or collective rights?

These questions flow from constitutional law, specifically from the **British North America Act, 1867**,[2] the **Constitution Act, 1982**,[3] and the **Canadian Charter of Rights and Freedoms**[4] contained in the latter. **Constitutional law** has been described as a "mirror reflecting the national soul,"[5] and as a means to "protect the values of a nation."[6] Within Canada's Constitution, we find the rules that define the powers of respective governments and, correspondingly, the rights of citizens.

Canada is, most significantly, a federal state—a number of governments within a common overarching organization. Each government has retained certain exclusive powers; each has also ceded to a central government other exclusive powers, most notably those related to income taxation, defence, and external affairs. Tension between the powers of Canada's central government and the powers of provincial governments is a significant source of our country's strength—and, arguably, of its weakness.

Constitutional law is different from other forms of statute law in that it cannot be changed by the mere passage of new law through the House of Commons and the Senate. Constitutional law is "entrenched" legislation, which can be changed only by a specific amending formula.

THE *BRITISH NORTH AMERICA ACT, 1867*

In order to understand the importance and contemporary relevance of entrenched legislation and its amending formula, it is necessary to turn to the *British North America Act, 1867*. This act, passed by the British Parliament for the colony of Canada, first united the provinces of Canada. **Sections 91 and 92** set out, respectively, the powers of the federal and provincial governments. Section 91 also gives the federal government a residual power to legislate in relation to matters that appear not to fall under any specific provincial or federal jurisdiction; it is to be invoked in order to affirm "the peace, order, and good government" of the country. As we will see later in this chapter, the specific powers of sections 91 and 92 remain in force today. The Act also provided for a national **bicameral Parliament** comprising an elected House of Commons and an appointed Senate. The House of Commons was to be based on the principle of representation by population; the Senate, on the principle of representation by region.

The 1867 statute that defined the new country of Canada was legislation passed by Britain, not by Canada. Although Britain rarely intervened in Canada's internal affairs, two events nearly 60 years later raised concerns about whether the country was still, in some respects, a colony. When Mackenzie King's Liberal minority government lost a vote of confidence in 1926, he asked Lord Byng, the governor general, to dissolve Parliament and call a general election. Surprisingly, the governor general, the monarch's representative in Canada, chose to exercise his discretionary authority and refused the prime minister's request for dissolution. He asked the Conservative leader, Arthur Meighen, to form a government. When Meighen's minority government was defeated in the House of Commons less than a week later, Lord Byng acceded to Meighen's request for the dissolution of Parliament and the calling of a general election. In the resulting election, Mackenzie King's Liberals won a majority, successfully exploiting Canadian independence as a campaign issue.

The other critical development of 1926 was the British Privy Council's decision in the case of *Nadan v. R.*[7] The Privy Council struck down an 1888 Canadian statute that had sought to abolish appeals to the Privy Council in criminal cases. It did so on the ground that Canada's abolition of the Privy Council's overview exceeded the colony's legislative powers; specifically, it was in direct conflict with the *British North America Act, 1867.*

The net effect of these two events was that Canada and other dominions of the British Empire lobbied the British government for their autonomy and for a mechanism that would remove their continuing colonial status. A 1930 conference of the dominions resulted in the declaration that "no law hereafter made by the Parliament of the United Kingdom shall extend to any dominion otherwise than at the request and consent of that dominion." In 1931, this declaration was reproduced as a preamble to the British government's Statute of Westminster. This change effectively precluded British intervention into the affairs of Canada's central and provincial governments. But the 1867 statute that set out Canada's Constitution remained a British statute. There was no established mechanism for amending this constitutional document—that is, for taking a British statute and reformulating it as a Canadian one, in both letter and spirit.

THE *CONSTITUTION ACT, 1982*

In 1967, constitutional scholar W.R. Lederman argued that there was a need to patriate the Canadian Constitution, "to make into law a set of amending procedures that can be carried out in Canada entirely by Canadian governments, legislative bodies, or electorates, acting severally or in combinations of some kind."[8] With the passage of the *Constitution Act, 1982,* **patriation** was accomplished.

The *Constitution Act, 1982* embodies two significant additions to Canadian constitutional law. The first is a formula to be applied in order to make future amendments to Canada's constitutional structure. The second is legislation in the mould of the U.S. Bill of Rights—the *Canadian Charter of Rights and Freedoms,* designed to be used by the courts to protect the rights accorded by the *Charter* to Canadian citizens.

THE AMENDING FORMULA OF THE *CONSTITUTION ACT, 1982*

Until the passage of the *Constitution Act, 1982,* there was no amending formula for the *British North America Act, 1867.* As mentioned, the *British North America Act, 1867* was unlike other federal or provincial statutes—it was a constitutional document and, as such, subject to a form of amendment different from that for other kinds of law. The 1964 Fulton-Favreau formula recommended unanimous consent of the federal and provincial governments for most significant amendments. The Victoria Charter of 1970 proposed less than unanimity among provincial governments, but gave veto powers to Quebec and Ontario on the ground that each had at least 25 percent of the country's population. The Trudeau government's amending-formula proposal of the early 1980s was based substantially on the Victoria Charter. It was strongly opposed by most provinces, largely because of the Ontario and Quebec veto. What ultimately emerged in 1982 as the amending formula for the Canadian Constitution was an elaborate compromise.

The **amending formula** created by the *Constitution Act, 1982* sets out three types of amendments. Section 38 of the act, the "general amending procedure," states that an amendment requires support from the House of Commons and the Senate, as well as from two-thirds of the provinces, provided that these provinces constitute at least 50 percent of the population of Canada.

> 38. (1) An amendment to the Constitution of Canada may be made by proclamation issued by the Governor General under the Great Seal of Canada where so authorized by
>
>   (a) resolutions of the Senate and the House of Commons; and
>
>   (b) resolutions of the legislative assemblies of at least two-thirds of the provinces that have, in the aggregate, according to the then latest general census, at least 50 percent of the population of all the provinces.

The so-called *seven-fifty formula* dictates that at least seven provinces must approve constitutional reform; given current populations, one of those provinces must be Ontario or Quebec. Significantly, however, no province has a veto over constitutional change. But section 38(3) softens the effect of the general amending formula by giving individual provinces, to a maximum of three, the power to "opt out" of constitutional amendments. If one, two, or three provinces with a cumulative population of no more than 50 percent of the total find a constitutional change unacceptable, they may declare that it will not apply within their jurisdictions.

The second type of amendment to constitutional law requires the unanimity of the federal government and all provincial governments. (The Northwest Territories, Yukon, and Nunavut fall under federal government jurisdiction until they become designated as provincial governments.) It is found in section 41 of the *Constitution Act, 1982*:

> 41. *An amendment to the Constitution of Canada in relation to the following matters may be made by proclamation issued by the Governor General under the Great Seal of Canada only where authorized by resolutions of the Senate and House of Commons and of the legislative assembly of each province:*
>
> (a) *the office of the Queen, the Governor General and the Lieutenant-Governor of a province;*
>
> (b) *the right of a province to a number of members in the House of Commons not less than the number of Senators by which the province is entitled to be represented at the time this Part comes into force;*
>
> (c) *subject to section 43, the use of the English or the French language;*
>
> (d) *the composition of the Supreme Court of Canada;*
>
> (e) *an amendment to this Part.*

Any of the matters named can be the subject of a constitutional amendment only if there is agreement from the federal government and every provincial government; in other words, every province has a veto. These issues—the monarchy, provincial representation in the House of Commons, the use of English or French, and the structure of the Supreme Court—are thought to be of such national significance that the unanimous consent of all governments is required.

Note that section 41 of the *Constitution Act, 1982* makes changes to the monarchical traditions of Canadian government a rather difficult task. Any legislation to eliminate the office of the queen, the governor general, or the lieutenant governor must have the consent of all federal and provincial governments. In Australia, in 1997 the federal government initiated a discussion about severing all political ties to the monarchy; in 1999 the Australian public voted to retain the queen as the titular head of state.

The third kind of constitutional amendment affects only certain provinces, as set out in section 43. For example, a number of language provisions in the *British North America Act, 1867* relate only to Manitoba, New Brunswick, and Quebec. These provisions can be changed with the consent of the federal government and the province affected; unaffected provinces have no say in the matter.

> 43. *An amendment to the Constitution of Canada in relation to any provision that applies to one or more, but not all provinces, including*
>
> (a) *any alteration to boundaries between provinces, and*
>
> (b) *any amendment to any provision that relates to the use of the English or French language within a province, may be made by proclamation issued by the Governor General under the Great Seal of Canada only where so authorized by resolutions of the Senate and House of Commons and of the legislative assembly of each province to which the amendment applies.*

Consider, in relation to these sections of the amending formula, the *Constitution Act, 1999* (Nunavut).[9] This legislation increased the number of senators from 104 to 105 and provided that Yukon Territory, the Northwest Territories, and Nunavut "are entitled to be represented in the Senate by one member each." The purpose of this constitutional amendment was to strengthen Nunavut's capacity to achieve political autonomy in the inaugural days of its newly established government. Because the representation of senators in other provinces is unaffected by this change, section 41 of the *Constitution Act, 1982* is not applicable.

SECTIONS 91 AND 92: THE DISTRIBUTION OF LEGISLATIVE POWER

As mentioned above, the original division of federal and provincial powers first set out in the *British North America Act, 1867* remained intact in the *Constitution Act* of 1982. Sections 91 and 92 are still central to the distribution of legislative responsibilities in Canada. The *British North America Act, 1867* was, under the *Constitution Act, 1982*, renamed the *Constitution Act, 1867*.[10]

Section 91 sets out the areas over which the federal government has jurisdiction.

> *91. It shall be lawful for the Queen, by and with the Advice and Consent of the Senate and House of Commons, to make Laws for the Peace, Order, and good Government of Canada, in relation to all Matters not coming within the Classes of Subjects by this Act assigned exclusively to the Legislatures of the Provinces; and for greater Certainty, but not so as to restrict the Generality of the foregoing Terms of this Section, it is hereby declared that (notwithstanding anything in this Act) the exclusive Legislative Authority of the Parliament of Canada extends to all Matters coming within the Classes of Subjects next herein-after enumerated; that is to say, ...*
>
> 1A.   *The Public Debt and Property.*
>   2.   *The Regulation of Trade and Commerce.*
> 2A.   *Unemployment Insurance.*
>   3.   *The raising of money by any Mode or System of Taxation.*
>   4.   *The Borrowing of Money on the Public Credit.*
>   5.   *Postal Service.*
>   6.   *The Census and Statistics.*
>   7.   *Militia, Military and Naval Service, and Defence.*
>   8.   *The fixing of and providing for the Salaries and Allowances of Civil and other Officers of the Government of Canada.*
>   9.   *Beacons, Buoys, Lighthouses, and Sable Island.*
> 10.   *Navigation and Shipping.*
> 11.   *Quarantine and the Establishment and Maintenance of Marine Hospitals.*
> 12.   *Sea Coast and Inland Fisheries.*

13. *Ferries between a Province and any British or Foreign Country, or between Two Provinces.*
14. *Currency and coinage.*
15. *Banking, incorporation of banks, and the Issue of Paper Money.*
16. *Savings Banks.*
17. *Weights and Measures.*
18. *Bills of Exchange and Promissory Notes.*
19. *Interest.*
20. *Legal Tender.*
21. *Bankruptcy and Insolvency.*
22. *Patents of Invention and Discovery.*
23. *Copyrights.*
24. *Indians, and Lands Reserved for the Indians.*
25. *Naturalization and Aliens.*
26. *Marriage and Divorce.*
27. *The Criminal Law, except the Constitution of Courts of Criminal Jurisdiction, but including the Procedure in Criminal Matters.*
28. *The Establishment, Maintenance, and Management of Penitentiaries.*
29. *Such classes of Subjects as are expressly excepted in the Enumeration of the Classes of Subjects by this Act assigned exclusively to the Legislatures of the Provinces.*

And any Matter coming within any of the Classes of Subjects enumerated in this Section shall not be deemed to come within the Class of Matters of a local or private Nature comprised in the Enumeration of the Classes of Subjects by this Act assigned exclusively to the Legislatures of the Provinces.

Section 92 catalogues the jurisdictional powers given to the provinces.

92. *In each Province the Legislature may exclusively make Laws in relation to Matters coming within the Classes of Subjects next herein-after enumerated; that is to say,*

1. *The Amendment from Time to Time, notwithstanding anything in this Act, of the Constitution of the Province, except as regards the Office of the Lieutenant-Governor.*
2. *Direct Taxation within the Province in order to the raising of a Revenue for Provincial Purposes.*
3. *The borrowing of money on the sole Credit of the Province.*
4. *The Establishment and Tenure of Provincial Offices and the Appointment and Payment of Provincial Officers.*
5. *The Management and Sale of the Public Lands belonging to the Province and of the Timber and Wood thereon*
6. *The Establishment, Maintenance, and Management of Public and Reformatory Prisons in and for the Province.*
7. *The Establishment, Maintenance, and Management of Hospitals, Asylums, Charities, and Eleemosynary Institutions in and for the Province, other than Marine Hospitals.*
8. *Municipal Institutions in the Province.*

9. *Shop, Saloon, Tavern, Auctioneer, and other Licences in order to the raising of a Revenue for Provincial, Local, or Municipal Purposes.*
10. *Local Works and Undertakings other than such as are of the following Classes:*
    a. *Lines of Steam or other Ships, Railways, Canals, Telegraphs, and other Works and Undertakings connecting the Province with any other or others of the provinces, or extending beyond the Limits of the Province:*
    b. *Lines of Steam Ships between the Province and any British or Foreign Country:*
    c. *Such Works as, although wholly situate within the Province, are before or after their Execution declared by the Parliament of Canada to be for the general Advantage of Canada or for the Advantage of Two or more of the Provinces.*
11. *The Incorporation of Companies with Provincial Objects.*
12. *The Solemnization of Marriage in the Province.*
13. *Property and Civil Rights in the Province.*
14. *The Administration of Justice in the Province, including the Constitution, Maintenance, and Organization of Provincial Courts, both of Civil and of Criminal Jurisdiction, and including Procedure in Civil Matters in those Courts.*
15. *The Imposition of Punishment by Fine, Penalty, or Imprisonment for enforcing any Law of the Province made in relation to any Matter coming within any of the Classes of Subjects enumerated in this Section.*
16. *Generally all Matters of a merely local or private Nature in the Province.*

QUESTIONS OF JURISDICTION: WHEN PROVINCIAL AND FEDERAL RESPONSIBILITIES COLLIDE

Sections 91 and 92 have been subject to shifting interpretations since they were legislated into being in 1867. The language of these sections is not always sufficiently precise to permit a clear sense of whether provincial or federal jurisdiction is to prevail. Moreover, section 91 contains the "peace, order, and good government" clause, which gives the federal government residual power over areas of jurisdiction not expressly noted in either section 91 or section 92. For example, punishment of those who commit narcotics offences has been deemed to be a federal power. In the 1979 decision in *R. v. Hauser*, the Supreme Court of Canada held that narcotics law cannot be traced to the federal power to legislate criminal law and procedure under section 91(27) but to the justification of "peace, order, and good government" in the preamble of section 91.[11] The residual power given to the federal government has meant that in perceived political, social, or economic emergencies, the federal government may act unilaterally in the interest of the country as a whole. Results of the use of residual federal power, in addition to narcotics control, include alcohol prohibition and runaway inflation.[12] (A separate federal statute, the *War Measures Act*, gives the federal government extraordinary powers in the event of war or a state of apprehended insurrection.)

More recently, conflict between the federal criminal law power and the province's jurisdiction over the provision of health services emerged in *Canada (Attorney General) v. PHS Community Services Society,* a 2011 decision of the Supreme Court of Canada.[13] At stake in this case was the conflict between the federal criminal law power to prosecute users of illegal drugs (under the *Controlled Drugs and Substances Act*) and the province's power to offer health services to these individuals. The court unanimously held in favour of the provincial facility offering assistance to injection drug users, ordering a continuing exemption from the operation of the federal *Controlled Drugs and Substances Act,* thereby allowing this public health initiative to continue. (Insite, a health facility in the downtown eastside of Vancouver, allows users to inject illegal drugs in a supervised environment with clean needles; the site also provides users with diagnostic services and referrals to various health services, including detoxification.)

The jurisdictions described within sections 91 and 92 have been the subject of many court battles, constitutional conferences, and elaborate delegations or interdelegations of federal and provincial power. The latter involve the granting of legal power by a federal or provincial government to a subordinate body in its own jurisdiction or to a subordinate body in another jurisdiction (federal or provincial) so that it may make law—pass statutes, bylaws, regulations, and so forth. An example of a potential source of conflict is section 91(2), which gives the federal government power to enact law in relation to "the regulation of trade and commerce." At what point does a commercial undertaking move from being an intraprovincial (hence, a provincially regulated) business to an interprovincial or extraprovincial business subject to federal control over "the regulation of trade and commerce"?

For some circumstances, the lack of precision in sections 91 and 92 has been clarified by the courts. The courts have determined that legislation is either *"intra vires"*—inside the jurisdiction—or *"ultra vires"*—outside the jurisdiction—of either the federal or the provincial government. However, more productive solutions have typically been found in the delegation of a federal power to a provincial body or tribunal, and in what constitutional scholars, such as Hogg, have described as "co-operative federalism":

> The essence of co-operative federalism is a network of relationships between the executives of the central and regional governments. Through these relationships mechanisms are developed, especially fiscal mechanisms, which allow a continuous redistribution of powers and resources without recourse to the courts or the amending process.... Changes in the financial arrangements have naturally altered the balance of powers within the federation. Yet the federal-provincial financial arrangements since the Second World War have been worked out by the executives of the various governments, at first almost at the dictation of the federal government, latterly by intergovernmental negotiation leading to genuine agreements.[14]

An example of co-operative federalism can be seen in the equalization payments made by the federal government to the poorer of the Canadian provinces each fiscal year, theoretically in order to provide a minimum standard of public services throughout the country. Although these payments do not flow from the *British North America Act,*

1867—since they originated in 1957—they are now mandated by section 36(2) of the *Constitution Act, 1982*:

> *36. (2) Parliament and the government of Canada are committed to the principle of making equalization payments to ensure that provincial governments have sufficient revenues to provide reasonably comparable levels of public services at reasonably comparable levels of taxation.*

Clearly, however, this section of the Act offers only a vague commitment to a principle of provincial equality of access to public services. The form and amount of equalization payments have been the subject of debate in federal-provincial conferences for almost 40 years, and they will, in all likelihood, continue to be so; the "have" and "have not" provinces have also changed somewhat in recent years. In the 2013/2014 fiscal year the provinces of Quebec, Ontario, Manitoba, New Brunswick, Nova Scotia, and Prince Edward Island are all receiving equalization provinces. The "have" provinces are currently Alberta, Saskatchewan, Newfoundland and Labrador, and British Columbia.

Despite some contentious areas, there are significant and unchanging parameters of provincial and federal jurisdictions that can be traced to sections 91 and 92 of the *British North America Act*. Section 91(27), as noted above, gives the federal government the exclusive power to legislate in relation to criminal law. (In the United States, by contrast, each of the 50 states is responsible for creating its own criminal law and attendant penalties.) But note that section 92(13) gives each province the power to legislate in relation to "property and civil rights." If a province creates law that, for example, censors certain kinds of films—effectively legislating in relation to propriety[15]—is it intruding upon the power of the federal government to decide, through the *Criminal Code*, what is obscene and hence prohibited?

Section 92(14) gives the provinces power to control the administration of justice, the organization of the courts, and the procedure to be employed in civil matters. When one adds to this the provinces' power to appoint the judiciary for family, small claims, and criminal courts (given by section 96 of the *British North America Act*), it is evident that the regional governments have a strong voice in defining and dispensing justice. More than 90 percent of all litigation takes place in small claims courts, family courts, and provincial courts (criminal division); only 10 percent is heard in the federally controlled criminal and civil courts.

At this point, one can already see that much of Canada's legal structure flows from the *British North America Act, 1867*; the *Constitution Act, 1982* is a lesser source of jurisdictional distribution. The division of powers therefore exists for reasons that are largely historical. But is it cast in stone? It is possible to construct a different configuration of federal and provincial powers. Why is it necessary, for example, for the federal government to have jurisdiction over the regulation of marriage and divorce, under section 91(26), when the solemnization of marriage and the regulation of matrimonial property and support are matters of provincial responsibility? Should the federal government continue to dictate immigration and agriculture policy to the provinces, in the manner envisaged by section 95?

> 95. *In each Province the Legislature may make Laws in relation to Agriculture in the Province, and to Immigration into the Province; and it is hereby declared that the Parliament of Canada may from Time to Time make laws in relation to Agriculture in all or any of the Provinces, and to Immigration into all or any of the Provinces; and any Law of the Legislature of a Province relative to Agriculture or to Immigration shall have effect in and for the Province as long and as far only as it is not repugnant to any Act of the Parliament of Canada.*

Should criminal law continue to be a national, rather than a provincial, concern? As is true of the other questions asked—about immigration, agriculture, and marriage and divorce—there is no "correct" answer, only grist for the mill of future constitutional discussions, arguments, and resolutions.

THE REJECTION OF THE *CONSTITUTION ACT, 1982* BY QUEBEC

Both the three types of amending formula described earlier in this chapter and the *Canadian Charter of Rights and Freedoms* were the product of thousands of hours of discussion, debate, and compromise. However, Quebec never approved the *Constitution Act, 1982*. In December 1981, the Quebec National Assembly passed a resolution rejecting the constitutional agreement reached by the federal government and the other provinces a month earlier. The Quebec government argued before the Supreme Court of Canada that the proposed constitutional amendments could not become law without Quebec's consent. The Supreme Court dismissed Quebec's arguments, noting that neither unanimity of governments nor the consent of the provinces was legally required for constitutional amendment. The Court added, however, that constitutional convention or custom requires that amendment by the federal government not proceed unilaterally.[16]

In April 1982, the new constitution became law, after passage through the House of Commons and the Senate, and its proclamation. But controversy about the *Constitution Act, 1982* has not diminished. The entrenchment of the *Charter* was strongly opposed (particularly by Alberta and Manitoba) during the negotiations that led to its introduction; and the arguments about its role and significance have not abated. In 2012, the 30th anniversary of the *Charter*, Prime Minister Stephen Harper declined any celebration of its anniversary. Furthermore, the absence of Quebec from the 1982 agreement led to a flurry of constitutional proposals, none of which proved acceptable. The most serious efforts were led by Conservative Prime Minister Brian Mulroney, whose government came to power in 1984. Mulroney was determined to amend the Constitution to make it acceptable to Quebec. The Quebec Liberal government of Robert Bourassa, elected in 1985, was equally interested in reconciliation with the rest of Canada. Both separatist and federalist politicians within Quebec generally felt that the *Constitution Act, 1982* had diminished the province's powers; if Quebec were to agree to the Constitution, concessions would have to be made by the rest of Canada.

THE WOOING OF QUEBEC: THE MEECH LAKE AND CHARLOTTETOWN ACCORDS

Packages of concessions ultimately surfaced in the form of the **Meech Lake Accord** and, later, the **Charlottetown Accord**.

THE MEECH LAKE ACCORD

In 1987, the Mulroney government's attempt to bring Quebec into the constitutional fold led to the Meech Lake Accord. The accord was an agreement reached by the federal government and provincial premiers at Meech Lake, Quebec, on June 3, 1987. In order for the accord to become law, it had to be ratified by the House of Commons, the Senate, and the legislatures of each province.

The Meech Lake Accord had essentially been initiated by the Quebec government in 1985. Premier Bourassa indicated at the time that Quebec would be willing to accept the *Constitution Act, 1982* if a number of conditions were met. Specifically, he called for the recognition of Quebec as a distinct society, a veto for Quebec on constitutional amendments, a provincial voice in appointments to the Supreme Court of Canada, and a greater role for the province in the development of immigration policy.

In general terms, the Meech Lake Accord met these conditions, designating Quebec as a "distinct society" and permitting some changes with respect to veto of constitutional amendments, Supreme Court appointments, and control over immigration. There were, however, a number of criticisms of the accord. Most telling, perhaps, was the argument that it had been negotiated in private by "eleven white men in suits": the fact that the future of the country was being decided behind closed doors by a small group of powerful insiders seriously compromised public support for the pact. There were other criticisms as well: Quebec was seen by some as no more deserving of distinct-society status than other provinces; Aboriginal Canadians, women, and people with disabilities had been excluded from the decision-making process. Ultimately, ratification of the accord did not succeed. The governments of Newfoundland, New Brunswick, and Manitoba changed between the negotiation period and the ratification deadline. The new premiers—Clyde Wells, Frank McKenna, and Gary Filmon—were, in varying degrees, unsupportive.

THE CHARLOTTETOWN ACCORD

After the collapse of the Meech Lake Accord, the Mulroney government made one more attempt to bring Quebec within the constitutional framework of the *Constitution Act, 1982*. The result—the Charlottetown Accord—was a very ambitious reworking of the Canadian Constitution, reached in Charlottetown on August 28, 1992, by the 10 premiers, the federal government, and Aboriginal and territorial leaders. All three then-existing major political parties—Conservatives, Liberals, and New Democrats—were represented in the agreement. The Charlottetown Accord not only addressed the issue of Quebec's representation within the country's Constitution, but also proposed changes to the Senate, the composition of the House of Commons, Aboriginal rights, and the amending formula, among other matters.

The Canada Clause

2. (1) The Constitution of Canada, including the Canadian Charter of Rights and Freedoms, shall be interpreted in a manner consistent with the following fundamental characteristics:

(a) Canada is a democracy committed to a parliamentary and federal system of government and to the rule of law;

(b) the aboriginal peoples of Canada, being the first peoples to govern this land, have the right to promote their languages, cultures, and traditions and to ensure the integrity of their societies, and their governments constitute one of three orders of government in Canada;

(c) Quebec constitutes within Canada a distinct society, which includes a French-speaking majority, a unique culture, and a civil law tradition;

(d) Canadians and their governments are committed to the vitality and development of official language minority communities throughout Canada;

(e) Canadians are committed to racial and ethnic equality in a society that includes citizens from many lands who have contributed, and continue to contribute, to the building of a strong Canada that reflects its cultural and racial diversity;

(f) Canadians are committed to a respect for individual and collective human rights and freedoms of all people;

(g) Canadians are committed to the equality of female and male persons; and

(h) Canadians confirm the principle of the equality of the provinces at the same time as recognizing their diverse characteristics.

(2) The role of the legislature and Government of Quebec to preserve and promote the distinct society of Quebec is affirmed.

(3) Nothing in this section derogates from the powers, rights, or privileges of the Parliament or the Government of Canada, or of the legislatures or governments of the provinces, or of the legislative bodies or governments of the aboriginal peoples of Canada, including any powers, rights, or privileges relating to language.

(4) For greater certainty, nothing in this section abrogates or derogates from the aboriginal and treaty rights of the aboriginal peoples of Canada.

The Canada Clause contained several controversial sections. Some Canadians, notably former prime minister Pierre Trudeau, objected to the classification of Quebec as a distinct society. (Trudeau dismissed the notion as a meaningless concession to "black-mailers.") The argument made by Trudeau and others was that Quebec is not the only "distinct" province or region of Canada. For others, the recognition of Aboriginal government as one of "three orders of government" was problematic, either because it was too substantial a concession or because the political ramifications were unclear, the essential justice of the position notwithstanding.

Proposed Amendments to the Senate

21. (1)   The Senate shall consist of 62 senators 42 of whom

    (a)   six shall be elected for each province, namely, Ontario, Quebec, Nova Scotia, New Brunswick, Manitoba, British Columbia, Prince Edward Island, Alberta, Saskatchewan, and Newfoundland;

    (b)   one shall be elected for each territory, namely, the Yukon Territory and the Northwest Territories; and

    (c)   [aboriginal representation]....

23. (1)   Subject to this Act, the Parliament of Canada may provide for all matters relating to the election of senators.

(2)   Subject to this Act, the legislature of any province or the legislative authority of any territory may provide for

    (a)   the indirect election of senators for the province or territory by the Legislative Assembly of that province or legislative authority of that territory, and all matters relating thereto;

    (b)   any special measures to provide for equal representation of male and female persons; and

    (c)   the determination of electoral districts and the boundaries thereof in relation to the election of senators.

(3)   Where a law of Parliament and a law of a province or territory under paragraph (2) (a) or (b) conflict, the law of the province or territory prevails to the extent of the conflict.

(4)   Where a law of Parliament and a law of a province or territory under paragraph (2) (c) conflict, the law of Parliament prevails to the extent of the conflict.

(5)   No law made under this section in relation to the direct election of senators shall apply in respect of a general election of senators for which the writs are issued within six months after the law receives the Queen's assent.

The amendments respecting the Senate represented major reform. The number of senators was to be cut to 62 from 104, and representation in the country's upper house was to be based not on population but on provincial status. Prince Edward Island, with a population of just over 100,000, was to have the same number of senators as Ontario, with a population of almost 10 million. The purpose of the change was to balance representation by population with representation by region. Some critics argued that the suggested changes to the Senate's structure went too far, ultimately undermining the principle of representation by population.

Section 23 of an amended Constitution Act would have provided for the election of senators, ending the present practice of appointment. Section 23(2)(b) would have permitted provinces to require an equal number of male and female senators. However, provinces could opt out of election and continue to appoint senators, since section 23(2) stated only that provinces "may provide" for the election of six senators. Quebec indicated, prior to the referendum, that it did not intend to hold Senate elections. The Senate would therefore be a hodgepodge: some senators would be elected, others would not; some provinces would insist upon gender equality, others would not. There was to be no consistent principle guiding Senate representation.

Other changes related to the powers of the Senate. Although the Charlottetown Accord would not have placed the Senate on an equal footing with the House of Commons, the upper chamber would possess expanded powers of legislative input, except in the crucial realms of revenue or expenditure bills, the taxation of natural resources, and bills affecting the French language or culture in Canada.

Proposed Amendments to House of Commons Representation

51A.(1) In readjusting the number of members in the House of Commons, the Parliament of Canada shall be guided by the principles that the proportion of members of the House of Commons representing a province shall be based on the proportion of the population of Canada from that province.

(2) Notwithstanding anything in this Act,

(a) a province shall always be entitled to a number of members in the House of Commons not fewer than the number of senators by which the province was entitled to be represented on April 17, 1982;

(b) Quebec shall always be entitled to a number of members in the House of Commons that is no fewer than 25 percent of the total number of members in the House of Commons;

(c) except as a result of the application of paragraph (b), no province shall have fewer members in the House of Commons than any other province that had, at the then latest general census, a smaller population;

(d) in any readjustment of the number of members in the House of Commons, no province shall have its representation reduced by more than one member; and

(e) the Yukon Territory and the Northwest Territories shall always be entitled to a number of members in the House of Commons not fewer than the number of members to which they were entitled on the coming into force of this section, and this entitlement applies to any new province established from either of them.

These amendments were among the most debated constitutional changes proposed by the Charlottetown Accord. Many critics particularly objected to Quebec's holding

25 percent of House of Commons seats in perpetuity, regardless of future population changes. Although demographers stressed that Quebec's share of Canada's population was unlikely to change by more than 1 percentage point over the next century, the principle of potentially unequal representation was strongly criticized. Opponents suggested that this was not an amendment of principle, but a political trade-off, not unlike those found in labour–management negotiations.

Proposed Amendments to Aboriginal Rights

35.1(1) The aboriginal peoples of Canada have the inherent right of self-government within Canada.

(2) The right referred to in subsection (1) shall be interpreted in a manner consistent with the recognition of the governments of the aboriginal peoples of Canada as constituting one of three orders of government in Canada.

(3) The exercise of the right referred to in subsection (1) includes the authority of duly constituted legislative bodies of the aboriginal peoples, each within its own jurisdiction,

> *(a) to safeguard and develop their languages, cultures, economies, identities, institutions, and traditions, and*
>
> *(b) to develop, maintain, and strengthen their relationship with their lands, waters, and environment, so as to determine and control their development as peoples according to their own values and priorities and to ensure the integrity of their societies....*

35.2(1) The government of Canada, the provincial and territorial governments, and the aboriginal peoples of Canada, including the Indian, Inuit, and Métis peoples of Canada, in the various regions and communities of Canada, shall negotiate in good faith the implementation of the right of self-government, including issues of

> *(a) jurisdiction,*
>
> *(b) lands and resources, and*
>
> *(c) economic and fiscal arrangements,*
>
> *with the objective of concluding agreements elaborating relationships between governments of aboriginal peoples and the government of Canada and provincial or territorial governments.*

This statement of support for Native self-government was seen as a major accomplishment, taking Canada's First Peoples beyond the current "recognition and affirmation of Aboriginal and treaty rights" within section 35 of the *Constitution Act, 1982*. Yet Canada's Aboriginal peoples were divided on the merits of the change. Some argued that section 35.2 committed the federal government and the provinces only to further negotiation to determine the nature and structure of Aboriginal self-government; in the absence of specifics, nothing of substance had been accomplished. On the other hand, the recognition of Aboriginal rule as one of three levels of government in Canada was a major breakthrough. Many who voted against the Charlottetown Accord were disappointed that this part of the agreement did not become a part of the Canadian Constitution.

The Amending Formula

41. An amendment to the Constitution of Canada in relation to the following matters may be made by proclamation issued by the Governor General under the Great Seal of Canada only where authorized by resolutions of the Senate and House of Commons and of the Legislative Assembly of each province:

(a) *the office of the Queen, the Governor General, and the Lieutenant-Governor of a province;*

(b) *the powers of the Senate and the election of senators;*

(c) *the number of senators by which a province or territory is entitled to be represented in the Senate and the qualifications of senators set out in the Constitution Act, 1867;*

[(c.1) the number of senators by which the aboriginal peoples of Canada are entitled to be represented in the Senate and the qualifications of such senators;]

(d) *an amendment to section 51A of the Constitution Act, 1867;*

(e) *subject to section 43, the use of the English or the French language;*

(f) *subject to subsection 42 (1), the Supreme Court of Canada;*

(g) *an amendment to section 2 or 3 of the Constitution Act, 1871; and*

(h) *an amendment to this Part.*

The proposed changes to the amending formula provoked substantial criticism. As in the case of the Meech Lake Accord, most significant parts of the Charlottetown Accord could be changed only with the unanimous consent of the federal and all provincial governments. Given the concerns raised by many of the proposed changes—the structure of Senate reform, a guarantee of 25 percent of Commons seats to Quebec, and uncertainty over both Aboriginal representation in the Senate and the form of Aboriginal self-government—the inflexible amending formula was a major stumbling block. Even its most ardent supporters acknowledged that the Charlottetown Accord was an imperfect compromise, and the amending formula would have cast that imperfect compromise in stone.

The Charlottetown Accord, unlike the Meech Lake Accord, was to be decided by a national referendum. It is probably not surprising that in October 1992 the voters of Canada rejected it by a margin of 55 to 45 percent. Although every government in the country had endorsed the accord, the Canadian people remained unconvinced. Former prime minister Pierre Trudeau had spoken out against the agreement, and a host of other politicians and interest groups had campaigned against its passage, albeit for often contradictory reasons.

In the end, the Charlottetown Accord probably failed because it tried to accomplish too much too quickly, lumping together the issues of Aboriginal rights, Senate reform, House of Commons representation, and distinct society status for Quebec. It did not help that its initiator, Prime Minister Brian Mulroney, together with his Conservative government, was both extremely unpopular and distrusted across the country at the time of the vote.

THE FUTURE OF CANADIAN FEDERALISM

With the demise of the Charlottetown Accord, the future of Canadian federalism became unclear and remains so, at least to some extent, more than 20 years later. There is widespread agreement among the federal and provincial governments to put constitutional reform on the back burner, although strong showings by the Bloc Québécois in federal elections between 1993 and 2008 (before its collapse in the 2011 election) and the exceptionally close referendum in Quebec in 1995 may require a rethinking of such sentiments. Additionally, the election of the Parti Québécois to minority government status in Quebec in 2012 suggests that the issue of constitutional reform is far from an easy resolution. In the interim, the numerous questions raised by the Charlottetown Accord remain unanswered. Can the goal of Aboriginal self-government be accomplished? Can Quebec be accommodated within the *Constitution Act, 1982*, or is separation inevitable? Can the Senate be reformed into a decision-making body that genuinely provides a sober second look at legislation passed by the House of Commons? Prime Minister Stephen Harper, first elected in 2006 and once a staunch advocate of Senate reform, has largely used Senate appointments for partisan political purposes, using his power of appointment to the Senate to further his legislative objectives in the House of Commons. Finally, can an amending formula be developed that embraces the bedrock character of constitutional law, yet permits future flexibility?

The answers to these questions will probably shape Canada's constitutional law in the next decade. Our task, as students, teachers, and citizens, is twofold: to involve ourselves in the changes that will ultimately define our country, and to understand the origins and consequences of these changes.

THE *CANADIAN CHARTER OF RIGHTS AND FREEDOMS*

The *Canadian Charter of Rights and Freedoms* (the *Charter*), which was entrenched in the *Constitution Act, 1982,* was the second significant addition to Canadian constitutional law in that year. Its passage signalled a controversial shift in power from the legislative to the judicial branches of government. It became the task of judges to determine whether the legislation of either the federal or the provincial governments offends the core values of the *Charter*, and by implication, the nation. Debates about whether judges interpret law or make law have become irrelevant; the *Charter* requires judges to set aside legislation that contravenes a protected right. However, it is not an easy matter to determine what is meant, in practice, by "cruel and unusual punishment," "freedom of religion," or various other terms now subject to judicial definition.

THE *CANADIAN BILL OF RIGHTS* OF 1960

The *Charter* was not the first Canadian law to deal with the rights of citizens. In 1960, the Conservative government of John Diefenbaker enacted the *Canadian Bill of Rights*[17] to protect the civil rights of Canadians. The *Bill of Rights* was not an entrenched constitutional document but a federal statute; it therefore applied only to federal laws and regulations.

The Canadian Bill of Rights

The Parliament of Canada, affirming that the Canadian Nation is founded upon principles that acknowledge the supremacy of God, the dignity and worth of the human person, and the position of the family in a society of free men and free institutions;

Affirming also that men and institutions remain free only when freedom is founded upon respect for moral and spiritual values and the rule of law;

And being desirous of enshrining these principles and the human rights and fundamental freedoms derived from them, in a *Bill of Rights* which shall reflect the respect of Parliament for its constitutional authority and which shall ensure the protection of these rights and freedoms in Canada:

Therefore Her Majesty, by and with the advice and consent of the Senate and House of Commons of Canada, enacts as follows:

1. *It is hereby recognized and declared that in Canada, there have existed and shall continue to exist without discrimination by reason of race, national origin, colour, religion, or sex, the following human rights and fundamental freedoms, namely,*

   (a) *the right of the individual to life, liberty, security of the person, and enjoyment of property, and the right not to be deprived thereof except by due process of law;*

   (b) *the right of the individual to equality before the law and the protection of the law;*

   (c) *freedom of religion;*

   (d) *freedom of speech;*

   (e) *freedom of assembly and association; and*

   (f) *freedom of the press.*

2. *Every law of Canada shall, unless it is expressly declared by an Act of the Parliament of Canada that it shall operate notwithstanding the Canadian Bill of Rights, be so construed and applied as not to abrogate, abridge, or infringe or to authorize the abrogation, abridgement, or infringement of any of the rights or freedoms herein recognized and declared, and in particular, no law of Canada shall be construed or applied so as to*

   (a) *authorize or effect the arbitrary detention, imprisonment, or exile of any person;*

   (b) *impose or authorize the imposition of cruel and unusual treatment or punishment;*

   (c) *deprive a person who has been arrested or detained*

      (i) *of the right to be informed promptly of the reason for his arrest or detention,*

      (ii) *of the right to retain and instruct counsel without delay, or*

      (iii) *of the remedy by way of habeas corpus for the determination of the validity of his detention and for his release if the detention is not lawful;*

(d) *authorize a court, tribunal, commission, board, or other authority to compel a person to give evidence if he is denied counsel, protection against self-crimination, or other constitutional safeguards;*

(e) *deprive a person of the right to a fair hearing in accordance with the principles of fundamental justice for the determination of his rights and obligations;*

(f) *deprive a person charged with a criminal offence of the right to be presumed innocent until proved guilty according to law in a fair and public hearing by an independent and impartial tribunal, or of the right to reasonable bail without just cause; or*

(g) *deprive a person of the right to the assistance of an interpreter in any proceedings in which he is involved or in which he is a party or a witness, before a court, commission, board, or other tribunal, if he does not understand or speak the language in which such proceedings are conducted.*

From the outset, some lawyers, judges, and politicians were disturbed by the possibility that the new law might be used to undermine the concept of **parliamentary supremacy** that lies at the heart of our version of democracy. The doctrine that Parliament is the supreme lawmaker has a corollary—namely, that no body or person has the legal right to override or set aside the law of Parliament.[18] Canada's British-based system of law is in marked contrast to the U.S. system, which cedes the legal protection of certain core rights to the courts.

Supporters of parliamentary supremacy feared that the *Bill of Rights* would move Canada closer to the U.S. model, in which the judiciary acts as a check on the possibility of abuse of legislative power. How, they asked, could an appointed judge, unaccountable to the voting public, be involved in making law or in interpreting the acceptability of a federal statute?

The counter argument to the concept of parliamentary supremacy is based on two points. First, there is a core of values to which all Canadians subscribe, enunciated in the *Bill of Rights* and later in the *Charter*. This core must be protected at all times, irrespective of the whims of legislators. Second, in view of the ongoing process of interpreting ambiguous law, Canadian judges were already involved in lawmaking before the *Bill of Rights* was enacted. Hence, it is probably overstatement to suggest that only the legislatures have ever had the exclusive right to create law.

Key sections of the *Bill of Rights* were first tested in 1969 in the case of *R. v. Drybones*.[19] Joseph Drybones, a Canadian Native, had been found intoxicated off a reserve, contrary to section 94(b) of the *Indian Act*. His counsel argued that this section of the Act contravened the *Bill of Rights*, discriminating against Drybones on the basis of race. Section 1(b) of the *Bill of Rights* prohibits discrimination on the basis of race and guarantees "the right of the individual to equality before the law." The *Indian Act* created an offence for which only Native Canadians could be charged and convicted.

The Crown argued that the *Bill of Rights* was a "canon of construction," a guide for legislators in the drafting of legislation and for the judiciary in the interpretation of federal statutes. It was, therefore, never intended to give courts the power to render inoperative those federal laws that ran afoul of the Bill's enumerated rights and freedoms.

Nevertheless, the Supreme Court determined in a 6–3 judgment that section 94(b) of the *Indian Act* was no longer enforceable. The Court noted in its decision that section 2 of the *Bill of Rights* provides that federal legislation not conforming to the Bill must clearly state its nonconformity in the specific legislation: "It must be expressly declared by an Act of the Parliament of Canada that it shall operate notwithstanding the *Canadian Bill of Rights*." In the absence of this express declaration, the relevant section of the *Indian Act* was inoperative.

The Supreme Court's decision in *Drybones* was greeted enthusiastically by civil libertarians as a sign that Canada's judiciary was prepared to use the new law in an activist manner to protect the rights of Canadians. The doctrine of parliamentary supremacy was being reshaped, they felt, bringing Canada closer to the U.S. model of providing judicial checks and balances upon the powers of the legislature.

But the jubilation was relatively short-lived. In 1974, the nine male justices of the Supreme Court brought down a decision in *Canada (A.G.) v. Lavell*.[20] The case involved another challenge to a section of the *Indian Act*, which provided that female band members who married non-status Indians would have their names (and those of the children of the marriage) struck from the Indian register. Male band members who married non-status Indians would not have their names so treated, and would therefore continue to enjoy the advantages accruing to status Indians. The argument advanced by Jeannette Lavell was that she was being discriminated against on the basis of gender, in much the same manner that Joseph Drybones had been discriminated against on the basis of race. As both race and gender are prohibited grounds for discrimination under section 1 of the *Bill of Rights*, section 12(1)(b) of the *Indian Act* should have been declared inoperative. The Supreme Court held in a 5–4 decision, however, that there was no violation of the principle of equality before the law. The majority of the Court argued that the *Indian Act* provides a framework for the internal administration of life upon reserves, and cannot be changed by the broad general language of the *Bill of Rights*.

Many academics, civil libertarians, and Canadian citizens saw the decision in *Lavell* as contradicting the *Drybones* decision. The fact that *Drybones* concerned a matter off the reserves and that *Lavell* concerned a matter internal to reserves was not seen to be the point, although some members of the Supreme Court found it a crucial distinction. The net effect of the Court's decision in *Lavell* was that the role of the *Bill of Rights* was now unclear. Was this legislation ultimately to be powerless against parliamentary supremacy?

ENTRENCHING THE RIGHTS OF CANADIANS: THE CONSTITUTION ACT AND THE CHARTER

The *Constitution Act, 1982* provided an answer to the above question. During the 1970s and early 1980s, debate continued among politicians, judges, academics, and other Canadians about the appropriate role of the judiciary with respect to the protection of individual rights. In the political arena, the premier of Manitoba, Sterling Lyon, led the advocates of parliamentary supremacy against Prime Minister Pierre Trudeau, who argued for an activist judiciary and a *Charter* that would be entrenched in the Constitution.

With the proclamation of the *Constitution Act, 1982,* Canada departed from strict adherence to the doctrine of parliamentary supremacy. Although weakened by opting-out provisions, the *Charter* nonetheless demanded—and continues to demand—that both federal and provincial laws be tested against the values it enshrines. If specific legislation is found to provide inadequate protection of *Charter* rights, then the legislation, or the relevant section or sub-section, is effectively terminated. The *Charter* is now clearly preeminent, as well as constitutional in its form.

THE "LIMITATIONS" CLAUSE OF THE *CHARTER*

Section 1 of the *Charter* is typically referred to as the "**limitations clause**" and is modelled on a number of European codes of civil rights. Unlike the *Bill of Rights,* the *Charter* makes explicit the reality that no right is absolute. The *Charter,* for example, guarantees the right of freedom of expression, but this does not extend to a right to yell "Fire!" in a crowded theatre without cause, or to libel another citizen.

> ### Guarantee of Rights and Freedoms
>
> *1. The Canadian Charter of Rights and Freedoms guarantees the rights and freedoms set out in it subject only to such reasonable limits prescribed by law as can be demonstrably justified in a free and democratic society.*

Section 1 sets out a two-part test to determine whether federal or provincial law can override a constitutional guarantee of protection within the *Charter*. First, the federal or provincial statute's limits on rights must be reasonable and prescribed by law. Second, the limits must be established, to the satisfaction of the presiding judge, to be demonstrably justified in a free and democratic society. In 1986, the Supreme Court of Canada expressed these criteria in more specific terms. In *R. v. Oakes*, Chief Justice Dickson wrote:

> To establish that a limit is reasonable and demonstrably justified in a free and democratic society, two central criteria must be satisfied. *First, the objective ... must be of sufficient importance* to warrant overriding a constitutionally protected right or freedom.... *Second* ... the party invoking s. 1 must show that the means chosen are reasonable and demonstrably justified. This involves *a form of proportionality test.*... There are, in my view, three important components.... First, the measures adopted must be carefully designed to achieve the objective in question. They must not be arbitrary, unfair, or based on irrational considerations.... Second, the means ... should impair as little as possible the right or freedom in question.... Third, there must be a proportionality between the effects of the measures and the objective which has been identified as of sufficient importance.[21] [Author's emphasis.]

In the **Oakes case**, the accused was charged with possession of a narcotic for the purpose of trafficking. He argued that section 8 of the *Narcotic Control Act* was unconstitutional. Section 8 required a two-stage trial on charges of possession for the purpose of trafficking. First, the prosecutor had to establish possession. Once convicted of possession, the accused had then to convince the judge or jury that he or she was not likely to be in possession of the narcotic for the purpose of trafficking. The argument against section 8 was that it undermined the presumption of innocence in criminal cases and, as a result, the right to a fair trial (guaranteed in section 11[d] of the *Charter*). The Supreme Court agreed with this argument, suggesting that although the objective of prohibiting narcotics was "sufficiently important," section 8 ultimately failed the test of proportionality. As Chief Justice Dickson noted, there is no "rational connection" between the fact of possession of an illegal drug, and the "presumed fact" of possession for the purpose of trafficking.

The Supreme Court's decision in *R. v. Oakes* does not suggest, however, that Canadian courts will generally entertain wide-ranging debate about the boundaries of section 1 of the *Charter*. In fact, the judiciary has spent relatively little time questioning the collision of federal and provincial legislation and the core values set out in the *Charter*. Whether existing legislation threatens individual rights to freedom of expression, the sanction against cruel and unusual punishment, or collective rights to freedom of association are issues too broad to be usefully placed on the agenda of the courts. Unlike legislatures, courts are not well equipped to debate and resolve broad philosophical issues; they *are* better equipped than legislatures, however, to resolve such issues as they arise within specific contexts. This is not true, however, of all jurisdictions. The German Supreme Constitutional Court has an exceptionally far-reaching competency in reviewing legislation; in contrast, the approach of Canada's judiciary could be seen as rather deferential.

Debates within the courts are usually quite circumscribed. In the *Oakes* case, there was a judicial insistence upon the right to be presumed innocent; the protection of this right was not seen to hamper the "sufficient importance" of apprehending and convicting narcotics users and distributors. In the event, neither police nor prosecutors have suggested that the removal of the reverse onus provisions in section 8 of the *Narcotic Control Act* has hampered their ability to act against illegal drug distributors.

The limitations clause ultimately presents two significant but not insurmountable obstacles to those who would use the *Charter* to advance social change. First, there are few circumstances for which no relevant precedents exist; the absence of precedents would permit existing government policies to be effectively challenged. Second, and perhaps more important, the cost of taking a claim of this kind to a provincial court of appeal or the Supreme Court of Canada is prohibitive for most individuals.

There is, nonetheless, a somewhat more recent example of a successful section 1 challenge in *Halpern v. R.* 225 D.L.R. (4th) 529 (2003). The applicants in this case challenged the constitutionality of legislation prohibiting same-sex marriage. The judgment of the Ontario Court of Appeal, excerpted below, was not appealed by the

Government of Canada, and legislation has since been passed (in June 2005) that legalizes same-sex marriages (civil unions):

The Attorney-General of Canada submits that marriage, as a core foundational unit, benefits society at large in that it has proven itself to be one of the most durable institutions for the organization of society. Marriage has always been understood as a special kind of monogamous opposite-sex union, with spiritual, social, economic and contractual dimensions, for the purposes of uniting the opposite sexes, encouraging the birth and raising of children of the marriage, and companionship.

No one is disputing that marriage is a fundamental societal institution. Similarly, it is accepted that, with limited exceptions, marriage has been understood to be a monogamous opposite-sex union. What needs to be determined, however, is whether there is a valid objective to maintaining marriage as an exclusively heterosexual institution. Stating that marriage is heterosexual because it always has been heterosexual is merely an explanation for the opposite-sex requirement of marriage; it is not an objective that is capable of justifying the infringement of a Charter guarantee.

We now turn to the more specific purposes of marriage advanced by the AGC: (i) uniting the opposite sexes; (ii) encouraging the birth and raising of children of the marriage; and (iii) companionship.

The first purpose, which results in favouring one form of relationship over another, suggests that uniting two persons of the same sex is of lesser importance. The words of Dickson C.J.C. in Oakes at 136 are instructive in this regard:

The Court must be guided by the values and principles essential to a free and democratic society which I believe embody, to name but a few, respect for the inherent dignity of the human person, commitment to social justice and equality, accommodation of a wide variety of beliefs, respect for cultural and group identity, and faith in social and political institutions which enhance the participation of individuals and groups in society. The underlying values and principles of a free and democratic society are the genesis of the rights and freedoms guaranteed by the Charter and the ultimate standard against which a limit on a right or freedom must be shown, despite its effect, to be reasonable and demonstrably justified.

Accordingly, a purpose that demeans the dignity of same-sex couples is contrary to the values of a free and democratic society and cannot be considered to be pressing and substantial. A law cannot be justified on the very basis upon which it is being attacked: Big M Drug Mart at 352.

The second purpose of marriage, as advanced by the AGC, is encouraging the birth and raising of children. Clearly, encouraging procreation and childrearing is a laudable goal that is properly regarded as pressing and substantial. However, the Attorney-General of Canada must demonstrate that the objective of maintaining marriage as an exclusively heterosexual institution is pressing and substantial: see Vriend at 554–57.

We fail to see how the encouragement of procreation and childrearing is a pressing and substantial objective of maintaining marriage as an exclusively heterosexual institution. Heterosexual married couples will not stop having or raising children because same-sex couples are permitted to marry. Moreover, an increasing percentage of children are being born to and raised by same-sex couples.

The Attorney-General of Canada submits that the union of two persons of the opposite sex is the only union that can "naturally" procreate. In terms of that biological reality, same-sex couples are different from opposite-sex couples. In our view, however, "natural" procreation is not a sufficiently pressing and substantial objective to justify infringing the equality rights of same-sex couples. As previously stated, same-sex couples can have children by other means, such as adoption, surrogacy and donor insemination. A law that aims to encourage only "natural" procreation ignores the fact that same-sex couples are capable of having children.

Similarly, a law that restricts marriage to opposite-sex couples, on the basis that a fundamental purpose of marriage is the raising of children, suggests that same-sex couples are not equally capable of childrearing. The AGC has put forward no evidence to support such a proposition. Neither is the AGC advocating such a view; rather, it takes the position that social science research is not capable of establishing the proposition one way or another. In the absence of cogent evidence, it is our view that the objective is based on a stereotypical assumption that is not acceptable in a free and democratic society that prides itself on promoting equality and respect for all persons.

The third purpose of marriage advanced by the AGC is companionship. We consider companionship to be a laudable goal of marriage. However, encouraging companionship cannot be considered a pressing and substantial objective of the omission of the impugned law. Encouraging companionship between only persons of the opposite sex perpetuates the view that persons in same-sex relationships are not equally capable of providing companionship and forming lasting and loving relationships.

Accordingly, it is our view that the AGC has not demonstrated any pressing and substantial objective for excluding same-sex couples from the institution of marriage. For that reason, we conclude that the violation of the Couples' rights under s. 15(1) of the Charter cannot be saved under s. 1 of the Charter.

FUNDAMENTAL FREEDOMS

Section 2 of the *Charter* sets out the fundamental freedoms that Canadians are said to possess.

Fundamental Freedoms

2. *Everyone has the following fundamental freedoms:*
   (a) *freedom of conscience and religion;*
   (b) *freedom of thought, belief, opinion and expression, including freedom of the press and other media of communication;*
   (c) *freedom of peaceful assembly; and*
   (d) *freedom of association*

The list shows similarities to the *Bill of Rights,* as well as some noteworthy differences. The Bill's conception of freedom of religion has been expanded to encompass both "freedom of conscience" and "freedom of religion." "Freedom of expression" has also been extended to cover more possibilities: "thought, belief, opinion and expression." And "freedom of assembly" has been more carefully restated as "freedom of peaceful assembly."

Even before the *Bill of Rights* and the *Charter* existed, Canadian courts tried cases in which certain statutes were alleged to violate fundamental freedoms. In the absence of legislation specifically related to rights and freedoms, the Supreme Court of Canada based its decisions on either the exclusivity of federal powers or the "peace, order, and good government" clause in section 91 of the *British North America Act.*

For example, in 1938, the Supreme Court was faced with the Alberta Press Bill. The government of Alberta had introduced legislation that compelled newspapers in the province to print the government's reply to any press criticism of it or its policies. The Supreme Court effectively killed the legislation, holding that the Press Bill was beyond the jurisdiction of the province: free political discussion is so vital to the life of a country that its control must be an exclusively federal power.[22] The Court did not accept the province's technical argument that the legislation could be justified as flowing from exclusive provincial jurisdictions: section 92(13), "property and civil rights," or section 92(16), "matters of a merely local or private nature," as specified in the *British North America Act.*

In 1953, in *Saumur v. City of Quebec,* the Supreme Court had to respond to a Quebec City bylaw that made the permission of the chief of police necessary before pamphlets could be distributed on city streets.[23] The purpose of the bylaw was to prevent the dissemination of certain kinds of materials—specifically, religious tracts published by the Jehovah's Witnesses. The Court again struck down the offending legislation, holding that it interfered with the federal power to legislate in relation to free speech.

Since the enactment of the *Charter,* Canadian courts have heard a range of cases concerning free expression and freedom of assembly and association. In *R. v. Butler,*[24] the accused challenged the constitutionality of obscenity provisions within the *Criminal Code,* specifically section 163(8):

> *163.(8) For the purposes of this Act, any publication a dominant characteristic of which is the undue exploitation of sex, or of sex and any one or more of the following subjects, namely, crime, horror, cruelty, and violence, shall be deemed to be obscene.*

Butler was the operator of a sex shop selling materials that emphasized explicit sex and depicted violence. The Supreme Court held that while the obscenity provisions in the *Criminal Code* do offend section 2(b) of the *Charter* and its guarantee of freedom of expression, these controls can be justified by section 1, the limitations clause. Justice Sopinka, writing for the majority of the Court, noted that while explicit sex in itself might well be justified, material that portrays explicit sex with violence or explicit sex that places women and occasionally men "in positions of subordination, servile submission, or humiliation" cannot be justified. Justice Sopinka further noted that these kinds of pornography are "perceived by public opinion to be harmful to society, particularly to women."

Debate about the legitimacy of pornography will continue, and it seems likely that the Supreme Court will be asked to rule again on the appropriate ambit of the criminal law. Since the late 1980s, free expression for pornographers has collided with other rights; specifically, the right of women to equal treatment, as guaranteed by section 15 of the *Charter*. Constitutional scholar Peter Hogg has commented on this shift: "[T]he advancement of the value of equality does constitute a far more important objective than the protection of conventional morality, and greatly strengthens the argument that can be made for s. 1 justification."[25] It should be noted, in relation to this issue of equality rights, that LEAF, the Women's Legal Education and Action Fund, was a key intervener in the *Butler* decision, discussed above. The argument advanced by LEAF in *Butler* was not one premised on the immorality of the pornography industry, but rather one premised on the damage that certain kinds of pornography impose on the equality rights of women.

In another case centring on freedom of expression, *RJR-MacDonald v. Canada (A.G.)*, the Quebec Superior Court was asked to rule on the constitutionality of the federal prohibition against the advertising of tobacco and tobacco products.[26] The court held that since the federal government was unable to prove a cause-and-effect relationship between a ban on advertising and a reduction in smoking, the legislation's limitation on freedom of expression could not be justified. Tobacco is a legal product, and a prohibition of the right to promote it contravenes section 2(b) of the *Charter*.

The federal government appealed this ruling, and the Quebec Court of Appeal reversed the judgment of the Superior Court.[27] A further appeal resulted ultimately in the Supreme Court of Canada deciding that the federal prohibition of tobacco advertising does contravene s. 2(b) of the *Charter* and that the limitation on freedom of expression imposed by that legislation cannot be justified under section 1.[28]

VOTING AND MOBILITY RIGHTS

The following sections of the *Charter* spell out the basic rights of Canadian citizens with respect to voting, electoral representation, and social mobility. Sections 3 to 5 essentially maintain previous constitutional practice, but section 6 asserts a new right: occupational mobility across Canadian provinces, subject to "reasonable residency requirements" and the operation of "discriminatory" laws aimed at the amelioration of social and economic disadvantage within specific provinces.

Democratic Rights

3. *Every citizen of Canada has the right to vote in an election of members of the House of Commons or of a legislative assembly and to be qualified for membership therein.*

4. (1) *No House of Commons and no legislative assembly shall continue for longer than five years from the date fixed for the return of the writs at a general election of its members*

   (2) *In time of real or apprehended war, invasion or insurrection, a House of Commons may be continued by Parliament and a legislative assembly may be continued by*

the legislature beyond five years if such continuation is not opposed by the votes of more than one-third of the members of the House of Commons or the legislative assembly, as the case may be.

5. *There shall be a sitting of Parliament and of each legislature at least once every twelve months.*

Mobility Rights

6. (1) *Every citizen of Canada has the right to enter, remain in and leave Canada.*
    (2) *Every citizen of Canada and every person who has the status of a permanent resident of Canada has the right*
    (a) *to move to and take up residence in any province; and*
    (b) *to pursue the gaining of a livelihood in any province.*
    (3) *The rights specified in subsection (2) are subject to*
    (a) *any laws or practices of general application in force in a province other than those that discriminate among persons primarily on the basis of province of present or previous residence; and*
    (b) *any laws providing for reasonable residency requirements as a qualification for the receipt of publicly provided social services.*
    (4) *Subsections (2) and (3) do not preclude any law, program or activity that has as its object the amelioration in a province of conditions of individuals in that province who are socially or economically disadvantaged if the rate of employment in that province is below the rate of employment in Canada.*

LEGAL RIGHTS

The following *Charter* sections focus on the legal rights of accused persons within the criminal justice system.

Legal Rights

7. *Everyone has the right to life, liberty and security of the person and the right not to be deprived thereof except in accordance with the principles of fundamental justice.*
8. *Everyone has the right to be secure against unreasonable search or seizure.*
9. *Everyone has the right not to be arbitrarily detained or imprisoned.*
10. *Everyone has the right on arrest or detention*
    (a) *to be informed promptly of the reasons therefor;*
    (b) *to retain and instruct counsel without delay and to be informed of that right; and*
    (c) *to have the validity of the detention determined by way of habeas corpus and to be released if the detention is not lawful.*
11. *Any person charged with an offence has the right*
    (a) *to be informed without unreasonable delay of the specific offence;*
    (b) *to be tried within a reasonable time;*
    (c) *not to be compelled to be a witness in proceedings against that person in respect of the offence;*

(d) *to be presumed innocent until proven guilty according to law in a fair and public hearing by an independent and impartial tribunal;*

(e) *not to be denied reasonable bail without just cause;*

(f) *except in the case of an offence under military law tried before a military tribunal, to the benefit of trial by jury where the maximum punishment for the offence is imprisonment for five years or a more severe punishment;*

(g) *not to be found guilty on account of any act or omission unless, at the time of the act or omission, it constituted an offence under Canadian or international law or was criminal according to the general principles of law recognized by the community of nations;*

(h) *if finally acquitted of the offence, not to be tried for it again and, if finally found guilty and punished for the offence, not to be tried or punished for it again; and*

(i) *if found guilty of the offence and if the punishment for the offence has been varied between the time of commission and the time of sentencing, to the benefit of the lesser punishment.*

12. Everyone has the right not to be subjected to any cruel and unusual treatment or punishment.

13. A witness who testifies in any proceedings has the right not to have any incriminating evidence so given used to incriminate that witness in any other proceedings, except in a prosecution for perjury or for the giving of contradictory evidence.

14. A party or witness in any proceedings who does not understand or speak the language in which the proceedings are conducted or who is deaf has the right to the assistance of an interpreter.

R. v. Morgentaler, perhaps the most significant legal case since the passage of the *Charter*, was based on section 7 and its protection of "life, liberty and security of the person."[29] Dr. Henry Morgentaler's challenge to state control over abortion was ultimately upheld by the Supreme Court of Canada when a majority of the justices found that the *Criminal Code*'s restrictions on abortion were contrary to the *Charter*. Specifically, the Court held that the requirement that abortions be approved by a therapeutic abortion committee created delays in treatment—delays that jeopardized the life, liberty, and security of the women subject to them.

The Supreme Court's interpretation of "life, liberty and security of the person" went beyond the narrow view that would simply have required protection of the physical health of the mother. The majority of the Court held that a woman's inability to control the termination of her pregnancy constituted an unjustifiable loss of "life, liberty and security of the person."

Section 7 of the *Charter* has also been used to protect the right of an accused not to make any statement when charged with a criminal offence. In *R. v. Hebert*, the accused exercised his right to retain counsel and told police that he did not wish to make any statement after being arrested.[30] He was then placed in custody with an undercover police officer to whom he unwittingly made an incriminating statement.

The issue for the Supreme Court of Canada was whether this statement was admissible in court. Seven members of the Court unanimously held that the statement was not admissible; the police officer had been employed to elicit an incriminating response from the accused—that is, to subvert the accused's constitutional right to remain silent in the face of police questioning.

During the past three decades, Canadian courts have been grappling with the *Charter*'s insistence under section 11(b) that "any person charged with an offence has the right to be tried within a reasonable time." The meaning of "within a reasonable time" has been the subject of more than a dozen cases decided by the Supreme Court and provincial Courts of Appeal. Courts have held that the reasonableness of a delay can be inferred from the following factors: the length of the delay before trial, the reasons for the delay, systemic or institutional delays, delays that may be attributable to the accused, and any prejudice visited upon the accused by the delay. Unfortunately, this naming of factors has not brought about much consistency in the determination of what is "reasonable." In one 2012 decision in Saskatchewan, a delay of two years and nine months was considered reasonable; another Alberta court decision in the same year found a delay of two years and six months unreasonable.[31]

The most significant case with regard to reasonableness was probably *R. v. Askov* in 1990.[32] The accused in *Askov* were charged with serious offences involving weapons and alleged threats of bodily harm. Thirty-four months elapsed between the original charges and the trial. The Supreme Court held that the jurisdiction in which the accused were charged (Ontario's Peel District) was one in which unreasonable delays were commonplace and that the accused could not be held responsible for these delays. The charges against Askov and his associates were therefore dismissed. Justice Cory, writing for a unanimous Supreme Court, argued that "a period of delay in a range of some six to eight months between committal and trial might be deemed to be the outside limit of what is reasonable."

The consequences of the *Askov* decision have been remarkable. Tens of thousands of charges, particularly in Ontario, have been withdrawn or stayed on the ground of delay. Although subsequent decisions by the Supreme Court have moderated Justice Cory's definition of six to eight months as an "outside limit," the Court has made clear that it will not tolerate "systemic" delays resulting from a lack of government resources. In *R. v. Morin*, the Court noted, "The government has a constitutional obligation to commit sufficient resources to prevent unreasonable delay, which distinguishes this obligation from many others that compete for funds with the administration of justice."[33]

Another provision of the *Charter* designed to protect the rights of the accused is section 12. The constitutional prohibition against cruel and unusual punishment was used in 1987 to strike down a section of the *Narcotic Control Act* that required a minimum term of seven years' imprisonment upon conviction for importing any amount of a narcotic, principally heroin, cocaine, or marijuana. In *R. v. Smith*, the Court held that, in some circumstances, the penalty of seven years' imprisonment could be seen to be "grossly disproportionate" to the offence committed.[34] Consider the example of a young person entering Canada with a couple of marijuana cigarettes. Would a seven-year sentence for such importation constitute cruel and unusual punishment? The Supreme Court answered this question in the affirmative.

In the case of *R. v. Luxton*,[35] however, the Court's response was much less sympathetic. The *Luxton* case challenged the *Criminal Code*'s minimum term of imprisonment for 25 years upon conviction for first degree murder. In 1976, when capital punishment was abolished in Canada, Parliament raised the minimum terms of imprisonment upon conviction for both first degree and second degree murder. These increases in the time to be served were a trade-off given by the government to those who favoured the death penalty in order to accomplish its goal of abolition.

There is no decisive evidence to support the contention that increased terms have a greater corrective efficacy than shorter terms. Nevertheless, Chief Justice Lamer, writing in *Luxton* for a unanimous Supreme Court of Canada, simply asserted that such "punishment is not excessive and clearly does not outrage our standards of decency." Constitutional scholar Peter Hogg, however, has found this logic less than compelling:

> [I]n my opinion, the mandatory sentence of 25 years without parole is so severe that it cannot meet the standard. Two of the three categories of first-degree murder do not include any element of premeditation, and therefore would encompass a wide range of moral turpitude. For example, it is not "far-fetched" to postulate a hypothetical offender—one who killed in panic, perhaps, or one who was merely an accomplice of the killer, perhaps—for whom the 25 years without parole would be grossly disproportionate. And yet the Court in *Luxton* did not test the sentence by reference to any hypothetical cases, or otherwise explain why the punishment was not grossly disproportionate.[36]

EQUALITY RIGHTS

The "equality" section of the *Charter* has expanded the protections set out in the *Bill of Rights* of 1960.

Equality Rights

15.(1) Every individual is equal before and under the law and has the right to the equal protection and equal benefit of the law without discrimination and, in particular, without discrimination based on race, national or ethnic origin, colour, religion, sex, age or mental or physical disability

(2) Subsection (1) does not preclude any law, program or activity that has as its object amelioration of conditions of disadvantaged individuals or groups including those that are disadvantaged because of race, national or ethnic origin, colour, religion, sex, age or mental or physical disability.

Section 15(1) of the *Charter* prohibits discrimination based on two new categories: mental and physical disability. As noted above, the Supreme Court of Canada's "equality" decisions during the 1970s appeared inconsistent: Joseph Drybones was determined to have suffered unequal treatment on the basis of race, but in strikingly similar circumstances Jeannette Lavell was said not to have suffered unequal treatment on the basis of gender.

Much of the difficulty in responding to allegations of unequal treatment, whether under the *Bill of Rights* or the *Charter,* is that inequality in itself is not considered to be an evil. There are many circumstances in which unequal treatment is not only justifiable but preferable and to be expected. Canadians who have not attained the age of majority are treated differently from those who have, most notably in relation to the right to vote, to drive an automobile, and to enter into contractual agreements; Canadians over 65 are treated differently from those under 65. The government responds to those convicted of criminal offences differently from those who have not been so convicted, and so on.

It is on the justification for unequal treatment that we must focus when looking at the protection offered by section 15. In addition to setting out prohibited grounds for discrimination—race, sex, age, and so forth—the section provides for an open-ended bar to unequal treatment, indicating that other forms of discrimination than those specifically set out may ultimately be determined to be constitutionally prohibited.

In *Andrews v. Law Society of British Columbia,* the Supreme Court was faced with Andrews's claim that the requirement of Canadian citizenship for the practice of law in British Columbia constitutes a denial of equality before the law. The Supreme Court held that the B.C. statute requiring lawyers to be Canadian citizens did create a lack of equality before the law, and the majority of the Court held that this inequality could not be justified by section 1 of the *Charter.* Justice La Forest compared citizenship to such personal characteristics as race, age, and mental or physical disability: "The characteristic of citizenship is one typically not within the control of the individual and, in this sense, is immutable. Citizenship is, at least temporarily, a characteristic of personhood not alterable by conscious action and in some cases, not alterable except on the basis of unacceptable costs."[37]

But section 15(2) of the *Charter* is also critical. In a 2008 decision of the Supreme Court of Canada, *R. v. Kapp,*[38] the appellants argued that their inability to participate in a communal fishery, granted only to Aboriginals, was a denial of equality before the law. They decided to fish in a manner similar to the Aboriginal fishers, and were convicted in provincial court for doing so; their convictions were upheld by the Supreme Court of Canada. The introductory comments of the Chief Justice set out the logic of the court's approach:

The appellants are commercial fishers, mainly non-aboriginal, who assert that their equality rights under s. 15 of the Canadian Charter of Rights and Freedoms were violated by a communal fishing licence granting members of three aboriginal bands the exclusive right to fish for salmon in the mouth of the Fraser River for a period of 24 hours on August 19–20, 1998.

The appellants base their claim on s. 15(1). The essence of the claim is that the communal fishing licence discriminated against them on the basis of race. The Crown argues that the general purpose of the program under which the licence was issued was to regulate the fishery, and that it ameliorated the conditions of a disadvantaged group. These contentions, taken together, raise the issue of the interplay between s. 15(1) and s. 15(2) of the Charter. Specifically, they require this Court to consider whether s. 15(2) is capable of operating independently of s. 15(1) to protect ameliorative programs from claims of discrimination—a possibility left open in this Court's equality jurisprudence.

We have concluded that where a program makes a distinction on one of the grounds enumerated under s. 15 or an analogous ground but has as its object the amelioration of the conditions of a disadvantaged group, s. 15's guarantee of substantive equality is furthered, and the claim of discrimination must fail. As the communal fishing licence challenged in this appeal falls within s. 15(2)'s ambit—one of its objects being to ameliorate the conditions of the participating aboriginal bands— the appellants' claim of a violation of s. 15 cannot succeed.

LANGUAGE RIGHTS

Sections 16 to 23 of the *Charter* are essentially self-explanatory. They are concerned with the protection of minority-language rights.

Official Languages of Canada

16.(1) English and French are the official languages of Canada and have equality of status and equal rights and privileges as to their use in all institutions of the Parliament and government of Canada.

(2) English and French are the official languages of New Brunswick and have equality of status and equal rights and privileges as to their use in all institutions of the legislature and government of New Brunswick.

(3) Nothing in this Charter limits the authority of Parliament or a legislature to advance the equality of status or use of English and French.

17.(1) Everyone has the right to use English or French in any debates and other proceedings of Parliament.

(2) Everyone has the right to use English or French in any debates and other proceedings of the legislature of New Brunswick.

18.(1) The statutes, records and journals of Parliament shall be printed and published in English and French and both language versions are equally authoritative.

(2) The statutes, records and journals of the legislature of New Brunswick shall be printed and published in English and French and both language versions are equally authoritative.

19.(1) Either English or French may be used by any person in, or in any pleading in or process issuing from, any court established by Parliament

(2) Either English or French may be used by any person in, or in any pleading in or process issuing from, any court of New Brunswick.

20.(1) Any member of the public in Canada has the right to communicate with, and to receive available services from, any head or central office of an institution of the Parliament or government of Canada in English or French, and has the same right with respect to any other office of any such institution where

> *(a) there is a significant demand for communications with and services from that office in such language; or*
>
> *(b) due to the nature of the office, it is reasonable that communications with and services from that office be available in both English and French.*

(2) Any member of the public in New Brunswick has the right to communicate with, and to receive available services from, any office of an institution of the legislature or government of New Brunswick in English or French.

21. Nothing in sections 16 to 20 abrogates or derogates from any right, privilege, or obligation with respect to the English and French languages, or either of them, that exists or is continued by virtue of any other provision of the Constitution of Canada.

22. Nothing in sections 16 to 20 abrogates or derogates from any legal or customary right or privilege acquired or enjoyed either before or after the coming into force of this Charter with respect to any language that is not English or French.

Minority Language Educational Rights

23.(1) Citizens of Canada

> *(a) whose first language learned and still understood is that of the English or French linguistic minority population of the province in which they reside, or*
>
> *(b) who have received their primary school instruction in Canada in English or French and reside in a province where the language in which they received that instruction is the language of the English or French linguistic minority population of the province, have the right to have their children receive primary and secondary school instruction in that language in that province.*

(2) Citizens of Canada of whom any child has received or is receiving primary or secondary school instruction in English or French in Canada, have the right to have all their children receive primary and secondary school instruction in the same language.

(3) The right of citizens of Canada under subsections (1) and (2) to have their children receive primary and secondary school instruction in the language of the English or French linguistic minority population of a province

> *(a) applies wherever in the province the number of children of citizens who have such a right is sufficient to warrant the provision to them out of public funds of minority language instruction; and*
>
> *(b) includes, where the number of those children so warrants, the right to have them receive that instruction in minority language educational facilities provided out of public funds.*

REMEDIES UNDER THE CHARTER

Section 24 of the *Charter* is the enforcement mechanism that gives courts the power to exclude evidence if "the admission of it in the proceedings would bring the administration of justice into disrepute."

Enforcement

24.(1) Anyone whose rights or freedoms, as guaranteed by this Charter, have been infringed or denied may apply to a court of competent jurisdiction to obtain such remedy as the court considers appropriate and just in the circumstances.

(2) Where, in proceedings under subsection (1), a court concludes that evidence was obtained in a manner that infringed or denied any rights or freedoms guaranteed by this Charter, the evidence shall be excluded if it is established that, having regard to all the circumstances, the admission of it in the proceedings would bring the administration of justice into disrepute.

Police organizations have attacked section 24(2), claiming that it permits the guilty to go free. Civil libertarians have argued, in response, that an exclusionary rule is needed to deter police from misconduct.

Prior to the passage of the *Charter*, Canadian courts followed the British approach to illegally obtained evidence: the evidence was admissible if relevant to the issues in dispute. Police misconduct did not limit the courts' use of this information; the misconduct was properly the subject of a separate hearing. U.S. courts, on the other hand, have adopted an exclusionary approach to illegally obtained evidence: if police in the United States use means contrary to the U.S. Bill of Rights to obtain evidence, then the evidence—the so-called fruit of the poison tree—is inadmissible.

Section 24(2) of the *Charter* represents a compromise between the British and U.S. positions. It instructs Canadian courts to engage in a balancing test, excluding illegally obtained evidence only when its admission would "bring the administration of justice into disrepute." Evidence would be potentially inadmissible if gained by means of some searches for illegal drugs, weapons, and/or stolen property, as well as through questionable confessions.

The case law to date reveals that a balancing test is, in fact, emerging. Generally speaking, good-faith errors by the police will not lead to exclusion, but intentional violations of the *Charter* will. For example, in *R. v. Greffe* police had no justifiable grounds for arresting the accused for a narcotics offence; they therefore arrested him for outstanding traffic tickets, conducted a rectal examination, and discovered heroin. The Supreme Court of Canada excluded the evidence of the heroin, arguing that the administration of justice would be brought into disrepute if Canadian courts were to permit the practice of rectal examination after arrest for outstanding traffic tickets, when no reasonable or probable grounds existed for believing that an accused had committed a criminal offence.[39]

On the other hand, in *R. v. Simmons* the accused was searched at the airport before being informed of her right to retain a lawyer; illegal drugs were discovered taped to her body. The police officers who conducted the search were not aware that it was necessary to inform the accused of her right to retain counsel at this initial stage of their investigation; they believed that such "investigative detention" did not require accused persons to be advised of their right to counsel. The evidence of the illegal drugs was admitted.[40]

In *Collins v. R.*, Justice Lamer set out three issues to be considered in determining whether the administration of justice has been brought into disrepute: (1) the nature and significance of the evidence obtained; (2) the quality of the police conduct that permitted the evidence to be obtained; and (3) the consequences for the justice system as a whole if the evidence is excluded.[41] As we move through the early twenty-first century, it is becoming clear that Canada is charting its own course with respect to the exclusion of evidence, adopting neither extreme of the British and U.S. approaches.

More recently, in *R. v. A.M.*,[42] the Supreme Court decided in a majority decision that the use of sniffer dogs in a public school without any knowledge or evidence that drugs were present (that is, a warrantless search) was contrary to section 8 of the *Charter* (the right to be secure against unreasonable search or seizure) and should be excluded under section 24(2). The majority quoted, with approval, the sentiments of the trial judge regarding section 24(2):

> This search was unreasonable from the outset. It is completely contrary to the requirements of the law with respect to the search in a school setting. To admit the evidence is effectively to strip A.M. and any other student in a similar situation of the right to be free from unreasonable search and seizure. It is effectively saying that persons in the same situation as A.M. have no rights. Such a finding would, to my mind, bring the administration of justice into disrepute, notwithstanding the other factors I have alluded to.

The dissenting minority argued that the breach of rights did not bring the administration of justice into disrepute:

> In this case, the use of the dog sniff was not based on a current, reasonable suspicion. As a result, the search was unreasonable for the purposes of s. 8 of the Charter. The evidence found in A.M.'s backpack, however, ought nonetheless have been admissible at trial. Section 24(2) of the Charter requires that evidence is only excluded when its admission would bring the administration of justice into disrepute, and admission in this case would not have that effect. As a result, I would have allowed the appeal on the limited basis that the evidence against A.M. ought to have been admitted at trial notwithstanding the breach of his s. 8 rights.

ABORIGINAL RIGHTS, GENDER EQUALITY, AND THE OPTING-OUT PROVISIONS

The key sections within sections 25 to 34 relate to the application of the *Charter*.

General

25. The guarantee in this Charter of certain rights and freedoms shall not be construed so as to abrogate or derogate from any aboriginal, treaty or other rights or freedoms that pertain to the aboriginal peoples of Canada including

    (a) *any rights or freedoms that have been recognized by the Royal Proclamation of October 7, 1763; and*

    (b) *any rights or freedoms that now exist by way of land claims agreements or may be so acquired.*

26. *The guarantee in this Charter of certain rights and freedoms shall not be construed as denying the existence of any other rights or freedoms that exist in Canada.*

27. *This Charter shall be interpreted in a manner consistent with the preservation and enhancement of the multicultural heritage of Canadians.*

28. *Notwithstanding anything in this Charter, the rights and freedoms referred to in it are guaranteed equally to male and female persons.*

29. *Nothing in this Charter abrogates or derogates from any rights or privileges guaranteed by or under the Constitution of Canada in respect of denominational, separate or dissentient schools.*

30. *A reference in this Charter to a province or to the legislative assembly or legislature of a province shall be deemed to include a reference to the Yukon Territory and the Northwest Territories, or to the appropriate legislative authority thereof, as the case may be.*

31. *Nothing in this Charter extends the legislative powers of any body or authority.*

Application of Charter

32.(1) *This Charter applies*

    (a) *to the Parliament and government of Canada in respect of all matters within the authority of Parliament including all matters relating to the Yukon Territory and Northwest Territories; and*

    (b) *to the legislature and government of each province in respect of all matters within the authority of the legislature of each province.*

(2) *Notwithstanding subsection (1), section 15 shall not have effect until three years after this section comes into force.*

33.(1) *Parliament or the legislature of a province may expressly declare in an Act of Parliament or of the legislature, as the case may be, that the Act or a provision thereof shall operate notwithstanding a provision included in section 2 or sections 7 to 15 of this Charter.*

(2) *An Act or a provision of an Act in respect of which a declaration made under this section is in effect shall have such operation as it would have but for the provision of this Charter referred to in the declaration.*

(3) *A declaration made under subsection (1) shall cease to have effect five years after it comes into force or on such earlier date as may be specified in the declaration.*

(4) *Parliament or the legislature of a province may re-enact a declaration made under subsection (1).*

(5) *Subsection (3) applies in respect of a re-enactment made under subsection (4).*

Citation

34. *This Part may be cited as the Canadian Charter of Rights and Freedoms.*

Section 32 makes it clear that the *Charter,* unlike the *Bill of Rights,* applies to both federal and provincial legislation. Arguably, section 33 most critically weakens the impact of the *Charter.* Section 33(1) permits governments to opt out of *Charter* provisions simply by stating that a specific piece of legislation will operate "notwithstanding" the fundamental freedoms of section 2, the rights afforded accused persons by sections 7 to 14, or the equality rights of section 15. Although there is some limitation on using the so-called **notwithstanding clause** to opt out of *Charter* provisions (section 33[3] terminates the exception after five years have elapsed), there is no bar to reenacting the override every five years (section 33[4] permits reenactment of exceptions to the *Charter*).

Provincial governments have opted out of *Charter* provisions in a number of instances. The government of Quebec declared shortly after the enactment of the *Charter* that all laws of the province would operate notwithstanding sections 2 and 7 to 15 of the *Charter.* This legislation was ultimately thrown out by the Quebec Court of Appeal.[43] The Quebec government later successfully applied the notwithstanding clause to legislation that restricted the use of English on commercial signs. The government of Saskatchewan has applied the notwithstanding clause to legislation that prohibits strikes by public-sector workers in "essential services." Saskatchewan did so to ensure that the fundamental freedoms afforded by section 2 of the *Charter* would not apply to its labour legislation.

STRENGTHS AND LIMITATIONS OF THE *CHARTER*

The *Charter* has been subject to many criticisms, and has received as many plaudits. The original objection—that it diminishes the doctrine of parliamentary supremacy—has not disappeared. It is argued that the passage of the *Charter* as a constitutional document gave Canada's judges the power to make law, a power that should never be given to individuals who are not democratically elected and hence not accountable to the general public.

Police have also criticized the *Charter*, suggesting that its emphasis on legal rights, particularly in sections 7 to 14, has hampered their ability to enforce the law effectively. Many police organizations have suggested that the *Charter* makes it more difficult for them to detect, arrest, and successfully prosecute criminals, and, more specifically, that more time must now be spent in the preparation of cases for the court.

Other opponents of the *Charter* have argued that its emphasis on the rights of private individuals tends to obscure and minimize the importance of collective rights, particularly in the economic sphere. Constitutional law scholar Andrew Petter has suggested that the focus on individual rights has combined with the substantial costs of litigation to yield a situation in which only the affluent can use this law to further their interests, with the net effect that the *Charter* can be used against the economically disadvantaged to uphold individual rights at the expense of the public good.[44] There is, in fact, nothing in the *Charter* about economic rights or economic equality.

Still other critics have pointed out that an entrenched Bill of Rights or Charter of Rights is no guarantee of the protection of civil liberties. Canada and Britain, in responding to crime, have shown less tendency to impose excessive punishments and to infringe liberty than the United States, which has had an entrenched Bill of Rights for more than 200 years.

Finally, some critics have claimed that the *Charter* has taken political issues out of the hands of citizens and given them to the judiciary. Lawyers and judges—representatives of the affluent—conduct expensive litigation without accountability to the electorate, resolving conflicting interests and, in the process, restructuring the nature of Canadian society. In the words of the late Osgoode Hall law professor Michael Mandel, the *Charter* has effectively permitted "the legalization of politics."[45]

Even those who find substantial merit in the *Charter*, and might be reluctant to accept any of these arguments, can find limitations in its present structure. Section 33 gives Parliament and the provinces the power to opt out of all significant *Charter* provisions and thereby, arguably, diminish its strength as a constitutional document.

The real test of the *Charter* is, however, to be found in the decisions that emanate from Canadian courts, as well as in the effect of these decisions on our social, political, and economic lives. In discussing the key sections of the *Charter* (the fundamental freedoms in s. 2, the rights afforded accused persons by ss. 7 to 14, and the equality provisions of s. 15) we have reviewed a number of the most significant decisions: *RJR-MacDonald*, *Morgentaler*, and, more recently, *R. v. Kapp* and *R. v. A.M.* But what can we conclude from the judgments issued by Canadian courts in these and other cases? With respect to the four cases just named, it appears that our courts have been willing to protect the legal rights of corporations to advertise a drug that kills about 35,000 Canadians every year. They have also been willing to declare the century-old criminalization of a woman's control over her reproductive ability a violation of fundamental justice. They have been willing to grant Aboriginal fishers rights that are not extended to non-Aboriginals, and they have also declared that bringing sniffer dogs into schools without warrant, and then laying charges against individuals in possession of illegal drugs, brings the administration of justice into disrepute.

CONCLUSION

What we make of these decisions, and hundreds of others, will depend upon the political, economic, and social values we hold. For example, for some, the Supreme Court's decision in *Morgentaler* is an abomination; for others it is justice. Hogg has said that the *Charter* "protects the values of a nation"—but how do we define "the values of a nation"? One person's freedom of religion may involve the imposition of offensive or alien beliefs on another person. The right to be secure against unreasonable search and seizure will be interpreted according to one's political values and, specifically, according to one's perceptions of specific crimes and their appropriate control.

Ultimately, at least in difficult cases, there are not clear overarching values to which all Canadians subscribe. Although almost all of us believe in the rhetoric of terms such as "equality" and "freedom of speech," we diverge on the practical specifics of the law's application. What we intend as fundamental freedoms, rights for the accused, or equality before the law are matters of debate. The court is a forum in which a contest of values, albeit circumscribed, takes place.

Consider, in closing, the recent controversy that has emerged over B.C's Trinity Western University, and its attempt to found a Christian law school unwilling to accept any homosexuality or sexual intimacy among its students unless they are man and wife. In early February of 2014, Trinity Western President Bob Kuhn stated that opposition to the law school "strikes at the very heart of religious freedom in Canada."[46]

But what of section 15 of the *Charter of Rights* and its protection of equality before the law? Canadian courts have used this section to protect individuals from discrimination on the basis of sexual orientation. Perhaps we have a clash of competing rights with Trinity Western's application. On the one hand, the university asserts a right to the protection of religious freedom, but on the other, critics can quite properly point to discrimination against homosexuality as a violation of equality rights. And which right should be preeminent?

Web Links

Constitution Acts: 1867 to 1982, Department of Justice
http://laws.justice.gc.ca/en/const/index.html
This website provides the full texts of the constitutional documents of Canada, including the *Canadian Charter of Rights and Freedoms.*

Library of Parliament, Parliamentary Research Branch
http://www2.parl.gc.ca/Sites/LOP/VirtualLibrary/ResearchPublications-e.asp
The Parliamentary Research Branch prepares research papers on matters of public interest.

Quebec's Politics on the Web
http://quebecpolitique.com
This website is dedicated to politics in Quebec and contains extensive information about Quebec's political history—for example, the province's political system and parties, its judicial system, all provincial elections since 1867, and the referendums.

Questions for Discussion

1. Should Canada's judges move toward a more restrictive interpretation of the *Canadian Charter of Rights and Freedoms*, thereby preserving the long-standing doctrine of parliamentary supremacy? Discuss.

2. The cases of *Kapp* and *Morris* raise questions about the conflict between federal and provincial governments and Aboriginal or treaty rights. Is the Supreme Court of Canada striking an appropriate balance in these cases?

3. Trinity Western Law School seeks to impose its religious beliefs on all who apply to study law; more important, the university is failing to respect legally established equality rights with respect to sexual orientation. Discuss the validity of this statement.

FURTHER READING

Beaudoin, G.A., and E. Mendes. *The Canadian Charter of Rights and Freedoms.* 4th ed. Toronto: Carswell, 2005.

> This legal text provides a comprehensive look at the application of the *Charter*. The authors analyze and interpret a wide range of *Charter* decisions that have served to alter the Canadian legal landscape. Their book also provides insight into their expectations of future judicial decisions within this realm.

Hogg, P.W. *Constitutional Law of Canada, 2013 Student Edition.* Toronto: Carswell, 2013.

> This student edition, an abridged version of the looseleaf two-volume 5th edition, is a remarkable and ongoing piece of work from Canada's foremost constitutional scholar. Peter Hogg of Blake, Cassels, and Graydon and Osgoode Hall Law School dissects constitutional law with a thorough and thoughtful analysis. There is no more comprehensive text available on the subject of Canadian constitutional law, with case law through to October of 2012.

Mandel, M. *The Charter of Rights and the Legalization of Politics in Canada: Revised Updated and Expanded.* Toronto: Thompson Educational, 1994.

> This is a well-researched and critical analysis of the emergence and continuation of the *Charter*. The late Professor Mandel suggests that the *Charter* has contributed to the decline of democracy in Canada, has promoted inequality, and has diminished collective rights in favour of a "fundamentally dishonest, authoritarian and above-all anti-democratic form."

NOTES

1. See http://www.canlii.org/en/ca/scc/doc/2006/2006scc59/2006scc59.html.
2. 30–31 Vict., c. 3 (U.K.).
3. Being Schedule B to the *Canada Act 1982* (U.K.), 1982, c. 11.
4. Part I of the *Constitution Act, 1982*, being Schedule B to the *Canada Act 1982* (U.K.), 1982, c. 11.
5. R. Cheffins and R. Tucker, *The Constitutional Process in Canada*, 2nd ed. (Toronto: McGraw-Hill Ryerson, 1976), 4.

6. P.W. Hogg, *Constitutional Law of Canada*. 3rd ed. (Toronto: Carswell, 1992), 1.

7. [1926] A.C. 482 (P.C.).

8. W.R. Lederman, "The Process of Constitutional Amendment for Canada," *McGill Law Journal* 12 (1967): 377.

9. *Constitution Act, 1999* (Nunavut)—1998, c. 15, Part 2, s. 47.

10. 30–31 Vict., c. 3 (U.K.), reprinted in R.S.C. 1985, App. II, no. 5.

11. *R. v. Hauser*, [1979] 1 S.C.R. 984, [1979] 5 W.W.R. 1, 8 C.R. (3d) 89, 98 D.L.R. (3d) 193, 46 C.C.C. (2d) 481, 26 N.R. 541, 16 A.R. 91.

12. See, for example, *Reference re Anti-Inflation Act*, [1976] 2 S.C.R. 373, 68 D.L.R. (3d) 452, 9 N.R. 541.

13. *Canada (Attorney General) v. PHS Community Services Society*, [2011] 3 S.C.R. 134.

14. Hogg, *Constitutional Law of Canada*, 131.

15. For a discussion of this issue see the Supreme Court of Canada's decision in *Re Nova Scotia Board of Censors and McNeil*, [1978] 2 S.C.R. 662, 84 D.L.R. (3d) 1.

16. *Patriation Reference (Re Resolution to Amend the Constitution)*, [1981] 1 S.C.R. 753.

17. S.C. 1960, c. 44, reprinted in R.S.C. 1985, App. III.

18. E.C.S. Wade, *Constitutional and Administrative Law* (Essex: Longman Group, 1985), 64.

19. [1970] 3 C.C.C. 355, 10 C.R.N.S. 334 (6:3).

20. (1973), 38 D.L. R. (3d) 481, [1974] S.C.R. 1439, 23 C.R.N.S. 197 (5:4).

21. *R. v. Oakes*, [1986] 1 S.C.R. 103 at 138–9.

22. *Re Alberta Statutes*, [1938] S.C.R. 100.

23. *Saumur v. City of Quebec*, [1953] 2 S.C.R. 299.

24. *Criminal Code*, R.S.C. 1985, c. C-46, s. 163(B), as cited in *R. v. Butler*, [1992] 1 S.C.R. 452.

25. Hogg, *Constitutional Law of Canada*, 977.

26. *RJR-MacDonald v. Canada (A.G.)* (1991), 82 D.L.R. (4th) 449 [hereinafter *MacDonald*].

27. *RJR-MacDonald v. Canada (A.G.)* (1993), 102 D.L.R. (4th) 289.

28. *RJR-MacDonald v. Canada* (A.G.), [1995] 3 S.C.R. 199.

29. *R. v. Morgentaler (No. 2)*, [1988] 1 S.C.R. 30.

30. *R. v. Hebert*, [1990] 2 S.C.R. 151.

31. See *R. v. Conway*, [1989] 1 S.C.R. 1659 and, alternatively, *R. v. Smith*, [1989] 2 S.C.R. 1120.

32. [1990] 2 S.C.R. 1199.

33. *R. v. Morin*, [1992] 1 S.C.R. 771 at 795.

34. *R. v. Smith*, [1987] 1 S.C.R. 1045.

35. [1990] 2 S.C.R. 711.

36. Hogg, *Constitutional Law of Canada*, 1135.

37. *Andrews v. Law Society of British Columbia*, [1989] 1 S.C.R. 143 at 195.

38. See http://www.canlii.org/en/ca/scc/doc/2008/2008scc41/2008scc41.html.

39. *R. v. Greffe* (1990), 55 C.C.C. (3d) 161, 75 C.R. (3d) 257, [1990] 1 S.C.R. 755.

40. *R. v. Simmons* (1988), 45 C.C.C. (3d) 296, [1988] 2 S.C.R. 495.
41. *Collins v. R.* (1987), 33 C.C.C. (3d) 1, [1987] 1 S.C.R. 265.
42. See http://www.canlii.org/en/ca/scc/doc/2008/2008scc19/2008scc19.html.
43. See also *Ford v. Quebec*, [1988] 2 S.C.R. 712.
44. A. Petter, "The Politics of the Charter," *Supreme Court Law Review* 8 (1986): 473–505; A. Hutchinson and A. Petter, "Private Rights/Public Wrongs: The Liberal Lie of the Charter," *University of Toronto Law Journal* 38 (1988): 278.
45. M. Mandel, *The Charter of Rights and the Legalization of Politics in Canada* (Toronto: Wall and Thompson, 1989).
46. In J. Bradshaw, "Religious Rights at Risk B.C. Law School with Gay-Intimacy Ban Warns Alumni," *The Globe and Mail*, Toronto, February 5, 2014.

REFERENCES

Abel, A.S. *Toward a Constitutional Charter for Canada*. Toronto: University of Toronto Press, 1980.

Bayefsky, A.F., and M.A. Eberts. *Equality Rights and the Canadian Charter of Rights and Freedoms*. Toronto: Carswell, 1985.

Berger, T. *Fragile Freedoms*. Toronto: Clarke Irwin, 1982.

Cheffins, R.I., and P.A. Johnson. *The Revised Canadian Constitution: Politics as Law*. Toronto: McGraw-Hill Ryerson, 1976.

Finkelstein, M. *The Right to Counsel*. Toronto: Butterworths, 1988.

Gibson, D. *The Law of the Charter: General Principles*. Calgary: Carswell, 1986.

Hogg, P.W. *Constitutional Law of Canada*. 2013 student edition. Toronto: Carswell, 2013.

– – –. *Meech Lake Constitutional Accord Annotated*. Toronto: Carswell, 1988.

Laskin, B. "The Canadian Constitution after the First Century, Part 1." *Canadian Bar Review* 45 (1967): 395.

– – –. *Laskin's Canadian Constitutional Law*. 5th ed. Revised by N. Finkelstein. Toronto: Carswell, 1986.

Lederman, W.R. *Continuing Canadian Constitutional Dilemmas*. Toronto: Butterworths, 1981.

– – –. "Unity and Diversity in Canadian Federalism: Ideals and Methods of Moderation." *Alberta Law Review* 14 (1976): 34.

Mackenzie, J.A. "Planning of the B.N.A. Act." *Ottawa Law Review* 6 (1974): 332.

McDonald, D.C. *Legal Rights in the Canadian Charter of Rights and Freedoms*. 2nd ed. Calgary: Carswell, 1989.

McDonald, R. St. J., and J.P. Humphrey, eds. *The Practice of Freedom*. Toronto: Butterworths, 1979.

McWhinney, E. "The Supreme Court of Canada and the Constitutional Division of Powers." *Supreme Court Conference* 55 (1986).

Mandel, M. *The Charter of Rights and the Legalization of Politics in Canada*. Toronto: Wall and Thompson, 1989.

Marshall, G. *Parliamentary Sovereignty and the Commonwealth*. Oxford: Clarendon Press, 1957.

Milne, D.A. *The Canadian Constitution*. 2nd ed. Toronto: James Lorimer, 1991.

Monahan, P. *Meech Lake: The Inside Story*. Toronto: University of Toronto Press, 1991.

———. *Politics and the Constitution: The Charter, Federalism and the Supreme Court of Canada*. Toronto: Carswell, 1987.

Morton, F.L., ed. *Law, Politics and the Judicial System in Canada*. Calgary: University of Calgary Press, 1984.

Morton, J.C., and S.C. Hutchison. *Presumption of Innocence*. Toronto: Carswell, 1987.

Petter, A. "The Politics of the Charter." *Supreme Court Law Review* 8 (1986): 473.

Russell, P.H. "Constitutional Reform of the Canadian Judiciary." *Alberta Law Review* 7 (1969): 103.

———. *The Judiciary in Canada: The Third Branch of Government*. Toronto: McGraw-Hill Ryerson, 1987.

Saywell, J., and G. Vegh. *Making the Law: The Courts and the Constitution*. Mississauga: Copp Clark Pitman, 1991.

Schmeiser, D.A. "The Case Against Entrenchment of a Canadian Bill of Rights." *Dalhousie Law Journal* 1 (1973): 15.

Scott, F.R. "Canadian Federalism: The Legal Perspective." *Alberta Law Review* 5 (1967): 262.

Strayer, B.L. *The Canadian Constitution and the Courts*. 3rd ed. Toronto: Butterworths, 1988.

Swinton, K. *The Supreme Court and Canadian Federalism*. Toronto: Carswell, 1990.

Tarnopolsky, W. "Just Desserts or Cruel and Unusual Treatment or Punishment? Where Do We Look For Guidance?" *Ottawa Law Review* 10 (1978): 1.

Tarnopolsky, W., and G.-A. Beaudoin, eds. *Canadian Charter of Rights and Freedoms: Commentary*. Toronto: Carswell, 1982.

Trudeau, P.E. "Constitutional Reform and Individual Freedoms." *Western Ontario Law Review* 8 (1969): 1.

Weiler, J., and R.M. Elliot, eds. *Litigating the Values of a Nation: The Canadian Charter of Rights and Freedoms*. Calgary: Carswell, 1986.

Weiler, P.C. "The Supreme Court of Canada and Canadian Federalism." *Osgoode Hall Law Journal* 11 (1973): 225.

CHAPTER 5

CANADA'S COURTS: THE PROCESSES OF DISPUTE RESOLUTION

The courts of this country should not be the places where resolution of disputes begins. They should be the place where the disputes end, after alternative methods of resolving disputes have been considered and tried.

(Sandra Day O'Connor)

Let me start by saying that the problem of access to justice is not a new one. As long as justice has existed, there have been those who struggled to access it. But as Canadians celebrated the new millennium, it became clear that we were increasingly failing in our responsibility to provide a justice system that was accessible, responsive and citizen-focused. Report told us that costs, delays, long trials, complex procedures and other barriers were making it impossible for more and more Canadians to exercise their legal rights.

(Chief Justice Beverley McLachlin, 2013)

With the first decade of the twenty-first century behind us, we can see that our models of response to legal conflict have been undergoing significant change. As Chief Justice McLachlin notes above, we are increasingly becoming wary of gaining access to justice. We are also concerned about too quick a resort to an adversarial court process, and have, for some time, been looking with interest at such concepts as restorative justice and alternative dispute resolution. Restorative justice is typically considered in the context of the criminal justice system, with a focus on the offender taking responsibility for the crime committed and attempting to repair or restore the damage done by his actions. The purpose of restorative justice is to promote a reconciliation of the victim, the offender, and the community; the approach has emerged from disenchantment with a criminal justice system focused on retribution and punishment, and leaving both victim and offender unhappy and discouraged by the outcome.

In contrast, alternative dispute resolution moves beyond the sphere of criminal law to the civil sphere, employing mediation, arbitration, negotiation, and conciliation as strategies preferable to courtroom litigation of conflict; mediation has become particularly significant in disputes arising out of marriage breakdown, and involving issues such as matrimonial property, child and spousal support, and custody arrangements.

Both restorative justice and alternative dispute resolution share a common interest in moving outside of an adversarial context, increasing access to justice, and resolving disputes in a manner that builds relationships, avoids conflicts, and promotes reconciliation. At the same time, however, the court process remains. But the burgeoning interest in these models for the delivery of justice suggests that we are collectively seeking alternatives to a costly win/lose model of justice, rooted within our court system, whether in the realm of family or criminal law or in disputes regarding land, personal property, or contractual obligations.

THE STRUCTURE OF CANADA'S COURT SYSTEM

Imagine the following scenario. A man steals a bottle of wine from a liquor store. After he leaves the store, while in the parking lot, he removes the bottle from under his jacket. He is noticed by a police officer, who begins to walk toward him.

The thief wields the bottle of liquor as a weapon and brings it crashing down on the police officer's jaw. With the police officer lying on the ground, the thief jumps into his car and drives off at high speed. He has gone no more than a kilometre when he loses control of the vehicle and plunges into a crowd of schoolchildren waiting for a bus. One child is killed.

The man is apprehended at the scene and jailed overnight. The next morning in **provincial court**, he faces an array of criminal charges: theft under $5,000, assaulting a police officer, impaired driving (his blood alcohol level was 0.18), and criminal negligence causing death.

One of the first things that he will learn from his lawyer is that in Canada's court system, our criminal courts, our superior courts, and our courts of appeal each have different jurisdictions. The man in the prisoner's dock can make some choices about where he appears to respond to these charges. He can elect, in some circumstances, to have his case determined by a jury of his peers, though this option is not available in our provincial courts.

And so it is crucial to understand the jurisdiction of each of Canada's courts—to understand the ultimate flow of power from the provincial courts to the **superior courts of the province**, on to the provincial courts of appeal, and from there to the **Supreme Court of Canada**.

Figure 5.1 sets out the flow of decision-making power within Canada's court system (www.canada.justice.gc.ca). As you can see, the first decision-making bodies that an individual will encounter are either the provincial courts (criminal, family, and small claims), the military courts, provincial administrative tribunals (e.g., workers' compensation, human rights, labour relations, landlord-tenant relations), or federal/administrative tribunals (e.g., parole, employment insurance, immigration). From these initial decision-making bodies one can appeal to higher courts, typically to

Figure 5.1
Outline of Canada's Court System

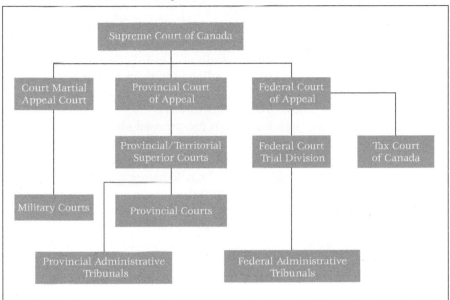

either the superior courts of the province or the federal court, trial division, and then from there to provincial and federal courts of appeal, and finally to the Supreme Court of Canada.

The Provincial Courts

CRIMINAL DIVISION AND *YOUTH CRIMINAL JUSTICE ACT*

- The Criminal Division of provincial court hears all summary conviction offences and all offences under provincial statutes, such as the *Motor Vehicle Act* and the *Liquor and Licensing Act*. The primary difference between summary and **indictable offences** is that indictable offences typically have more serious consequences than summary offences.
- The court has absolute jurisdiction to hear all matters listed under section 553 of the *Criminal Code*.[1] Section 553 states that "the jurisdiction of a provincial court judge to try an accused is absolute and does not depend on the consent of the accused where the accused is charged ... with theft or obtaining money or property by false pretences." Section 553 goes on to require that only thefts under $5,000 in value must be heard in provincial court. A few other offences are set out in section 553: keeping a gaming house, bookmaking, keeping a common bawdy house,

driving while disqualified, and possession of illegal drugs (contrary to section 4 (4) of the *Controlled Drugs and Substances Act*) are crimes that also fall within the absolute jurisdiction of the provincial court.

- The court may hear most indictable offences under the *Criminal Code* and the *Controlled Drugs and Substances Act,* except those listed under section 469 of the *Code*—essentially, murder, treason, piracy, sedition, and the bribing of the judiciary. Section 469 establishes an exclusive jurisdiction in the superior courts for the hearing of all charges of murder (and treason, piracy, and the others). This court also hears charges under the *Youth Criminal Justice Act.*

- The court hears all preliminary hearings when the accused elects to proceed with a preliminary hearing prior to a possible trial. Proposals have been put forward to eliminate more preliminary inquiries; an onus would be placed on an accused to demonstrate why a preliminary inquiry should be held before a trial; court backlogs and unnecessary costs could, arguably, be reduced.

Our man in the dock, charged with criminal negligence causing death, among other offences, could plead guilty to all his charges in provincial court. The charge of theft of the bottle of wine must be heard in provincial court since it is an offence under section 553 of the *Criminal Code.* But the accused could also elect to have his three indictable charges of impaired driving, criminal negligence causing death, and assaulting a police officer dealt with in provincial court.

In fact, only criminal negligence causing death is exclusively an indictable offence. The other two charges—impaired driving and assaulting a police officer—are classified as hybrid offences. With these hybrid offences, a prosecutor chooses to proceed either summarily or by indictment, depending upon the seriousness of the accused's specific actions. In this case, because of the loss of life and the conduct of the accused, the prosecutor might well proceed by indictment in relation to impaired driving and assaulting a police officer.

Before turning to the superior courts of the provinces, the next step upward in the hierarchy of judicial decision making, we must first take a look at the other provincial courts. There are essentially two other kinds of provincial court: the youth and family courts, and the small claims courts. The youth and family courts, as the name implies, respond to the problems created by young offenders and attempt to resolve family disputes. The small claims courts are designed for citizens without lawyers; these courts allow the resolution of small financial disputes, currently up to a maximum of $25,000; that maximum amount may vary from one province to another.

FAMILY DIVISION

- The court in the Youth and Family Division hears matters arising out of disputes within families: separation, maintenance of children and spouses, custody, adoption, guardianship, child welfare, and divorce, where a unified family court system is in place.

- The family court, with its emphasis on reconciliation and family harmony, is characterized by a greater informality and a less adversarial atmosphere than the Criminal Division.

SMALL CLAIMS DIVISION

- The Small Claims Division hears minor civil matters outside the context of the family; in this court the average citizen can seek compensation without the assistance of a lawyer.
- The court is primarily concerned with the fields of contract and tort law, and is limited in its monetary jurisdiction—in most provinces, to amounts of less than $25,000.

THE SUPERIOR COURTS OF THE PROVINCES

TRIAL DIVISION

- The Trial Division of the provincial superior court hears indictable offences under section 469 (murder, piracy, bribery of the judiciary), as well as indictable offences by election of the accused. Trial can take place before a provincial court judge, a superior court judge sitting alone, or a superior court judge and jury.
- The court hears all civil cases within a given monetary jurisdiction—amounts larger than those permitted in either small claims court or county court.
- The court hears all libel and defamation actions.
- The court hears appeals from provincial court Criminal Division and Family Division, depending upon the jurisdiction in which the appeal is launched.
- The court hears divorces, except in those jurisdictions where unified family courts exist.

APPEAL DIVISION

- The court hears civil and family law appeals from the superior court (Trial Division) on questions of law, fact, and a mixture of law and fact.
- The court hears appeals of criminal cases from the superior court (Trial Division) on questions of law, fact, and a mixture of law and fact.

THE SUPREME COURT OF CANADA

- The Supreme Court of Canada has been the court of last resort in the country since 1949. Composed of eight justices and one chief justice, the Court hears cases in panels of three, five, seven, or all nine members.
- The Court hears appeals in criminal cases from provincial courts of appeal when there has been dissent on a question of law in a three- or five-member decision. The Court also grants leave to hear appeals in criminal cases from provincial courts

of appeal when there has been no dissent. Leave to appeal is a request for an appeal; the issue advanced in such circumstances must have public significance beyond the private interest of the party affected.

- The Court grants leave to hear appeals in civil cases if an issue of sufficient public importance is at stake.
- The Court hears references regarding constitutional matters, the division and sphere of powers for the federal and provincial governments, and any other matter of law that might be referred to it.
- Like provincial courts of appeal, the Supreme Court of Canada is a lawyer's court: lawyers typically appear before it to argue points of law, but the parties to a dispute do not appear.

THE FEDERAL COURT OF CANADA

TRIAL DIVISION

- The Trial Division of the **Federal Court of Canada** has jurisdiction over civil matters—specifically, disputes created by actions of the federal government, its officers in the Armed Forces, and its employees.
- The court responds to disputes over trademarks, copyrights, patents of invention, and maritime law.
- The court may also hear appeals from citizenship courts and, with the consent of the parties, federal-provincial disputes.

APPEAL DIVISION

- The Appeal Division hears appeals from the Trial Division of the Federal Court of Canada.
- The division may hear appeals from decisions of federal boards, commissions, and tribunals, such as the Immigration Board, the Parole Board, and the Tax Appeal Board.

One final note about these different court jurisdictions. Provincial court judges—criminal court, family court, and small claims court judges—are all appointed by the provincial government. The judges sitting in the supreme courts of the provinces, the Federal Court, and the Supreme Court of Canada are federally appointed, on the advice of provincial bar associations.

THE COURTS, LAW, AND SOCIAL CONTROL

Our man in the dock at the outset of this chapter would likely go to jail for his crimes, regardless of his lawyer and which court and which judge heard his case. More than

90 percent of those convicted of criminal offences plead guilty to all charges in the Criminal Division of provincial court. The overwhelming majority of those convicted do not appeal their conviction or sentence.

Canada's judges impose penalties, financial and otherwise; they require the fulfillment of contracts; order compensation for individual or corporate negligence; try to settle claims that arise between the federal and provincial governments; and perform numerous other tasks related to the resolution of disputes. It is against the complex and varied backdrop of public and private law that the courts try to reconcile competing interests within certain kinds of relationships: husband and wife, creditor and debtor, consumer and producer or distributor, the state and the deviant, one government and another.

In doing so, the courts set directions for social control in many areas of life. Sociologist Donald Black has argued that all forms of law and all courts ultimately invoke one or more of four styles of social control: compensation, conciliation, punishment, or treatment. Criminal law, for example, is typically concerned with punishment and treatment, but can also provide compensation and conciliation. Family law is typically concerned with compensation and conciliation, but, on occasion, can impose punishment and/or treatment. The essential task of the court is to arrive at a productive and helpful blend of these ingredients, regardless of the specific context of private or public law. Note the comments at the outset of this chapter; we appear to be entering an era in which more consideration is being given to compensatory and conciliatory styles of social control—these styles are viewed as more likely to produce positive and productive outcomes for both the individual and the community than are regimes of punishment or forced treatment.

Canadian Courts: Essential Characteristics

The Adversarial System

The most obvious characteristic of Canadian courts is that they bring down decisions within the context of an **adversarial system**. It has been assumed that "the truth" is most likely to emerge from a contest of two competing arguments. In Canada's courts, the strengths of one lawyer's claim are pitted against the strengths of the opposing claim, and, in the process of this "duel," the judge or **jury** is to arrive at a just decision or verdict. Accordingly, the adversarial system places its confidence in the counsel who appear before the court. The most common alternative to an adversarial system of justice is an **inquisitorial system**. This approach places greater expectations on judges, for they are required to ask relevant questions and to direct the investigation of the issues of a given case.

Law professor S.M. Waddams has noted of the adversarial system, "Procedural rules are designed to see that each party gets a fair hearing. The role of the judge is not to discover what he may conceive to be 'the truth' but to act as an impartial arbiter. It is often said, without apology, that litigation is a game played according to rules of which the judge is umpire."[2] The adversarial system is therefore not ultimately concerned with finding "the" truth, but with choosing from among the truths presented by two competing advocates.

Herein lies a critical weakness of the adversarial system: counsel are equal neither in ability nor in cost. The strength and thoroughness of an individual's legal argument will depend, to a significant extent, upon the resources at his or her disposal. In other words, wealth can provide an individual—or a corporation—with particularly skilled counsel and meticulously researched, well-documented arguments, irrespective of the merits of the case. The response to this allegation concerning inequality is that all lawyers must meet the provincial law societies' minimum standards of competence in order to graduate from law school and enter the practice of law. That process provides the public with a minimum guarantee of competence.

OPEN ACCESS TO THE COURTS

Canadian courts are also characterized by openness and accessibility to the public. Any member of the public can enter virtually any courtroom in the country and watch and listen to justice being dispensed. We have come a long way from the days of the **Star Chamber**, the British Privy Council's home from the fourteenth to the sixteenth centuries. The Star Chamber was an apartment in the royal palace where, protected from public scrutiny, the judiciary handed down often arbitrary judgments.

There is, however, one exception to the general rule of open courts. Under the *Youth Criminal Justice Act,* the proceedings of Canada's youth courts may be held *in camera* when, in the opinion of the judge, it is in the public interest to bar access. Section 132 of the *Youth Criminal Justice Act* states that the public may be excluded from all or part of the proceeding where "it would be in the interest of public morals, the maintenance of order, or the proper administration of justice to exclude any or all members of the public from the courtroom." In the early 1980s, a constitutional challenge to the validity of this exclusion was not successful. The Southam newspaper chain argued that the ban on access constituted a denial of the *Charter*'s guarantee of freedom of expression; the Ontario Court of Appeal ultimately rejected this argument.[3]

During the mid 1990s, in the trial of serial rapist and killer Paul Bernardo, his own videotapes of his sex crimes were not made public in criminal court. Only the audio portion of the tapes was played in the courtroom; there was no compelling reason for the public to watch these crimes taking place, particularly given the impact that such a presentation might have on the families and friends of Bernardo's young victims.

More common than a ban on access to Canadian courts is a ban on publication of their proceedings. The names of those convicted in youth court cannot, in most circumstances, be published. The rationale is that the stigma of arrest and conviction will be reduced, and that young offenders will be given an opportunity to change their behaviour without being publicly labelled as criminals. There are two exceptions to this publication ban. First, if a young person's trial is transferred to adult court, the defendant is treated as an adult offender and his or her name may be published. Second, a judge may permit the identification of a young person who is believed to have committed a crime and is at large when the judge is satisfied that "(a) there is reason to believe that the young person is dangerous to others; and (b) publication of the report is necessary to assist in apprehending the young person."[4]

In adult courts, counsel for the accused can (and usually does) request a ban on publication of the proceedings of a preliminary inquiry. The finding of the inquiry—the name of the accused, and whether there was sufficient evidence to commit the accused to trial—may be published, but specific evidence heard by the court cannot be published, since this might jeopardize the accused's right to receive a fair trial or the accused's standing within the community. The concern is that the press could communicate a misleading impression to potential judges or jurors, prior to a trial of the matter.

The preliminary hearing publication ban raises a fundamental question concerning the publication of the name of an accused prior to conviction. The right of the public to know who has been charged with criminal offences must be balanced against the presumption of innocence. By publishing the name of the accused, we run the risk that in the event of an acquittal, the individual will still be stigmatized by the initial charges. The public may be inclined to believe that a criminal charge is tantamount to a conviction, and ultimate acquittal may do little to alter this perception, particularly since acquittals seldom receive as much media attention as the laying of criminal charges. The contrary argument is that the public has the right to know—for its own safety and the safety of the community. A trial may take place months after initial charges have been laid, and the final disposition, after all appeals, may not take place until years later. In many senses, however, the issue is empirical: Is there evidence that public safety will be adversely affected by restricting publication of an accused's name until after a conviction has been handed down by the court that first hears the case?

There is one other context in which a limitation is placed on the open nature of courtroom proceedings. Section 486(1) of the *Criminal Code* states:

> Any proceedings against an accused shall be held in open court, but where the presiding judge, provincial court judge, or justice, as the case may be, is of the opinion that it is in the interest of public morals, the maintenance of order, or the proper administration of justice to exclude all or any members of the public from the courtroom for all or part of the proceedings, he may so order.

The section, with its focus on the ambiguous concept of "public morals," is typically applied to sexual offences. Although Canadian courts have held that embarrassment of the complainant is not a sufficient reason to bar the public from the courtroom, the public *was* excluded in one definitive Ontario case after the court determined that the complainant would otherwise be too nervous to give her testimony.[5] Section 486(3) of the *Code* also provides Canadian judges with the power to direct that the identity of the complainant in a sexual offence or an offence of extortion "shall not be published in any document or broadcast in any way." The purpose of this ban on publication is to protect the privacy of the potential victim of a sexual offence or an extortion; this section has withstood constitutional challenge.

Finally, it is worth noting that, at present, only print journalists have full access to the proceedings of Canadian courts. Television cameras and tape recorders are generally not permitted to record the testimony of witnesses or the commentary of the judiciary, although Ontario typically permits audio recording devices, but not cameras or any visual recording apparatus. During the past two decades there has been substantial discussion about granting access to broadcast journalists; in the United States, such access has been commonplace for almost two decades. The trial of O.J. Simpson, conducted before a television audience of millions, highlighted the differences between Canadian and U.S. approaches to media coverage of the trial process. In the aftermath of the Simpson trial, however, many U.S. jurisdictions began rethinking the wisdom of permitting cameras in the courtroom; in 1996, the year after his acquittal on homicide charges, Simpson's civil trial for wrongful death was not televised. In 2007 Simpson was convicted of robbery in Nevada and sentenced to a term of imprisonment of at least nine years. Although this trial was televised, only the verdict and sentencing of Simpson attracted significant public attention.

Opponents of cameras in the courtroom have pointed to the often sensationalistic tendencies of this visual medium. The rationale and complexity of court decisions may be ignored in favour of dramatic testimony or individual showmanship. It has also been suggested that by presenting only parts of a trial or of judicial commentary, the television camera will necessarily distort the full context of a case. In a worst-case scenario, a defendant may be judged more on physical attractiveness, race, gender, accent, eloquence—or his taste in ties—than on the specifics of the testimony.

The Supreme Court of Canada does permit television cameras in its courtroom (the Supreme Court is, of course, wholly concerned with matters of law and policy), and courts in Ontario will permit cameras if the judiciary and both counsel are supportive. But there is no access as a matter of right. To date, constitutional challenges to the restriction, on the ground of freedom of speech or freedom of expression, have been unsuccessful. The argument in favour of television coverage is that few Canadians attend courts; accordingly, few understand the structure of the court, the procedure employed, and the kinds of arguments typically made. A television camera can educate and inform the public, for example about Canada's criminals and judges and why they do what they do, or about family disintegration and the underlying social scripts. Print journalism conveys a sense of these issues and social problems, but broadcast journalism can add another layer of complexity to our understanding. There is some merit in the claim that a picture is worth a thousand words, but that merit can be seriously undermined by a sensationalist cutting and pasting of the trial or sentencing process

THE FORMALITY OF THE COURTS

A third characteristic of Canadian courts is their air of formality. Justice is delivered by judges and justices who wear ritual garments and are elevated above the participants in the courtroom. Norwegian criminologist Nils Christie said of this display that the court's function is to appropriate the conflict of the citizens who appear before it. The conflict is appropriated through law enforcement and prosecution; it is reconstructed by the language and the drama of the courtroom.[6]

The atmosphere of formality in Canadian courts, like so much in Canadian law, has its origins in British practices. The forms of address for those who sit in judgment reflect the level of court: Your Honour, Your Worship, My Lord. The use of these terms is more historical reflex than an accurate expression of the sentiments of counsel; the terms do, however, indicate respect for the significance of the process. In the United States, these vestiges of a monarchical past have been excised, though much of the formality of the court process has been retained.

It is imperative that a country's system of courts be worthy of its citizens' respect. Supporters of formality, such as the late law professor Gerald Gall, have argued that it is therefore important that courtroom procedure be conducted within an "atmosphere of dignity and decorum":

> While some may argue that these formalities constitute a certain stuffiness, if not elitism, on the part of judges and lawyers, the counter-argument is more persuasive. This argument holds that by conforming to certain formalities, the court achieves the prestige it deserves, given the important function it exercises in society.[7]

The criticism of Gall's argument is that it equates manners with merit. More important, it may not adequately reflect upon the attitudes and values of those subject to the rulings of Canadian courts, particularly those who do not share the educational, social, and economic backgrounds of an essentially upper-middle-class and largely male judiciary. Consider, for example, the perception that many Aboriginal Canadians have of the court system:

> The general impression Dene people have of the court circuit is that a bunch of strangers, most of whom are non-Native people, have come to town. They see the court proceedings as very strict and formal, and for most of them, scary.
>
> I was always impressed with a Cree who is involved in the James Bay communities in the courts. He was asked by the translator to put his hand on the Bible and swear to tell the truth, the whole truth, and nothing but the truth. He replied: "I would never be able to tell the whole truth and nothing but the truth; all I would be able to do is tell you what I know."

The psychology of the legal system is a very complex one, especially to Native people who are not bilingual. People who do not speak both languages are passive in the administration of justice. They know what the sentence is and how long they can go to jail, but they do not really know the intricacies of the legal system. The communication process should not be a one-way exchange. People should not be bystanders; they should be participants who know what is happening to them.[8]

It is not only Aboriginal Canadians who may be restricted in their dialogue with the courts. Legal representation is a costly enterprise, particularly if one wishes to pursue one's case through the court hierarchy. Most economically disadvantaged Canadians experience Canadian courts only in the context of criminal or family law; their trag-edies and conflicts are determined and resolved for better or for worse. From their research interviews with more than 100 individuals charged with criminal offences, sociologists Richard Ericson and Patricia Baranek concluded:

Given that the accused rarely speaks or is given the opportunity to speak, it is highly unlikely that a benevolent, well-meaning court would have any knowledge of the accused's comprehension. Rather than the court attempting to make the pro-ceedings comprehensible, the onus is on the accused to inform the court that he does not understand. However, given the anxiety and stage fright that most accused suffer, this is unlikely.... [E]ven when asked if they understand, accused are reluc-tant to say no because they feel powerless, they don't want to appear incompetent, and/or they are too nervous to say anything.

It might be assumed that it is the lawyer's role to ensure that the accused com-prehends the court's discourse. On the contrary, the lawyer is usually left to "do the understanding" for the accused and to order the accused in a way that does not encourage the accused even to seek understanding, let alone acquire it.[9]

This is a harsh indictment of our court system, standing in marked contrast to Gall's claim that Canadian courts have "achieved the prestige [they] deserve." Perhaps the differences between Gall's perceptions and those of Ericson and Baranek are explained by considering the lens through which these academics are observing "the ordering of justice." From the point of view of the judiciary, judicial administrators, and most lawyers, Canadian courts operate in an atmosphere of prestige, dignity, and decorum that mirrors their nature. To those who are subject to the courts' judgments but are not stakeholders in the system, the atmosphere and the very nature of the courts might, if only occasionally, be described as somewhat confusing and a little self-congratulatory.

THE PURPOSES OF CANADIAN COURTS AND THE STANDARDS FOR JUDGMENTS

As mentioned earlier, the four styles of social control used by the courts are compen-sation, conciliation, punishment, and treatment. No single one of these purposes is common to all Canadian courts. Canada's civil courts respond to disputes between a plaintiff and a respondent; the plaintiff may be asserting rights in relation to a contract, a will, a failed marriage, or the negligence of the respondent. In these circumstances, the task of the court is to compensate the plaintiff or to seek some means of reconciling the parties. The nature and form of compensation or resolution will vary according to the type of law before the court. The outcome in civil cases depends upon a balance of probabilities: a plaintiff must establish that his or her claim is more probable than not in order to be successful. In other words, the plaintiff's case must be given a better than 50 percent likelihood of legitimacy. If the respondent's defence or counterclaim is seen to be equally or more valid, the plaintiff's action will be lost.

Criminal courts act on behalf of the state—that is, in the collective interests of all Canadians. In the realm of criminal law, punishment and treatment are preeminent. The court has two separate tasks: first, it must establish the guilt of the accused; second, it must prescribe an appropriate punishment or treatment. In prescribing treatments and/or punishments, criminal courts are guided by the principles of (1) general deterrence—deterring the general public from committing the crime; (2) specific deterrence—deterring the specific defendant from committing future crimes; and (3) rehabilitation—assistance to prepare the convicted person for community reintegration and ultimate abstinence from criminal activity.

The former chief justice of the Supreme Court of Canada Antonio Lamer suggested that courts fulfill two functions in Canadian society: they provide a **conflict resolution** service and perform a "dramatization function."[10] The dramatization function is held to be particularly applicable to criminal law, wherein the penalties serve dramatically to reaffirm societal values. It is not clear, however, that a core of commonly held values exists in all realms of the criminal law. While crimes against persons and against property are almost universally seen as offending societal values, there is substantial debate about so-called victimless crimes, including certain kinds of drug use, consensual sexual behaviours, and gambling. In these realms, it is more difficult to assert that criminal punishments reaffirm core values. What they reaffirm, instead, is a somewhat controversial status quo—a dominant majority typically asserts its world-view over a reluctant minority.

Even in the case of crimes against persons or property, it can be argued that there may be less consensus about the need to dramatize commonly held values (or the extent of the dramatization required) than the former chief justice has suggested. While Canadians overwhelmingly reject and abhor violence, theft, and fraud, we have no consensus on the form that punishments should take in response, or to use the language of the former chief justice—the form that the dramatization function should take. The debate, for example, regarding the role of restorative justice is an example of this lack of consensus.

In criminal courts, the judge or jury must be satisfied that an accused's guilt has been established beyond a reasonable doubt by the prosecuting lawyer. This standard is difficult to quantify. The judge or jury may be less than 100 percent certain of guilt—perhaps 90 to 95 percent certain—yet convict the accused. Convictions are probably assigned when levels of certainty of guilt are in the range of 90 or 95 percent. In other words, the balance that criminal courts strike between convicting the guilty and protecting the rights of the innocent is not absolute; there are likely to be occasional mistakes. Human beings are not infallible; consequently, a human system of criminal justice is not infallible.

THE CASE OF DAVID MILGAARD: RESPONDING TO THE FALLIBILITY OF THE COURTS

On the morning of January 31, 1969, Gail Miller left her rooming house in Saskatoon to take a bus to her job as a nurse's assistant at a local hospital. It was –42°C and visibility was poor because of ice crystals in the air. Gail Miller never arrived at work; shortly after dawn, her body was discovered in a back alley near her home. She had been raped and stabbed 11 times.

A little more than four months later, David Milgaard was arrested and charged with the murder of Gail Miller. Milgaard was a 16-year-old who had been driving through Saskatoon on the morning of the killing with two teenaged companions, Nichol John and Ron Wilson. The three teenagers were looking for their friend Albert "Shorty" Cadrain. After finding him several hours later, all four left the city about noon to buy marijuana in Alberta.

The prosecution argued at trial that shortly before 7:00 on the morning of the murder, the teenagers' car had become stuck in snow and ice. Milgaard was said to be away from the car for about 15 minutes, ostensibly looking for help. It was during this time that he is alleged to have found Miller, raped her, and stabbed her to death. He then returned to the car, and he and his companions continued to search for the home of Cadrain, obtaining a map at a motel within about 20 minutes of the killing. The motel manager testified at trial that Milgaard was polite and friendly in asking for directions. He did not see any blood on Milgaard or any indication that he had just participated in a struggle.

At trial, Milgaard's companions implicated him in the murder. Although Wilson, John, and Cadrain had all initially rejected suggestions that any one of them was responsible, they later provided damning testimony. Wilson and Cadrain testified that they had seen blood on Milgaard that morning, and John told police that she had seen Milgaard stab a woman, then drag her into an alley, ostensibly to rape her.

The jury convicted Milgaard of non-capital murder, and in January 1970, he was sentenced to life imprisonment. His appeals to the provincial court of appeal and the Supreme Court of Canada were unsuccessful. Throughout 22 years of imprisonment, Milgaard never ceased to maintain that he did not kill Gail Miller. In the late 1980s, with the assistance of Winnipeg lawyers Hersh Wolch and David Asper, Milgaard applied to the minister of justice, Kim Campbell, requesting that his case be reopened.

A mistake had been made by the court, he argued. Like all Canadians who have exhausted their appeals, he relied on section 690 of the *Criminal Code* (now revised as section 696.1 of the *Code,* with some regulatory revisions):

> *690. The Minister of Justice may, upon an application for the mercy of the Crown by or on behalf of a person who has been convicted in proceedings by indictment ...*
>
> (a) *direct, by order in writing, a new trial ... before any court that he thinks proper, if after inquiry he is satisfied that in the circumstances a new trial or hearing, as the case may be, should be directed;*
>
> (b) *refer the matter at any time to the court of appeal for hearing and determination by that court as if it were an appeal by the convicted person ... or*
>
> (c) *refer to the court of appeal at any time, for its opinion, any question on which he desires the assistance of that court, and the court shall furnish its opinion accordingly.*

There was also new evidence in the *Milgaard* case. Wilson, who had testified that he had seen blood on Milgaard at trial, told private investigators that he had lied in order to "get the police off my back." He said that he and John had agreed to "sink" Milgaard in order to stop persistent police questioning. John's claim that she witnessed the stabbing had been revealed, even at trial, to be an impossibility. Her description required that there be knife cuts in Miller's dress; there were none, since the dress had been removed before Miller was stabbed. And Cadrain, the first to claim that he had seen blood on Milgaard, was found to be a highly unreliable witness. Within a year of the trial, he was committed to a psychiatric institution. In the early 1970s, he alleged that another individual had committed a crime. This allegation was found by police to be without foundation.

In 1990, an alternative scenario emerged for the morning of the murder. The defence learned of an unusual coincidence: a serial rapist by the name of Larry Fisher had been living in the basement of the Cadrain home at the time of the murder. In the months before the Miller murder, Fisher had abducted three women in Saskatoon, held knives to their throats, and raped them in back alleys. On other occasions, he had stabbed and beaten his rape victims; everything done to Miller, he had done to other women. Fisher was not a suspect at the time of the Miller murder, though Saskatoon police reported to the media immediately after the killing that they believed the crime was related to a number of unsolved rapes in the neighbourhood. Fisher was not apprehended for these rapes until months after David Milgaard's conviction.

The minister of justice, faced with this evidence, initially turned down Milgaard's application for a new trial. In a 12-page decision handed down in February 1991, Campbell claimed that Wilson's testimony was not credible, that Cadrain's was credible, and that there was no good evidence against Fisher. The following November, she changed her mind, after front-page stories about the case in *The Globe and Mail* and the *Toronto Star*. Campbell ordered a hearing before the Supreme Court of Canada. At the conclusion of that hearing, David Milgaard was set free after more than 23 years in jail.

The *Milgaard* case raises questions about the justice system and the manner in which it responds to its inevitable fallibility. What is the burden of proof that must be met by an accused in section 690 of the *Criminal Code*? Should an accused have to establish innocence on a balance of probabilities? Or beyond a reasonable doubt? The section gives no guidance as to the standard to be employed in those instances in which fallibility in the justice system is alleged.

The courts have made mistakes on other occasions as well. Donald Marshall was set free in the 1980s and financially compensated after being wrongfully convicted of a murder that another man ultimately confessed to. However, the issue is not that the Canadian justice system, like all other justice systems, makes mistakes. Rather, it is whether our justice system is equipped to respond fairly and effectively to allegations of wrongful conviction.

In its review of David Milgaard's conviction, the Supreme Court set out to answer three key questions: Can Milgaard establish his innocence beyond a reasonable doubt? Is it more likely than not that Milgaard is innocent? If a new trial were to be held today, would there be a similar result? The Supreme Court concluded that Milgaard's innocence could not be established either beyond a reasonable doubt or on a balance of probabilities. As regards the third question, the Court could not be sure that if a new trial were held, a conviction would be forthcoming. Accordingly, it decided that a new trial was in order. The Province of Saskatchewan decided not to proceed with a new trial, however, citing cost and compassion, and David Milgaard was set free in April 1992. He was not found to be either innocent or guilty; nor was he found to be deserving of any compensation.

It was not until the summer of 1997 that the Province of Saskatchewan changed its approach to the *Milgaard* case, apologizing to him for his wrongful conviction and offering compensation. DNA test results from London, England, had confirmed what many observers of the case had believed for years: there was no DNA match between Milgaard and Gail Miller; there was, however, a DNA match with Larry Fisher. Fisher is now in jail, after being convicted in 1999 of the first degree murder of Gail Miller.

For those who followed the *Milgaard* case, or the cases of Guy Paul Morin and Donald Marshall, or, more recently, Thomas Sophonow, Kyle Unger, James Driskell, and Steven Truscott, questions remain—particularly about the way in which our justice system responds to claims of fallibility within its courts. With Milgaard, Saskatchewan convened an inquiry into his conviction; that inquiry concluded with a report issued in September 2008 calling for a new independent body in Canada to review allegations of wrongful convictions. The inquiry also concluded that while the justice system failed David Milgaard, the police did not appear to act in bad faith during their investigation.

More generally, however, what should be the standard—the burden of proof—in circumstances in which allegations of wrongful conviction are made? Equally critical, what procedure should the minister of justice employ in evaluating claims like Milgaard's—an independent body of investigation, as recommended in the *Milgaard*

Inquiry Report of 2008? And, finally, in what circumstances should compensation be contemplated?

There is one additional lesson from many wrongful conviction cases. We should probably be skeptical of human abilities in the realm of determination of guilt. In many instances it has been science—the technology of DNA testing—that has set innocent men free; our system of justice was exposed as more fragile and fallible. In the context of an issue such as capital punishment, this fragility and fallibility is particularly critical, given our long-standing commitment to the notion that it is better to let a guilty man go free than to convict—and execute—an innocent man.

BY A JURY OF ONE'S PEERS

In Canada's superior courts, the general public is involved in the determination of guilt through the mechanism of the jury. There are also jury trials, albeit in more limited circumstances, in civil cases. In the United States, jury trials are common in both criminal and civil cases. In fact, it has been estimated that 80 percent of all the world's jury trials take place there. It is also permissible in the United States to speak to jurors after the trial about the jury's deliberation. In Canada, by contrast, section 649 of the *Criminal Code* makes disclosure of jury proceedings a summary conviction offence, punishable by a fine of up to $2,000 and imprisonment of up to six months. The Canadian position is that post-deliberation inquiries can serve only to impeach or undermine jury verdicts, thereby weakening the value of the jury to the justice system.

Considerable debate has taken place about the value of the jury to the court structure. Critics assert that the business of law is too complex to be left to "amateurs." The former dean of Harvard Law School, E.N. Griswold, once noted, "The jury trial is the apotheosis of the amateur. Why should anyone think that twelve persons brought in from the street, selected in various ways for their lack of general ability, should have any special capacity for deciding controversies?"[11] Similarly, the British legal scholar Glanville Williams remarked, "[I]t is an understatement to describe a jury ... as a group of twelve men of average ignorance."[12] And the American jurist and academic Jerome Frank asserted, "While the jury can contribute nothing of value so far as the law is concerned, it has infinite capacity for mischief, for twelve men can easily misunderstand more law in a minute than the judge can explain in an hour."[13]

Those who defend the jury system maintain that the collective intelligence of 12 decision makers is almost always an improvement upon the fact-finding abilities of a single judge. And, as jury experts Hans and Vidmar have noted, juries will often apply standards of community fairness and equity to a case, whereas a judge, preoccupied with the technicalities of the law, would tend to ignore these essentially democratic principles:

> Newspapers recently carried an article about a woman who shot her common-law husband. For fifteen years, she had suffered physical abuse and threats of

death from him. He threatened to kill her if she reported the assaults to the police. Finally, she purchased a gun. When her husband again attacked her in a drunken rage, she took the gun and shot him in the leg. Because of the premeditated nature of her act, a judge would have felt compelled to follow the letter of the law and find her guilty, but the jury acquitted her. In short, the jury differs from the judge on the values it brings to the case and on the freedom to apply those values.[14]

The *Morgentaler* case offers another illustration of the jury's imposition of democratic values upon the authority of the courts. The law respecting abortion was ultimately struck down by the Supreme Court of Canada in 1988; one of the catalysts for this legal change was the continued inability of prosecutors to obtain jury convictions,[15] although the case was ultimately decided on constitutional grounds.

The trial of O.J. Simpson in California also raised questions about the role of the jury in criminal and civil cases. Simpson, a black male, was acquitted by a largely black jury in October 1995, after a lengthy trial in which DNA evidence had clearly connected him to his two victims, Nicole Brown Simpson and Ronald Goldman. The jury heard, however, of the alleged racism of one white police officer and of claims that some members of the Los Angeles Police Department may have conspired to frame Simpson for these horrific crimes. The jury, with a legacy of oppression against blacks in the United States as its backdrop, chose to exercise a reasonable doubt in favour of Simpson. A year later, the largely white civil jury that convened to hear a claim of wrongful death against Simpson was more inclined to believe the DNA evidence; it rendered a substantial financial judgment against the former football star. In both these instances, juries imposed their own long-standing perceptions of justice, crime, and race in their verdicts.

The injection of community sentiments into the determination of guilt in criminal cases, or even into civil cases, raises questions about the limits that should be imposed upon the power of the jury. The many examples of juries in Canada, England, and the United States refusing to support unpopular laws ring alarm bells for those concerned about the dangers of juries displacing lawmakers. While a jury may well embrace progressive and democratic sentiments within its decisions, it is as likely to embody community prejudices that reaffirm racism, religious bigotry, sexism, and other kinds of bias and intolerance.

Recently, in some U.S. trials the jury's role has moved away from the principle of community representation. U.S. law typically demands jurors to be "death-qualified"— that is, to serve on a jury in most states permitting capital punishment, a citizen must support the death penalty. In California, for example, jurors must be willing to vote for guilt or innocence, and, in the second stage of the trial, to vote for death. In one California study, researchers found that 21 percent of the population would not find an accused guilty if they knew that the death penalty could be imposed. A further 17 percent said that they could not vote for the death penalty, but would be willing to determine guilt in a capital case with an open mind. Thus, almost 40 percent of the state's population is excluded from jury trials in capital cases. Hans and Vidmar commented on these research findings:

> These figures tell us that a significant number of otherwise eligible jurors will automatically be excluded from capital-murder juries.... Women and blacks are more likely to be in both of these groups. So are Jews, atheists, and agnostics. So are poor people and Democrats. To put it the other way around, the typical juror in a capital-murder trial is more likely to be wealthier, a Protestant or a Catholic, a Republican, male, and white. In short, juries in death-penalty cases are not representative of the population, or similar to other juries.[16]

In a Canadian survey of jury responsibilities, psychologist Anthony Doob asked both the general public and the Canadian judiciary whether individual jurors should decide cases according to their own consciences, ignoring the law if doing so would produce a just result. More than 75 percent of the general public believed that jurors should have the right to nullify unfair laws, but fewer than 5 percent of Canadian judges were in favour of giving this power to citizens.[17]

COURTROOM DELAY: THE RIGHT TO BE TRIED "WITHIN A REASONABLE TIME"

In Chapter 4, we discussed the *Askov* case as a significant development of the *Canadian Charter of Rights and Freedoms* focusing on the rights of the accused. For Canada's court system, *Askov* was even more significant, since it represented a call from the judiciary to government about the need for more court resources.

Askov and his associates did not initially appear to be the sort of accused who were likely to gain the sympathy of the court. They provided nightclubs with exotic dancers, and had been charged with possession of a prohibited weapon, possession of a weapon for a purpose dangerous to the public peace, pointing a firearm, and assault with a weapon. The three accused were at first denied bail. They remained in jail from November 1983 until May 1984. They were then released, pending the outcome of the trial, on a recognizance of $50,000 each. They were required to report to police on a regular basis, as well as to abstain from communicating with one another.

A preliminary hearing for the three men began in July 1984, but could not be completed because of a conflict in the court's timetable. The preliminary was finally completed in late September 1984, almost 10 months after the initial arrests. Because of a crowded court schedule, the first available date for the trial of the accused was in October 1985, almost two years after the arrests. When the date arrived, it became clear that there would not be sufficient time for the trial to be held during the fall sitting after all. Accordingly, the case was put over to September 1986—almost three years after the initial arrests. At that time, counsel for the accused argued that a stay of proceedings should be entered since the right of the accused to a fair trial within a reasonable time had been unfairly violated by courtroom delays. The presiding judge agreed, taking the position that the delay was not attributable to the accused, but the result of institutional problems. District Court Judge Bolan wrote: "I am satisfied that the reason for the delay was caused by the insufficient institutional resources in the Judicial District of Peel.... It is obvious that this jurisdiction lacks sufficient resources to meet the demands and administer the criminal justice system with minimal delay. This has caused a systemic delay in the administration of justice."[18]

Delays in Canadian courts had been a matter of judicial and political concern since the early 1980s. In 1986, Justice Thomas Zuber of the Ontario Court of Appeal was appointed to conduct a study of the Ontario court system in response to escalating court costs, together with increasingly lengthy delays in gaining access to the courts. Justice Zuber released his report in 1987, noting, among other things, that some districts were particularly slow in bringing cases to court for disposition, and that a "delay reduction strategy" was imperative. The Ontario government's response to Justice Zuber's report was to introduce such a strategy, which included pilot projects in six areas of the province identified as having the most serious problems of delay. The government also suggested funding for increased staff—13 judges, 24 Crown attorneys, and support staff—and improvements to existing facilities.

The decision handed down by Judge Bolan in *Askov* was taken to the Ontario Court of Appeal, which upheld the prosecutor's argument that the rights of the accused to trial within a reasonable time had not been infringed. The Court of Appeal found, first, that there was no misconduct on the part of the Crown with respect to the delay; second, that there was no objection made by any of the accused to the various adjournments; and third, that there was no evidence of prejudice to the accused as a consequence of the delay.

Askov and his associates appealed to the Supreme Court of Canada, which issued its decision in October 1990. The Court noted a number of factors to be taken into account when determining whether a court delay is sufficient to deprive an accused of the right to trial within a reasonable time: the length of the delay, the explanation for the delay (such as the conduct of the Crown, systemic or institutional delays, or the conduct of the accused), the accused's waiver of rights, and prejudice to the accused. On this basis, the Supreme Court rejected the Ontario Court of Appeal's claim that the accused in *Askov* had waived their right to trial within a reasonable time. Justice Cory wrote:

> [T]here was no explicit waiver of their rights by the appellants.... The term "waiver" indicates that a choice has been made between available options. When the entire record of the proceedings ... is read, it becomes crystal clear that the appellants had no choice as to the date of the trial.... The silence of the appellants or their failure to raise an objection to a long delay is certainly not enough in the circumstances to infer waiver. Rather, the onus rests upon the Crown to demonstrate that the actions of the accused amounted to an agreement to the delay, or waiver of their right.[19]

The Supreme Court also noted that the delays in the judicial district of Peel were more substantial than in virtually all other districts in the country. This deviation from the norm became an important part of the decision: "The usual delays in Peel are more than four times as long as those of busy metropolitan districts in the Province of Quebec and the delay in this case, is more than eight times as long."[20]

The *Askov* case highlights a conflict between competing interests. On the one hand, the crimes that the accused were alleged to have committed were very serious; armed violence stands in stark opposition to the values of a civilized society. But the *Charter* enshrines the right to be tried within a reasonable time. Justice Cory commented on this conflict:

> Extortion and threatened armed violence tear at the basic fabric of society. To accede to such conduct would constitute a denial of the rule of law and an acceptance of a rule that unlawful might makes right.... There can be no doubt that it would be in the best interest of society to proceed with the trial of those who are charged with posing such a serious threat to the community. Yet, that trial can only be undertaken if the *Charter* right to trial within a reasonable time has not been infringed. In this case, that right has been grievously infringed and the sad result is that a stay of proceedings must be entered.[21]

Other cases heard since the *Askov* decision have clarified and refined the right to be tried within a reasonable time.[22] But the tensions that gave rise to *Askov* have not disappeared. If anything, concerns have expanded from the problem of delay to the more fundamental issue of access to justice and its decision-making processes. In 2013, a group of legal experts released a report, "Access to Civil and Family Justice: A Roadmap for Change."[23] The report began with a very positive introduction to its content from the Chief Justice Beverley McLachlin, and it highlighted not only delays in access to family and civil matters in Canadian courts, but also the lack of access that most Canadian experience in relation to "everyday legal problems." The authors noted that the poor and the vulnerable are particularly badly served and that both the cost of legal services and the length of legal proceedings has continued to grow over the last two decades. The report urged an expansion of focus, widening concerns from dispute resolution to education and prevention, the creation of services for early resolution of legal issues, improving accessibility to legal information, increasing legal aid services and funding, and making courts and tribunals and their procedures more accessible to more Canadians.

EMERGING MODELS OF CONFLICT RESOLUTION: MEDIATION AND RESTORATIVE JUSTICE

There has been an understandable frustration with the time and cost required for courtroom litigation of both civil and criminal disputes. In the realm of family law it is often fairly said that all parties lose when they proceed to contest their claims in the courtroom. And while the adversarial system of justice remains in place within family law, developments over the past two decades have at least modified the centrality of the adversarial approach in resolving the breakdown of relationships.

Mediation involves the use of an independent third party whose task is to attempt to bring the parties to agreement. The goal of the mediator is not to impose a decision on the two litigants but to encourage them to come to a mutual agreement about the issues in dispute—matrimonial property, support, and/or custody of children. If mediation fails, the court process is the obvious fallback position. But there are many good reasons for engaging in mediation: it is usually much less expensive, the parties themselves can come to terms rather than having terms imposed upon them, and an ongoing monitoring of the settlement can also be a part of the agreement (allowing for greater future flexibility, since the situations of the parties will inevitably change).

At the same time, however, no clear standards have been set out with respect to the qualifications required of a mediator. The mediator may or may not be a lawyer. In fact, many mediators have no legal training, but rely rather on their training and skills in social work, psychology, or psychiatry for their expertise; still others have no formal educational training. Given this backdrop, there is a significant risk for the consumer of these services. Law is, after all, the system that prescribes appropriate remedies for disputes, whether in the realm of family law, contract, or property. And those who trust their legal rights to individuals who have no legal training may well be doing themselves a great disservice. Perhaps the future of mediation can be found in what has been termed "collaborative divorce," a term that might seem, at first glance, to be an oxymoron. Collaborative divorce brings an interdisciplinary team of professionals to the task at hand: a lawyer with a specialty in family law, a psychologist or social worker, and a financial counsellor. Courses that canvass and detail this process of collaborative separation and divorce are now offered, for example, by provincial legal education societies.

Those who practise criminal law have also seen the emergence of alternative models to the judiciary's traditional sentencing paradigms of punishment and treatment. More specifically, section 718.2(e) of the *Criminal Code* states: "(e) [A]ll available sanctions other than imprisonment that are reasonable in the circumstances should be considered for all offenders, with particular attention to the circumstances of [A]boriginal offenders." This section directs the judiciary to hand down a sentence to the Aboriginal offender that is different from sentences for other offenders. In *R. v. Gladue,* the Supreme Court held that because of systemic discrimination and markedly different circumstances, principles of **restorative justice** must be applied alongside or in place of the more traditional sentencing principles. The Court held that an Aboriginal offender's community will often understand the nature of a just penalty very differently from non-Aboriginal communities.

Both the *Gladue* decision and the legislation that spawned it (section 718.2(c) of the *Criminal Code*) have been subject to considerable public criticism, from both within and outside Aboriginal communities. It remains to be seen whether this different treatment will ultimately be perceived as just by the Aboriginal community, and/or by the larger national community of Canadians. In the interim, the decision does appear to prompt a number of empirical questions: Is crime committed by Aboriginals "different" in its origins and its consequences? Is there a consensus within Aboriginal communities to support this kind of restorative rather than punitive approach to the sentencing of offenders? Is this simply a productive approach to sentencing that ought to be extended to the general community? And does the broader community view this response as a violation of equality provisions—or as an important initiative consistent with section 15(2) of the *Charter,* an approach that has both its intent and its consequences in the amelioration of the conditions of one category of especially disadvantaged Canadians? We can only await the verdict of the next few decades.

But regardless of the ultimate impact of *Gladue,* it is clear that restorative justice has emerged within the past decade as a significant development within the criminal justice systems of Canada and most other Western industrialized nation-states. The following question-and-answer posting from Justice Canada's website highlights the increasing importance of restorative justice[24]:

> In the face of crime and conflict, RJ is a philosophy and an approach that views crime and conflict principally as harm done to people and relationships. It strives to provide support and safe opportunities for the voluntary participation and communication between those affected (victims, offenders, and community) to encourage accountability, reparation, and a movement towards understanding, feelings of satisfaction, healing, safety and a sense of closure.
>
> RJ is a non-adversarial, non-retributive approach to justice that emphasizes healing in victims, meaningful accountability of offenders, and the involvement of citizens in creating healthier, safer communities.
>
> The RJ approach is based on values and principles that emphasize:
> - *Recognition of Harm*
> - *Inclusion*
> - *Accountability*
> - *Facilitated Dialogue*
> - *Truth*
> - *Voluntary Participation*
> - *Safety*
> - *Choice*
> - *Holism*
> - *Humanism*
> - *Reparation*

How is Restorative Justice Applied?

RJ views crime as a violation of people and relationships. RJ is an approach that seeks to determine who has been hurt, what their needs are, and how these needs can be addressed. RJ uses processes that are collaborative and inclusive to all parties affected—victim, offender and community.

RJ processes include but are not limited to:

- *Victim-Offender Mediation*
- *Restorative Conferencing*
- *Circle Processes*

What are the Benefits of RJ Processes?

Victims can tell their story; be certain the offender understands the impact; find answers to questions; hold the offender accountable; and if possible, identify what can be done to repair the harm.

Offenders can tell their story; accept responsibility for and acknowledge the harm caused; hear how their behaviour affected others; and participate in determining how to repair the harm.

Communities can be empowered to gain a better understanding of the root causes of crime, engage in a process to express and reduce their fears, and contribute to an understanding of the wider impacts of crime.

CONCLUSION: FUTURE PROSPECTS FOR THE COURTS AND COURT REFORM

Among other topics, this chapter has discussed two difficulties currently facing Canadian courts: first, issues of delay and access in the administration of justice, and second, the legal response to the inevitable fallibility of judges and juries in making decisions. The resolution of the problems of delay and access appears to require certain changes in the jurisdictions most affected, including the construction of new facilities; the provision of more judges, Crown attorneys, lawyers and duty counsel, and support staff; and new mechanisms to enhance access to legal remedies for the poor and the vulnerable. The problem of the fallibility of the courts is more difficult, particularly in the case of criminal trials. The existing law, section 696.1 of the *Criminal Code,* does not meet the standards proposed in the Milgaard Inquiry Report of 2008; until governments can acknowledge the inevitability of mistakes—and create a system of investigation at arm's length from government—it seems unlikely that the necessary reforms will take place.

Various movements within the Canadian court system have taken shape within the last few decades. First, there is an increasing use of diversion for first-time offenders, particularly young offenders. The purpose of diversion—a community-based response—is twofold: to reserve the courts for the most serious cases and, by taking the offender out of the court process, to lessen the likelihood of stigmatization of the offender by the judicial and correctional processes.

Related to the practice of diversion is the increasing involvement of the community within the justice system. This development can take the form of the community-service orders that flow from both youth and adult courts; lobby groups created as a reaction against specific crimes (Victims of Violence, Mothers Against Drunk Driving); or the development of alternative systems of dispute resolution, particularly within Aboriginal communities.

A third movement in the court system appears in the considerable amount of administrative law designed to enable boards, commissions, and tribunals to become alternatives to courts when specific expertise in decision making is deemed necessary. The National Parole Board, the Workers' Compensation Review Board, the Industrial Relations Council, and the Labour Relations Board are federal and provincial agencies that currently function as courts within specified spheres of expertise. They tend to be less formal and less rigorously structured than the court system.

Canada's court structure has its strengths—openness and accessibility—but it also has its weaknesses—delay and fallibility. There are also many possibilities for improvement in making the courtroom more accessible and more democratic, and in the construction of a better legal mechanism for responding to allegations of judge and jury fallibility. The task ahead is to build on what we have accomplished, mindful that the open court, operating with public support, remains the linchpin of any civilized nation-state.

WEB LINKS

Department of Justice Canada: Publications

http://www.justice.gc.ca/eng/dept-min/pub/index.asp

This page of the website of the Department of Justice Canada provides details of Canada's court system. The site also offers extensive information on the Justice Department and its programs and services, including matters such as access to information, child access and custody, electronic commerce, youth justice, and victims of crime.

Justice Manitoba

http://www.gov.mb.ca/justice/index.shtml

This is the home page for Manitoba's Justice Department. It has links to matters of provincial jurisdiction such as family law, including information about domestic violence.

Manitoba Justice: Court Processes

http://www.gov.mb.ca/justice/court/index.html

A site accessed through Manitoba's Justice Department, this page provides an excellent resource for information on the court system in Manitoba.

Supreme Court of Canada
http://www.scc-csc.gc.ca/
This is the home page of the court of last resort in Canada. Its functions and mandate are explained on the website, which also contains links to judgments.

Federal Court of Canada
http://www.fct-cf.gc.ca/index_e.html
The website of the Federal Court of Canada provides details of the court's work: its functions and mandate; its judges, decisions, and publications. It is linked to the online Federal Court Reports, which can be accessed through a search engine.

Australian Law Reform Commission
http://www.alrc.gov.au/publications/index.htm
Canada and Australia share a similar juridical history because of their shared links to Britain and their implementation of a common-law system. Australians have been struggling with issues of law and justice reform, which are similar to some of the issues of concern in Canada. This website provides access to online publications of the Australian Law Reform Commission on diverse topics, such as judicial reform, children in the legal system, and matrimonial law review.

Department of Justice Canada: Annual Report Regarding Alleged Miscarriages of Justice
http://www.justice.gc.ca/eng/rp-pr/cj-jp/ccr-rc/rep13-rap13/p1.html
This link to the Department's site publishes an annual report for Canadians on applications to the minister of justice for reviews of alleged "miscarriages of justice."

The Continuing Legal Education Society of British Columbia
www.cle.bc.ca
The website of the Continuing Legal Education Society of British Columbia offers up-to-date information on a variety of legal issues, as well as links to law faculties of universities in B.C. and decisions of B.C. courts.

QUESTIONS FOR DISCUSSION

1. Is the jury, as Lord Devlin suggests, "the lamp that shows that freedom lives," or as Dean Griswold suggests, "twelve persons brought in from the street, selected in various ways for their lack of general ability"?
2. Could restorative justice ever become the dominant response to most criminal conduct, displacing the criminal courts? Discuss.
3. What were the key errors or issues leading to the conviction of David Milgaard? Discuss. Is an independent commission of review needed to address the possibility of wrongful conviction in Canada?

FURTHER READING

Action Committee on Access to Justice in Civil and Family Matters, *Access to Civil and Family Justice: A Roadmap for Change*, Ottawa, October 2013.

> This is a report that documents a range of systemic difficulties in relation to access to civil and family courts in Canada. The 38-page report notes the inability of the legal system to deal effectively with the legal problems of the poor and vulnerable, and makes a number of practical suggestions for change. The report begins with a statement of support from Chief Justice Beverley McLachlin.

Canadian Centre for Justice Statistics. *The Juristat Reader: A Statistical Overview of the Canadian Justice System, Unit 3:* Court Statistics. Toronto: Thompson Educational Publishing, 1999.

> An excellent empirical description of the work done by Canadian courts, highlighting the kinds and numbers of cases heard by various levels of court, the characteristics of the accused in criminal cases, dispositions, sentencing, and case processing. *The Juristat Reader* is a very useful complement to the statute and case law that governs Canada's courts.

Queen's Printer, Saskatchewan. *Report of the Commission of Inquiry into the Wrongful Conviction of David Milgaard,* Volumes 1 and 2, September 2008.

> A thorough analysis of the David Milgaard case, with testimony from key witnesses and stakeholders. The report, although indicating that all involved in the prosecution and defence of Milgaard acted in good faith, also notes that the justice system failed Milgaard, and makes a number of recommendations aimed at preventing future injustices of this kind—most notably the creation of an independent commission to review allegations of wrongful conviction.

Canada. Royal Commission on Aboriginal Peoples. *Final Report of the Royal Commission on Aboriginal Peoples.* 5 vols. Ottawa: Canada Communications Group, 1996.

> The final report of the Royal Commission on Aboriginal Peoples is a compilation that could be cited as critical further reading for a number of chapters in this text. The royal commission was given the task of developing recommendations on a wide range of issues, including the right of self-government, land claims, living conditions in Aboriginal communities, and programs to improve the lives of Aboriginal Canadians. The more than 400 recommendations have had and continue to have a significant impact on the development of Canadian law and policy.

Karp, C., and C. Rosner. *When Justice Fails: The David Milgaard Story.* Toronto: McClelland & Stewart, 1991.

> A comprehensive analysis of the Milgaard case, a wrongful conviction that dramatically demonstrated the fallibility of a human justice system. The authors point to the factors that culminated in Milgaard's conviction, providing the reader with a good grasp of the variables that underlie such cases.

NOTES

1. R.S.C. 1985, c. C-46.
2. S.M. Waddams, *Introduction to the Study of Law*. 4th ed. (Toronto: Carswell, 1992), 123.
3. *Re Southam Inc. and The Queen* (1984), 16 C.C.C. (3d) 262, 48 O.R. (2d) 678 (H.C.J.), aff'd 53 O.R. (2d) 663 (C.A.).
4. *Youth Criminal Justice Act,* R.S.C. 1985, c. Y-1, s. 38 (1.2).
5. See *R. v. Quesnel and Quesnel* (1979), 51 C.C.C. (2d) 270 (Ont. C.A.). For a more restrictive interpretation, see *R. v. Lefebvre* (1984), 17 C.C.C. (3d) 277 (Que. C.A.).
6. N. Christie, "Conflicts of Property," *British Journal of Criminology* 17 (1977): 1–15.
7. G. Gall, *The Canadian Legal System,* 3rd ed. (Toronto: Carswell, 1990), 135.
8. C.T. Griffiths and D. Chunn, eds., *Circuit and Rural Court Justice in the North: A Resource Publication* (Burnaby, B.C.: The Northern Conference and Simon Fraser University, 1986), 1–6 to 1–7.
9. R. Ericson and P. Baranek, *The Ordering of Justice: A Study of Accused Persons as Dependants in the Criminal Process* (Toronto: University of Toronto Press, 1982), 186.
10. A. Lamer, "Are We Over-Judicialized?" Address delivered to the Canadian Institute for the Administration of Justice, February 1977. Cited in Gall, *The Canadian Legal System,* 137.
11. E.N. Griswold, cited in H. Kalven and H. Zeisel, *The American Jury* (Boston: Little, Brown, 1966).
12. G. Williams, *The Proof of Guilt* (1963), cited in Kalven and Zeisel, ibid., 6.
13. G. Williams and J. Frank, cited in V. Hans and N. Vidmar, *Judging the Jury* (New York: Plenum Press, 1986), 114–5.
14. Hans and Vidmar, *Judging the Jury,* 116.
15. *R. v. Morgentaler, Smoling and Scott* (1988), 37 C.C.C. (3d) 449, 62 C.R. (3d) 1, [1988] 1 S.C.R. 30.
16. Hans and Vidmar, *Judging the Jury,* 232.
17. A.T. Doob, "The Canadian Trial Judges' View of the Criminal Jury Trial," in *Law Reform Commission of Canada, Background Studies on the Jury* (1979).
18. Bolan D.C.J., cited in *R. v. Askov* (1991), 59 C.C.C. (3d) 449, rev'g 37 C.C.C. (3d) 289, 60 C.R. (3d) 277, 33 C.R.R. 319 [hereinafter *Askov*].
19. *Askov,* 494–5.
20. Ibid., 490.
21. Ibid.
22. See, for example, *R. v. Bennett* (1991), 64 C.C.C. (3d) 449 and *R. v. Morin* (1992), 71 C.C.C. (3d) 1. *Morin* remains a critical case in 2010.
23. Action Committee on Access to Justice in Civil and Family Matters, *Access to Civil and Family Justice: A Roadmap for Change,* Ottawa, October 2013.
24. *Restorative Justice Factsheet,* http://www.csc-scc.gc.ca/restorative-justice/003005-0004-eng.shtml. Correctional Service Canada, 2012. Reproduced with the permission of the Minister of Public Works and Government Services, 2014.

REFERENCES

Beckton, C.F. *Law and the Media*. Toronto: Carswell, 1982.

Elliott E., and R.M. Gordon. *New Directions in Restorative Justice: Issues, Practice, Evaluation*. Portland: Willan Publishing, 2005.

Ericson, R., and P. Baranek. *The Ordering of Justice: A Study of Accused Persons as Dependants in the Criminal Process*. Toronto: University of Toronto Press, 1982.

Gall, G. *The Canadian Legal System*. 5th ed. Toronto: Carswell, 2004, Chapter 6.

Griffiths, C.T., and D. Chunn, eds. *Circuit and Rural Court Justice in the North: A Resource Publication*. Burnaby, B.C.: The Northern Conference and Simon Fraser University, 1986.

Hans, V., and N. Vidmar. *Judging the Jury*. New York: Plenum Press, 1986.

Henry, D.J. "Televised Court Proceedings: The Case for Implementation Today." *Advocates' Society Journal* 3 (1984): 19.

Kalven, H., and H. Zeisel. *The American Jury*. Boston: Little, Brown, 1966.

Karp, C., and C. Rosner. *When Justice Fails: The David Milgaard Story*. Toronto: McClelland & Stewart, 1991.

Kesterton, W.H. *The Law and the Press in Canada*. Carleton University Library Series. Toronto: McClelland & Stewart, 1976.

Lepofsky, D. *Open Justice: The Constitutional Right to Attend and Speak About Criminal Proceedings*. Toronto: Butterworths, 1985.

Marks, J.B. "An Overview of Alternative Dispute Resolution Techniques, Successes and Obstacles." *Antitrust Law Journal* 53 (1984): 283.

Mewett, A.W. "Television in the Courtroom." *Criminal Law Quarterly* 26 (1984): 385.

Pirie, A.J. "The Lawyer as Mediator: Professional Responsibility Problems or Profession Problem?" *Canadian Bar Review* 63 (1985): 378.

Robertson, S. *Courts and the Media*. Toronto: Butterworths, 1981.

Vidmar, N. "The Small Claims Court: A Reconceptualization of Disputes and an Empirical Investigation." *Law and Society Review* 18 (1984): 515.

Zuber, T.G. *Report of the Ontario Courts Inquiry*. Toronto: Government of Ontario, 1987.

THE STUDY OF LAW, LAWYERS, AND JUDGES: THE EVOLVING NATURE OF THE LEGAL PROFESSION

The legal industry in Canada is not immune to the major macro trends that are transforming virtually every industry in the world. The globalization of commerce and the rapid spread and adoption of technology are having significant effects on the Canadian legal industry. In many cases economic power has shifted to the consumer or client side, with buyers demanding more say on what lawyers do, how they do it, and how much and how they charge for it. With new competitors already in the marketplace—such as paralegals, global legal publishers, and legal process outsourcers (LPO)—and more on the horizon—law firms and individual lawyers will have to make important decisions on how to maintain a competitive advantage in the provision of legal services in Canada and globally. While these decisions may seem daunting to some people, they also present a vast range of opportunities for the profession to reinvent itself and thereby ensure that it remains dynamic and confident....

Demographics will play an important role in the future of the legal industry in Canada. The number of practicing lawyers in Canada is growing at a rate faster than the general population. While more women and historically marginalized groups are entering the profession, there are still few women in top management positions in firms. In fact, many female practitioners are choosing to work outside of private practice or as corporate counsel. As the Canadian Bar ages, inter-generational conflicts may arise, as older lawyers put off retirement, blocking career advancement for the younger cohort....

While demographics are shifting, so too are values and motives. Many lawyers are seeking a better work/life balance through part-time, contract, or work-at-home arrangements. Younger lawyers who are used to the new speed of communication and the democratization of discourse and planning through social media may expect similar management and decision-making processes in legal organizations...

Finally, access to justice ... remains a critical consideration for the legal profession in Canada. A commitment to the availability of affordable legal services to a broad range of Canadians must be part of any responses to change in the next decade.*

This excerpt makes the point that the teaching and the practice of law cannot be divorced from the ever-changing political, social, and economic context that underpins everyday life. Legal education and legal practice are, to a large extent, shaped

---

*Executive Summary, The Future of Legal Services in Canada: Trends and Issues, Canadian Bar Association, June 2013. Reprinted with permission of the Canadian Bar Association.

by developments outside the walls of the law school and the courtroom. With demographic shifts, the globalization of legal practice and changing conceptions of the appropriate provision of legal services, neither legal education nor the practice of law can be at all static.

It is perhaps because of these structural changes that one must not lose sight of the need to study and to think about law in settings that do something more than deliver a range of career choices. More specifically, legal education must continue to be focused on critical inquiry, and in this respect, it may be that the teaching of law outside of law schools performs an especially useful function, whether this takes place in our high schools or in our universities. For example, the Department of Law at Carleton University points to this strength in describing its program:

> Carleton University offers the most comprehensive Bachelor of Arts in Law in the country. Our programs reflect the growing demand for legal studies outside the professional LL.B., placing law and legal issues within a social context. Our courses move beyond the study of legal rules, to examining what we know about the law and how it works in our society.[1]

A BRIEF HISTORY OF LEGAL EDUCATION IN CANADA

How are Canada's lawyers chosen? How are they educated? What do Canadians expect from them when they undertake legal practice? Some 60 years ago, no formal university education in law existed in Canada; law students apprenticed with practising lawyers, wrote a few examinations, and gradually earned their admission to the bar. The 1983 Arthurs report *Law and Learning* noted that:

> [U]ntil after World War II, legal education consisted of practical training in law offices, supplemented by attendance on a part-time basis at lectures offered for the most part by practitioners, and by a very few full-time law teachers. The content and direction of the curriculum were heavily influenced by the desire to impart knowledge quickly, with an emphasis upon "black letter" law and the rules of procedure. There was little time—and often less incentive—to reflect on matters of jurisprudence.[2]

In 1949, debate over legal education in the Province of Ontario led to a schism within Toronto's Osgoode Hall. On one side were legal academics who argued that academic views and values were not adequately dealt with by the law school curriculum. On the other side were law teachers supporting the existing curriculum, which was aimed at training practitioners—setting out statute and case law and the rules of procedure—with little attention to the more theoretical questions of jurisprudence; legal philosophy; or the social, economic, and political contexts of law. The debate was resolved when a number of full-time Osgoode faculty established a university-based study of law at the University of Toronto, creating a clear choice for lawyers-to-be between a broad academic approach and practical training.

During the 1950s and 1960s, the university-based model of legal education gained ascendance. Law was to be studied for three years at university **law schools** approved by provincial **law societies**. Typically, the three years would follow at least two years of undergraduate study in another discipline. A period of apprenticeship, called **articling**, would follow the successful completion of courses in law, after which examinations, to be developed by provincial law societies, would admit successful candidates to the bar. Both the number and the size of law schools in Canada have expanded considerably since then. There were, for example, fewer than 50 law professors in Canadian law schools in 1950; in the late 1990s, there were more than 600 (since that time there has been relatively little growth in the size of the population of Canada's law professors). Furthermore, as the Arthurs report noted, there has been a substantial expansion of the traditional law school curriculum over the past 40 years:

> [A] growing emphasis on interdisciplinary work; a commitment to legal research and writing programs; the proliferation of new courses and seminars, including some in nontraditional areas such as poverty law; the teaching of legal skills; and new concepts of teaching such as clinical programs, intensive full-term programs in specific areas, and opportunities for individual, directed research.[3]

MEASURES OF ELIGIBILITY FOR LAW SCHOOL ADMISSION

In 2014 and likely beyond, applicants to law school are selected on the basis of their grade point averages (GPA) and their scores on a U.S.-designed aptitude test, the Law School Admission Test, or **LSAT**. Canada's law schools typically combine the two measures in varying proportions in order to determine eligibility for admission, usually assigning a greater statistical weight to previous university performance than to LSAT scores.

There have been many criticisms of the adequacy of these measures. Some have suggested that these essentially academic indices are too narrow, that students should be interviewed to determine such social attributes as their community involvement, relevant employment, and so on. Academic excellence, in itself, is no guarantee that a person will be able or willing to serve the community as a trained advocate. Like doctors, dentists, engineers, and other professionals, lawyers are trained in specialized areas in order to fulfill a function intended to serve the public good. Most Canadian law schools admit a small number of "mature," First Nations, and other differently qualified students in addition to those admitted on the basis of traditional entrance requirements. Mature students are those who have demonstrated academic ability through a combination of the LSAT score and some academic coursework, but do not have the undergraduate university degree that is typically required for entrance. Their work histories to date are set in the balance, however, and they are granted entrance to the law school because they have demonstrated this combination of academic promise and relevant work experience; the mature student brings a diversity of experience to the law school classroom.

The additional categories of Aboriginal and differently qualified applicants are also very common in Canadian law schools. For example, while Osgoode Hall Law School has both "Aboriginal applicant" and "general applicant" categories for admission, in addition to a mature student classification, in 2014/2015 they also express interest in a "Personal Statement and Supplemental Information." More specifically, they ask students to address issues of equity, work or life experience, performance considerations, and diversity.

Part B of the Personal Statement—Specific Considerations

Equity Factors

How well an applicant is able to demonstrate that he or she overcame challenges, such as financial difficulty, illness, family conflict, social or cultural prejudice, language barriers, and changes. It is helpful to provide some insight into their own character or understanding of abilities.

Work or Life Experience

Opportunity to show how his or her employment/volunteer or extra-curricular activities were demanding, important, and led to skill development (i.e., leadership, confidence, courage).

Preferable if can explicitly link efforts to an explanation of academic achievement and interest in legal studies.

We consider how well-rounded the applicant is, and how he or she has balanced the demands of study, work and community involvement and how they have grown from their experiences.

Performance Considerations

An applicant may explain any anomalies in their academic records or LSAT performances.

We assess how the applicant has written about and reflected upon their performances. We consider how the irregularities in performance came about, what they realized when they became aware of their results, and what they decided to do to improve their performance.

Diversity

We look for how the applicant explains how he or she would contribute to the diverse population at the law school and the legal profession. This is not meant for explaining how one supports diversity theoretically.

Applicants note how they are culturally, socially, racially diverse, and explain how these qualities have strengthened them.

We look for explicit connections between the applicant's diversity and their intentions to contribute meaningfully to the law school and the profession.[4]

Of its Aboriginal applicant category, the law school noted in 2014 that:

It is a priority of Osgoode Hall Law School to encourage the participation of Aboriginal students in the legal community. To that end, we have: a distinct admissions category for Aboriginal applicants; diverse programming related to Aboriginal law: and, custom student services to enhance the Aboriginal law student experience.... The

> Admissions Committee's decision to admit a candidate ultimately depends on its judgment of the candidate's ability to successfully complete law school. Applicants must provide some form of documentation corroborating identification with and connection to their Aboriginal community.[5]

In other words, although a certain number of spaces may be set aside for Aboriginal applicants, these spaces will not be occupied unless the law school is convinced the student will be able to graduate and make a contribution to the practice of law.

Osgoode has noted that challenges may involve language, financial difficulty, or myriad other disabilities. Similar kinds of categories of access now exist at most Canadian law schools. For example, the University of Western Ontario has created a category called "Access" for applicants who have disabilities or who fit into other categories including mature and Aboriginal.

The nontraditional criteria used to admit student applicants seem to work well; as noted, these students appear to perform as well as those admitted through traditional criteria. In the United States, however, such "preferential" treatment is often viewed as reverse discrimination, denying equality before the law to applicants who are not First Nations, or, more typically in the U.S. situation, to applicants who are not Black.

One argument in favour of affirmative action is that First Nations peoples (and Blacks) have suffered both legal and non-legal oppression and colonization. Second, these groups are underrepresented within the legal profession, and affirmative action is a useful means of correcting the imbalance. Moreover, it encourages the assumption of leadership roles within the community. Finally, proponents of such measures note that, once admitted to law school, black and First Nations students are evaluated by the same standards as all other students.

The *Canadian Charter of Rights and Freedoms* (unlike the U.S. Bill of Rights) states that affirmative-action programs are consistent with the protection of rights and freedoms. Section 15(2) states that the guarantees of equality within section 15(1) do not "preclude any law, program, or activity that has as its object the amelioration of conditions of disadvantaged individuals or groups including those that are disadvantaged because of race, national or ethnic origin, colour, religion, sex, age or mental or physical disability."

There have also been many criticisms of the use of the LSAT. Some critics argue that a U.S.-oriented aptitude test should not determine admissions to Canadian law schools. Others believe that the test is biased toward the language and orientation of a white middle-class culture; still others hold that it has no predictive abilities and that the cumulative weight of three years of university courses taken from a wide range of professors is all that is needed to determine eligibility. Indeed, supporters of the LSAT are not able to provide convincing evidence that test scores can adequately predict success in law school and within legal practice.

As imperfect as LSAT scores and grade point averages may be, it has been difficult to create alternative standards for admission that are either more useful to the law schools and Canada's communities or more fair to prospective applicants. Evaluation by interview is highly subjective, potentially biased by the attitudes, beliefs, and values of interviewers. A lottery system appears to produce law students at least marginally less capable than those admitted with traditional qualifications.

Legal academics have focused on the admissions processes in Canadian law schools, however, suggesting that the underpinnings of admissions decisions have not been rigorously evaluated or debated. Dawna Tong and Wes Pue wrote in the *Osgoode Hall Law Journal* in 1999 about the cultural imposition of the LSAT, a U.S. aptitude test, and more pointedly of the goals that underlie the admissions process itself. They noted:

> [T]he public interest requires a legal profession that is both "competent" and "diverse." A profession consisting entirely of extremely competent, hard-working, selfless, and ethical individuals who were all, nonetheless, exclusively drawn from a narrow social group would not be well placed to serve the public interest. It could understand nothing beyond its own narrow sectoral interests. The foundation of liberal democracy lies not in the denial of diversity but in finding creative ways of negotiating difference so as to make life-in-common possible, tolerable and just.[6]

Tong and Pue are wary, then, of admissions decisions that are based only on grade point average and LSAT scores. They imply that such an approach will compromise diversity and hence diminish the law's capacity for tolerance and justice.

INSIDE THE LAW SCHOOLS: NUMBERS AND CURRICULA

In 1962, Canada graduated fewer than 1,000 lawyers; in the late 1990s, nearly 3,000 lawyers were graduating each year. Since that time (between 2000 and 2014) there has been relatively little change, though the law's complexity and breadth has, arguably, continued to grow. In a broader context, looking back at the past 50 plus years, the Canadian population has grown by about 50 percent, while the number of lawyers increased by about 300 percent. The cumulative effect of these changes has been substantial: 10,000 lawyers were practising in Canada in 1962; today there are more than 60,000. In 1962, women formed fewer than 5 percent of each law school class; currently, they make up about 40 percent of law graduates.

The increased contribution of women to the legal profession has developed largely because of growing demands for gender equality. The disproportionate growth in the numbers of Canadian lawyers relative to many other occupations flows, at least in part, from the increased complexity of social life and the related need for regulation and dispute resolution. There has been a substantial rise in both the law and litigation relating to such matters as labour relations, radio and television communications, welfare, unemployment insurance, workers' compensation, immigration, family relationships, and correctional administration. Furthermore, market surveys reveal that an increasing percentage of graduating law students do not intend to practise law as such; they have chosen a legal education in order to pursue an academic, government, or corporate/commercial career.

Law degrees are also useful for those who wish to pursue a career outside the practice of law. A small percentage of each graduating class goes on to complete a master's or a doctorate in law, typically embarking upon an academic career at the conclusion of this further degree. And many other students contemplating a career in either business or government service have found a law degree to be a useful springboard for such work.

There has been considerable debate over the past three decades about whether Canada's law schools are graduating a surplus of lawyers. Most agree that it is mainly enrolment increases that account for the 300-percent increase between 1960 and 2000. But, as legal historians David Stager and Harry Arthurs noted, that increase was not linear:

> Law school enrolment in Canada more than doubled between 1964 and 1970; this represented an average annual increase of 12.4 percent. Between 1971 and 1976, enrolment increased at an annual average of 3.6 percent, and since the mid-1970s, enrolment has increased at an average yearly rate of only 1 percent. This virtual plateau appears to represent a return to long-run equilibrium in the lawyers' market. Moreover, the proportion of law graduates entering private practice in Canada has continued to decline because of increasing demand for lawyers in government and business, and lawyers finding employment in non-legal fields.[7]

Not surprisingly, in the face of increased enrolments and increased diversity within the profession, the law school curriculum has also expanded. While the basics of the first-year **LL.B.** program have generally remained intact—torts, real property, personal property, criminal law, jurisprudence, constitutional law, and contracts— the second and third years now typically permit a wide range of courses and of approaches to law.

When deans of Canadian law schools were asked to rank the three most important goals of their programs, the value of training students for the practice of law was not seen to have overwhelming importance. Of almost equal importance were the tasks of "providing students with an understanding of the relationship of law and society," "developing interest in law as a scholarly discipline," and "developing critical reflection on legal practice."[8] These goals reflect a change in the understanding of the purpose and nature of legal education, as well as an effort to respond to public concerns about the nature of legal practice. Today's graduate in law is asked to understand not only the literal content of statute and case law, but also the social, political, and economic contexts in which such law both operates and develops.

The role of legal education continues to be the subject of considerable debate and disagreement, within both law schools and the legal profession. Many students complain that faculty members who emphasize an understanding of the relationship between law and society or critical reflection on legal practice are not adequately preparing them for the exigencies of the profession. They urge, together with some faculty, greater emphasis on the attainment of technical skills, on so-called black letter law. Their argument is that discussion of the values and principles that underlie specific forms of law is relevant only if it contributes directly to their effectiveness as practitioners.

With the advent of the *Canadian Charter of Rights and Freedoms* (the *Charter*), this kind of argument has less persuasiveness. The *Charter* forces Canada's lawyers to litigate the values of the nation—to engage in debate about such principles as freedom of expression, cruel and unusual punishment, and so forth. Even if the *Charter* did not exist, however, it seems doubtful that a university education in law could now be justified by the attainment of technical skills. A university education in law was designed to supplement, not replace, apprenticeship. The pre-1949 structure of apprenticeship and the current structure of articling and bar admission examinations are systems designed to test the attainment of technical skills.

Thus, a university education in law is, at least in theory, designed to provide students with a broad base of understanding in the form of insight into the history, purpose, principles, and controversies within specific areas of the legal system. It is unclear, however, whether the refocused law school curriculum will change the trajectory of legal practice for most students. Lawyer Robert Kerry Wilkins argues:

> [W]e absorb the politics of aspiration while we practice refining the rhetoric of justice. The price of success in the program is learning to treat the one as the other. It is an exercise shot through with bogus necessity. The harm and dislocation many law students suffer have their origins in just such contortions. They change us, often in ways we had not noticed, do not understand, and may not like.[9]

At the conclusion of the LL.B. program, law school graduates typically apply for articles and register for the bar admission program in the province in which they intend to practise. Each province sets its own requirements with respect to the length of both the articling period and the bar admission examinations. In most provinces, a lawyer can be called to the bar after one year to 18 months of articling and examinations. Transferring to practise in another province typically requires the writing of transfer examinations.

THE LAWYER IN PRACTICE

The past three decades represent a significant evolution in the role of law and lawyers within our culture. As noted earlier, there are both more laws and more lawyers. It is perhaps to be expected, then, that there should also be more negative attitudes toward lawyers. Practitioners of law are the subject of any number of derisive jokes, caricatured as greedy and amoral, driven more by material considerations than by principles. In short, the profession does not always succeed in convincing the public that justice, rather than material gain, is the linchpin of legal practice. In the words of Wilkins:

> The power and prestige that lawyers as a group enjoy remain contingent ... on certain unvoiced public assumptions about lawyers' roles in our culture: that the work they do is essential to the realization of justice, for example, and that it is beyond the competence of ordinary mortals acting alone. These assumptions (and others like them) underpin the correlation in people's minds between privilege and desert. Any serious erosion of them would invite inconvenient questions about the whole notion of legal profession-alism: about the tasks and attitudes appropriate to it, and about its moral and functional legitimacy within a system dedicated, nominally at least, to marketing justice.[10]

Within public culture, there are other, more neutral, images of the Canadian lawyer: corporate technocrat, crusading litigator, general practitioner serving a small community, and so on. The most dominant of these is the image of the courtroom advocate. In fact, however, even lawyers who are litigators spend very little of their time in the courtroom, engaged in advocacy. A survey of lawyers in private practice in the United States revealed that almost two-thirds of their time was taken in drafting documents, interviews with clients, correspondence, library research, orally counselling clients, and office administration. Time in the courtroom amounted to about 5 percent of the legal practice.

From this list of tasks, we may conclude that Canada's lawyers have conflicting obligations. They must fulfill responsibilities to their clients, their professional societies, the criminal and civil courts, and their communities. Many of these obligations are common to lawyers in other countries, as well as to other professionals such as medical practitioners and accountants.

There is one essential distinction, however, between lawyers and other professionals. Lawyers, like physicians, can claim that communications between themselves and their clients are "privileged"—that is, any written or oral communication between lawyer and client may not be revealed to a court, board, or tribunal without the client's permission. The purpose of privilege is, in theory, to give clients the assurance that their interests will supersede those of the other participants within the justice system, notably the prosecutor, the police, and the judiciary. But some critics have suggested that the existence of solicitor–client privilege is not sufficient to ensure that clients' interests will indeed be paramount. Sociologists Richard Ericson and Patricia Baranek, after an empirical study of hundreds of accused within the criminal process, made the following observation:

> The accused does not typically have a relationship with his lawyer that would allow trust to be built up and used on either side to accept evidence at face value; further-more, the accused and lawyer do not have the same stake in a future relationship.... The accused's trust in his lawyer is, thus, ... a forced faith that his lawyer will act in his best interests.... [T]he accused has little choice but to accept matters on blind faith when his lawyer attempts out-of-court settlements with the police and Crown attorney. He is nearly always excluded from these transactions and therefore must rely on his lawyer's account of what happened and what it is possible to achieve.[11]

The provincial law societies are typically more demanding than clients in the structuring of their relationships with the lawyers within their jurisdictions. These professional societies establish the relevant standards and construct examinations for admission to the bar, set and collect annual fees from practising lawyers, administer government-funded systems of legal aid for the working poor and the indigent, arrange insurance for their membership, and discipline lawyers who fall short of their existing standards of professional conduct.

During the 1990s, the problem of gender bias in the legal profession emerged as a source of both concern and empirical scrutiny. A task force of the Canadian Bar Association produced a report on gender equality, "Touchstones for Change: Equality, Diversity and Accountability." This 1993 report set out more than 100 recommendations on topics ranging from barriers to entry into the profession and barriers to equality within the profession to problems encountered by women in private and government practices. Most pointedly, the report presented four critical findings resulting from studies of women in legal practice: (1) the vast majority of women surveyed reported both the perception and the experience of gender bias in the legal profession; (2) the vast majority of female lawyers face barriers to career advancement, and this is evidenced in the patterns of access to legal positions, areas of practice, partnership, and remuneration; (3) female lawyers with child-care responsibilities are discriminated against because of the lack of accommodation by the profession, resulting in lost income and reduced opportunities for advancement; and (4) more than one in three female lawyers have experienced sexual harassment in the form of unwanted sexual advances.[12]

Some empirical evidence of these dissatisfactions can be found in the percentage of women who leave the practice of law. Kay and Brockman have reported that women are leaving the profession at higher rates than men. By 1990, for example, 22 percent of women called to the bar in British Columbia between 1974 and 1988 had left the profession, in contrast to 13 percent of men called to the bar during that time. But it would also be a mistake to portray the lot of women in law as one of a unidimensional gendered misery. A 1996 study of more than 1,500 Ontario lawyers revealed no significant differences in job satisfaction between men and women in the province, except with respect to issues of parental leave arrangements and job security (admittedly, though, very significant issues).[13] Additionally, the percentage of women serving as judges in Canada has increased from less than 10 percent of the judicial population in 1990 to approximately 30 percent in 2014.

THE CANADIAN BAR ASSOCIATION'S *CODE OF PROFESSIONAL CONDUCT*

The professional conduct expected of Canada's lawyers has been a subject of considerable discussion. In 2009, after consultations with provincial law societies, the

Canadian Bar Association published an updated *Code of Professional Conduct*, generally held to be reflective of established opinion within the legal profession.[14]

RULES OF THE CANADIAN BAR ASSOCIATION

Code of Professional Conduct (Revised 2009)

Chapter I: Integrity

The lawyer must discharge with integrity all duties owed to clients, the court or tribunal or other members of the profession and the public.

Chapter II: Competence and Quality of Service

1. The lawyer owes the client a duty to be competent to perform any legal services undertaken on the client's behalf.

2. The lawyer should serve the client in a conscientious, diligent and efficient manner so as to provide a quality of service at least equal to that which lawyers generally would expect of a competent lawyer in a like situation.

Chapter III: Advising Clients

The lawyer must be both honest and candid when advising clients.

Chapter IV: Confidential Information

Maintaining Information in Confidence:

1. The lawyer has a duty to hold in strict confidence all information concerning the business and affairs of the client acquired in the course of the professional relationship, and shall not divulge any such information except as expressly or impliedly authorized by the client, required by law or otherwise required by this Code.

Public Safety Exception:

2. Where a lawyer believes upon reasonable grounds that there is an imminent risk to an identifiable person or group of death or serious bodily harm, including serious psychological harm that would substantially interfere with health or well-being, the lawyer shall disclose confidential information where it is necessary to do so in order to prevent the death or harm, but shall not disclose more information than is required.

3. The lawyer who has reasonable grounds for believing that a dangerous situation is likely to develop at a court or tribunal facility shall inform the person having responsibility for security at the facility and give particulars, being careful not to disclose confidential information except as required by paragraph 2 of this Rule. Where possible the lawyer should suggest solutions to the anticipated problem such as:

(a) the need for further security;

(b) that judgment be reserved;

(c) such other measure as may seem advisable.

Disclosure Where Lawyer's Conduct in Issue:

4. Disclosure may also be justified in order to establish or collect a fee, or to defend the lawyer or the lawyer's associates or employees against any allegation of malpractice or misconduct, but only to the extent necessary for such purposes.

Chapter V: Impartiality and Conflict of Interest between Clients

1. The lawyer shall not advise or represent both sides of a dispute and, except after adequate disclosure to and with the consent of the clients, preferably after receiving independent legal advice, shall not act or continue to act in a matter when there is a conflicting interest.

2. The lawyer may act in a matter which is adverse to the interests of a current client provided that:

   (a) the matter is unrelated to any matter in which the lawyer is acting for the current client; and

   (b) no conflicting interest is present.

Chapter VI: Conflict of Interest between Lawyer and Client

1. Except after adequate disclosure to and with the consent of the client, preferably after receiving independent legal advice, the lawyer shall not act for the client where the personal interests of the lawyer, or a partner or associate of the lawyer, give rise to a substantial risk of material and adverse effect on representation of the client by the lawyer.

2. The lawyer should not enter into a business transaction with the client or knowingly give to or acquire from the client an ownership, security or other pecuniary interest unless:

   (a) the transaction is a fair and reasonable one and its terms are fully disclosed to the client in writing in a manner that is reasonably understood by the client;

   (b) the client is given a reasonable opportunity to seek independent legal advice about the transaction, the onus being on the lawyer to prove that the client's interests were protected by such independent advice; and

   (c) the client consents in writing to the transaction.

3. The lawyer shall not enter into or continue a business transaction with the client if:

   (a) the client expects or might reasonably be assumed to expect that the lawyer is protecting the client's interests;

   (b) there is a significant risk that the interests of the lawyer and the client may differ.

4. The lawyer shall not act for the client where the lawyer's duty to the client and the personal interests of the lawyer or an associate are in conflict.

5. The lawyer shall not prepare an instrument giving the lawyer or an associate a substantial gift from the client, including a testamentary gift.

6. The lawyer must comply with the terms of all professional liability insurance policies.

Chapter VII: Outside Interests and the Practice of Law

The lawyer who engages in another profession, business or occupation concurrently with the practice of law must not allow such outside interest to jeopardize the lawyer's professional integrity, independence or competence.

Chapter VIII: Preservation of Clients' Property

The lawyer owes a duty to the client to observe all relevant laws and rules respecting the preservation and safekeeping of the client's property entrusted to the lawyer. Where there are no such laws or rules, or the lawyer is in any doubt, the lawyer should take the same care of such property as a careful and prudent owner would when dealing with property of like description.

Chapter IX: The Lawyer as Advocate

When acting as an advocate, the lawyer must treat the tribunal with courtesy and respect and must represent the client resolutely, honourably and within the limits of the law.

Chapter X: The Lawyer in Public Office

The lawyer who holds public office should, in the discharge of official duties, adhere to standards of conduct as high as those that these rules require of a lawyer engaged in the practice of law.

Chapter XI: Fees

The lawyer shall not:

    (a) *stipulate for, charge or accept any fee that is not fully disclosed, fair and reasonable;*

    (b) *appropriate any funds of the client held in trust or otherwise under the lawyer's control for or on account of fees without the express authority of the client, save as permitted by the rules of the governing body.*

Chapter XII: Withdrawal

The lawyer owes a duty to the client not to withdraw services except for good cause and upon notice appropriate in the circumstances.

Chapter XIII: The Lawyer and the Administration of Justice

The lawyer should encourage public respect for and try to improve the administration of justice.

Chapter XIV: Advertising, Solicitation and Making Legal Services Available

Lawyers should make legal services available to the public in an efficient and convenient manner that will command respect and confidence, and by means that are compatible with the integrity, independence and effectiveness of the profession.

Chapter XV: Responsibility to the Profession Generally

The lawyer should assist in maintaining the integrity of the profession and should participate in its activities.

Chapter XVI: Responsibility to Lawyers and Others

The lawyer's conduct toward all persons with whom the lawyer comes into contact in practice should be characterized by courtesy and good faith.

Chapter XVII: Practice by Unauthorized Persons

The lawyer should assist in preventing the unauthorized practice of law.

Chapter XVIII: Public Appearances and Public Statements by Lawyers

The lawyer who engages in public appearances and public statements should do so in conformity with the principles of the Code.

Chapter XIX: Avoiding Questionable Conduct

The lawyer should observe the rules of professional conduct set out in the Code in the spirit as well as in the letter.

Chapter XX: Non-Discrimination

The lawyer shall respect the requirements of human rights and constitutional laws in force in Canada, and in its provinces and territories. Except where differential treatment is permitted by law, the lawyer shall not discriminate with respect to partnership or professional employment of other lawyers, articled students or any other person, or in professional dealings with other members of the profession or any other person on grounds including, but not limited to, an individual's ancestry, colour, perceived race, nationality, national origin, ethnic background or origin, language, religion, creed or religious belief, religious association or activities, age, sex, gender, physical characteristics, pregnancy, sexual orientation, marital or family status, source of income, political belief, association or activity, or physical or mental disability.

Chapter XXI: The Lawyer as Mediator

1. A lawyer who acts as a mediator shall, at the outset of the mediation, ensure that the parties fully understand that:

    (a) the lawyer is not acting as a lawyer for either party but, as mediator, is acting to assist the parties to resolve the matters in issue, and

    (b) although communications pertaining to and arising out of the mediation process may be covered by some other common law, civil law, principles, statutory or other privilege or rule, they will not be covered by the solicitor-client privilege.

2. A lawyer shall not act as a mediator if the lawyer or the lawyer's firm has acted or is acting in a matter that may reasonably be expected to become an issue during the mediation, except with the informed consent of all parties.

Chapter XXII: Independence of the Bar

1. The lawyer must exercise independent professional judgment in providing legal advice, services and representation to a client.

2. The lawyer must conduct himself or herself in a manner that respects, protects and advances the independence of the bar.

The rules in the 22 "chapters" set out in the *Code of Professional Conduct* take the form of guidelines; they are not precise or specific in their instructions to practising lawyers. The Code has no legal force within a given province until adopted by that jurisdiction's law society.

INFRINGEMENTS OF THE *CODE OF PROFESSIONAL CONDUCT*

When the *Code of Professional Conduct* states that the lawyer must discharge duties "owed to clients, the court, other members of the profession, and the public ... with integrity," it is not clear about what kinds of behaviour are acceptable or unacceptable. Fortunately, in its discussion of the rules, the Canadian Bar Association has given illustrations of the kinds of actions that are likely to infringe the Code[15]:

    (a) committing any personally disgraceful or morally reprehensible offence that reflects upon the lawyer's integrity (of which a conviction by a competent court would be prima facie evidence);

    (b) committing, whether professionally or in the lawyer's personal capacity, any act of fraud or dishonesty, for example by knowingly making a false tax return or falsifying a document, whether or not prosecuted for so doing;

(c) *making an untrue representation or concealing a material fact from a client, with dishonest or improper motive;*

(d) *taking advantage of the youth, inexperience, lack of education or sophistication, ill health, or unbusinesslike habits of a client;*

(e) *misappropriating or dealing dishonestly with a client's money or other property;*

(f) *receiving money or other property from or on behalf of a client for a specific purpose and failing, without the client's consent, to pay or apply it for that purpose;*

(g) *knowingly assisting, enabling or permitting any person to act fraudulently, dishonestly, or illegally;*

(h) *failing to be absolutely frank and candid in all dealings with the Court or tribunal, fellow lawyers, and other parties to proceedings, subject always to not betraying the client's cause, abandoning the client's legal rights or disclosing the client's confidences; and*

(i) *failing to honour the lawyer's word when pledged even though, under technical rules, the absence of writing might afford a legal defence.*

These nine illustrations suggest that dishonesty and "morally reprehensible" conduct are at the heart of behaviour that would infringe the Code. Significantly, the first illustration shows that conviction for a criminal offence does not, in itself, constitute an infringement. What is at issue is that the crime must be either "personally disgraceful" or "morally reprehensible" to infringe the Code. We might, therefore, wonder what kinds of convictions might be seen to be "personally disgraceful" or "morally reprehensible."

This question reveals that the specificity of the Code and its nine illustrations are not as clear as its rhetoric might imply. First, we must remember that the legal profession is self-regulated, so we might expect its professional code of conduct to reflect primarily the interests of lawyers, not those of the general public. Second, what behaviours do the ambiguous illustrations actually prohibit?

It can be argued, concerning the first illustration, that conviction for any criminal offence is evidence of disrespect for the law and effectively compromises a lawyer's standing before the law society and the public. On the other hand, certain offences may be said to reflect only personal weakness or indulgence, and a criminal conviction for such crimes does not constitute conflict of interest for a defence counsel. For a prosecutor or judge, however, any criminal conviction represents conflict of interest. The prosecutor who seeks conviction and penalty and the judge who determines guilt and penalty cannot be seen as impartial if they have engaged in criminal acts outside the court that they respectively prosecute and sanction within the court. But another point of view argues that judges and prosecutors are drawn from a select, typically upper-middle-class segment of society. Hence, they are insulated from the classes of people who appear in criminal courts, and their lack of association with criminal conduct may be as much a badge of ignorance as it is a qualification for employment.

We are still left with the question of what kinds of crimes can be considered to be personally disgraceful or morally reprehensible. A property offence might be said to reveal a fundamental dishonesty, and an offence involving violence might be termed disgraceful or reprehensible. But what of the categories of vice—possession of an illegal drug or the non-criminal use of the services of a prostitute? Would a lawyer who helped to arrange an abortion for a teenager be taking improper advantage of the youth or ill health of a client (illustration [d])? Should a distinction be drawn between a handful of parking tickets and impaired driving?

Canada's provincial law societies have disciplined and reprimanded lawyers convicted of illegal drug possession, impaired driving, or using the services of prostitutes, but they have generally not disbarred them for such behaviours. In some instances, lawyers have been fined and suspended from practice for a period of time (typically less than one year); in others, they have received reprimands. Paradoxically, impaired driving convictions have typically been tolerated to a greater extent than drug possession convictions, perhaps because alcohol is a more socially established drug of choice, even though it usually presents a greater risk to others than some illegal substances. But lawyers who have acted dishonestly are most often disbarred. Within Canada and most other Western nations, lawyers have been disbarred for the misappropriation of trust funds, monies entrusted to them by members of the public. This and other violations of the lawyer–client relationship are dealt with by illustrations (b) to (i).

Illustration (h)—the requirement that lawyers be "absolutely frank and candid in all dealings with the Court or tribunal, fellow lawyers, and other parties to proceedings"— raises a quite different issue from the betrayal of a client's economic interests. This illustration confronts the ethical problems surrounding the disclosure of information relevant to a case before the court. Specifically, it suggests that in matters of criminal law, there is an obligation on the part of the prosecutor to inform the defence fully of the evidence against the accused. In the instance of indictable offences, the Crown prosecutor is generally required to disclose to the accused all evidence relevant to the charge, regardless of whether this evidence will be used at trial and regardless of whether the evidence is inculpatory or exculpatory. In *R. v. Stinchcombe,*[16] a case that highlights the importance of disclosure, the Supreme Court of Canada determined that in the case of an unrepresented accused, a trial judge should not take a plea unless this accused has been informed of his right to disclosure by the Crown.

Allegations of nondisclosure by Crown counsel continue to be a major issue in many criminal cases. However, while nondisclosure in criminal cases is rarely found to be deserving of disbarment or reprimand, it is significant that the bar association's *Code of Professional Conduct* mandates disclosure as a professional responsibility.

By considering recent cases of disciplinary action taken against four lawyers in Ontario between 2011 and 2014,[17] we can examine more closely at least a few of the circumstances in which provincial law societies will take action against individual lawyers for their misconduct, and the range of penalties that they will impose. Note that forms of theft such as misappropriation of a client's trust funds—a violation of honesty—are treated much more harshly than criminal convictions for illegal drug possession or even money laundering, where honesty is not the critical issue at stake. Much more common, however, are disciplinary proceedings for failing to respond to an investigation by the law society or failing to keep adequate books and records:

- Donald Sumner Baker was found to have engaged in professional misconduct for failing to serve his client in a family law matter that was contested and for simultaneously failing to take appropriate steps in relation to a conflict of interest—hiring opposing counsel in this family law matter (an associate in his firm, thereby creating a situation in which there was likely to be a conflict of interest). He was reprimanded, asked to pay costs to the Law Society of $2,500 and to make a charitable donation of $1,000 to the Law Society Foundation.
- Lawrence John Burns was found to have engaged in professional misconduct for misappropriating approximately $80,000 from the funds he held on behalf of one client, and misappropriating approximately $300,000 from funds held on behalf of another client. His licence to practise law was revoked and he was ordered to make a $92,500 payment to the compensation fund, along with $20,000 in costs to the Law Society.
- Kevin John MacTavish was found to have engaged in professional misconduct for failing to reply promptly to communications from the Law Society and for failing to co-operate with an investigation. He was suspended for one month, or indefinitely until he provided a complete response to requests from two written communications; he was also fined $1,000 and ordered to pay costs to the Law Society of approximately $4,300.
- Terence John Robinson was found to have engaged in conduct unbecoming for having been convicted of the criminal offence of aggravated assault. He was suspended from practice for 12 months, and ordered to provide evidence to the Law Society, in the form of a medical report from a qualified medical practitioner, prior to resuming practice, to establish that he is not incapable of doing so; he was also to complete 25 hours of professional development within the first year of resuming practice.

What conclusions are we to draw from these admittedly few cases? (Approximately 100 lawyers may be disciplined in Ontario in a given year.) Dishonesty in economic relationships between lawyer and client is most likely to be punished. Individual issues relating to personal conduct seem to be taken less seriously than the more fundamental issues of honesty and trust. The most common form of discipline in recent years (2011 to 2014), typically involving a suspension and some financial reparation, appears to be for failing to respond to an investigation by the Law Society, for consistently failing to respond to requests for documentation, or for failing to keep proper records of transactions.

Disciplinary cases raise another issue. Who should be responsible for disciplining lawyers, making decisions to reprimand, fine, or disbar? Should the provincial law societies be more accessible to and controllable by public interest? Why are lawyers permitted to police themselves, with little input from those outside the profession? If the practice of law must be in the public interest, it would seem to follow that the public should play a major role in helping the legal profession define the boundaries of unacceptable conduct for its membership.

THE CODE OF PROFESSIONAL CONDUCT AND THE COST OF LEGAL SERVICES

One other matter concerning the ethical responsibilities of Canada's lawyers requires some discussion. The issue of the fees charged to clients is covered in chapter 11 of the *Code of Professional Conduct*: "[All fees should be] fully disclosed, fair, and reasonable." There is little guidance, however, as to what constitutes a "fair and reasonable" fee. The Canadian Bar Association's discussion of this rule in chapter 11 notes only that the size of a lawyer's fee will depend upon

> the time and effort required and spent; the difficulty and importance of the matter; whether special service or skill has been required and provided; the customary charges of other lawyers ... in like matters and circumstances; in civil cases the amount involved ...; in criminal cases the exposure and risk to the client; the results obtained; tariffs or scales authorized by local law; ... the urgency and uncertainty of reward; any relevant agreement between the lawyer and the client.[18]

These criteria indicate that the economic value of the legal dispute, or, in criminal cases, the seriousness of the charge, will necessarily affect the value of the legal services provided.

The *Code of Professional Conduct* also makes it clear that the practice of charging contingency fees is an acceptable one, although some provinces prohibit it. When contingency fees are agreed upon by lawyer and client, the lawyer provides services on the basis that the client will be billed only if the action is successful. The amount charged will typically be a percentage of the total award, potentially providing a greater enrichment than the lawyer would have received if the legal tariff had been applied irrespective of the result in the case. In any event, the Code dictates that the contingency fee must again be "fair and reasonable."

These principles aside, there are significant differences in the fees charged by Canada's lawyers for similar kinds of work. Some lawyers have reputations and abilities that can justify more substantial levies. This discrepancy raises the question of whether access to justice is dependent on the ability of individuals or corporations to pay for legal services.

It was mentioned earlier that over the past four decades the provision of legal services within Canada has changed markedly. For most of the twentieth century, the consumers of legal services were individuals with significant assets, businesses, governments, or the poor; the latter class of clients was typically involved only in litigation related to crime or accident. Since the 1960s, however, Canadian lawyers have increasingly become involved in serving corporate clients; in drawing from provincial legal-aid plans (particularly in relation to criminal law); and in servicing the needs of more complex kinds of government regulation and legislation in such areas as family law, administrative law, real property, and wills and estates.

The greater affluence of the Canadian population in the postwar era is a leading factor in the increased demand for legal services; the primary use of legal services has been to protect growing individual and corporate wealth. As many legal commentators have observed, these changes have had the effect of creating considerable diversification within the practice of law, leading to substantially different structures for the delivery of legal services. During the past 30 years we have witnessed the merger of individual law firms into a small number of multi-city international practices serving a wide range of corporate and government clients. Computer technology and Internet access have also dramatically changed the nature of legal research, introducing economies of scale that benefit all practitioners.

There have been fewer rewards for lawyers concerned with the rights of the disadvantaged or the legal problems of the middle class. Although legal-aid clinics and consumer and environmentally driven practices have become more common, their numbers and their economic well-being pale when placed alongside the rosy financial health of Canada's major corporate law firms. In the face of such discrepancies, could we imagine a system of universal insurance for the provision of all forms of legal assistance—a government-funded program along the lines of Medicare? Is "judicare" a logical next step in the construction of Canada's system of government services?

Medicare proceeds on the premise that all citizens are equally entitled to health care as a matter of right, regardless of wealth, disability, or social contribution—at the least, to a basic minimum of health care. It is not clear, however, that this premise would fairly apply to the provision of all legal services. While a Canadian citizen might be said to have a right to a lawyer when facing family separation, a criminal charge, deportation, or the consequences of an accident, it is not clear that there is a corresponding right to use legal services to facilitate and protect the accumulation of real property, stocks and bonds, and similar assets. Thus, if a system of judicare were to be constructed, it would have to take account of the diverse uses of legal services within Canadian society. As noted earlier, corporations, governments, and the wealthy are the major consumers of the product. Most working-class or middle-class Canadians will typically use a lawyer within a fairly restricted set of circumstances: to write a will, purchase a property, facilitate a family separation, or face a charge relating to the criminal law or the operation of a motor vehicle. For these restricted purposes, it may be reasonable to consider a private or government legal insurance program, financed by individual or taxpayer contributions.

PARALEGALS: AN EMERGING ROLE FOR THE PROVISION OF LEGAL SERVICES

A number of Canadian colleges now offer programs in paralegal studies. Paralegals may provide advocacy for clients appearing before such specialized tribunals as landlord and tenant and other administrative tribunals; they may also appear in small claims court or work as legal researchers, court monitors, or investigators with an appreciation and understanding of the working of the law in Canada.

Because of the importance and legal significance of the services paralegals provide, the Law Society of Upper Canada has begun regulating their work. After June 30, 2010, all paralegals applying for regulation must have completed an accredited legal services program in one of 10 colleges in Ontario, and ultimately be licensed by the Law Society of Upper Canada. In response to the question *What is the permitted scope of practice for paralegals*, the Law Society of Upper Canada sets out the following[19]:

> The regulatory scheme set out in the Law Society's By-Law 4 permits paralegals to practise in what were already permitted areas of practice. Subsection 6 (2) authorizes licensed paralegals to represent someone:
>
> * *in Small Claims Court*
> * *in the Ontario Court of Justice under the Provincial Offences Act*
> * *on summary conviction offences where the maximum penalty does not exceed six months' imprisonment*
> * *before administrative tribunals, including the Financial Services Commission of Ontario.*
>
> A person with a paralegal licence can do the following in the course of representing a client in any of the above-mentioned proceedings:
>
> * *give legal advice concerning legal interests, rights or responsibilities with respect to a proceeding or the subject matter of a proceeding*
> * *draft or assist with drafting documents for use in a proceeding*
> * *negotiate on behalf of a person who is a party to a proceeding.*

The future of paralegal services appears to be quite positive, as the relatively high costs of legal representation and the complexity of modern life have combined to create a need for this set of skills.

JUDICIAL RECRUITMENT AND STANDARDS OF CONDUCT

In November 1981, British Columbia Supreme Court Justice Thomas Berger criticized the federal government's abandonment of support for Aboriginal rights during the negotiations that led to the patriation of the Constitution. Berger told the press:

> Our leaders felt it was in the national interest to sacrifice the rights. They felt they were serving the greater good in reaching an agreement. It was mean-spirited. There are a million and more Natives in Canada: Indians, Inuit, and Métis, and for the most part, they are poor and powerless. They were the people who were

sacrificed in this deal. That is the whole point of minority rights, that they should not be taken away for any reason.[20]

Berger's statement elicited a strong response from the prime minister, Pierre Trudeau; from Bora Laskin, then chief justice of the Supreme Court; and, ultimately, from the **Canadian Judicial Council**. The council convened a committee to consider allegations that Justice Berger's comments were detrimental to the interests of an impartial judiciary. It concluded that the comments were "unwise, inappropriate, and indiscreet," but that they were not sufficient to justify his removal from the bench. The committee urged "members of the judiciary [to] avoid taking part in controversial political discussions except only in respect of matters that directly affect the operation of the Courts."[21] Justice Berger, dissatisfied with this restriction on his right to free expression, resigned from the bench. "I believe a judge has the right, a duty, in fact, to speak out on an appropriate occasion on questions of human rights and fundamental freedoms," he told the press.[22]

The so-called Berger affair highlights the issue of an impartial judiciary. As legal academic Paul Weiler has noted, there are essentially two competing models for judicial recruitment, one stressing the impartiality and neutrality of the judiciary and the other stressing the prospective judge's policy-making skills, political beliefs, and past practices. Weiler wrote of the model of impartiality, currently in use within Canada:

> [T]he most necessary prerequisite for judicial office is legal training which must be accompanied by some degree of moral probity and respectability; the judge does not campaign for office on the basis of a policy program, but rather is selected for his legal ability, as adjudged primarily by his peers in the profession; once in office, the judge has tenure for life until retirement age, subject only to removal for misbehaviour: the latter ground for impeachment should never include substantive results in particular decisions.[23]

The competing model of judicial recruitment, found in the United States, dictates that a judge will not be impartial and that the political views of the prospective candidate will play a key role in determining eligibility to serve. Weiler notes:

> [T]he logic of the system demands that these (individuals) be evaluated in some manner other than an apolitical appointment process. Instead, judges should either be directly elected, or the various groups whose interests are affected by the judges' decisions should have some more formalized and legitimized form of participation in the making of the selection.[24]

Under both systems of recruitment, it appears that members of the judiciary bring certain political values to the courts, which inform the decisions they make. Legal academic Sidney Peck initially found, for example, that justices of the Supreme Court of Canada show patterns of legal decision making that either support an extended interpretation of civil liberties or oppose such an extension.[25] This research has been extended in more recent years by Ostberg and Wetstein, and demonstrates a similar point—that judges have patterns of decision making that reflect different political or ideological viewpoints, particularly in responding to contentious or pointedly ambiguous cases. The provincial governments have consistently pushed for input into Supreme Court appointments, knowing that prospective members of the Court will have markedly different views on the division of powers between the federal and provincial governments. The assumption is clear: these political views will find expression in action, specifically, within a wide range of constitutional decisions.

The assumption that the members of Canada's judiciary act as value-neutral, impartial arbiters is difficult to support in empirical terms. A claim of impartiality has rhetorical value, but it is probably more accurate to say that Canadian judges are simply able to act independently of political forces if appointed to their positions.

The question whether the judiciary, once appointed, should be able to express views on the law is at the heart of the Berger affair. Research on the issue shows that judges do, in fact, bring their economic, social, and political values to the tasks they face on the bench. Moreover, as the esteemed sociologist John Porter once observed, many members of the judiciary in Canada were formerly political elite: Cabinet ministers, members of Parliament, and provincial representatives. "They constitute what must be one of the most curious of occupational systems, one in which a person whose political role is marked by partiality, irrationality, and opinion-expressing assumes a judicial role marked by impartiality, rational inquiry, and attention to fact."[26] Thus, there is an air of disingenuousness in the assumption that the judiciary is or should be impartial. It is not clear that a judge's commitments—to specific human rights or provincial powers, for example—will limit judicial independence or create disrespect among the public toward the legal system. After all, the members of the judiciary are already chosen from a relatively restricted range of political, economic, and social opinion. Canada's federally appointed judges are chosen almost exclusively from the ranks of men and women who support the Conservative and Liberal parties. Those who seek judicial appointment typically support what may fairly be termed "status quo" or "mainstream" political views. The potential judicial appointee must, as has often been said by critics, chart a careful course between the Scylla of reformist activism and the Charybdis of bureaucratic inertia.

In its report on Justice Berger, the committee of the Canadian Judicial Council argued that once appointed, he descended to the impropriety of reformist activism:

> It is apparent that some of the Native peoples are unhappy with section 35 of the *Canadian Charter of Rights and Freedoms*. If Justice Berger should be called on to interpret that section, for example, the meaning to be given to the word "existing" in the phrase, "the existing aboriginal and treaty rights of the aboriginal peoples of Canada," would the general public have confidence now in his impartiality?[27]

The potential flaw in the council's logic may be that the question whether treaty rights exist is not only a legal question, but also a matter of political, economic, and social interpretation. The interpretation of which Aboriginal rights are existing and, correspondingly, which rights have been extinguished is not ultimately a technical matter, but a legal and a moral issue about which judges, lawyers, and other citizens are likely to disagree. To the extent that we continue to ask those who sit in judgment within our legal system to refrain from the expression of political opinion, we continue to confuse the value of judicial independence with the impossibility of judicial impartiality.

CONCLUSION: LAW, LAWYERS, AND THE PUBLIC INTEREST

The legal profession in Canada has been dramatically restructured since the Second World War, and particularly since the cultural changes of the late 1960s and early 1970s. The advent of more complex systems of criminal, family, environmental, and consumer law and regulation has increased the need for legal representation. Likewise, the growing complexity of corporate law and regulation has increased government and corporate investment in legal services.

Legal historians Stager and Arthurs argue that the legal profession in Canada is no longer a single profession but a collection of distinct groups of lawyers, lacking political, economic, or cultural cohesion:

> Lawyers who never practice in court are still capable of identifying with the profession's heroes who made their reputations as advocates, but office-bound lawyers will also develop a subculture that is largely foreign to the advocate. For example, the ritual surrounding the "closing" of certain formal transactions has no courtroom counterpart, and the terms used to describe clients, staff, and tasks vary between— and even within—the two types of practice. This accumulation of cultural differences and gradual dissolution of unifying cultural symbols are both the effects and causes of the diminishing cohesion of the profession.[28]

The road ahead for lawyers, judges, and the public is uncertain. For the most part, lawyers are, at least by their own standards, a relatively honest if often quite privileged lot. In Ontario, from 1921 to the present, fewer than 1 percent of the province's lawyers have been disciplined in any given year; in fact, the average yearly rate of discipline is close to one-tenth of 1 percent of the profession. Can we demand more of the men and women who practise law, and of those who sit in judgment of others? Probably. Can we actually achieve greater public regulation of the legal industry? Or a greater professional commitment to the elusive Holy Grail of justice, as opposed to adherence to existing political, economic, and moral structures and conventions? The answers to these questions are likely to define the landscape of legal practice for generations to come.

WEB LINKS

Canadian Law Schools

http://www.ccld-cdfdc.ca/index.php/law-schools

This excellent website created by the Council of Canadian Law Deans provides information for prospective law students. There are links to all Canadian law schools, to colleges and universities in Canada, as well as to the Law School Admission Council, which administers the LSAT.

Federation of Law Societies of Canada

http://www.flsc.ca/

Admission to the bar of each province is controlled by the provincial law societies. This is the website of the umbrella organization of the 14 law societies in Canada. The site provides information about admission to the profession generally, as well as links to member societies and their programs.

Canadian Judicial Council

http://www.cjc-ccm.gc.ca/

The Canadian Judicial Council's website provides details about the council and its work. One of its functions is the handling of complaints against federally appointed judges. The website has links to media releases and advisories concerning its investigations, as well as the reports and decisions of its committee. It also publishes frequently asked questions dealing with the procedure for making complaints against judges.

National Judicial Institute

http://www.nji-inm.ca/

This is the website of the National Judicial Institute, an educational resource for Canada's federal, provincial, and territorial judges. Its programs reflect "Canada's cultural, racial, and linguistic diversity, as well as the changing demands on the judiciary."

QUESTIONS FOR DISCUSSION

1. Do Osgoode Hall Law School's standards for admission of various categories of applicants in 2014 have sufficient breadth, or would they have more fairness if they more narrowly focused on grade point average and LSAT score?
2. Should a lawyer be disbarred if convicted of the offence of cultivation of marijuana? What about impaired driving, shoplifting, auto theft, robbery, or manslaughter? Should the standard for disbarment depend on whether the person convicted is a defence counsel, Crown counsel, or judge?
3. Should we expect impartiality of those we appoint as judges? Or should legal skills and competencies be of greater importance than the political perspectives of the potential appointee to the bench?

FURTHER READING

Canadian Bar Association. *The Future of Legal Services in Canada: Trends and Issues,* Ottawa: Canadian Bar Association, June 2013.

> This report canvasses the changing business of legal practice, concomitant changes currently going on within the industry of law in Canada, the trends of client empowerment, downward pressure on prices for some legal services, technology and innovation, legal education, regulatory issues, and prospects for the future.

Canadian Bar Association. *Touchstones for Change: Equality, Diversity and Accountability.* Ottawa: Canadian Bar Association, 1993.

> This 300-page task force report looks at the legal profession in Canada and its difficulties in establishing both equality and diversity within the practice and administration of law. The report covers the issues of barriers to entry into the profession; women in the legal profession; barriers to equality; and problems in private, government, and corporate practice, faculties of law, administrative tribunals, and the judiciary. The report concludes with more than 100 recommendations regarding equality and diversity.

Kay, F.M., and J. Brockman. "Barriers to Equality in the Canadian Legal Establishment." *Feminist Legal Studies* 8, 4 (2000): 169–98.

> This article chronicles current difficulties faced by women in achieving equality within the Canadian legal profession. The authors canvass the historical exclusion of women from the legal profession, contemporary patterns of inequality, the gap in wages, departures from practice, and difficulties in accommodating family and the workplace.

Tong, D., and W. Wesley Pue. "The Best and the Brightest? Canadian Law School Admissions." *Osgoode Hall Law Journal* 37, 4 (1999): 843–79.

> Tong and Pue examine the process of law school admission, questioning the relevance of the LSAT (law school admission test) and the reliance placed by admissions committees on the combination of grade point average and LSAT score. The authors discuss the goals of legal education and the values of diversity and social equity within the legal profession. The authors then query the extent to which current admissions policies are able to reflect these values of diversity and social equity.

NOTES

1. See Carleton University Department of Law website (www.carleton.ca/cu/ed4life/brochures/law.html).
2. H. Arthurs, *Law and Learning* (Ottawa: Supply and Services, 1984), 13.
3. Ibid.

4. See http://www.osgoode.yorku.ca/prospective-students/jd-program/applying/jd-application-procedures/first-year-program/personal-statement.

5. See http://www.osgoode.yorku.ca/prospective-students/jd-program/applying/aboriginal-applicants.

6. D. Tong and W. Wesley Pue, "The Best and the Brightest? Canadian Law School Admissions," *Osgoode Hall Law Journal* 37, 4 (1999): 843–79.

7. D.A.A. Stager and H.W. Arthurs, *Lawyers in Canada* (Toronto: University of Toronto Press, 1990), 318.

8. Ibid.

9. R.K. Wilkins, "The Person You're Supposed to Become: The Politics of the Law School Experience," *University of Toronto Faculty of Law Review* (1987): 45.

10. Ibid., 140.

11. R. Ericson and P. Baranek, *The Ordering of Justice: A Study of Accused Persons as Dependants in the Criminal Process* (Toronto: University of Toronto Press, 1982), 14.

12. Canadian Bar Association, *Touchstones for Change: Equality, Diversity and Accountability* (Ottawa: Canadian Bar Association, 1993), 74.

13. F.M. Kay and J. Brockman, "Barriers to Gender Equality in the Canadian Legal Establishment, *Feminist Legal Studies* 8 (2000): 169–198.

14. Reprinted with permission of the Canadian Bar Association.

15. Reprinted with permission of the Canadian Bar Association.

16. [1991] 3 S.C.R. 326, 68 C.C.C. (3d) 1.

17. The Law Society of Upper Canada: http://www.lsuc.on.ca/.

18. *Code of Professional Conduct,* pp. 79–80.

19. © Copyright 2011-2014 The Law Society of Upper Canada. All Rights Reserved. Reprinted with permission of The Law Society of Upper Canada.

20. T. Berger, cited in F.L. Morton, ed., *Law, Politics and the Judicial System in Canada* (Calgary: University of Calgary Press, 1984), 109.

21. "Report of the Committee of Investigation to the Canadian Judicial Council," in *Law, Politics and the Judicial System in Canada,* edited by Morton, ibid., 120.

22. Berger, in *Law, Politics and the Judicial System in Canada,* ibid., 109.

23. P. Weiler, "Two Models: Judicial Recruitment," *Canadian Bar Review* (1968): 406.

24. Ibid.

25. S.R. Peck, "Patterns in Judicial Decision Making within the Supreme Court of Canada," *Osgoode Hall Law Journal* (1969): 323. See also, more recently, C. Ostberg and M. Wetstein, *Attitudinal Decision Making in the Supreme Court of Canada* (Vancouver: UBC Press, 2007).

26. John Porter, *The Vertical Mosaic* (Toronto: University of Toronto Press, 1965), 415.

27. "Report of the Committee of Investigation to the Canadian Judicial Council," vol. III in *Law, Politics and the Judicial System in Canada,* edited by Morton.

28. Stager and Arthurs, *Lawyers in Canada.*

REFERENCES

Arthurs, H.W. *Law and Learning*. Ottawa: Supply and Services, 1984.

———. "Poor Canadian Legal Education: So Near to Wall Street, So Far from God," *Osgoode Hall Law Journal* 381, 38 (2000).

Brockman, J. "Leaving the Practice of Law: The Wherefores and the Whys." *Alberta Law Review* 32, 1 (1994): 116–76.

Colvin, E. "The Executive and the Independence of the Judiciary." *Provincial Judges' Journal* 11 (1987): 229.

Dickson, B. "Legal Education." *Canadian Bar Review* 64 (1986): 374.

Erickson, P.G. "Legalistic and Traditional Role Expectations for Defence Counsel in Juvenile Court." *Canadian Journal of Criminology and Corrections* 17 (1975): 78.

Ericson, R., and P. Baranek. *The Ordering of Justice: A Study of Accused Persons as Dependants in the Criminal Process*. Toronto: University of Toronto Press, 1982.

Finlayson, G.D. "Self-Government of the Legal Profession—Can It Continue?" *Advocates Society Journal* 4 (1985): 1.

Gall, G. *The Canadian Legal System*. 3rd ed. Toronto: Carswell, 1990, Chapter 9.

Johnston, D.L. "Role of the Lawyer in Our Society." *Gazette* 13 (1979): 119.

Laskin, B. "The Lawyer's Responsibility in the Supervision of the Legal Order." *Gazette* 4 (1970): 210.

LeDain, G. "The Quest for Justice: The Role of the Profession." *University of New Brunswick Law Journal* 19 (1969). 18.

Martin, G.A. "The Role and the Responsibility of the Defence Advocate." *Criminal Law Quarterly* 12 (1970): 376.

Morton, F.L., ed. *Law, Politics and the Judicial Process in Canada*. Calgary: University of Calgary Press, 1989.

Peck, S.R. "Patterns in Judicial Decision Making within the Supreme Court of Canada." *Osgoode Hall Law Journal* (1969): 323.

Pirie, A.J. "The Lawyer as Mediator: Professional Responsibility Problems or Profession Problems?" *Canadian Bar Review* 63 (1985): 378.

Stager, D.A.A., and H.W. Arthurs. *Lawyers in Canada*. Toronto: University of Toronto Press, 1990.

Starr, G., L. Fisher, and L. Katz. "By Choice, by Chance, by Birthright: The First Three Years of an Admissions Policy." In *Essays on Legal Education,* edited by N. Gold. Toronto: Butterworths, 1982.

Taman, L., and F. Zemans. "The Future of Legal Services." *Canadian Bar Review* 5 (1973): 32.

Tong, D., and W. Wesley Pue. "The Best and the Brightest? Canadian Law School Admissions." *Osgoode Hall Law Journal* 37, 4 (1999): 843–79.

Weiler, P. "Two Models: Judicial Recruitment." *Canadian Bar Review* (1968).

Wilkins, R.K. "The Person You're Supposed to Become: The Politics of the Law School Experience." *University of Toronto Faculty of Law Review* 45 (1987): 98.

PART 3
Substantive Law

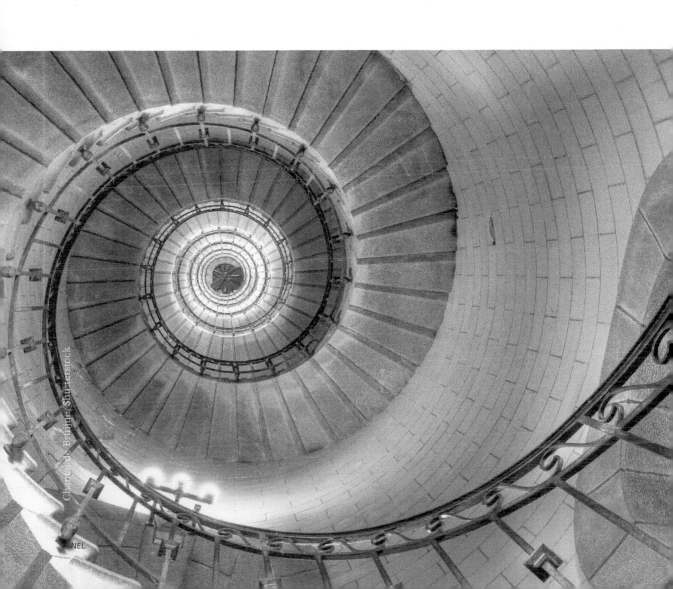

CHAPTER 7

TORTS OF INTENTION AND NEGLIGENCE: PRIVATE LAW, PUBLIC INTEREST

In summer time, village cricket is the delight of everyone. Nearly every village has its own cricket field where the young men play and old men watch. In the village of Lintz in County Durham, they have their own ground, where they have played these last 70 years. They tend it well. The wicket area is well rolled and mown. The outfield is kept short. It has a good clubhouse for the players and seats for the onlookers. The village team plays there on Saturdays and Sundays. They belong to a league, competing with the neighbouring villages. On other evenings after work, they practise while the light lasts. Yet now after these 70 years, a judge of the High Court has ordered that they must not play there any more. He has issued an injunction to stop them.

He has done it at the instance of a newcomer (the plaintiff) who is no lover of cricket. This newcomer has built, or has had built for him, a house on the edge of the cricket ground, which four years ago was a field where cattle grazed. The animals did not mind the cricket. But now this adjoining field has been turned into a housing estate. The newcomer bought one of the houses on the edge of the cricket ground. No doubt the open space was a selling point. Now he complains that when a batsman hits a six, the ball has been known to land in his garden or near his house. His wife has got so upset about it that they always go out at weekends. They do not go into the garden when cricket is being played. They say that this is intolerable. So they asked the judge to stop the cricket being played. And the judge, much against his will, has felt that he must order the cricket to be stopped with the consequence, I suppose, that the Lintz Cricket Club will disappear. The cricket ground will be turned to some other use. I expect for more houses or a factory. The young men will turn to other things instead of cricket. The whole village will be much the poorer. And all this because of a newcomer who has just bought a house there next to the cricket ground.

(Lord Denning, *Miller v. Jackson*)

The situation described above is in the realm of **torts**, the remedying of private wrongs. The word "tort" is derived from Latin *tortus*: "crooked" or "wrong." In the contemporary world, "tort" is defined by *The Oxford Reference Dictionary* as "a breach of a legal duty, other than under contract, with liability for damages."* In Anglo-Saxon England, there was no clear distinction between a crime and a tort. The offending individual within a given clan or group would be required to compensate the offended

---

*The Oxford Reference Dictionary, edited by Joyce M. Hawkins, Clarendon Press, Oxford, 1986, Pg. 868.

clan or group for damages, and to pay the king some sum of money for breaching the peace. With the centralization of political authority, taken first by the monarchy and later by elected governments, the separation between tort and crime became significant. From the eleventh century onward, tort and crime were distinguished in Britain.

CRIME AND TORT: DISTINCTIONS AND SIMILARITIES

We now define a crime as a public wrong, an offence against the public interest. We define a tort as a private wrong, an offence against the private interest of an individual, corporation, or government. At first glance, however, tort and crime seem easily equated. If you are walking down the street and you are assaulted by a man with a baseball bat, the assault is both a crime and a tort. The man is liable to be charged by the police for his violation of the assault provisions of the *Criminal Code*. But you may also pursue a civil claim in tort for this assault, going to court to recover damages from the man for his intentional infliction of physical harm. The object of the tort system is to compensate victims of either intentional acts or negligent acts. There is no guilt in tort, only a testing of individual or collective liability. Criminal law, on the other hand, does not exist to compensate victims of various prohibited acts, but to punish wrongdoers and, in so doing, protect the general community (i.e., the country).

The purposes and scope of criminal law are broader than those of tort law. Criminal law is designed to respond to infringements against the public interest; sanctions are imposed in order to deter specific offenders from further crime, as well as to deter the general public from the commission of prohibited acts. Criminal law is also designed to rehabilitate offenders, so that they may be usefully reintegrated into the community. Its final purpose, independent of the effectiveness of deterrence or rehabilitation, is to express moral condemnation of proscribed behaviours.

Perhaps the case that best illustrates the distinction between criminal law conviction and tort liability is that of O.J. Simpson, the former football star who was charged with the murder of his wife, Nicole Brown, and her friend, Ron Goldman. Simpson was found not guilty after a long criminal trial; but when the Goldman and Brown families went to civil court to claim damages from Simpson for the wrongful deaths of their children, they were successful. The criminal court jury concluded that the public offence of murder had not been proven beyond a reasonable doubt; but when the case was heard as a private matter (between Simpson and the families of his victims), a civil jury determined that it was more probable than not that Mr. Simpson was responsible for these deaths. On the basis of the jury's finding of tortious liability, substantial damages were ordered to be paid by Simpson to the Goldmans and the Browns.

Tort law exists only to compensate for private wrongs. An action may be brought in either **intentional tort**—in response to the intentional infliction of mental or physical harm to persons or property—or, more commonly, in **negligence**—in response to the failure of an individual or collectivity to conform to a standard of reasonable care.

Negligence may be premised upon doing something that a **reasonable person** would not be expected to do, or upon a failure or omission to do something that a reasonable person would be expected to do. In *Miller v. Jackson*, the famous British case from which the quotation at the start of the chapter was taken, the **plaintiffs** alleged negligence on the part of the cricketers—that is, they claimed the cricketers were doing something that a reasonable person would not be expected to do.[1]

The standards of tort liability and criminal conviction are very different in another important respect. Tort liability is premised upon meeting a balance of probabilities test, whereas criminal conviction demands proof of the offence beyond a reasonable doubt. Hence, it is much less difficult to find liability in tort; the plaintiff has only to make a case that is more probable than not.

Finally, criminal law premises criminal conviction upon a coincidence of *mens rea* and *actus reus*: an evil mind and an evil act. In order to be found guilty of a crime, an accused must have both committed the evil act and possessed an evil intention. In other words, the accused must be aware of, or able to appreciate, his or her responsibility for the crime. For example, an accused in possession of either stolen property or an illegal drug must have knowledge of possession—an evil intention. A person who has committed the evil act of murder must be able to appreciate what he or she has done in order to be found criminally culpable. Without awareness of this kind, a verdict of not criminally responsible by reason of mental disorder might result (section 16 of the *Criminal Code*). In tort law, particularly in the realm of negligence, there is no requirement of *mens rea*—evil intention.

Despite these important differences between criminal and tort law, there are areas in which they coincide, as noted earlier. An assault may be both a crime and an intentional tort, thereby giving rise to both criminal court proceedings and a civil tort action against the aggressor in order to recover damages for the intentional infliction of physical harm. In practice, however, very few victims of assault commence tort actions against their attackers, typically because the defendant in such cases has virtually no financial resources. Justice as a private matter can often be extracted only from the wealthy. In an attempt to remedy this defect, most provinces have created criminal injury compensation boards or tribunals; these agencies make financial awards, on behalf of the state, to victims of violent crime.

There is one other coincidence of tort law and criminal law: the **Criminal Code**[2] defines certain kinds of negligence as criminal. Sections 219 and 220 of the *Code* create offences of criminal negligence and criminal negligence causing death.

219. (1) *Every one is criminally negligent who*

    (a) *in doing anything, or*

    (b) *in omitting to anything that it is his duty to do,*

    (c) *shows wanton or reckless disregard for the lives or safety of other persons.*

(2) *For the purposes of this section, "duty" means a duty imposed by law.*

220. *Every one who by criminal negligence causes death to another person is guilty of an indictable offence and is liable to imprisonment for life.*

This apparent overlap in the jurisdictions of tort and crime notwithstanding, the purposes of tort law remain both quite distinct from and more limited than those of criminal law. As stated previously, tort law exists primarily to compensate those who have been wronged either by the intentional infliction of harm or by acts of negligence. While it is often argued that a complementary function of tort law is to impose **punitive damages** in order to deter negligent conduct and the intentional infliction of harm, this is far from a universally accepted principle. According to this view, the court's adjudication and ultimate award to a wronged plaintiff can have what has been termed an "appeasement" or "denunciation" function, serving simultaneously to condemn publicly the conduct of the defendant and to vindicate the rights of the plaintiff.[3]

THE ROLE OF DETERRENCE AND PUNITIVE DAMAGES IN TORT

There can be difficulties with the punitive-deterrence and appeasement or denunciation functions of tort law. First, an emphasis on punitive damages in tort may duplicate the existing imposition of sanctions by the criminal court system, potentially imposing two sets of punishment upon an accused. Second, because the overwhelming majority of tort actions are to be found in the realm of negligence, specifically, in the realm of non-criminal negligence, the goals of punishment and denunciation are more difficult to justify. At the same time, however, particularly in circumstances where a criminal trial is not a possibility, Canadian courts have held that the pursuit of principles such as deterrence and punishment is a reasonable objective in tort law.

Consider the Supreme Court of Canada's decision in 2002 in *Whiten v. Pilot Insurance*. In this particular instance the insurance company's conduct raised the issue of punitive damages. The facts, as set out by Justice Binnie:

The appellant, Daphne Whiten, bought her home in Haliburton County, Ontario, in 1985. Just after midnight on January 18, 1994, when she and her husband Keith were getting ready to go to bed, they discovered a fire in the addition to their house. They and their daughter, who had also been upstairs, fled the house wearing only their night clothes. It was minus 18 degrees Celsius. Mr. Whiten gave his slippers to his daughter to go for help and suffered serious frostbite to his feet for which he was hospitalized. He was thereafter confined to a wheelchair for a period of time. The fire totally destroyed the Whitens' home and its contents, including their few valuable antiques and many items of sentimental value and their three cats.

The appellant was able to rent a small winterized cottage nearby for $650 per month. Pilot made a single $5,000 payment for living expenses and covered the rent for a couple of months or so, then cut off the rent without telling the family, and thereafter pursued a hostile and confrontational policy which the jury must have concluded was calculated to force the appellant (whose family was in very poor financial shape) to settle her claim at substantially less than its fair value. The allegation that the family had torched its own home was contradicted by the local fire chief, the respondent's own expert investigator, and its initial expert, all of whom said there was no evidence whatsoever of arson. The respondent's position, based on wishful thinking, was wholly discredited at trial. Pilot's appellate counsel conceded here and in the Ontario Court of Appeal that there was no air of reality to the allegation of arson.

Justice Binnie noted:

This case raises once again the spectre of uncontrolled and uncontrollable awards of punitive damages in civil actions. The jury was clearly outraged by the high-handed tactics employed by the respondent, Pilot Insurance Company, following its unjustified refusal to pay the appellant's claim under a fire insurance policy (ultimately quantified at approximately $345,000). Pilot forced an eight-week trial on an allegation of arson that the jury obviously considered trumped up. It forced her to put at risk her only remaining asset (the insurance claim) plus approximately $320,000 in legal costs that she did not have. The denial of the claim was designed to force her to make an unfair settlement for less than she was entitled to. The conduct was planned and deliberate and continued for over two years, while the financial situation of the appellant grew increasingly desperate. Evidently concluding that the arson defence from the outset was unsustainable and made in bad faith, the jury added an award of punitive damages of $1 million, in effect providing the appellant with a "windfall" that added something less than treble damages to her actual out-of-pocket loss. The respondent argues that the award of punitive damages is itself outrageous.

Binnie concludes:

Compensatory damages also punish. In many cases they will be all the "punishment" required. To the extent a defendant has suffered other retribution, denunciation or deterrence, either civil or criminal, for the misconduct in question, the need for additional punishment in the case before the court is lessened and may be eliminated. In Canada, unlike some other common law jurisdictions, such "other" punishment is relevant but it is not necessarily a bar to the award of punitive damages. The prescribed fine, for example, may be disproportionately small to the level of outrage the jury wishes to express. The misconduct in question may be broader than the misconduct proven in evidence in the criminal or regulatory proceeding. The legislative judgment fixing the amount of the potential fine may be based on policy considerations other than pure punishment. The key point is that punitive damages are awarded "if, but only if" all other penalties have been taken into account and found to be inadequate to accomplish the objectives of retribution, deterrence, and denunciation. The intervener, the Insurance Council of Canada, argues that the discipline of insurance companies should be left to the regulator. Nothing in the appeal record indicates that the Registrar of Insurance (now the Superintendent of Financial Services) took an interest in this case prior to the jury's unexpectedly high award of punitive damages....

The respondent and its supporting intervener suggest that an award of $1 million in punitive damages is out of line because compensatory damages were ultimately assessed only at about $345,000. The result, they argue, is an improper ratio. It is apparent from what has already been said, however, that proportionality is a much broader concept than the simple relationship between punitive damages and compensatory damages. That relationship, moreover, is not even the most relevant because it puts the focus on the plaintiff's loss rather than where it should be, on the defendant's misconduct. If a ratio is to be used what should the ratio measure? The fact that compensatory damages are quantified in dollars and cents is temptingly useful, but wholly inadequate, for example, in a case where outrageous misconduct has fortuitously (and fortunately) resulted in a small financial loss. Potential, as well as actual, harm is a reasonable measure of misconduct, and so are the other factors, already mentioned, such as motive, planning, vulnerability, abuse of dominance, other fines or penalties, and so on. None of these features are captured by the ratio of punitive damages to compensatory damages. Adoption of such a ratio, while easy to supervise, would do a disservice to the unavoidable complexity of the analysis. It would in fact undermine the nuanced principles on which the concept of punitive damages has been justified. There is no doubt at all that evaluation of outrageous conduct in terms of dollars and cents is a difficult and imprecise task, but so is evaluating the worth of a cracked skull, a lost business opportunity or a shattered reputation. Yet all these things are done every day in the courts in the calculation of compensatory damages without resort to formulae or arbitrary rules such as ratios.

I would not have awarded $1 million in punitive damages in this case but in my judgment the award is within the rational limits within which a jury must be allowed to operate. The award was not so disproportionate as to exceed the bounds of rationality. It did not overshoot its purpose. I have already outlined the reasons why I believe this to be the case.

And now, back to the cricketers. What of their plight in *Miller v. Jackson?* Lord Denning concluded:

This case is new. It should be approached on principles applicable to modern conditions. There is a contest here between the interest of the public at large and the interest of a private individual. The public interest lies in protecting the environment by preserving our playing fields in the face of mounting development, and by enabling our youth to enjoy all the benefits of outdoor games, such as cricket and football. The private interest lies in securing the privacy of his home and garden without intrusion or interference by anyone. In deciding between these two conflicting interests, it must be remembered that it is not a question of damages. If by a million-to-one chance a cricket ball does go out of the ground and causes damage, the cricket club will pay. There is no difficulty on that score. Nor is it a question of an injunction. And in our law, you will find it repeatedly affirmed that an injunction is a discretionary remedy. In a new situation like this, we have to think afresh as to how discretion should be exercised. On the one hand, Mrs. Miller is a very sensitive lady who has worked herself up into such a state that she exclaimed to the judge:

I just want to be allowed to live in peace. Have we got to wait until someone is killed before anything can be done?

If she feels like that about it, it is quite plain that, for peace in the future, one or other has to move. Either the cricket club has to move, but goodness knows where. I do not suppose for a moment there is any field in Lintz to which they could move. Or Mrs. Miller must move elsewhere. As between their conflicting interests, I am of opinion that the public interest should prevail over the private interest. The cricket club should not be driven out. In my opinion, the right exercise of discretion is to refuse an injunction; and, of course, to refuse damages in lieu of an injunction. Likewise as to the claim for past damages. The club was entitled to use this ground for cricket in the accustomed way. It was not a nuisance, nor was it negligence of them so to run it. Nor was the batsman negligent when he hit the ball for six. All were doing simply what they were entitled to do. So if the club had put it to the test, I would have dismissed the claim for damages also. But as the club very fairly says that they are willing to pay for any damage, I am content that there should be an award of 400 pounds to cover any past or future damage.

Lord Denning's decision is noteworthy in that it pits the private interests of tort law against more general principles of public policy—as did *Whiten v. Pilot Insurance.* Although decisions in tort involve the resolution of the competing claims of private interests (in this case, the Lintz Cricket Club and the Millers), they may also involve the imposition of an overriding public interest on the decision-making process.

How might Lord Denning's decision have changed with changes in circumstances? What if the Millers' suit against the cricket club had resulted from a ball hit through the window, crashing into the side of Mrs. Miller's face, breaking her jaw, and knocking out her teeth? Alternatively, what if a member of the Lintz Cricket Club had intentionally thrown a cricket ball through the window, frustrated with the Millers' opposition to the use of the cricket ground?

In the first instance of a claim in negligence, it is not clear, given Lord Denning's logic, that the outcome would have been any different. The severity of Mrs. Miller's injuries would have been acknowledged as regrettable, but Lord Denning's principle governing *Miller v. Jackson* would still hold: "As between their conflicting interests, I am of opinion that the public interest should prevail over the private interest. The cricket club should not be driven out. In my opinion, the right exercise of discretion is to refuse an injunction; and, of course, to refuse damages in lieu of an injunction."

What about the second hypothetical situation—what if injuries to Mrs. Miller had resulted from an intentional tort, such as a ball tossed through the window while she was walking in front of it? Could the Lintz Cricket Club continue to claim that there should be no liability? Might criminal charges be warranted? The simple answer is that an intentional tort of this kind would attract liability, possibly only to the individual responsible, and, more remotely, to the Lintz Cricket Club.

INTENTIONAL INFLICTION OF MENTAL OR PHYSICAL HARM: THE SCOPE OF LIABILITY

A wide range of circumstances exist—assault and battery, false imprisonment, malicious prosecution, and the intentional infliction of mental harm—where **liability** in tort can flow from intentional conduct. Two key questions arise in these cases: Is the standard for liability similar to the standard imposed in instances of negligence? Is it similar to the standard imposed for conviction in criminal cases?

THE STANDARD IN INTENTIONAL CONDUCT VERSUS THE STANDARD IN NEGLIGENCE

Consider, with respect to the first question above (Is the standard for liability similar to the standard imposed in instances of negligence?), the case of *Bettel v. Yim.*

Borins, County Court Judge: The events giving rise to this action took place on May 22, 1976, in a variety store owned and operated by the defendant, Ki Yim, situated in a small commercial plaza located in Metropolitan Toronto....

The defendant testified that the plaintiff, together with six or seven other boys, entered the store and went to the area of the pinball machines. Some of the boys were playing with a toy football and toy guns and the defendant told them to leave his store. Half of the boys, including the plaintiff, left and went outside. The defendant saw the plaintiff lighting matches and throwing them into the store. On the first occasion, the plaintiff entered the store and retrieved a burning match. The second match that was thrown into the store burned itself out. Then the plaintiff re-entered the store, proceeded toward the pinball machines and said, "What's the smell?" The defendant smelled nothing, but after 20 or 30 seconds, he saw flames coming from the bag of charcoal and proceeded to remove the bag from the store, unassisted by the plaintiff, who remained inside. The defendant did not see who had thrown the match which started the fire.

As the defendant returned to the store, he saw the plaintiff walking toward the door. He grabbed the plaintiff by the arm as he did not want the plaintiff to leave. The plaintiff denied that he set the fire. The plaintiff did not try to leave. He stood where he was. Because the plaintiff denied setting the fire, the defendant grabbed him firmly by the collar with both hands and began shaking him. His purpose in doing so was to obtain a confession from the plaintiff before he called the police. The plaintiff's constant denials had made the defendant unhappy. He shook the plaintiff two or three times and then his head came down and struck the plaintiff's nose. He relaxed his hold on the plaintiff, who fell to the ground. The defendant obtained some kleenex for the plaintiff, who was bleeding from the nose, and helped him to his feet. The defendant then telephoned the police.

In explaining the incident, the defendant said: "I shook him maybe three times and my head and his nose accidentally hit; I didn't intend to hit him." In cross-examination, he stated that he did not mean to hit the plaintiff with his head and that is why he said it was an accident....

The Law

The plaintiff has framed his action in assault. Properly speaking, the action should have been framed in battery, which is the intentional infliction upon the body of another of a harmful or offensive contact. However, in Canada, it would appear that the distinction between assault and battery has been blurred and when one speaks of an assault, it may include a battery.... [Note to students: Assault has occurred when there is a reasonable apprehension of bodily harm; battery has occurred when bodily harm is actually inflicted.]

On the defendant's evidence, his act in grabbing the plaintiff with both his hands and shaking him constituted the intentional tort of battery. It is obvious that he desired to bring about an offensive or harmful contact with the plaintiff for the purpose of extracting a confession from him. Viewed as such, the defendant's own evidence proves, rather than disproves, the element of intent insofar as this aspect of his physical contact with the plaintiff is concerned. Indeed, the defendant's admitted purpose in grabbing and shaking the plaintiff does not fit into any of the accepted defences to the tort of battery—consent, self-defence, defence of property, necessity, and legal authority....

That there is no liability for accidental harm is central to the submission of defence counsel who argues that the shaking of the plaintiff by the defendant and the striking of the plaintiff by the defendant's head must be regarded as separate and distinct incidents. While he concedes that the defendant intentionally grabbed and shook the plaintiff, he submits that the contact with the head was unintentional. I have, of course, accepted the defendant's evidence in this regard. This, in my view, gives rise to the important question: Can an intentional wrongdoer be held liable for consequences which he did not intend? Another way of stating the problem is to ask whether the doctrine of foreseeability as found in the law of negligence is applicable to the law of intentional torts. Should an intentional wrongdoer be liable only for the reasonably foreseeable consequences of his intentional application of force, or should he bear responsibility for all the consequences which flow from his intentional act?...

It is my respectful view that the weight of opinion is that the concept of foreseeability as defined by the law of negligence is a concept that ought not to be imported into the field of intentional torts.... In the law of intentional torts, it is the dignitary interest, the right of the plaintiff to insist that the defendant keep his hands to himself, that the law has for centuries sought to protect. In doing so, the morality of the defendant's conduct, characterized as "unlawful", has predominated the thinking of the Courts and is reflected in academic discussion. The logical test is whether the defendant was guilty of deliberate, intentional, and unlawful violence or threats of violence. If he was, and a more serious harm befalls the plaintiff than was intended by the defendant, the defendant, and not the innocent plaintiff, must bear the responsibility for the unintended result. If physical contact was intended, the fact that its magnitude exceeded all reasonable or intended expectations, should make no difference. To hold otherwise, in my opinion, would unduly narrow recovery where one deliberately invades the bodily interest of another with the result that the totally innocent plaintiff would be deprived of full recovery for the totality of the injuries suffered as a result of the deliberate invasion of his bodily interests.

     To import negligence concepts into the field of intentional torts would be to ignore the essential difference between the intentional infliction of harm and the unintentional infliction of harm resulting from a failure to adhere to a reasonable standard of care, and would result in bonusing the deliberate wrongdoer who strikes the plaintiff more forcefully than intended.[4]

The decision of Judge Borins in this case draws a line between a standard to be employed with torts of negligence and a standard to be employed with intentional torts. His argument is that the concept of foreseeability, while integral to a tort of negligence, would unfairly diminish the prospects for a plaintiff's recovery in cases involving an intentional tort. With intentional torts, it is sufficient that the **defendant** intended harm, and it is no answer to claim that some amount of the damage was not foreseeable. In the *Bettel v. Yim* case, the fact that Yim did not intend to strike Bettel's nose with his head, or could not foresee that he would do so, does not limit his liability for the assault.

DEFENCES TO INTENTIONAL TORT

In the *Bettel v. Yim* case, the Court mentioned the defences to claims of damages from intentional torts: consent, self-defence, defence of property, necessity, and legal authority. Examples of these defences are relatively easy to imagine. A police officer's use of force might, if undertaken by a citizen, constitute a tortious act; the police officer could be said to have acted under legal authority. Similarly, a person might intrude upon or damage another person or another person's property in order to avoid a physically threatening event; the defence would be necessity.

    Self-defence is almost self-explanatory. If one harms another in defence of oneself, no liability arises. However, the extent and appropriateness of the response to a threat may give rise to liability.

    Consent to an intentional tort can also apply as a defence, either in relation to sexual contacts or in relation to sporting contests in which injuries and damages are sustained. Consent is especially important in the context of sexual assault. Unlike most other assaults, consent is relatively common in sexual interactions. While it is virtually unthinkable for individuals to consent to being punched, kicked, stabbed, or shot, consent to sexual contact is considerably more common than sexual contact without consent. In suits to recover damages for sexual assault, the most common defence is that the person, typically the woman, consented to sexual activity. Therefore, the factual issue of consent is usually central to allegations of sexual assault.

Similarly, contact sports permit assaults that would otherwise be actionable. In boxing, football, hockey, and the like, it is fair to say that the participants consent to some forms of assault; these normally tortious acts fall within the rules of the game. In boxing, for example, the object of the game is to punch one's opponent into unconsciousness. In football and hockey, assaults that leave an individual with a concussion or a broken leg can be well within the rules of the game. Nonetheless, some assaults in sport may be outside the rules, leading to criminal charges and/or claims in tort. The task of determining tortious liability in such circumstances is necessarily focused on the specifics of what a person consents to when he or she steps onto the football field or hockey rink or into the boxing ring. While it is clear that assault with a knife would fall outside the rules of all these sports and hence be actionable, liability for inflicting an injury immediately after the conclusion of the match or liability for using a hockey stick as a weapon during the course of the game is much less certain.

NEGLIGENCE AND THE STANDARD OF THE REASONABLE PERSON

We noted at the outset of this chapter that the most common form of claim in tort is a claim in negligence. Claims in negligence began to appear in England at the time of the Industrial Revolution, placing a duty of care upon citizens within certain relationships. In 1856, in the case of *Blyth v. Birmingham Water Works,* the Court of Exchequer defined negligence in the following manner: "Negligence is the omission to do something which a reasonable man, guided upon those considerations which ordinarily regulate the conduct of human affairs, would do, or doing something which a prudent and reasonable man would not do."[5] (The gender-specific nature of reasonableness is, of course, a reflection of the era in which this judgment was written. Women had yet to secure the right to vote; the question of their reasonableness in relation to negligence was moot.)

In 1932, in the landmark negligence case of *Donoghue v. Stevenson*, Lord Atkin further defined the concept.

> The rule that you are to love your neighbour becomes in law, you must not injure your neighbour, and the lawyer's question, Who is my neighbour? receives a restricted

reply. You must take reasonable care to avoid acts or omissions which you can reasonably foresee would be likely to injure your neighbour. Who, then, in law is my neighbour? The answer seems to be persons who are so closely and directly affected by my act that I ought reasonably to have them in contemplation as being so affected when I am directing my mind to the acts or omissions which are called in question.[6]

Donoghue v. Stevenson was a landmark case because of its extension of the doctrine of negligence to the products of manufacturers. The plaintiff, Donoghue, brought an action to recover damages from the manufacturer of a bottle of ginger beer. In the process of consuming part of a bottle of the defendant's ginger beer, the plaintiff had discovered the decomposing remains of a snail. This discovery caused the plaintiff to suffer shock and severe gastroenteritis. She argued that the defendant manufacturer should have had a system of inspection sufficient to prevent snails and other contaminants from getting into ginger beer bottles. Britain's House of Lords allowed the plaintiff's appeal, supporting their decision with the following logic:

Lord Atkin: The question is whether the manufacturer of an article of drink sold by him to a distributor in circumstances which prevent the distributor or the ultimate purchaser or consumer from discovering by inspection any defect is under any legal duty to the ultimate purchaser or consumer to take reasonable care that the article is free from defect likely to cause injury to health....

My Lords, if your Lordships accept the view that this pleading discloses a relevant cause of action, you will be affirming the proposition that by Scots and English law alike, a manufacturer of products, which he sells in such a form as to show that he intends them to reach the ultimate consumer in the form in which they left him with no reasonable possibility of intermediate examination, and with the knowledge that the absence of reasonable care in the preparation or putting up of the products will result in an injury to the consumer's life or property, owes a duty to the consumer to take that reasonable care.

It is a proposition which I venture to say no one in Scotland or England who was not a lawyer would for one moment doubt. It will be an advantage to make it clear that the law in this matter, as in most others, is in accordance with sound common sense. I think that this appeal should be allowed.

Lord Macmillan: ... [A]s I have pointed out, it is not enough to prove the respondent to be careless in his process of manufacture. The question is, Does he owe a duty to take care, and to whom does he owe that duty?

Now I have no hesitation in affirming that a person who for gain engages in the business of manufacturing articles of food and drink intended for consumption by members of the public in the form in which he issues them is under a duty to take care in the manufacture of these articles. That duty, in my opinion, he owes to those whom he intends to consume his products. He manufactures his commodities for human consumption; he intends and contemplates that they shall be consumed....

It must always be a question of circumstances whether the carelessness amounts to negligence, and whether the injury is not too remote from the carelessness. I can readily conceive that where a manufacturer has parted with his produce and it has passed into other hands, it may well be exposed to vicissitudes which may render it defective or noxious, for which the manufacturer could not in any view be held to be to blame. It may be a good general rule to regard responsibility as ceasing when control ceases. So, also, where between the manufacturer and the user there is interposed a party who has the means and opportunity of examining the manufacturer's product before he reissues it to the actual user. But where, as in the present case, the article of consumption is so prepared as to be intended to reach the consumer in the condition in which it leaves the manufacturer, and the manufacturer takes steps to ensure this by sealing or otherwise closing the container so that the contents cannot be tampered with, I regard his control as remaining effective until the article reaches the consumer and the container is opened by him. The intervention of any exterior agency is intended to be excluded and was in fact in the present case excluded.

The test of product liability for negligence, as set out by Lord Atkin and Lord Macmillan, focuses on the extent to which the product in question can be altered after leaving the manufacturer. If it is possible that individuals other than the manufacturer could affect the form or safety of the product before it reaches the consumer, the manufacturer's liability may be limited or terminated.

In contemporary cases of product liability, the legal issues in dispute have been compounded. The courts not only must sort out responsibility for a plaintiff's loss, but also must determine whether sufficient information has been provided to potential consumers, asking, in the specific case, whether adequate warnings and instructions were given to the plaintiff.

Consider this recent 2011 decision of the B.C. Court of Appeal regarding the safety of a hockey helmet manufactured by Bauer Hockey Corporation; the following is an excerpt from the reasons for judgment of Madam Justice Levine, concurred in by Mr. Justice Tysoe and Madam Justice Bennett.[7]

Justice Levine: Darren More suffered a serious head injury in a hockey game in 2004, when he was 17 years old. He was wearing a hockey helmet designed and manufactured by Bauer Hockey Corp. and certified to the minimum standards of the Canadian Standards Association (CSA). Darren More and his parents claimed Bauer was negligent in the design and manufacture of the helmet he wore, and CSA was negligent in failing to develop and adopt a more rigorous standard for hockey helmets. The trial judge dismissed these claims.

The trial judge dealt with the issue of causation:

By alleging either negligent misrepresentation or failure to warn, the plaintiffs are saying that the CSA did not provide enough information for the plaintiffs to make an informed choice of whether to use the helmet. They say that the CSA knew that users of CSA certified helmets would assume that the certification label would apply to all kinds of injuries, would rely on CSA certification as a representation regarding safety, and that users would not understand the limited nature of CSA testing that underlies the certification labels.

The plaintiffs focus solely on the small CSA label on the helmet that simply says "Certified Hockey Helmet". They ignore the larger label also on the helmet that states severe head and brain injuries may occur despite wearing the helmet. Considering the effect of the smaller CSA sticker without taking the larger sticker into account is misleading.

The plaintiffs also ignore the owner's information that was originally attached to the chin strap of the Bauer helmet. The owner's information had a warning which included the following statement: "This helmet affords no protection from neck, spinal, or certain types of brain injuries including those that may be caused by rotational forces. Severe head, brain, and spinal injuries including paralysis or death may occur despite using this helmet." The box that the helmet originally came in had a similar warning on it. It is unclear on the evidence whether CSA mandated these warnings, or whether Bauer provided them of their own volition.

Taking both warnings on the helmet together, there is insufficient evidence for a finding of negligent misrepresentation because the labels were not misleading and Darren did not rely on them in any event. As stated in *Queen v. Cognos,* 1993 CanLII 146 (SCC), [1993] 1 S.C.R. 87, both of these preconditions must be present to ground a finding of negligent misrepresentation.

The CSA labels on the helmet are in no way misleading. The larger label clearly states that severe brain injuries may occur despite wearing the helmet. The label informs the prospective user that even if they wore the helmet they may suffer injury.

The same reasoning applies to the claim that the CSA breached its duty to warn. In *Buchan v. Ortho Pharmaceutical (Canada) Ltd.* 1986 CanLII 114 (ON CA), (1986), 54 O.R. (2d) 92 (C.A.), Robins J. aptly describes the duty to warn at paras. 16–18:

As a matter of common law, it is well settled that a manufacturer of a product has a duty to warn consumers of dangers inherent in the use of its product of which it knows or has reason to know. The guiding principle of liability underlying the present law of products liability in this country was formulated by Lord Atkin in his classic statement in M'Alister (or Donoghue) v. Stevenson, *[1932] A.C. 562 at p. 599 (H.L.):*

… a manufacturer of products, which he sells in such a form as to show that he intends them to reach the ultimate consumer in the form in which they left him with no reasonable

possibility of intermediate examination, and with the knowledge that the absence of reasonable care in the preparation or putting up of the products will result in an injury to the consumer's life or property, owes a duty to the consumer to take that reasonable care.

This statement has been the source of subsequent developments in products liability law based on negligence. The rationale is that one who brings himself into a relation with others through an activity which foreseeably exposes them to danger if proper care is not observed must exercise reasonable care to safeguard them from that danger. It can now be taken as a legal truism that the duty of reasonable care which lies at the foundation of the law of negligence commonly comprehends a duty to warn of danger, the breach of which will, when it is the cause of injury, give rise to liability: see, generally, Fleming, The Law of Torts, *6th ed. (1983), at p. 459 ff., and Linden,* Canadian Tort Law, *3rd ed. (1982), at p. 563 ff.*

Once a duty to warn is recognized, it is manifest that the warning must be adequate. It should be communicated clearly and understandably in a manner calculated to inform the user of the nature of the risk and the extent of the danger; it should be in terms commensurate with the gravity of the potential hazard, and it should not be neutralized or negated by collateral efforts on the part of the manufacturer. The nature and extent of any given warning will depend on what is reasonable having regard to all the facts and circumstances relevant to the product in question.

The CSA had a duty to warn the public of the amount of protection a CSA helmet provides. As discussed earlier, the CSA certifies helmets for public use. Consumers cannot buy a hockey helmet in Canada unless the CSA certifies it. Therefore, the CSA must exercise reasonable care to safeguard users of certified helmets by informing them that injury can occur while playing hockey despite wearing a certified helmet.

The question then is whether the CSA's warning was adequate. The warning does not mention whether the helmet protects from linear or rotational injuries or both. Such wording is unnecessary in this situation. While there are situations where more detailed warnings are necessary, adding technical terms such as "rotational" or "linear" to the CSA warning adds little to a typical consumer's understanding of the type of injury the helmet protects against. The warning on the helmet is clear that serious injury may occur despite wearing the helmet.

Darren also had other warnings of the type of injuries one could sustain while wearing a helmet and chose to continue playing hockey regardless of those warnings. One was attached to the helmet's chin strap when he bought it and clearly stated the helmet did not provide protection from rotational injuries.

Equally important, before his accident Darren was aware that people suffer head injuries while playing hockey despite wearing the CSA approved helmets. Darren himself suffered two concussions prior to the accident, and at least one other teammate had suffered a concussion while wearing a CSA approved helmet. Darren was clearly aware of the risks associated with playing hockey, even while wearing a helmet, and like hundreds of thousands of other Canadians, chose to play anyway.

The plaintiffs' claims against the CSA for negligent misrepresentation and failure to warn are dismissed. The plaintiffs failed to prove any statement or omission on the CSA's part contributed in any way to Darren's injury.

In the result, the trial judge dismissed all of the appellants' claims....

Conclusion

In the result, whether the trial judge found that the impact was primarily rotational or translational was irrelevant. The case was dismissed on the basis that the appellants had not proved any negligence in designing or manufacturing the helmet, the helmet met and exceeded any increased standard suggested by the appellants' expert, and the appellants had failed to prove there was any failure to warn and if there was, that it bore any causal relationship to Darren's injury.

For all of these reasons, I would dismiss the appeal.

The Supreme Court of Canada returned to the realm of products liability in 2008 in *Mustapha v. Culligan of Canada*. In this case, Mustapha sued his bottled water supplier, Culligan, for psychiatric harm suffered by seeing a dead fly and part of another dead fly in an unopened replacement bottle of water. Chief Justice McLachlin summarized the issues before the court:

The plaintiff, Mr. Mustapha, sues for psychiatric injury sustained as a result of seeing the dead flies in a bottle of water supplied by the defendant, Culligan. In the course of replacing an empty bottle of drinking water with a full one, Mr. Mustapha saw a dead fly and part of another dead fly in the unopened replacement bottle. He became obsessed with the event and its "revolting implications" for the health of his family, which had been consuming water supplied by Culligan for the previous 15 years. The plaintiff developed a major depressive disorder with associated phobia and anxiety. He sued Culligan for damages.

The trial judge found that seeing the flies in the water resulted in psychiatric injuries to Mr. Mustapha, and awarded him $80,000 in general damages, $24,174.58 in special damages, and $237,600 in damages for loss of business ((2005), 32 C.C.L.T. (3d) 123). The Ontario Court of Appeal overturned the judgment on the basis that the injury was not reasonably foreseeable and hence did not give rise to a cause of action ((2006), 84 O.R. (3d) 457). The issue before this Court is whether the cause of action has been established. For different reasons than the Court of Appeal, I conclude that it has not.

A successful action in negligence requires that the plaintiff demonstrate (1) that the defendant owed him a duty of care; (2) that the defendant's behaviour breached the standard of care; (3) that the plaintiff sustained damage; and (4) that the damage was caused, in fact and in law, by the defendant's breach. I shall examine each of these elements of negligence in turn. As I will explain, Mr. Mustapha's claim fails because he has failed to establish that his damage was caused in law by the defendant's negligence. In other words, his damage is too remote to allow recovery.

Chief Justice McLachlin explained this remoteness at a later point in her judgment:

> The remoteness inquiry depends not only upon the degree of probability required to meet the reasonable foreseeability requirement, but also upon whether or not the plaintiff is considered objectively or subjectively. One of the questions that arose in this case was whether, in judging whether the personal injury was foreseeable, one looks at a person of "ordinary fortitude" or at a particular plaintiff with his or her particular vulnerabilities. This question may be acute in claims for mental injury, since there is a wide variation in how particular people respond to particular stressors. The law has consistently held—albeit within the duty of care analysis—that the question is what a person of ordinary fortitude would suffer: see *White v. Chief Constable of South Yorkshire Police*, [1998] 3 W.L.R. 1509 (H.L.); *Devji v. Burnaby (District)* (1999), 180 D.L.R. (4th) 205, 1999 BCCA 599; Vanek. As stated in *White*, at p. 1512: "The law expects reasonable fortitude and robustness of its citizens and will not impose liability for the exceptional frailty of certain individuals."[8]

DEFENCES TO NEGLIGENCE

What of potential defences to claims of negligence: **contributory negligence**, accident, voluntary participation, and voluntary assumption of risk? Although obviously not relevant to the decision in *Mustapha*, the defence of contributory negligence is often used to diminish or even eliminate the plaintiff's liability for damages. The defence is based on an argument that the plaintiff has either contributed to or created the negligence complained of.

A second defence is that the negligence complained of took place in the context of voluntary participation in a criminal or antisocial action. In *Tallow v. Tailfeathers*,[9] the plaintiffs were passengers in a stolen car driven by the defendant, who fell asleep at the wheel and hit a telephone pole. One of the passengers was killed, and the rest were injured. At no time did the plaintiffs object to the defendant's driving of the car, even though he had been drinking very heavily, was very tired, and was clearly travelling at an illegal speed at the time of the accident.

The court found that the plaintiffs had no claim in negligence, premising its decision on the Latin maxim ***ex turpi causa, non oritur actio***. This maxim was perhaps best explained by Lord Diplock in a 1964 British case:

> All that rule means is that the courts will not enforce a right which would otherwise be enforceable if the right arises out of an act committed by the person asserting the right (or by someone who is regarded in law as his successor) which is regarded by the court as sufficiently antisocial to justify the court's refusing to enforce that right.[10]

In *Tallow v. Tailfeathers*, the Alberta Court of Appeal concluded:

> Here, as I have said, the appellants participated with their driver in the theft of the car and in its unlawful use in the course of which the accident occurred that has

given rise to their claims. The driving of the car was a continuation of the theft and it was that driving and the manner of it that caused the accident. I agree with Dechene, J. that the appellants' claims arise *ex turpi* and should not be entertained by the Court.

A third defence to a claim of negligence is the assertion that the event in question was simply an accident, which no reasonable person could or ought to have foreseen. This defence is often expressed as the defence of inevitable accident, set out in an 1892 British case by Lord Esher: "In my opinion, a person relying on inevitable accident must shew that something happened over which he had no control, and the effect of which could not have been avoided by the greatest care and skill."[11]

Consider the application of the defence of accident to *Blyth v. Birmingham Water Works Co.*, a tort claim to recover damages for the flooding of the plaintiff's premises. The defendant had installed a fire plug in the vicinity; because of an exceptionally severe frost in the winter of 1855, the fire plug was damaged, resulting in the flooding complained of. The fire plug had worked adequately for 25 years.

> Alderson, B.: A reasonable man would act with reference to the average circumstances of the temperature in ordinary years. The defendants had provided against such frosts as experience would have led men, acting prudently, to provide against; and they are not guilty of negligence, because their precautions proved insufficient against the effects of the extreme severity of the frost of 1855, which penetrated to a greater depth than any which ordinarily occurs south of the polar regions. Such a state of circumstances constitutes a contingency against which no reasonable man can provide. The result was an accident, for which the defendants cannot be held liable.[12]

The final defence to negligence is voluntary assumption of risk. It can be argued that, in some circumstances, plaintiffs have voluntarily assumed the risks of a given activity, thereby nullifying any tort claim that they might bring. This defence was successfully used in the British Columbia case of *King v. Redlich*.

Carrothers, J.A.: The appellant was a 32-year-old postman. Both parties were regularly engaged on different teams in recreational hockey played on an unscheduled basis by men ranging in age from 30 to their early 40s, in the interests of keeping fit and enjoying a game played since childhood. They are whimsically known as Old Timers.

During the pregame warm-up, the respondent took a practice shot at the goal. The puck hit the goal post, ricocheted and struck the head of the appellant who was not wearing a helmet. The evidence is that the appellant would not have suffered the injuries he did had he been wearing a helmet.

The trial judge also found that the practice shot was taken at the moment that the appellant emerged from behind the goal and when hit was several feet away from the left side of the goal toward which the respondent aimed his practice shot.

The appellant suffered permanent brain damage which impaired his speech and word selection, although he was able to continue with his employment. The appellant's involvement in sports and social relationships was severely curtailed. Had the respondent been held liable at trial, general damages of $40,000 would have been awarded....

In regard to the matter of liability, the trial judge held that the respondent was not negligent, the warm-up shot was normal, and within the reasonable expectations of the appellant. The trial judge found that warm-up shots are usual during pregame rehearsal and injury from a puck is not uncommon. The appellant was deemed to have accepted and assumed the risk of injury during warm-up....

In dismissing the appellant's action, Spencer, J. said this:

Since it is an accepted part of the game for players to practise shots during the warm-up, and since on all the witnesses' evidence I find that injury from a flying puck is not uncommon, I am of the opinion that a player like the plaintiff must be deemed to accept and assume a risk of injury during the warm-up. While it may be a wrongful act for one player, during a warm-up, to shoot deliberately at another, knowing him to be unaware, it was not negligent for the defendant in this case to shoot at the goal, having allowed the plaintiff to skate from behind it and under circumstances where the puck deflected at random off the post and struck the plaintiff. The plaintiff's action must be dismissed.

In my view, that finding cannot be faulted on the facts. The appellant challenges this finding of absence of negligence on the part of the respondent on the law. The appellant argues that notwithstanding the lessened duty of care which prevails in recreational hockey during warm-up, any higher risk which is perceived or ought to be perceived by the prudent player about to take a practice shot automatically elevates the level of the duty of care so that by proceeding to take the practice shot without taking that extra care, the player is negligent; any higher risk here would be due to the presence of the appellant behind the goal.

While the time frame of the practice shot would only be a few seconds, I think it can be fairly said that the respondent perceived the higher risk because on noting the appellant behind the goal post, the respondent momentarily delayed his practice shot to allow the appellant to clear the goal. In so doing, he correspondingly increased the care, which he took by delaying his practice shot until the appellant was, in the respondent's judgement, out of immediate danger. The respondent then proceeded with his practice shot. The respondent did not foresee and could not be expected to foresee the ricochet which redirected the puck and caused the injury of the appellant.

In these circumstances, I would not interfere with the trial judge's finding of no negligence and would dismiss the appeal.[13]

COMPENSATION FOR TORTS OF INTENTION AND NEGLIGENCE

Both intentional torts and torts of negligence are largely, perhaps overwhelmingly, concerned with compensation. This finding prompts the question whether tort law is the best means we can devise to compensate individuals for the negligence of others. Canadian legal scholars Solomon, Feldthusen, and Mills have noted:

> [T]he present system of tort law cannot be explained or justified as a mechanism of accident compensation. First, tort law provides compensation to a relatively small number of accident victims and then only in very limited circumstances. Second, the accident victim must make a substantial financial investment to initiate the process. Third, the plaintiff must prove fault, not need, and will only recover if he is fortunate enough to be injured by a tortfeasor with assets. Finally, it is generally accepted and clearly documented that tort law is an extremely inefficient mechanism for providing compensation.[14]

The purpose of tort law can therefore be said to be somewhat elusive. While access to the courts may provide compensatory redress for certain individuals or corporations, it is not clear that the broad social goal of compensation can be adequately met by the present structure of the law.

Automobile accidents and work-related accidents are significant areas in which tort law has not provided an efficient mechanism of compensation. In Canada and most other industrialized states, compensation plans have therefore displaced the use of claims in tort for such accidents. In the case of automobile accidents, no-fault compensation is provided by either private insurers or government agencies. The compensation displaces tort in virtually every circumstance, though a plaintiff may seek damages in the courts in the unusual event that his or her losses exceed awarded benefits. Thanks to workers' compensation boards and tribunals, injuries at work have also been largely removed from the scope of tort claims. Workers' compensation schemes, funded for the most part by employers, have been in place in Canada since just after the turn of the 20th century. The boards and tribunals are public bodies created by statute; they provide less costly, more efficient and comprehensive compensation for accidents in the workplace than courtroom claims in tort. Unlike actions in tort, however, the plans do not provide for the possibility of compensation for pain and suffering.

The system of claims in tort works well in restricted circumstances when there is a coincidence of key features: in intentional torts, a defendant with the financial capacity to compensate; in torts of negligence, an action with a highly significant impact for which no system of insurance or other form of compensation exists. There are many examples of the latter kind of claim: individual claims for medical or legal malpractice; collective, or class-action, claims to recover damages for the consequences of the Dalkon shield and thalidomide, failure to screen blood products for HIV, and defects in automobiles or other consumer products.

Vicarious Liability and Social Host Liability

Consider an intentional tort with a defendant who has the financial capacity to compensate, and the thorny question of vicarious liability. The decision of the Supreme

Court of Canada in *John Doe v. Bennett*,[15] excerpted below, raises the possibility of the vicarious liability of the Roman Catholic Church for a sexual assault:

Over a period of almost two decades, Father Kevin Bennett, a Roman Catholic priest in Newfoundland in the Diocese of St. George's, sexually assaulted boys in his parishes. Two successive bishops failed to take steps to stop the abuse. Ultimately, in 1979, a victim revealed the abuse to the Archbishop of the neighbouring diocese, St. John's, who was also Metropolitan of the broader ecclesiastical province. He referred the complaint to Bennett's Bishop but again nothing was done. The unnamed plaintiffs, 36 in number, suffered greatly as a consequence of the abuse. Now adults, they remain deeply wounded.

The plaintiff-respondents sued for the wrongs that had been done to them. They sued Father Bennett; the Roman Catholic Episcopal Corporation of St. George's ("St. George's"); the bishop of St. George's at the time the lawsuit was commenced, Raymond Lahey; the archbishop of St. John's at the time of the abuse, Alphonsus Penney; the archbishop of St. John's at the time the lawsuit was commenced, James MacDonald; the Roman Catholic Episcopal Corporation of St. John's ("St. John's"); and the Roman Catholic Church. Father Bennett's liability is not at issue before this Court. The main issue is the liability of St. George's.

The trial judge found Bennett directly liable; St. George's and Bishop Lahey vicariously liable, and Archbishop Penney liable in negligence. He dismissed the claims against Archbishop MacDonald, St. John's and the Roman Catholic Church ((2000), 190 Nfld. & P.E.I.R. 277).

The Court of Appeal set aside the findings of personal liability against Archbishop Penney and Bishop Lahey, and upheld the dismissal of the action against Archbishop MacDonald, St. John's and the Roman Catholic Church. The majority found St. George's directly but not vicariously liable ((2002), 218 D.L.R. (4th) 276, 2002 NFCA 47). St. George's appealed the finding of direct negligence to this Court, and argued in addition that the Roman Catholic Church was liable. The plaintiff-respondents replied that St. George's is not only directly, but also vicariously liable for Bennett's wrongs. The plaintiff-respondents also filed a cross-appeal asserting the liability of Lahey, MacDonald, Penney, St. John's and the Roman Catholic Church. However, they also asserted that the cross-appeal was conditional on the success of St. George's appeal from liability and need not be considered in the event St. George's appeal was dismissed.

The main issue on the appeal is whether St. George's is liable to the plaintiff-respondents and if so, on what basis. St. George's contends it is neither directly nor vicariously liable; the plaintiff-respondents assert they are liable on both grounds. St. George's also argues that the Roman Catholic Church is liable.

A. Direct Liability

All of the abuse took place in the diocese of St. George's. A Roman Catholic diocese is a territorial enterprise, composed of a number of parishes and administered by a bishop or archbishop. Dioceses are constituted by the Pope, who also appoints bishops and archbishops. A number of dioceses may form an ecclesiastical province. It is common for legislation to

incorporate bishops and archbishops as episcopal corporations. I conclude that the episcopal corporation is the secular arm of the bishop or archbishop for all purposes. The office
of bishop/archbishop, the enterprise of the diocese and the episcopal corporation are legally
synonymous.

The argument for direct liability of St. George's is as follows:

(1) The bishops of St. George's in charge of Bennett (Bishops O'Reilly and McGrath
successively) knew or ought to have known that Bennett was abusing the plaintiff-
respondents and negligently did nothing to stop the assaults from continuing;

(2) The bishops (successively) constituted the corporation sole of St. George's under
the relevant legislation and acted on its behalf;

(3) Therefore St. George's is directly liable for these acts and omissions.

St. George's concedes the first proposition (the negligence of Bishops O'Reilly and
McGrath) and does not seriously dispute the second. Its only argument is that St. George's
is not liable for the Bishops' negligence, because the corporation's sole activities and
powers are confined to holding property and do not extend to the placement, direction
and discipline of priests.

The narrow issue is therefore whether the corporation sole's activities and liability are
confined to matters pertaining to its property. The courts below rejected this proposition.
So would I. I base this conclusion on the legislation creating the corporation sole and on its
function or purpose.

The purpose for which ecclesiastical corporations like St. George's are created is to
serve as a point of legal interface between the Roman Catholic Church and the community
at the diocesan level. The Church is at one and the same time a spiritual presence in the
community and a secular actor in the community. The task of the corporation sole is to provide
a bridge between the two spheres for the diocese. On a secular level, the Church interacts
with members of the diocesan community in a host of ways. It carries on a variety of religious,
educational and social activities. It makes contracts with employees. It transports parishioners.
It sponsors charitable events. It purchases and sells goods and property. To do these things,
it requires a legal personality. That personality is the corporation sole. To restrict the purpose
of the corporation sole to the acquisition, holding and administration of property is to capture
only a portion of the purpose it is intended to serve and to artificially truncate its functions.

The role of the corporation sole as a legal interface between the Church and the community is set forth in the legislation creating it, *An Act to Incorporate the Roman Catholic
Bishop of St. George's,* S.N. 1913, c. 12. The Act, quite simply, incorporates the office of
bishop, in all its aspects. It does not confine itself to the holding of property belonging to the
diocese.

Section 1 of the Act states that "the Roman Catholic Bishops from time to time of the
Diocese of St. George's ... shall be a body corporate ... for the purpose of holding lands and
property, personal or otherwise." However, the language of other sections makes it clear the
Corporation's powers are not confined to property. Section 3 provides:

The Corporation shall have perpetual succession and a corporate seal, with power
to alter the same, and by the name of the Roman Catholic Episcopal Corporation of

St. George's shall be capable in law of suing and being sued, pleading and being impleaded in all Courts and places whatsoever, and shall have power to take and to hold lands, and all other property whatsoever for ecclesiastical, charitable and educational purposes and uses of the Roman Catholic Church, and to lease, sell, convey and dispose of the same.

This section permits the Corporation to be sued on all matters, not just those relating to property....

I would confirm the conclusion below that the Roman Catholic Episcopal Corporation of St. George's is directly liable for the wrongs to the plaintiff-respondents resulting from its bishops' failure to properly direct and discipline Father Bennett.

B. Vicarious Liability

The plaintiff-respondents also seek a finding that the Roman Catholic Episcopal Corporation of St. George's is vicariously liable for Father Bennett's assaults, as his employer. The doctrine of vicarious liability imputes liability to the employer or principal of a tortfeasor, not on the basis of the fault of the employer or principal, but on the ground that as the person responsible for the activity or enterprise in question, the employer or principal should be held responsible for loss to third parties that result from the activity or enterprise.

The trial judge found St. George's vicariously liable for the assaults committed by Father Bennett. The majority of the Court of Appeal, per Marshall J.A., reversed this finding, emphasizing that Bennett's actions violated the norms of the Church and the charitable, non-profit nature of the diocese's activities. The dissenting justice, Cameron J.A., held vicarious liability to be established. In my view, the majority of the Newfoundland and Labrador Court of Appeal erred on this point and the view of the dissent is to be preferred.

This Court considered the application of the doctrine of vicarious liability to the tort of assault of children in *Bazley v. Curry*, [1999] 2 S.C.R. 534, *Jacobi v. Griffiths*, [1999] 2 S.C.R. 570, and *K.L.B. v. British Columbia*, [2003] 2 S.C.R. 403, 2003 SCC 51. The decisions affirm the same test for vicarious liability.

In *Bazley*, the Court suggested that the imposition of vicarious liability may usefully be approached in two steps. First, a court should determine whether there are precedents which unambiguously determine whether the case should attract vicarious liability. "If prior cases do not clearly suggest a solution, the next step is to determine whether vicarious liability should be imposed in light of the broader policy rationales behind strict liability": *Bazley*, at para. 15; *Jacobi*, at para. 31. Vicarious liability is based on the rationale that the person who puts a risky enterprise into the community may fairly be held responsible when those risks emerge and cause loss or injury to members of the public. Effective compensation is a goal. Deterrence is also a consideration. The hope is that holding the employer or principal liable will encourage such persons to take steps to reduce the risk of harm in the future. Plaintiffs must show that the rationale behind the imposition of vicarious liability will be met on the facts in two respects. First, the relationship between the tortfeasor and the person against whom liability is sought must be sufficiently close. Second, the wrongful act must be sufficiently connected to the conduct authorized by the employer. This is necessary to ensure that the goals of fair and effective compensation and deterrence of future harm are met: *K.L.B., supra,* at para. 20.

In determining whether there is a sufficient connection in the case of intentional **torts**, factors to be considered include, but are not limited to the following (*Bazley, supra,* at para. 41):

(a) the opportunity that the enterprise afforded the employee to abuse his or her power;

(b) the extent to which the wrongful act may have furthered the employer's aims (and hence be more likely to have been committed by the employee);

(c) the extent to which the wrongful act was related to friction, confrontation or intimacy inherent in the employer's enterprise;

(d) the extent of power conferred on the employee in relation to the victim;

(e) the vulnerability of potential victims to wrongful exercise of the employee's power.

The employer's control over the employee's activities is one indication of whether the employee is acting on his or her employer's behalf: *K.L.B., supra,* at para. 22. At the heart of the inquiry lies the question of power and control by the employer: both that exercised over and that granted to the employee. Where this power and control can be identified, the imposition of vicarious liability will compensate fairly and effectively.

In *Bazley, supra,* vicarious liability was imposed on a non-profit association operating residential care facilities for children, in an action brought by a former resident for sexual assault by a child care counsellor. The Court unanimously rejected the argument that non-profit bodies should be protected from tort liability in the public interest. The relationship between the employer and employee was sufficiently close, while the wrongful act was a manifestation of risks inherent in the employer's enterprise.

In the companion case, *Jacobi, supra,* the majority of the Court found a nonprofit Boys' and Girls' Club not vicariously liable for sexual assaults committed by its employee, the program director, some of them in the course of excursions relating to the children's sports activities. Applying the test set out in *Bazley, supra,* the majority found the required connection between the employer's enterprise and the wrong had not been established. In the view of the majority, the facts established a much weaker connection than in *Bazley:* the level of intimacy was much less; the job did not require the employee to be alone with the child; the offence occurred off-premises and outside working hours; and the employee had established his own "bait" of home attractions. These facts, the majority held, negated the required strong connection between the risks inherent in the employer's enterprise and the wrong. Whatever power Griffiths used, Binnie J. wrote, it was not conferred by the Club, nor was it characteristic of the type of enterprise the Club put into the community. A minority of three justices found vicarious liability to be established, notwithstanding these differences.

In my respectful opinion, the majority of the Court of Appeal erred in reading *Jacobi* as suggesting that its effect is that non-profit employers should not be held vicariously liable for sexual assaults by their employees. The unanimous opinion in *Bazley,* which also involved a non-profit employer, and both the majority and dissenting opinions in *Jacobi,* are all inconsistent with this conclusion. The majority reasons in *Jacobi* suggest that non-profit status may sometimes negatively impact on the policy rationales that underlie the imposition of vicarious liability; however, they do not state that non-profit employers should not be held vicariously liable; nor do they affirm the old doctrine of charitable immunity. In the result, the majority held (at para. 78) that

"fairness" to these non-profit organizations is entirely compatible with vicarious liability provided that a strong connection is established between the enterprise risk and the sexual assault. [Emphasis in original.]

The majority in *Jacobi* grounds its conclusion firmly in the factors relevant to the connection between the employer's creation of risk and the wrong complained of as expressed in *Bazley*, notably the absence of job-conferred power.

In the present case, the relevant precedents dealing with church-related activities do not clearly determine the issue, although they tend to support the imposition of vicarious liability on the episcopal corporation. In *McDonald v. Mombourquette* (1996), 152 N.S.R. (2d) 109 (leave to appeal refused, [1997] 2 S.C.R. xi), the Nova Scotia Court of Appeal reversed the trial judge's finding that the Roman Catholic & Episcopal Corporation of Antigonish was vicariously liable for sexual assaults committed by a priest on children in the parish. A key factor was that the priest had acted "totally contrary to the religious tenets which he has sworn to uphold" (para. 47). In *K. (W.) v. Pornbacher* (1997), 32 B.C.L.R. (3d) 360 (S.C.), the court declined to follow *Mombourquette* and held the Catholic Church, through its Bishop of Nelson, to be both negligent and vicariously liable for sexual assaults committed by a priest. The trial judge emphasized the job-conferred power of a priest over church youth. Although the case law does not provide a clear answer, the facts of *Pornbacher* (as well as *Mombourquette*) more closely resemble *Bazley* than *Jacobi*.

The relationship between the bishop and a priest in a diocese is not only spiritual, but temporal. The priest takes a vow of obedience to the bishop. The bishop exercises extensive control over the priest, including the power of assignment, the power to remove the priest from his post and the power to discipline him. It is akin to an employment relationship. The incidents of control far exceed those characterizing the relationship between foster parents and the government, discussed in *K.L.B.*, and, as will become evident below, the priest is reasonably perceived as an agent of the diocesan enterprise. The relationship between the bishop and the priest is sufficiently close. Applying the relevant test to the facts, it is also clear that the necessary connection between the employer-created or enhanced risk and the wrong complained of is established.

First, the bishop provided Bennett with the opportunity to abuse his power. As noted by the trial judge, at para. 26, "the vast majority of all the activities which [Bennett] organized and in which he was always accompanied by boys, were activities which he organized and controlled in his capacity as parish priest." Canon 528 of the *Code of Canon Law* directs a parish priest to "have a special care for the catholic education of children and young people," and involvement with children was clearly an expected role for a parish priest. As priest, Bennett directed altar boys, led a parish band, involved boys in renovation and construction projects, was active in the Boy Scout troop, and engaged boys in various fundraising and parochial activities. All of these opportunities came via his appointment and placement as parish priest by the bishop.

Second, Bennett's wrongful acts were strongly related to the psychological intimacy inherent in his role as priest. As explained by Cameron J.A., at para. 184: "The Church encourages psychological intimacy between a priest and the members of the parish. A priest may not have to bath children [as in *Bazley*] but he, like parents, teaches them right from wrong, he represents God and they are to accept his instructions in spiritual matters." This psychological intimacy encourages victims' submission to abuse and increases the opportunity to abuse, partly by satisfying parents "that their children [are] in good hands while in the care and control of their priest" (trial decision, at para. 21). A church member's personal identity is closely intertwined with his or her faith and its institutional expression, which may nurture trust in the institution's hierarchy from a young age, granting it considerable power.

Third, the bishop conferred an enormous degree of power on Bennett relative to his victims. The power imbalance was intensified in St. George's diocese due to a number of factors. The parishes in which Bennett worked were geographically isolated, impacting on the opportunities for, and extent and frequency of, the sexual assaults and contributing to their remaining unchecked for many years. The communities were entirely Roman Catholic and the devoutly religious inhabitants placed the Church at the centre of their daily lives. There were few other authority figures; the communities lacked municipal government, diverse business activities, secular organizations, police, courts or any other form of community leadership, leaving that role entirely to the parish priest. The only schools were denominational, and as such, were influenced by the priest, who served as the only local representative of the distant school board.

Bennett had enormous stature because of his position as parish priest, both to the boys and to their parents. The plaintiffs perceived him as a "god"—quite logically given his centrality in the community and the disparity in lifestyles between himself and his parishioners. As the school principal, Kerry Dwyer, testified, "It was like having a celebrity in the community that you had to treat properly. … [T]here were incidents where I found people believed that the priest could turn you into a goat." Or, as one victim stated, when he asked his father if he should sleep over at Bennett's house as Bennett had requested, "my dad said of course, he's the priest." While Bennett had a particularly forceful personality, the root of his power over his victims lay in his role as a priest, conferred by the bishop. The trial judge summed it up eloquently, at para. 28: "The awe in which Father Bennett was held by the community at large contributed to his ability to control his victims and thus to satisfy a prodigious appetite for constant sexual gratification."

In summary, the evidence overwhelmingly satisfies the tests affirmed in *Bazley*, *Jacobi* and *K.L.B.* The relationship between the diocesan enterprise and Bennett was sufficiently close. The enterprise substantially enhanced the risk which led to the wrongs the plaintiff-respondents suffered. It provided Bennett with great power in relation to vulnerable victims and with the opportunity to abuse that power. A strong and direct connection is established between the conduct of the enterprise and the wrongs done to the plaintiff-respondents. The majority of the Court of Appeal erred in failing to apply the right test. Had it performed the appropriate analysis, it would have found the Roman Catholic Episcopal Corporation of St. George's vicariously liable for Father Bennett's assaults on the plaintiff-respondents.

I conclude that the Roman Catholic Episcopal Corporation of St. George's is vicariously liable for the wrongs done to the plaintiff-respondents.

III. The Liability of the Roman Catholic Church

The appellant St. George's argues that the Roman Catholic Church should be found liable. The trial judge and the Court of Appeal unanimously rejected this proposition. I decline to deal with this argument on the record before us in this case.

The Roman Catholic Church is a religious organization operating in many countries of the world, including Canada. It possesses a hierarchical structure with the Pope at its apex, and works through diverse orders, groups and individuals. On the record before us, it is impossible to answer the questions as to procedure and remedies for recovery which the claim against the Church raises. The record does not provide the clear picture of the details of the Church's hierarchy or of the relationship between the Church and its constituent parts, necessary to delineate the boundaries of the institution, the nature of its legal status, and its potential liability. Nor does the record offer much assistance on the procedural questions that would need to be answered before the Church, as a global institution, could be found liable for the wrongs committed by Father Bennett in the diocese of St. George's. Although named as a party, the Church was not represented during the proceedings in this case, and issues relating to procedure and remedies for recovery were left unexplored.

Without suggesting that the full organizational structure of the Roman Catholic Church and its relations with its various constituent organizations must be apparent on the evidence before a finding of Church liability could be made, I am satisfied that the record before us is too weak to permit the Court in this case to responsibly embark on the important and difficult question of whether the Roman Catholic Church can be held liable in a case such as this.

For these reasons, I decline to deal with the appellant's second argument.[16]

Social concepts of private wrongs vary, not only from one individual to another but also in relation to social change within a given society. The case of *John Doe v. Bennett* demonstrates, among other things, that the claims of victims of sexual abuse, in tort and elsewhere, are taken more seriously today than they were even a decade or two ago. Additionally, the ability to make a claim, the willingness of social institutions to consider such a claim, and the justifications for recovery have necessarily changed over time. See, additionally, the Supreme Court of Canada's decision in *E.B. v. Order of the Oblates of Mary Immaculate in the Province of British Columbia*, a 2005 judgment that comes to a relatively similar conclusion regarding the church's vicarious liability for sexual assaults during the late 1950s and early 1960s in a residential school for First Nations children in British Columbia. The majority of the court held that there was not a sufficiently "strong connection" between the sexual assault committed by the employee, Saxey, and what employees of the residential school were expected to do in the course of their employment—that Saxey's actions were sufficiently separate and apart from the actions of the Oblates. The minority judgment in this case, written by Justice Abella, concluded that there was a sufficient connection between the "employment enterprise" and the sexual assaults, a connection that would justify an imposition of vicarious liability on the employer for the wrong committed by his employee.[17]

SOCIAL HOST LIABILITY: *CHILDS V. DESORMEAUX*

The facts, as set out by Chief Justice McLachlin:

This case arises from a tragic car accident in Ottawa in the early hours of January 1, 1999. At 1:30 a.m., after leaving a party hosted by Dwight Courrier and Julie Zimmerman, Desmond Desormeaux drove his vehicle into oncoming traffic and collided head-on with a vehicle driven by Patricia Hadden. One of the passengers in Ms. Hadden's car was killed and three others seriously injured, including Zoe Childs, who was then a teenager. Ms. Childs' spine was severed and she has since been paralyzed from the waist down. Mr. Desormeaux and the two passengers in his car were also injured.

Mr. Desormeaux was impaired at the time of the accident. The trial judge found that he had probably consumed 12 beers at the party over two and a half hours, producing a blood-alcohol concentration of approximately 235 mg per 100 ml when he left the party and 225 mg per 100 ml at the time of the accident—concentrations well over the legal limit for driving of 80 mg per 100 ml. Mr. Desormeaux pleaded guilty to a series of criminal charges arising from these events and received a 10-year sentence.

The party hosted by Dwight Courrier and Julie Zimmerman at their home was a "BYOB" (Bring Your Own booze) event. The only alcohol served by the hosts was three-quarters of a bottle of champagne in small glasses at midnight. Mr. Desormeaux was known to his hosts to be a heavy drinker. The trial judge heard evidence that when Mr. Desormeaux walked to his car to leave, Mr. Courrier accompanied him and asked, "Are you okay, brother?" Mr. Desormeaux responded "No problem", got behind the wheel and drove away with two passengers.

Ms. Childs sued Mr. Desormeaux and the hosts of the party, Dwight Courrier and Julie Zimmerman, arguing that a reasonable person in their position would have foreseen that Mr. Desormeaux might drive away from their home, intoxicated, become involved in an accident, and injure someone. The Chief Justice concluded, in finding no liability on the social host:

[H]osting a party at which alcohol is served does not, without more, establish the degree of proximity required to give rise to a duty of care on the hosts to third-party highway users who may be injured by an intoxicated guest. The injury here was not shown to be foreseeable on the facts as found by the trial judge. Even if it had been, this is at best a case of nonfeasance. No duty to monitor guests' drinking or to prevent them from driving can be imposed having regard to the relevant cases and legal principles. A social host at a party where alcohol is served is not under a duty of care to members of the public who may be injured by a guest's actions, unless the host's conduct implicates him or her in the creation or exacerbation of the risk.

In contrast, note the commentary of Mothers Against Drunk Driving Canada:
> While Childs obtained partial recovery from Desormeaux, the Supreme Court of Canada rejected her claim against the social hosts. Surprisingly, the Court held that hosting an alcohol-related event does not create a risk sufficient to warrant imposing a legal duty on the social host. Accordingly, social hosts have virtually no legal responsibility for intoxicated guests who drive away and injure other users of the road. The decision is troubling on several grounds. For instance, the Court's analysis of the risks of social hosting is inconsistent with statistics showing that there are more impaired drivers on Canadian roads coming from private homes than from commercial licensed establishments.[18]

Which of these positions is more compelling? The evidence did establish that Mr. Desormeaux had consumed about 12 beers in less than three hours and, as noted above, was known by the hosts to be a heavy drinker. The contrary position is that unlike commercial establishments, social hosts do not profit from the sale of alcohol, and in this instance they were not serving drinks—it was a "bring your own booze" party. One parting thought, however: who is in the best position to know about the risks that a drunken individual may pose to others, the social host or the commercial host? And, from an empirical standpoint, which form of gathering leads to the greatest number of accidents on the road, drinking in a commercial establishment, or drinking at a party, amongst friends?

CONCLUSION: TORT LAW AS A MIX OF PRIVATE AND PUBLIC INTERESTS

Tort law is clearly a mix of private and public interests. Should the collective interests of the Lintz Cricket Club supersede the private interests of the Millers? Should a company providing bottled water be found liable for negligence if a customer suffers an unusual psychiatric breakdown because of viewing the shoddy nature of their product? In what circumstances should a Roman Catholic diocese be held responsible for the actions of one of its priests? Should social hosts be held liable when they fail to intervene to protect the public, particularly when they are aware of the danger that one of their guests might pose? In each of these cases, the courts were concerned with more than a simple resolution of the private claims of the parties. The collective right to recreation, the extent of corporate responsibility in response to the issuing of a faulty product, the social responsibility of a church and the responsibility of a social host are fundamentally issues of public interest. When the system of tort law fails—as it does with most forms of injury and accident, whether negligent or not—it is public interest that dictates the failure. And so it is true of torts, as of contract law, property law, wills and estates—in short, all forms of private law: it may be the realm of private wrongs, but it is the public interest that lies at the heart of the matter.

WEB LINKS

Lord Denning: An Affectionate Remembrance

http://lawtrain.blogspot.com/2006/04/lord-denning-affectionate-remembrance.html
This essay was written by an Ottawa lawyer as a eulogy to the judge who many regarded as the most interesting of all times.

Faculty of Law, University of Cambridge

http://www.law.cam.ac.uk
One of the most comprehensive academic legal sites in the U.K. is located at the University of Cambridge. For excellent essays and materials on legal history as well as links to British cases and statutes, this site is a good resource.

Cornell University: The Legal Institute

http://www.law.cornell.edu/topics
Listed as a topical index, the materials on the Cornell University website include explanations of key legal principles in concise and clear language.

Lexum

https://lexum.com/en/
This site offers an excellent topical index for substantive law in Canada.

Legal Portal

http://www.gahtan.com/links
Maintained by internationally known Canadian Internet and technology lawyer Alan Gahtan, this site offers good definitions and explanations of topical areas of law. It also has numerous links to other Web pages and search engines with similar material.

David Friedman, Santa Clara School of Law

http://www.daviddfriedman.com/
A prodigious author and academic, David Friedman has an excellent topical website that links tort and crime from an economics perspective.

QUESTIONS FOR DISCUSSION

1. Is the Supreme Court correct in saying that the injuries sustained by Mr. Mustapha are too remote to justify liability on the part of the Culligan company?
2. What are the strengths and weaknesses of the tort system as a mechanism of compensation? Is the awarding of punitive damages, as in *Whiten v. Pilot Insurance*, an appropriate function for the resolution of claims in tort?
3. In *Childs v. Desormeaux*, which view of social host liability is more compelling—that of the Supreme Court of Canada, or that of Mothers Against Drunk Driving? Why?
4. In *More v. Bauer Nike Hockey Inc.*, is the corporation's duty to warn of the limitations of the hockey helmet sufficient, as the B.C. Court of Appeal has asserted?

FURTHER READING

Carolyn Sappideen and Prue Vines, *Fleming's the Law of Tort.* 10th ed. Sydney: Australia Lawbook Co., 2011.

> This is the 10th edition of Fleming's now classic work on the subject of tort law. This text of more than 800 pages is required reading for many Canadian and U.S. law school courses on torts. Although the book emanates from Australia, it clearly canvasses both timeless principles and new developments.

Solomon, R., M. McInnes, E. Chamberlain, and S Pitel. *Cases and Materials on the Law of Torts.* 8th ed. Toronto: Carswell, 2011.

> This book, in its eighth edition, provides a thorough analysis of the realm of torts, exploring intentional torts; torts of negligence; defences to intentional torts; defences to torts of negligence; issues of causation, remoteness, and assessment of damages; updates on vicarious liability and defamation; and the theories, criticisms, and alternatives to tort law as a mechanism of compensation. The authors provide a good coverage of Canadian tort law.

Wigmore, J.H. *Select Cases on the Law of Torts, with Notes and a Summary of Principles.* Boston: Little, Brown, 1912.

> This book by the celebrated jurist John Henry Wigmore sets out the foundations of tort liability. Although the case law is specific to a rather different era, the book provides an insight into current developments within tort law, and allows the reader to understand the historical context from which this area of law has emerged.

NOTES

1. *Miller v. Jackson*, [1977] Q.B. 966, [1977] 3 All E.R. 338 at 366 (C.A.).
2. R.S.C. 1985, c. C-46.

3. R. Solomon, B. Feldthusen, and S. Mills, *Cases and Materials on the Law of Torts*, 2nd ed. (Toronto: Carswell, 1986).
4. *Bettel v. Yim* (1978), 20 O.R. (2d) 617 at 632, 88 D.L.R. (3d) 543 at 558 (Ont. Co. Ct.).
5. *Blyth v. Birmingham Water Works* (1856), 11 Ex. 781 at 784, 156 E.R. 1047 at 1049 (Ex. Ct.).
6. *M'Alister (or Donoghue) v. Stevenson*, [1932] A.C. 562.
7. *More v. Bauer Nike Hockey Inc.*, 2011 BCCA 419 (CanLII), http://canlii.ca/t/fnl40.
8. *Mustapha v. Culligan of Canada Limited*, [2008] 2. S.C.R. 114.
9. [1973] 6 W.W.R. 732, 44 D.L.R. (3d) 55 (Alta. C.A.).
10. *Hardy v. Motor Insurers' Bureau*, [1964] 2 All E.R. 742 at 750.
11. *The Schwan* [1892], cited in *McIntosh v. Bell*, [1932] O.R. 179 at 179–89.
12. *Blyth v. Birmingham Water Works*.
13. *King v. Redlich* (1985), 24 D.L.R. (4th) 636 at 636–638, aff'g [1984] 6 W.W.R. 705, 30 C.C.L.T. 247 (B.C.C.A.).
14. Solomon, Feldthusen, and Mills, *Cases and Materials on the Law of Torts*, 23.
15. *John Doe v. Bennett* [2004], 1 S.C.R. 436.
16. Ibid.
17. *E.B. v. Order of the Oblates of Mary Immaculate in the Province of British Columbia*, 2005 SCC 60, [2005] 3 S.C.R. 45 (see http://scc-csc.lexum.com/scc-csc/scc-csc/en/item/2241/index.do).
18. Mothers Against Drunk Driving Canada, *Being Sued Can Ruin a Good Party: A Social Host's Guide to Avoiding Legal Liability*, page 11, MADD, Oakville, 2006.

REFERENCES

Abel, E.L. "A Socialist Approach to Risk." *Modern Law Review* 41 (1982): 695.

Brown, R. "Deterrence and Accident Compensation Schemes." *University of Western Ontario Law Review* 17 (1978–79): 111.

Englard, P. "The System Builders: A Critical Appraisal of Modern American Tort Theory." *Journal of Legal Studies* 9 (1980): 27.

Galanter, M. "When Legal Worlds Collide: Reflections on Bhopal, the Good Lawyer, and the American Law School." *Journal of Legal Education* 36 (1986): 292.

Hutchinson, A., and J. Morgan. "The Canengusian Connection: The Kaleidoscope of Tort Theory." *Osgoode Hall Law Journal* 22 (1984): 69.

Ison, T. "The Infusion of Private Law in Public Administration." *Cahiers de Droit* 17 (1976): 799.

Linden, A., L. Klar, and B. Feldthusen. *Canadian Tort Law: Cases, Notes and Materials*. 12th ed. Toronto: Butterworths, 2004.

Ontario Law Reform Commission. *Report on Motor Vehicle Accident Compensation*. Toronto: Government Services, 1973.

Pierce, R. "Encouraging Safety: The Limits of Tort Law and Government Regulation."
    Vanderbilt Law Review 33 (1980): 1281.

Posner, R. "A Theory of Negligence." *Journal of Legal Studies* 1 (1972): 29.

Solomon, R., M. McInnes, E. Chamberlain, and S. Pitel. *Cases and Materials on the
    Law of Torts.* 7th ed. Toronto: Carswell, 2007.

Sugarman, S. "Doing Away with Tort Law." *California Law Review* 73 (1985): 555.

CHAPTER 8

THE CHANGING FAMILY AND FAMILY LAW: MARRIAGE, DIVORCE, SUPPORT, AND CUSTODY

Canadians do not have adequate access to family justice. For many years now reports have been telling us that cost, delay, complexity and other barriers are making it impossible for many Canadian to exercise their legal rights. More recently, a growing body of research has begun to quantify the extent of unmet legal need in our communities and to describe the disquieting individual and social consequences of failing to respond adequately to family legal problems.

We have in Canada a highly evolved and comprehensive body of substantive family laws designed to help provide direction to families about the rules that apply when issues arise on separation. Unfortunately, the procedures by which this substantive law is invoked are increasingly complex, unaffordable and inaccessible. Without access to the mechanisms to implement them, the substantive rules have limited value....

We identify two primary barriers to change. One is the limited resources available for the family justice system. Despite the pervasiveness of family justice problems, the general public, media and politician are far more engaged with criminal law matters. This heightened interest fuels criminal law reform efforts and often translates into funding support for criminal justice as a priority over family law.

The implementation gap is also a function of the culture of the justice system and its incomplete embrace of non-adversarial or consensual dispute resolution processes. While progress has been made on this front, the potential of non-adversarial programs and consensual processes in family law has not yet been fully realized. Accordingly, we see further culture change as one of the more important options for enhanced access to family justice.*

There is probably no other substantive area of law in Canada that has changed as much in the past 50 years as has family law. The grounds for divorce have been dramatically restructured; the rules that guide the provision of both spousal and child support have also changed, as have both the definition of matrimonial property and the principles that determine appropriate allocation. And perhaps most fundamentally, the conception of marriage itself has been altered, both within our communities and in our laws.

In July 2005 Canada passed Bill C-38, an act that provides for same-sex marriage for civil purposes. Although many in the religious communities argued against the

---

*Action Committee on Access to Justice in Civil and Family Matters, *Meaningful Change for Family Justice: Beyond Wise Words*, Ottawa, April, 2013.

bill, it was clear from the outset that the standards of these communities would not be affected by the legislation; these religious organizations could continue to bar homosexual men and women from marriage within their churches, synagogues, or mosques. More specifically, Bill C-38 simply provided for the equality of heterosexual and homosexual men and women within civil unions, extending these existing rights in British Columbia and Ontario to all provinces and territories of Canada. The text of the legislation is excerpted below.

An Act respecting certain aspects of legal capacity for marriage for civil purposes

[Assented to 20th July, 2005]

Preamble

WHEREAS the Parliament *of* Canada is committed to upholding the Constitution of Canada, and section 15 of the *Canadian Charter of Rights and Freedoms* guarantees that every individual *is equal* before and under the law and has the right to equal protection and equal benefit of the law without discrimination;

WHEREAS the courts in a majority of the provinces and in one territory have recognized that the right to equality without discrimination requires that couples of the same sex and couples of the opposite sex have equal access to marriage for civil purposes;

WHEREAS the Supreme Court of Canada has recognized that many Canadian couples of the same sex have married in reliance on those court decisions;

WHEREAS only equal access to marriage for civil purposes would respect the right of couples of the same sex to equality without discrimination, and civil union, as an institution other than marriage, would not offer them that equal access and would violate their human dignity, in breach of the *Canadian Charter of Rights and Freedoms*;

WHEREAS the Supreme Court of Canada has determined that the Parliament of Canada has legislative jurisdiction over marriage but does not have the jurisdiction to establish an institution other than marriage for couples of the same sex;

WHEREAS everyone has the freedom of conscience and religion under section 2 of the *Canadian Charter of Rights and Freedoms*;

WHEREAS nothing in this Act affects the guarantee of freedom of conscience and religion and, in particular, the freedom of members of religious groups to hold and declare their religious beliefs and the freedom of officials of religious groups to refuse to perform marriages that are not in accordance with their religious beliefs;

WHEREAS it is not against the public interest to hold and publicly express diverse views on marriage;

WHEREAS, in light of those considerations, the Parliament of Canada's commitment to uphold the right to equality without discrimination precludes the use of section 33 of the *Canadian Charter of Rights and Freedoms* to deny the right of couples of the same sex to equal access to marriage for civil purposes;

WHEREAS marriage is a fundamental institution in Canadian society and the Parliament of Canada has a responsibility to support that institution because it strengthens commitment in relationships and represents the foundation of family life for many Canadians;

AND WHEREAS, in order to reflect values of tolerance, respect and equality consistent with the *Canadian Charter of Rights and Freedoms,* access to marriage for civil purposes should be extended by legislation to couples of the same sex;

NOW, THEREFORE, Her Majesty, by and with the advice and consent of the Senate and House of Commons of Canada, enacts as follows;

1. *This Act may be cited as the Civil Marriage Act.*

2. *Marriage, for civil purposes, is the lawful union of two persons to the exclusion of all others.*

3. *It is recognized that officials of religious groups are free to refuse to perform marriages that are not in accordance with their religious beliefs.*

3.1 *For greater certainty, no person or organization shall be deprived of any benefit, or be subject to any obligation or sanction, under any law of the Parliament of Canada solely by reason of their exercise, in respect of marriage between persons of the same sex, of the freedom of conscience and religion guaranteed under the Canadian Charter of Rights and Freedoms or the expression of their beliefs in respect of marriage as the union of a man and woman to the exclusion of all others based on that guaranteed freedom.*

4. *For greater certainty, a marriage is not void or voidable by reason only that the spouses are of the same sex.*

The Canadian family of 2014 is dramatically different from the Canadian family of the 1960s. In this new millennium nuclear families, single-parent families, and blended families are common, and the divorce rate is four times that of 1960. Same-sex marriage, within a civil context, is now a legal reality. Moreover, the prevalence of **common-law relations** has led to legal recognition of spousal obligations in the absence of marriage, and, more recently, to requirements of allocation of matrimonial property after two years of cohabitation. Such changes have been summarized by sociologist John Conway:

The growing diversity of family forms is self-evident. New "unorthodox" family forms—especially dual-earner and single-parent families—will become the orthodox family forms of the future as they characterize the experience of a growing majority of Canadians. Families are smaller and less stable, and family life is more episodic as we marry later, as divorce and separation rates grow, and as remarriage touches more and more of our lives. Many more Canadians are opting for single lifestyles, and fewer are feeling it obligatory to have children. More women are choosing to have children as single mothers and to remain single for significant portions of their lives. Materially, people have more choices, and ideologically, people are more willing to exercise them.[1]

SOCIAL CHANGE AND THE *DIVORCE ACT* OF 1968

At the turn of the century, **divorce** was a rarity in Canada, a complex and cumbersome legal process. In some provinces, a "parliamentary divorce" was the only option: a private member's bill had to pass first reading in both the Commons and the Senate; after second reading in the House of Commons, it could be heard by a special divorce committee. James Snell observed from his study of divorce in Canada between 1900 and 1940:

> Divorce in Canada was squarely founded on a belief in innocence and guilt, which meshed nicely with the moral pathology of divorce. The process itself, through mandatory confrontation, always and with impressive assurance assigned those attributes to the participating parties. Few divorces were granted through either the judicial or the legislative process, and the matter was not of particular concern in the dominion.[2]

Changes in social attitudes with respect to divorce began before the Second World War, but it was not until the 1960s that the law changed to reflect the new realities. The *Divorce Act* of 1968, the first federal divorce statute, took a first step toward "no fault" divorce, permitting dissolution of a **marriage** if the partners had lived "separate and apart" for a period of three or five years.

Some have argued that the increase in divorce during the late 1960s and early 1970s can be tied to the sexual liberation and feminist movements. The slogans "Make love, not war," "If it feels good, do it," and "Love the one you're with" epitomized the viewpoint of the era. Sexual activity, with or without emotional commitment, was set out as a valuable experience fulfilling both physical and social needs. In this social climate, the commitments of traditional marriage were effectively undermined. Feminist arguments in favour of gender equality were also in conflict with traditional cultural conceptions. The bride's solemn vow to honour and obey the groom epitomized a pre-feminist family power structure. Feminism helped to rewrite this cultural script. Conservatives and liberals have been arguing ever since, with conservatives insisting that feminism is to blame for the increased divorce rate, and liberals suggesting that divorce is not an evil in itself, and that less restrictive divorce laws have helped to give women a greater range of choices.

Behind these changes in attitude and conflicts in philosophy were a number of technological and social developments. In the early 1960s, the birth control pill became widely available, allowing women in most Western industrial cultures a measure of the sexual freedom that men had traditionally enjoyed. The ability to engage in sexual relations with minimal risk of pregnancy created the material conditions in which an ideology of sexual liberation could flourish. More important, women's control over their fertility was linked to change in the economic and social structure of the family. Women were entering the labour force in unprecedented numbers for both material and ideological reasons. In 1966, 2.3 million women were in the labour force in Canada; by 1975, the number had reached more than 5.5 million women; in 2001, the figure had reached almost 7.5 million women, and by 2013, more than 9 million. The number of married women in the labour force increased by almost 70 percent during the same period. Today, dual-earner families are the most common type of family.[3]

JURISDICTION OVER FAMILY LAW

The power to legislate in relation to marriage and divorce is given to the federal government in the *British North America Act, 1867*. The power to solemnize marriage is given to the provinces by section 92(12) of the same act, but the key jurisdictional section for the purpose of family law is section 92(13), which is concerned with "property and civil rights." It gives the provinces the right to legislate in relation to matrimonial property, the support of **spouses** and children, and custody; it also confers jurisdiction over the related matters of succession, adoption, and guardianship. Therefore, Canada has a divided jurisdiction in matters of family law. The *Divorce Act* is federally constructed and applied in federal courts, pursuant to petitions for divorce. But other family-related matters—custody, property, and support—are heard in provincial courts only if they are not determined in the context of a divorce action.

THE LEGAL DEFINITION OF "FAMILY"

This brings us to the question of what the term "family law" really means. *The Oxford Reference Dictionary* defines "family" as "the members of a household."* But how, then, do we define what is meant by "household"? Is the legality of marriage a precondition for a household, and hence a family? Can same-sex couples constitute a household and, hence, a family? Do obligations with respect to property, support, and child custody arise in the absence of marriage? The clear answer to the last question is yes—the state is willing to intervene, in the absence of marriage, to confer familial obligations upon individual citizens. Consider, for example, the 2013 enactment of the *Family Law Act* in British Columbia, with measures mandating matrimonial property division in the event of the dissolution of common-law relationships. The law of contract, implied or express, gives rise to many of these commitments.

In the face of conflicting definitions and beliefs about the nature of family and sexuality, some Canadians advocate a return to an allegedly more simple time when Father was the breadwinner and Mother stayed at home raising the children. As sociologist Roberta Hamilton has noted, feminists, wage-earning women, homosexuals, and lesbians—inasmuch as each represents a changing family form—have all become, in some circles, targets of disaffection. Hamilton argues that the enduring and defining feature of the family over the past 2000 years has been the contributions of women, most often made in difficult circumstances:

> Women have always had to support their families. In feudal society, they toiled without respite to support themselves and their children. In capitalist society, they

---

The Oxford Reference Dictionary, edited by Joyce M. Hawkins, Clarendon Press, Oxford, 1986, Pg. 292.

have had to supplement their husbands' incomes through work done at home, through seeking waged work, and making whatever arrangements they could for their children.... Because of death, sickness, desertion, or unemployment, many have been sole supporters of their children. The particular contingencies of women's lives today emerged on the world stage with the transition to capitalism three hundred years ago.[4]

As mentioned above, the law of contract gives rise to such familial obligations as **child custody**, **child support**, and **spousal support**. The question then arises: Is family law different from the law of contract in any way? Is the family simply one more context in which two individuals enter into a legally enforceable contract, express or implied? If that is the case, marriage is simply a statement of benefits and obligations existing over time. In legal terms, its only significance is that it serves to simplify definition of the contractual relationship. Although marriage might be said to have originated within the context of either property or ecclesiastical law, it is, in the contemporary world, best situated within the realm of contract.

Despite this narrowly legalistic viewpoint, the family, broadly defined, remains an important structure in cultural and community life, providing guidance to the future generation. The restructuring of the Canadian family over the past few decades has produced dramatic increases in the numbers of children raised in poverty. While 10 percent of single-male-parent families live in poverty, more than 60 percent of single-female-**parent** families do so.[5] These figures are not adequately explained by the principles of contract; nor do such principles explain the recent recognition of homosexual marriage, which is, rather, an extension of the definition of family. And in child-custody disputes, the legal matter of the best interests of the child is typically seen in the context of nurturance and support, not in the law of contract. All in all, family law is, in both human and conceptual terms, quite distinct from an essentially economic bargain.

GROUNDS FOR DIVORCE UNDER THE *DIVORCE ACT* OF 1968

The *Divorce Act* of 1968 imposed uniform standards for divorce on all the provinces and territories. The grounds for petitioning for divorce were set out in sections 3 and 4. For the most part, a petitioner still had to rely upon the notion of fault. Section 3 granted a divorce on the grounds of adultery, sodomy, bestiality, rape, bigamy, and physical and mental cruelty. Section 4 granted divorce in the instance of imprisonment, addiction to drugs without prospect of rehabilitation, failure to consummate the marriage, and, most significantly, varying periods of living separate and apart.

Section 4(1)(e)(i) provided that a divorce could be granted after three years of **separation** if the petitioner had been "deserted" by the respondent. In order to prove desertion, the petitioner had to establish that there had been an intention to desert, proof of living separate and apart as well as proof of lack of consent to the separation, and no just cause for the separation. Section 4(1)(c)(ii) allowed a petition for divorce after living separate and apart for five years, with no requirement of establishing desertion.

Between 1968 and the early 1980s, the number of divorces granted in Canada continued to increase, from just under 30,000 in 1970 to more than 70,000 in 1982. Although marital offences of adultery and mental and physical cruelty continued as the most common grounds for divorce, almost one-third of petitions were granted on the new ground of separation.[6]

Pressure for the reform of divorce law continued to mount throughout the 1970s. Critics argued that the 1968 legislation was too restrictive. The three- and five-year periods of separation were assailed as impractical, and as serving to produce lengthy conflict between the parties. Critics also argued that the grounds for divorce remained tied to the outdated practice of assigning fault for marriage breakdown, further intensifying rather than diminishing the existing conflict between husband and wife.

THE *DIVORCE ACT* OF 1985

In 1985, a new *Divorce Act* was enacted which remains in force today, albeit with some amendments relating to child custody passed in 1997. In its introduction to the act, the Ministry of Justice noted:

> [S]hortening the separation period to one year from the present requirement of three years is designed to reduce the conflict between the spouses. At the same time, it is considered long enough to allow for second thought, and to avoid rash and hasty divorces, especially since the law will allow for periods of resumption of cohabitation for the purpose of reconciliation without interrupting the period of separation.[7]

Section 8 of the 1985 *Divorce Act* reads as follows:

> 8.(1) A court of competent jurisdiction may, on application by either or both spouses, grant a divorce to the spouse or spouses on the ground that there has been a breakdown of their marriage.
>
> (2) Breakdown of a marriage is established only if
>
>   (a) the spouses have lived separate and apart for at least one year immediately preceding the determination of the divorce proceeding and were living separate and apart at the commencement of the proceeding; or
>
>   (b) the spouse against whom the divorce proceeding is brought has, since celebration of the marriage,
>
>   (i) committed adultery, or
>
>   (ii) treated the other spouse with physical or mental cruelty of such a kind as to render intolerable the continued cohabitation of the spouses.

Grounds for Divorce under the *Divorce Act* of 1985

The Canadian Bar Association had urged the federal government to adopt a different form of legislation, one which focused on *whether* a marriage had broken down, not *why*. The association urged abandonment of any notion of fault as an element of marriage breakdown, proposing this wording for the legislation:

A petition for divorce on breakdown of marriage:

> (a) *shall be established if the husband and wife have lived separate and apart for a period of one year that immediately precedes, includes, or immediately follows the date of presentation of the petition;*
>
> (b) *may be established on proof satisfactory to the Court that a marriage has irretrievably broken down.*[8]

But the Canadian Bar Association's recommendations were not accepted. Current law maintains a focus on fault, within section 8(2) of the act. Proof of wrongdoing—adultery or mental or physical cruelty—continues to be required in the case of petitions filed pursuant to section 8(2)(b), even though such petitions are now rare.

ADULTERY

Is it even useful to inquire about fault, if the goal of the act is simply to establish whether a marriage has broken down? Furthermore, as a technical matter, how is adultery to be proven? Consider the dilemma of *Shaw v. Shaw*.

Dubinsky, J.: At the conclusion of the hearing in this case, I granted a decree nisi in the divorce petition by Mrs. Shaw on the ground of cruelty. I reserved my decision on the counter-petition by Mr. Shaw on the ground of adultery.

Harold Bellefontaine, the corespondent named in the counter-petition, denied that he had committed adultery with Mrs. Shaw, the respondent by the counter-petition.

I am on safe ground in saying that there is no direct evidence of any adulterous relationship between Mrs. Shaw and Mr. Bellefontaine. It follows, therefore, that if adultery is to be found herein on the part of the respondent (the respondent by the counter-petition), it must be inferred from the proven facts.

Power on Divorce, 2nd ed., 1964, p. 425, states as follows:

Since it is almost never possible to adduce direct evidence of the act of adultery, its commission is permitted to be proven by evidence of acts or a course of conduct which convinces the court that it should infer that it did occur.

The inference can be drawn although both parties deny their guilt. The drawing of the inference must always be with caution and evidence that creates only a suspicion of adultery is insufficient.

It is now settled that the standard of proof required in a divorce action wherein no question of legitimacy arises is not that applicable to criminal cases, where the prosecution must prove guilt beyond a reasonable doubt, but is the standard required in civil actions where the preponderance of probabilities determines the issues....

It is impossible to lay down any general rule defining the circumstances which are sufficient in an action for divorce to justify a finding of adultery, except that the circumstances must be such as lead by fair and reasonable inference to that conclusion. Each case depends on its own particular facts. Evidence of familiarities between the parties and of facts showing opportunity for the commission of adultery raise a prima facie case that adultery has been committed, but the inference should always be drawn with extreme caution and it has been held should not be drawn unless there is proof of an inclination to commit adultery.

It would, in my opinion, be a reasonable and guarded inference from the facts that Mrs. Shaw and Mr. Bellefontaine, a married man with two children, were seeing so much of each other that the opportunities for her to commit adultery were present. However, Lord Atkin in *Ross v. Ellison (Ross),* [1930] A.C. 1 at 23, points out:

That there were opportunities for committing adultery is nothing; **there must be circumstances amounting to proof that the opportunities would be used.** *(The boldface is mine.)*

... I would regard it as a sorry day if a married person could not have and enjoy the warm friendship of one of the opposite sex, without being stamped with the stigma of impropriety.

In two fairly recent cases, where the same sort of situation existed, I did draw the inference that adultery had been committed. In each of these cases, there was something which led me to find as I did. In the first case, there was evidence that on one occasion the respondent and corespondent, who were both present at a party, were found lying fully clothed on the bed of a darkened bedroom. This uncontradicted piece of evidence led me to conclude that they were there for an amorous purpose. This incident, coupled with other evidence, led me to infer that adultery had taken place between the respondent and corespondent.

In the other cases, there was introduced a letter which had been written by the respondent to the corespondent and which referred to the great love that existed between them, as well as other things. That letter, when added to other evidence which had been given, led me to infer that adultery had been committed.

In each of these two cases, I had in mind what Lord Buckmaster said in *Ross v. Ellison (Ross),* supra, at p. 7:

Adultery is essentially an act which can rarely be proved by direct evidence. It is a matter of inference and circumstance. It is easy to suggest conditions which can leave no doubt that adultery has been committed, but the mere fact that people are thrown together in an environment which lends itself to the commission of the offence is not enough unless it can be shown **by documents, e.g. letters and diaries, or antecedent conduct that the association of the parties was so intimate and their mutual passion so clear that adultery might reasonably be assumed as the result of an opportunity for its occurrence.** *(The boldface is mine.)*

In short, keeping in mind the authorities quoted above and reviewing all the evidence given in the present case touching upon the allegation of adultery, I am not led to the conclusion that adultery was committed by Mrs. Shaw and Mr. Bellefontaine. Accordingly, I dismiss the counter-petition.[9]

Shaw v. Shaw illustrates the difficulty of proof of adultery and simultaneously leads to the question whether such proof is ultimately relevant to a finding of marriage breakdown. As the Canadian Bar Association has argued, perhaps the inquiry of the court ought to be directed to the simpler question of whether the marriage has broken down, not to the factually difficult requirement of proof of specific acts that often accompany marriage breakdown.

MENTAL OR PHYSICAL CRUELTY

With the issues of mental or physical cruelty, the requirement of proof poses similar difficulties as adultery. Consider the following excerpts from the cases *Knoll v. Knoll* and *S. (J.G.) v. S. (W.O.J.)*. The first case was decided under the *Divorce Act* of 1968, prior to the 1985 reconstruction of the legislation; the second case was decided in 2004. The relevant section in *Knoll v. Knoll* was section 3(d), which is virtually identical to section 8(2)(b)(ii) of the current act:

> 3. *Subject to section 5, a petition for divorce may be presented to a court by a husband or wife, on the ground that the respondent, since the celebration of the marriage ...*
>
>> (d) *has treated the petitioner with physical or mental cruelty of such a kind as to render intolerable the continued cohabitation of the spouses.*

Knoll v. Knoll was an appeal by the wife to the Ontario Court of Appeal following the dismissal of her petition for divorce at trial. She had sought divorce on the ground of physical or mental cruelty. Evidence at trial revealed that her husband became very abusive toward her when he drank. He had both assaulted her and verbally abused her on a number of these occasions.

Schroeder, J.A.: Over the years, the courts have steadfastly refrained from attempting to formulate a general definition of cruelty. As used in ordinary parlance, "cruelty" signifies a disposition to inflict suffering; to delight in or exhibit indifference to the pain or misery of others; mercilessness or hard-heartedness as exhibited in action. If in the marriage relationship, one spouse, by his conduct, causes wanton, malicious, or unnecessary infliction of pain or suffering upon the body, the feeling, or emotions of the other, his conduct may well constitute cruelty which will entitle a petitioner to dissolution of the marriage if, in the court's opinion, it amounts to physical or mental cruelty "of such a kind as to render intolerable the continued cohabitation of the spouses." ...

    Care must be exercised in applying the standard set forth in s. 3(d) that conduct relied upon to establish cruelty is not a trivial act, but one of a "grave and weighty" nature, and not merely conduct which can be characterized as little more than a manifestation of incompatibility of temperament between the spouses. The whole matrimonial relations must be considered, especially if the cruelty consists of reproaches, complaints, accusations, or constant carping criticisms. A question most relevant for consideration is the effect of the conduct complained of upon the mind of the affected spouse. The determination of what constitutes cruelty in a given case must, in the final analysis, depend upon the circumstances of the particular case, having due regard to the physical and mental condition of the parties, their character, and their attitudes toward the marriage relationship.

In the present case, it is the cumulative effect of the acts of the defendant upon the petitioner which must be considered and given proper weight. The wife's return to her home after a day's work only to find her husband in an inebriated state, given to quarrelsomeness and abuse, heaping insult upon insult and indignity upon indignity, was clearly conduct amounting to mental cruelty of such a kind as to render intolerable the continued cohabitation of the spouses. I cannot be convinced that our community standards require a wife to tolerate such an intolerable situation.[10]

Consider, on the other hand, the rationale in an excerpt from the more recent case of *S. (J.G.) v. S. (W.O.J.)*, with its acknowledgement that cruelty has become an increasingly uncommon ground for divorce.[11]

Macaulay J.: I am concerned only with the necessary proof of cruelty as the one year separation before determination of the divorce proceeding as required by s. 8(2)(a) will not occur until November 8, 2004.

The application for divorce based on cruelty does not require any wait. The *Divorce Act* permits an application for a divorce based on the breakdown of the marriage due to cruelty at any time if:

8(2)(b) the spouse against whom the divorce proceeding is brought has, since celebration of the marriage,

> *(ii) treated the other spouse with physical or mental cruelty of such a kind as to render intolerable the continued cohabitation of the spouses.*

I am not satisfied that the plaintiff established cruelty within the meaning of the subsection and accordingly, the application for a divorce on such basis is dismissed. I am not dismissing the action for divorce as the plaintiff will be able to reapply in due course for a divorce under the alternative ground.

Applications for divorce based on cruelty are rare. The partial explanation may be that parties choose instead to apply under the so-called no fault provision set out in s. 8(2)(a). Parties choosing to rely on alleged cruelty should take care to place a proper evidentiary basis before the court. The evidence in the present case fell well short of meeting the objective and subjective test for establishing cruelty.

In her affidavit sworn March 3, 2004, in support of the application for a desk order divorce, the plaintiff deposed:

The facts alleged in the Statement of Claim as particulars of the cruelty with which I have been treated since the celebration of marriage are true and particulars of such cruelty include the following:

a. The Defendant ignored me and withheld affection from me and refused to have any relationship with me for approximately the last five years and would continuously refuse to have any intimate contact with me.

b. The Defendant, to my knowledge, has been involved in grotesque and deviant sexual relationships with other female persons. I have photographic and other evidence of these relationships, but do not wish to produce them in these proceedings as they are very disturbing.

As stated earlier, this evidence is inadequate.

While evidence of refusal to have intimate contact over an extended period of time may be objectively capable of constituting cruelty, there is no evidence here of the subjective impact of the refusal on the plaintiff. As to the conduct referred to in (b) above, there are problems with both the objective and subjective tests.

I cannot determine whether the plaintiff learned of the defendant's conduct with other women before, during or after the fact. It is also not clear whether the conduct occurred before or during the marriage. Assuming it occurred during the marriage, the timing and manner in which the plaintiff learned of it and the aftermath might have assisted in objectively establishing cruelty.

The *Divorce Act* only permits a divorce when the marriage breaks down because one spouse treated the other cruelly so as to render continued cohabitation intolerable. It does not permit a divorce simply on the basis that one party may have mistreated other persons. In this case, the plaintiff failed to adequately address how the defendant's conduct rendered cohabitation intolerable.

The court should not be left to speculate on any of these questions. The plaintiff failed to establish marriage breakdown due to cruelty within the meaning of the *Divorce Act*.

The *Divorce Act* of 1985 and the Question of Support

The question of support for a spouse in the event of marriage breakdown typically generates considerable discussion and controversy. The relevant sections—15, 15.1(1), 15.2(1) to (6), 15.3(1), (2), and 17(7)—of the *Divorce Act* of 1985 state:

15. In sections 15.1 to 16, "spouse" has the meaning assigned by subsection 2(1), and includes a former spouse.

15.1 (1) A court of competent jurisdiction may, on application by either or both spouses, make an order requiring a spouse to pay for the support of any or all children of the marriage....

15.2 (1) A court of competent jurisdiction may, on application by either or both spouses, make an order requiring a spouse to secure or pay, or to secure and pay, such lump sum or periodic sums, or such lump sum and periodic sums, as the court thinks reasonable for the support of the other spouse.

(2) Where an application is made under subsection (1), the court may, on application by either or both spouses, make an interim order requiring a spouse to secure or pay, or to secure and pay, such lump sum or periodic sums, or such lump sum and periodic sums, as the court thinks reasonable for the support of the other spouse, pending the determination of the application under subsection (1).

(3) The court may make an order under subsection (1) or an interim order under subsection (2) for a definite or indefinite period or until a specified event occurs, and may impose terms, conditions or restrictions in connection with the order as it thinks fit and just.

(4) In making an order under subsection (1) or an interim order under subsection (2), the court shall take into consideration the condition, means, needs and other circumstances of each spouse, including

(a) the length of time the spouses cohabited;

(b) the functions performed by each spouse during cohabitation; and

(c) any order, agreement or arrangement relating to support of either spouse.

(5) In making an order under subsection (1) or an interim order under subsection (2), the court shall not take into consideration any misconduct of a spouse in relation to the marriage.

(6) An order made under subsection (1) or an interim order under subsection (2) that provides for the support of a spouse should

(a) recognize any economic advantages or disadvantages to the spouses arising from the marriage or its breakdown;

(b) apportion between the spouses any financial consequences arising from the care of any child of the marriage over and above any obligation for the support of any child of the marriage;

(c) relieve any economic hardship of the spouses arising from the breakdown of the marriage; and

(d) in so far as practicable, promote the economic self-sufficiency of each spouse within a reasonable period of time....

15.3 (1) Where a court is considering an application for a child support order and an application for a spousal support order, the court shall give priority to child support in determining the applications.

(2) Where, as a result of giving priority to child support, the court is unable to make a spousal support order or the court makes a spousal support order in an amount that is less than it otherwise would have been, the court shall record its reasons for having done so.

17. (7) A variation order varying a spousal support order should

(a) recognize any economic advantages or disadvantages to the former spouses arising from the marriage or its breakdown;

    (b) apportion between the former spouses any financial consequences arising from the care of any child of the marriage over and above the obligation for the support of any child of the marriage;

    (c) relieve any economic hardship of the former spouses arising from the breakdown of the marriage; and

    (d) in so far as practicable, promote the economic self-sufficiency of each former spouse within a reasonable period of time.

Sections 15.2(6)(d) and 17(7)(d) set out an important general principle with respect to claims for spousal support: an expectation of self-sufficiency "within a reasonable period of time." In the mid-1970s, both the Ontario Law Reform Commission and the Law Reform Commission of Canada had called for the reform of spousal maintenance obligations in the event of marriage breakdown. Prior to the passage of the *Divorce Act* of 1985, there was very little guidance as to the principles applicable to spousal support. Section 11 of the *Divorce Act* of 1968 provided for awards of maintenance to husband or wife, "if (the court) thinks it fit and just to do so having regard to the conduct of the parties and the condition, means, and other circumstances of each of them." The current *Divorce Act* provides more guidance, asserting equality between spouses, basing support on the principle of need, and assuming self-sufficiency of each spouse "within a reasonable period of time." The meanings to be attributed to these concepts were delineated by the Supreme Court of Canada in the landmark case of *Moge v. Moge.*

Consider the following excerpt from the Supreme Court of Canada's unanimous decision,[12] handed down in late 1992:

L'Heureux-Dubé, J.: At the heart of this appeal lies the question of spousal support. Specifically, the Court is asked to determine the circumstances under which spousal support ought to be varied or terminated pursuant to s. 17 of the *Divorce Act....* In a broader sense, however, this case turns upon the basic philosophy of support within the Act as a whole.

Mrs. Moge was born in 1937. The parties were married in Poland in the mid-'50s. It is unclear from the evidence or the recollection of the parties whether the marriage took place in 1955 or 1957, but the discrepancy is immaterial for the purposes of this appeal. They decided to emigrate and moved to Manitoba in 1960. Three children were born of the marriage. The two elder children, Elizabeth and Victor, were born in Poland prior to the family's coming to Canada. The youngest, Edward, was born in 1966 and at the time of the application at issue, was studying at the University of Manitoba.

Mrs. Moge has a Grade 7 education. Prior to coming to this country, she worked briefly as a sales clerk. During the marriage, she was responsible for the day-today care of the children and did the laundry, housework, shopping, cooking and so on. She was also employed in the evenings working from 5:00 p.m. until 11:00 p.m. cleaning offices, except for a brief period in 1963–64 when she worked as a seamstress. In his pleading, Mr. Moge attempted to persuade the Court that this was a marriage in which both contributed to the domestic chores, she during the day while he worked as a welder with Motor Coach Industries, and he in the evening while she worked. However, Twaddle J.A., whose reasons in the Court of Appeal I will examine in more detail later, found based on the evidence that:

There is no suggestion that the wife's outside employment was undertaken for any reason other than the need to supplement her husband's income. Nor is there any suggestion that the husband undertook additional responsibilities at home to counterbalance the wife's efforts in the external work force. In all respects, this was a traditional relationship of the kind which was common then and which was in conformity with the social conventions of the time.

In 1973, the parties separated and on November 22, 1974, Nitikman J. of the Manitoba Court of Queen's Bench granted the separation and made an order awarding custody of the children to Mrs. Moge. Mr. Moge was ordered to pay $150 per month spousal and child support. After the separation, Mrs. Moge continued to work outside the home. From 5:00 p.m. until 11:00 p.m. she cleaned at the Fort Garry Hotel in Winnipeg. During this time she remained responsible for the care of the children, and while she was out of the home in the evenings, the older children apparently helped out with Edward.

A divorce petition was filed by Mr. Moge in 1980. It was not opposed by Mrs. Moge and she did not appear on the hearing of the petition to oppose her husband's proposal that he continue to pay $150 per month toward her maintenance and that of the remaining dependent child. Mr. Moge remarried in 1984 but continued to pay support to his former wife.

Mrs. Moge was employed at the Fort Garry Hotel from 1975 until January of 1987 when it closed down.... The evidence disclosed that, at the time she was laid off in 1987, she was earning approximately $795 net per month. Her net monthly income (excluding support) was reduced to $593 in unemployment insurance benefits. The evidence further discloses that during the period she was out of work, she unsuccessfully sought employment with 38 prospective employers. Mr. Moge was then earning approximately $2,000 in gross monthly income and also derived a small amount from investments. He and his second wife had purchased a home.

Mrs. Moge applied to vary the spousal and child support order pursuant to which she was continuing to receive $150 per month. She was successful and a variation order was made by Mullally J. of the Manitoba Court of Queen's Bench on October 14, 1987. The order provided for spousal support of $200 per month and child support of $200 per month, thereby increasing her total monthly support from $150 to $400.

Between December 14, 1987 and June 30, 1989, Mrs. Moge was able to secure part-time and intermittent cleaning work with the province of Manitoba. The longest period of work began on November 14, 1988 and ended on June 30, 1989. During this period, she worked from early to mid-morning for a total of 20 hours per week and received $9.28 per hour or approximately $800 gross per month. By way of comparison, though by no means independently wealthy, Mr. Moge was earning approximately $2,200 per month. His second wife was also employed.

In May of 1989, Mr. Moge applied to vary both the child and spousal support orders of October 14, 1987. This second application also came before Mullally J. By an order pronounced September 29, 1989 and signed on December 7, 1989, child support was terminated and spousal support was to cease on December 1, 1989. The wife appealed on the issue of spousal support only. On April 5, 1990, the Court of Appeal allowed Mrs. Moge's appeal in part and ordered spousal support in the amount of $150 per month for an indefinite period beginning January 1, 1990. Mr. Moge now appeals that decision to this court....

The Trilogy and Its Jurisprudence

The position of Mr. Moge before this Court is that his support obligation to his ex-wife should be terminated on the basis of the reasoning in *Pelech,* supra, *Richardson v. Richardson,* [1987] 1 S.C.R. 857, and *Caron v. Caron,* [1987] 1 S.C.R. 892, the so-called "trilogy." He submits that though those cases specifically concerned situations in which the parties had set out their respective rights and obligations following the dissolution of the marriage by agreement, the Court was advocating a model of support to be relied upon even in the absence of a final settlement.

That model, he says, is characterized by such notions as self-sufficiency and causal connection. Effectively, his position is that his ex-wife should have been self-sufficient by now and, if she is not, no link may be drawn between that lack of self-sufficiency and the marriage (i.e., no causal connection). In other words, her current financial position is no concern of his....

The question that arises is the extent to which the causal connection test articulated in *Pelech,* supra, decided under the 1970 *Divorce Act,* applies to nonconsensual dispositions under the Act, as is the case here....

Introduction

Before dealing squarely with the main issue raised by this appeal, there are a number of preliminary observations that I wish to make.

The first has to do with the argument raised by Mr. Moge that, quite apart from the trilogy, the Act espouses a self-sufficiency model as the only basis of spousal support.... Mrs. Moge disagrees. She points out that self-sufficiency is only one of many objectives which the Act directs a court of competent jurisdiction to consider in exercising its discretion under ss. 17(4) and 17(7) and that even then, the objective of self-sufficiency in s. 17(7) is modified by such terminology as "insofar as practicable." She further submits that there is now appellate court jurisprudence which recognizes that in cases such as her own, self-sufficiency will not be practicable, largely due to the residual effects of being outside the labour market for a protracted period of time.

The self-sufficiency model advanced by Mr. Moge has generally been predicated on the dichotomy between "traditional" and "modern" marriage. Often, in order to draw the line after which no more support will be ordered, courts have distinguished between "traditional" marriages in which the wife remains at home and takes responsibility for the domestic aspects of marital life, and "modern" ones where employment outside the home is pursued.... [A]s Judge Rosalie S. Abella wrote ... "it is hard to be an independent equal when one is not equally able to become independent." ... [C]ourts have frequently been more amenable to finding that "traditional" marriages survive the so-called "causal connection" test (more often) than "modern" ones....

The second observation I wish to make is that, in determining spousal support, it is important not to lose sight of the fact that the support provisions of the Act are intended to deal with the economic consequences, for both parties, of the marriage or its breakdown. Marriage may unquestionably be a source of benefit to both parties that is not easily quanti-fied in economic terms. Many believe that marriage and the family provide for the emotional, economic, and social well-being of [the] members. It may be the location of safety and comfort, and may be the place where its members have their most intimate human contact. Marriage and the family act as an emotional and economic support system as well as a forum for intimacy. In this regard, [they] serve vital personal interest, and may be linked to building a "comprehensive sense of personhood." Marriage and the family are a superb environment for raising and nurturing the young of our society by providing the initial environment for the development of social skills. These institutions also provide a means to pass on the values that we deem to be central to our sense of community.

Conversely, marriage and the family often require the sacrifice of personal priorities by both parties in the interests of shared goals. All of these elements are of undeniable importance in shaping the overall character of a marriage. Spousal support in the context of divorce, however, is not about the emotional and social benefits of marriage. Rather, the purpose of spousal support is to relieve economic hardship that results from "marriage or its breakdown." Whatever the respective advantages to the parties of a marriage in other areas, the focus of the inquiry when assessing spousal support after the marriage has ended must be the effect of the marriage in either impairing or improving each party's economic prospects....

A third point worthy of emphasis is that this analysis applies equally to both spouses, depending on how the division of labour is exercised in a particular marriage. What the Act requires is a fair and equitable distribution of resources to alleviate the economic conse-quences of marriage or marriage breakdown for both spouses, regardless of gender. The reality, however, is that in many if not most marriages, the wife still remains the economically disadvantaged partner. There may be times where the reverse is true and the Act is equally able to accommodate this eventuality....

The Objectives of the Act

The most significant change in the new Act when compared to the 1970 *Divorce Act* may be the shift away from the "means and needs" test as the exclusive criterion for support to a more encompassing set of factors and objectives which requires courts to accommodate a much wider spectrum of considerations. This change, of course, does not signify that "means and needs" are to be ignored. Section 15(5) [now 15.2(4)] of the Act specifically states that "the court shall take into consideration the condition, means, needs and other circumstances of each spouse." ...

All four of the objectives defined in the Act (under section 17(7)) must be taken into account when spousal support is claimed or an order for spousal support is sought to be varied. No single objective is paramount. The fact that one of the objectives, such as economic self-sufficiency, has been attained does not necessarily dispose of the matter....

Many proponents of the deemed self-sufficiency model effectively elevate it to the pre-eminent objective in determining the right to, quantum and duration of spousal support. In my opinion, this approach is not consonant with proper principles of statutory interpretation. The objective of self-sufficiency is only one of several objectives enumerated in the section and, given the manner in which Parliament has set out those objectives, I see no indication that any one is to be given priority. Parliament, in my opinion, intended that support reflect the diverse dynamics of many unique marital relationships....

An examination of the economic position of single mothers is also useful in assessing the effects of dissolution of marriage since about 30 percent of single mothers are divorced: Statistics Canada, *Women in Canada: A Statistical Report* (2nd ed.) 1990. In 1987, 57 per-cent of single mothers lived below the poverty line....

Reports such as these have led many Canadian commentators to draw direct links between female poverty and the financial consequences of the dissolution of marriage. While Eichler emphasizes the limits of family law in addressing poverty in "The Limits of Family Law Reform, or The Privatization of Female and Child Poverty" (1990–1991), *7 C.F.L.Q.*, she rec-ognizes that family law nevertheless has a role to play in alleviating poverty for single mothers when she writes at p. 60:

What are the consequences of divorce for women, men, and children, besides emotional pain? They are very different. Men tend to maintain the standard of living they had before the divorce, while women and children sink into instant poverty....

Findings in the *Report of the Social Assistance Review Committee, Transitions* (1988), show that support can be a significant factor in alleviating some of these negative eco-nomic effects. The report notes that recipients of social assistance who receive support payments are more likely to leave the program than those who do not and that the length of time a recipient receives social assistance is inversely proportional to the total amount of support received. At page 44, the report states:

The nearly 50 percent of single parents receiving family benefit allowance who receive no support payments at all averaged between 3.5 and 4 years in the program. The 11 percent receiving between $10 and $100 per month averaged 2.5 to 3 years, while those receiving between $100 and $200 per month averaged 2 to 2.5 years. Finally, the mere 6 percent receiving in excess of $200 per month averaged less than 2 years in the program....

Application to the Case at Bar

... The sole remaining consideration is whether the application of Mr. Moge to terminate support ought to have been granted in this case. In my view, it should not have and the majority of the Court of Appeal was right in finding an error of principle on the part of the trial judge. I agree with Twaddle J.A., supra, at p. 177:

> ... even if some degree of economic self-sufficiency is practicable, the level at which the wife can become self-sufficiency may be lower than the husband's level of self-sufficiency. This disadvantage will often be attributable to the marriage. In such a case, the court will best meet the objectives prescribed by Parliament by supplementing the wife's earning ability with some maintenance. It would be contrary to those objectives to foreclose a traditional wife from all maintenance.

> In the case at bar, the learned judge in Motions Court did just that. In the passage from his reasons which I have quoted, he makes it clear that, in his view, this wife should have achieved total financial independence. With the greatest respect to him, I think that is an error in principle. He failed to consider the disparity between the earning ability of each former spouse: he failed to have regard to the fact that the wife, having married in a traditional arrangement, was disadvantaged by it.

The four objectives of spousal support orders under s. 17(7) of the Act, as explicated above and applied by the Court of Appeal, are met in this case. For this reason, the following specific findings are in order based on the evidence in the record:

1. Mrs. Moge has sustained a substantial economic disadvantage "from the marriage or its breakdown" within the meaning of s. 17(7)(a) of the Act.
2. Mrs. Moge's long-term responsibility for the upbringing of the children of the marriage after the spousal separation in 1973 has had an impact on her ability to earn an income so as to trigger the application of s. 17(7)(b) of the Act.
3. Mrs. Moge continues to suffer economic hardship as a result of the "breakdown of the marriage" within the meaning of s. 17(7)(c) of the Act.
4. Mrs. Moge has failed to become economically self-sufficient notwithstanding her conscientious efforts.

These findings are irrefutable even in the absence of expert evidence relating to the appropriate quantification of spousal support. It follows that in view of all of the objectives of spousal support orders set out in s. 17(7) of the Act, continuing support is in order in this case. Accordingly, there was no error in the Court of Appeal....

McLachlin, J.: Parties sometimes argue that the economic disadvantage of their spouse was not caused by the marriage or its breakdown, or that her economic hardship was not caused by the termination of the marriage. Shades of these arguments surfaced in this case. It was said that Mrs. Moge voluntarily elected to be the primary homemaker and caregiver; that it was her choice and not the marriage that caused the resultant economic disadvantage.

Similarly, it was suggested that her present need and lack of self-sufficiency was not the product of the marriage but of her failure to choose to upgrade her education so she could earn more money.

A formalistic view of causation can work injustice in the context of s. 17(7), as elsewhere. The question under s. 17(7)(a) is whether a party was disadvantaged or gained advantages from the marriage, as a matter of fact; under s. 17(7)(c) whether the marriage breakdown in fact led to economic hardship for one of the spouses. Hypothetical arguments after the fact about different choices people could have made which might have produced different results are irrelevant, unless the parties acted unreasonably or unfairly. In this case, for example, Mrs. Moge, in keeping with the prevailing social expectation of the times, accepted primary responsibility for the home and the children and confined her extra activities to supplementing the family income rather than to getting a better education or to furthering her career. That was the actual domestic arrangement which prevailed. What Mrs. Moge might have done in a different arrangement with different social and domestic expectations is irrelevant.

Similarly, in determining whether economic hardship of a spouse arises from the breakdown of the marriage, the starting point should be a comparison of the spouse's actual situation before and after the breakdown. If the economic hardship arose shortly after the marriage breakdown, that may be a strong indication that it is caused by the family breakdown. Arguments that an ex-spouse should be doing more for herself must be considered in light of her background and abilities, physical and psychological. It may be unreasonable to expect a middle-aged person who has devoted most of her life to domestic concerns within the marriage to compete for scarce jobs with youthful college graduates, for example. Even women who have worked outside the home during the marriage may find that their career advancement has been permanently reduced by the effort which they devoted to home and family instead of their jobs, whether the woman be a janitor like Mrs. Moge or a well-trained professional. Sometimes the breakdown of the marriage may have left the woman with feelings of inadequacy or depression which make it difficult for her to do more. In short, the whole context of her conduct must be considered. It is not enough to say in the abstract that the ex-spouse should have done more or be doing more, and argue from this that it is her inaction rather than the breakup of the marriage which is the cause of her economic hardship. One must look at the actual social and personal reality of the situation in which she finds herself and judge the matter fairly from that perspective.[13]

The decision in *Moge v. Moge* shows clearly that the importance and relevance of the factors to be considered in awarding support will depend upon the nature of the marriage, as well as on the relationship between marriage breakdown and the economic status of the respective spouses. Critics have asserted that the decision serves to undermine the principle of equality between men and women; supporters have applauded *Moge v. Moge* for providing a realistic assessment of the consequences of divorce for many, if not most, Canadian women. In any event, the case demonstrates first that economic self-sufficiency is only one variable to be considered in awards of spousal support, and second that the importance of this factor may be eclipsed by the other considerations set out in section 17(7).

After their finding in *Moge*, the Supreme Court of Canada made a similar determination in relation to spousal support in *Hickey v. Hickey*.[14] In this case, the Court was asked to determine the validity of an increase in spousal and child support granted to Patricia Hickey in 1996. The Hickeys (Walter and Patricia) were married in 1971 and divorced in 1987. They had two children, a girl born in 1977 and a boy born in 1980. In 1987, at the time of the divorce, Walter Hickey was paying his wife $1,000 monthly in spousal support and $1,500 in child support ($750 for each of the two children). In March 1996, when the older daughter moved out of her mother's home, her father brought a motion to eliminate support for his daughter, asking that his total monthly payment be decreased from $2,500 to $1,750. His former wife agreed to this removal of support for her daughter, but asked that the remaining spousal and child support be increased. The motions judge agreed and increased her spousal support to $1,300 and child support for her son to $1,500, thereby increasing the original amount of support from $2,500 to $2,800. The Court heard that in 1995 Walter Hickey had an annual income of almost $220,000 and that Patricia Hickey had an income of a little more than $30,000, most of which was from support payments made by her former husband since 1987. She had tried to start a small business, but this enterprise had not been very successful. Mr. Hickey appealed to the Manitoba Court of Appeal, which agreed with him, reducing the amount awarded for child support to $750 and finding the original amount of $1,000 for spousal support to be sufficient.

The Supreme Court of Canada, however, overturned the Court of Appeal's decision and restored the motions judge's decision requiring Mr. Hickey to pay $2,800 per month in spousal and child support. The Court noted that in the instance of child support the increased means of the payor spouse, the increased needs of a child as he or she grows older, and the fiscal reality of inflation all justified an upward variation of the award of support. In the instance of spousal support, the Court noted that all four criteria set out in section 17(7) of the *Divorce Act* must be taken into consideration: the economic disadvantage to the former spouse arising from marriage breakdown, the financial consequences of child care, the economic hardship of a former spouse arising from marriage breakdown, and the promotion of the economic self-sufficiency of each former spouse. The Court argued that an upward variation of the support order in this case was consistent with the objectives set out in section 17(7) of the Act.

Moreover, the Supreme Court held that appeal courts should not overturn support orders made by trial courts unless there is a significant error in principle, a significant misunderstanding of the evidence, or the award is, on its face, clearly wrong. In other words, the Supreme Court has indicated that in matters of support awards the discretion of the trial court is to be respected; a trial judge is in the best position to appreciate all the facts in the case. An appeal court is not entitled to overturn a support order simply because it would have balanced factors somewhat differently—to permit such appeals is to create a greater incentive for appeal, to produce added expenses for litigants, and to delay an important need for finality in family law litigation. In any event, both *Moge* and *Hickey* make clear that, at least in certain circumstances, a spouse may well have a lifetime financial obligation to support a former spouse.

A 2003 decision of the Supreme Court of Canada, *Miglin v. Miglin,*[15] extends the logic of *Moge* and *Hickey,* at least to some extent. In this case the Miglins separated after 14 years of marriage. They were joint owners of Killarney Lodge in Ontario's Algonquin Park, and they signed an agreement whereby Mrs. Miglin agreed to give up her interest in this lucrative business in exchange for Mr. Miglin's interest in the family home. She believed that she would be able to get by on child support from Mr. Miglin, and on a small annual consulting fee related to the lodge business. As a consequence, she waived her right to any payment of spousal support.

When she found it more difficult than expected to support herself financially, Mrs. Miglin went to court to argue for relief from the agreement she had signed, saying that it was unfair. Ultimately, a majority of the Supreme Court of Canada did not agree that she should be awarded support, but not before indicating that, while judges should be reluctant to overturn private agreements regarding support, there will be circumstances in which it is legitimate to do so. When there is a significant and unforeseen change in the parties' financial circumstances—one that could not reasonably have been foreseen—it will be appropriate for a court to review and possibly amend the terms of the support agreement, irrespective of the apparent finality of the waiver of rights at the time of the initial agreement. Again, the Supreme Court of Canada has made it clear that there are legitimate circumstances in which a spouse may well have a lifetime obligation of support to a former spouse. In this regard, note the Supreme Court's 2006 decision in *Leskun v. Leskun,* further clarifying the role of spousal support (and cited at greater length in Chapter 3 of this text). Note, additionally, that in March 2010 the federal Department of Justice released spousal support guidelines, developed by two law professors, Carol Rogerson and Rollie Thompson, "The Spousal Support Advisory Guidelines: A New and Improved User's Guide to the Final Version." These guidelines, although they do not have the force of law, are consulted routinely by counsel. They include tables that establish an anticipated range of financial support; the variables of relevance are the length of the marriage, varying levels of income, the work history of each spouse, the number of children, if any, of the marriage, and issues of variation and review.[16]

THE *DIVORCE ACT* OF 1985 AND THE QUESTION OF CUSTODY

Section 16 of the *Divorce Act* of 1985 sets out the terms and conditions applying to orders for custody, pursuant to a petition for divorce. Custody may also be dealt with in provincial courts, pursuant to provincial legislation.

> 16. *(1) A court of competent jurisdiction may, on application by either or both spouses or by any other person, make an order respecting the custody of or the access to, or the custody of and access to, any or all children of the marriage.*
>
> *(2) Where an application is made under subsection (1), the court may, on application by either or both spouses or by any other person, make an interim order respecting the custody of or the access to, or the custody of and access to, any or all children of the marriage pending determination of the application under subsection (1).*
>
> *(3) A person, other than a spouse, may not make an application under subsection (1) or (2) without leave of the court.*
>
> *(4) This court may make an order under this section granting custody of, or access to, any or all children of the marriage to any one or more persons.*
>
> *(5) Unless the court orders otherwise, a spouse who is granted access to a child of the marriage has the right to make inquiries, and to be given information, as to the health, education and welfare of the child.*
>
> *(6) The court may make an order under this section for a definite or indefinite period or until the happening of a specified event and may impose such other terms, conditions, or restrictions in connection therewith as it thinks fit and just.*
>
> *(7) Without limiting the generality of subsection (6), the court may include in an order under this section a term requiring any person who has custody of a child of the marriage and who intends to change the place of residence of that child to notify, at least thirty days before the change or within such other period before the change as the court may specify, any person who is granted access to that child of the change, the time at which the change will be made, and the new place of residence of the child.*
>
> *(8) In making an order under this section, the court shall take into consideration only the best interests of the child of the marriage as determined by reference to the condition, means, needs, and other circumstances of the child.*
>
> *(9) In making an order under this section, the court shall not take into consideration the past conduct of any person unless the conduct is relevant to the ability of that person to act as a parent of a child.*

The *Divorce Act* does not provide substantial statutory guidance as to the principles that should guide an award of custody, inasmuch as the test of "the best interests of the child" appears to be highly subjective. Family law professor Robert Mnookin has argued as follows concerning child custody adjudication:

> Deciding what is best for a child poses a question no less ultimate than the purposes and values of life itself. Should the judge be concerned with the

economic "productivity" of the child when he grows up? Are the primary values of life in warm, interpersonal relationships, or in discipline and self-sacrifice? Is stability and security for a child more desirable than intellectual stimulation? These questions could be elaborated endlessly. And yet, where is a judge to look for a set of values that should inform the choice of what is best for the child? Normally, the custody statutes do not themselves give content or relative weights to the pertinent values. And if the judge looks back to society at large, he finds neither a clear consensus as to the best child-rearing strategies nor an appropriate hierarchy of ultimate values.[17]

In light of these views, how are we to analyze the issues that arise in *Barkley v. Barkley*? Are homosexual and heterosexual relationships treated equally by Canadian courts?

Nasmith, Family Court Judge: Lynn is a 10-year-old girl whose mother and father are each applying ... for sole custody of her. The mother is homosexual and much of the evidence has sprung from this fact.

There are serious differences between the parents and I have ruled out the possibility of an order extending the "joint custody" rights with which they both came into this action. It apparently must be determined whether it is in Lynn's best interests for me to order that the mother have sole custody or that the father have sole custody.

Mr. and Mrs. B. were married in 1962 and they adopted three children. They separated in May 1977, shortly after Mr. B returned from a lengthy posting with the armed forces in Egypt. Upon separation, all three children resided with the father, but at the time of trial, only Robert, aged 13, and Douglas, aged 15, remained with their father. There is no dispute about the boys and no order is sought to cover them.

The mother had generous access to the children following the separation, and she often moved back into the house to look after them during extended absences by the father. The evidence is that Lynn became increasingly unhappy living with her father and developed a desire to be with her mother on a full-time basis. The turning point in this arrangement came when the mother was upset at the father for allegedly leaving the children unattended. In March 1979, she unilaterally decided to keep Lynn with her. That move gave rise to these proceedings to settle Lynn's custody.

There is no allegation by the father as to any deficiencies in the parenting performance of the mother during the period of their cohabitation. The unique feature of the case, I think, is that the father's sole concern arises out of Mrs. B's being a declared homosexual and his case is built on that. From his evidence, I am convinced that he sincerely believes it would be harmful to his daughter to be raised in what he sees as a homosexual environment....

The court made a referral of the family to the family court clinic for an assessment and report on the question of which of the two placements was more likely to serve the best interests of Lynn. Mr. Robert Gardner, M.S.W., has given evidence and has filed a nine-page opinion with a lengthy bibliography of the literature on homosexual parenting. The intimate clinical analysis apparently satisfied Mr. Gardner that both parents had a reasonably good relationship with Lynn. But he concluded that Lynn felt a much greater closeness with Mrs. B, and some distance between herself and her father. The evidence was that Lynn was doing very well, and it was Mr. Gardner's opinion that Lynn's needs could be more adequately met, given a decision to allow her to remain with her mother. It is clear that Lynn's own preference to reside with her mother was a significant part of Mr. Gardner's considerations....

Three Canadian cases have been cited by counsel and from my own research, these would seem to be the only Canadian cases reported.

In *Case v. Case* (1974), 18 R.F.L. 132 (Sask. Q.B.) MacPherson J. stipulated that homosexuality was not a bar to an award of custody and that it was simply a factor to be considered along with others. On the facts, as he found them, custody of a 10-year-old daughter and a 4-year-old son were granted to the father as against the homosexual mother. The court was influenced by what it saw as unfair and exaggerated charges by the mother as to the father's conduct, and I think he was concerned about the fact that the mother slept in the same bed with her homosexual partner and that he had not had the benefit of having the partner as a witness. Reference was made to the mother's hiding her partner from the court. The extent to which the homosexuality weighed against the mother may have been given away by the closing comments....

I greatly fear that if these children are raised by the mother, they will be too much in contact with people of abnormal tastes and proclivities.

In the subsequent case of *K. v. K.* 23 R.F.L. 58 ... Rowe Prov. J. of the Alberta Provincial Court distinguished the *Case* decision.

His Honour agreed with the Saskatchewan court as to homosexuality being one factor to be considered along with all the others. In awarding custody to a homosexual mother, who also slept in the same bed as her partner, and did not engage in any sexual contact in the presence of the children, the trial judge was supported by strong evidence from a psychologist who testified that the mother and the child had a close relationship, which was one of the best mother–child interactions she had seen in her professional practice. The psychologist noted that the child was happy, well-adjusted, and doing very well in school, and concluded:

... [T]he manner in which one fulfills one's sexual needs does not relate to the abilities of being a good parent.

... In *D. v. D.* (1978), 20 O.R. (2d) 722, 3 R.F.L. (2d) 327 ... Smith Co. Ct. J. dealt with an application to vary a decree nisi. The decree had been silent as to custody and the father later sought custody of 13- and 8-year-old children who had been in his *de facto* custody since the separation. It was clear that the father was bisexual but that he was involved in a continuing homosexual relationship. The trial judge treated his homosexuality as ...

a problem which may damage the children's psychological, moral, intellectual, or physical well-being, and their orderly development and adaptation to society.... The court's concern ought to be the children's position in their peer group, the children's sexual orientation, and the manner in which the relationship of children to parent is or can be affected by the deviation from the norm in the latter's sexual preferences.

In awarding custody of the children to the father, which confirmed the status quo, the trial judge's concerns about the "problem" of homosexuality were apparently modified by the following findings:

(a) The father was bisexual;

(b) The father was discreet;

(c) He was not an exhibitionist;

(d) The public did not know about his sexual orientations;

(e) He did not flaunt his homosexual activities;

(f) He was not a militant homosexual;

(g) The court felt that he could "cope with" the problems;

(h) There was no evidence that the children would become homosexual;

(i) The main homosexual partner made a favourable impression on him.

It would appear that the net result of the analysis of the homosexual question was the placing of very little weight on the homosexuality of the father.

In the present case, a focus on the quality of the parent-child relationship here produces a good case for the mother as the more appropriate person to have custody of Lynn.

As in *D. v. D.*, any possible ill effects for Lynn from the mother's sexual orientation have been minimized by the following circumstances:

(1) She is not militant;

(2) She does not flaunt her homosexuality;

(3) She does not seem to be biased about Lynn's orientation, and seems to assume that Lynn will be heterosexual;

(4) There is no overt sexual contact apart from sleeping in the same bed;

(5) The sexual partner has a reasonably good relationship with the child.

Whatever significant risks remain in the area of Lynn's necessary adjustments to our "homophobic" society, they are too esoteric and speculative for me to attach much weight to. I think they must give way here to the more concrete indicia of "best interests."

An order will go granting custody of the child to the respondent with reasonable access to the applicant.... [18]

Although *Barkley v. Barkley* was decided before the amendments to the *Divorce Act* of 1985, it remains a valid statement of the law today (the 1985 amendments did not touch upon the issue raised in *Barkley*). For a more recent case that has taken a similar approach to that in *Barkley*, see *Daller v. Daller*.[19] In *Daller*, the Ontario Court of Appeal declined to remove a child from the lesbian mother's custody, on the basis that the homosexual relationship was not having a detrimental effect on the child, and it was not in the child's best interest to grant the father's claim for custody. Similarly, in *Monk v. Doan*[20] the court awarded custody to a lesbian aunt whose life with a long-term partner was conducted in a manner that was said to be discreet and dignified. At the same time, however, some Canadian courts have used a homosexual lifestyle as a bar to an award of custody. In *Saunders v. Saunders*,[21] a British Columbia judge denied a gay father overnight **access** to his child on the basis that the father's sleeping with another man during these visits was necessarily exposing his child to an "unnatural" relationship.

CONCLUSION: FAMILY LAW AS THE CRUCIBLE OF CULTURE

Legislation and judicial decisions relating to the family in Canada provide us with a lens through which to look back at the changes within our culture over the past 50 years. Perhaps more than any other type of law, family law affords the opportunity of understanding how the way we relate to each other has changed, for better or for worse, and perhaps mostly for the better. We have witnessed legal amendments that permit divorce more easily, strengthen the position of women in the event of marriage breakdown, and endorse same-sex marriage. Whether these kinds of developments will continue is uncertain. What is certain, however, is that family law will continue to be a part of the fabric upon which the evolution of our culture is written.

WEB LINKS

Community Legal Information Association of Prince Edward Island
http://www.cliapei.ca
The website of the Community Legal Information Association of Prince Edward Island has a very good section on common-law relationships, typically a matter of provincial jurisdiction.

Manitoba Justice
http://www.gov.mb.ca/justice/family/familyindex.html
This user-friendly Web page provides information on family law in Manitoba. It contains links to other sites dealing with family law issues.

Gene C. Colman—Family Law Centre
http://www.complexfamilylaw.com
Toronto lawyer Gene Colman's website has extensive information about family law, with an Ontario perspective. Colman has detailed discussion and references on family law issues with respect to children.

Public Legal Information Association of Newfoundland
http://www.publiclegalinfo.com/about.html
The website of the Public Legal Information Association of Newfoundland offers information about the law, legal processes, and the administration of justice. This association is a component of the Public Legal Education Association of Canada, a national network of legal education societies, to which it has links.

Department of Justice Canada: Child Support
http://www.justice.gc.ca/eng/pi/fcy-fea/sup-pen/index.html
This Web page contains the federal child support guidelines from the Department of Justice, and has links to extensive information on child-support laws.

Duhaime's Canadian Family Law Centre
http://www.duhaime.org/legalresources/familylaw.aspx
The website of Victoria family law lawyer Lloyd Duhaime is extremely useful for its articles on many areas of family law. He also has links to other primary sites for statutes and regulations.

The Alberta Law Foundation
http://www.albertalawfoundation.org/
This Web page provides information on frequently asked questions about Canada's *Divorce Act* and has links to other aspects of family law.

QUESTIONS FOR DISCUSSION

1. Are same-sex civil unions a threat to the institution of marriage? Discuss.
2. What are the strengths and weaknesses of the Supreme Court's decisions in *Moge, Hickey, Leskun,* and *Miglin*? Are the Spousal Support Advisory Guidelines consistent with the decisions in these cases?
3. What do you think of the Canadian Bar Association's insistence that divorce be premised on *whether* a marriage has broken down, not *why*? Take account of the relevant sections of the *Divorce Act* in your response.

FURTHER READING

Action Committee on Access to Justice in Civil and Family Matters. *Meaningful Change for Family Justice: Beyond Wise Words*, Ottawa, April 2013.

> This report provides a good description and summary of the major challenges facing family justice in Canada within our current context. Two of the most significant difficulties include first, access to family justice that is affordable and actually works to resolve conflict, and second, the continuing intransigence of elements of an adversarial approach within legal practice. The authors suggest a range of potential remedies for these and other problems.

Conway, J. *The Canadian Family in Crisis*. Toronto: Lorimer, 1990.

> This book provides a very useful historical backdrop for understanding our contemporary construction of family life, documenting changes in family structure and ideology over the past century. The book is required reading for those who are interested in the social and historical evolution of the family form.

Dekeseredy, W., and R. Hinch. *Woman Abuse: Sociological Perspectives*. Toronto: Thompson, 1991.

> This is a useful introduction to the problems of domestic violence and the difficulties in conceptualizing the problem and in the ability to attach the criminal sanction to various forms of assault and harassment. The book is a useful addendum to the more legalistic materials canvassed within this chapter.

Hovius, B., and M.J. Maur. *Family Law: Cases, Notes and Materials*. 8th ed., Toronto: Carswell, 2013.

> The most comprehensive compilation of family law materials in Canada. Professor Hovius and Mary Jo Maur cover marriage, divorce, family property, spousal and child support, custody and access, domestic contracts, and the issues of child protection and adoption. Additionally, this text looks in some depth at domestic violence, same-sex marriage, and the use of the best-interests-of-the-child test in determining custody and access. Spousal support advisory guidelines are also covered in this edition.

NOTES

1. J. Conway, *The Canadian Family in Crisis* (Toronto: Lorimer, 1990), 36.
2. J. Snell, *In the Shadow of the Law: Divorce in Canada, 1900–1939* (Toronto: University of Toronto Press, 1991), 9.
3. Statistics Canada, *Income Trends in Canada* (Ottawa, 2002).
4. R. Hamilton, "Women, Wives and Mothers," in *Reconstructing the Canadian Family: Feminist Perspectives*, edited by N. Mandell and A. Duffy (Toronto: Butterworths, 1988), 20.

5. National Council of Welfare, "Canada, Poverty Profile, 1996," Spring 1998, Ottawa, Canada.
6. Statistics Canada, *Marriages and Divorces: Vital Statistics*, vol. 2 (Ottawa: Supply and Services, 1985).
7. Ministry of Justice, *Information Paper C-47* (Ottawa: Supply and Services, 1985).
8. Canadian Bar Association, "Submission Regarding Bill C-10 and the Proposed Amendments to the Divorce Act," 1985, 37.
9. *Shaw v. Shaw* (1971), 4 R.F.L. 392 at 392–398, 7 N.S.R. (2d) 77 at 77–84 (T.D.).
10. *Knoll v. Knoll* (1970), 1 R.F.L. 141 at 149–150, [1970] 2 O.R. 169 at 176–7 (C.A.).
11. *S. (J.G.) v. S. (W.O.J.)*, 2004 B.C.S.C. 749 (CanLII), http://canlii.ca/t/1h8t9.
12. See also, on the issue of economic self-sufficiency, *Messier v. Delage* (1983), 35 R.F.L. (2d) 337 (S.C.C.) and *Richardson v. Richardson* (1987), 7 R.F.L. (3d) 304 (S.C.C.).
13. *Moge v. Moge*, [1992] 3 S.C.R. 813 at 824–882.
14. [1999] 2 S.C.R. 518.
15. [2003] 1 S.C.R. 303.
16. Department of Justice Canada, Spousal Support Advisory Guidelines, March 2010 (see http://www.justice.gc.ca/eng/fl-df/spousal-epoux/topic-theme/ug_a1-gu_a1/index.html).
17. P. Mnookin, "Child-Custody Adjudication: Judicial Functions in the Face of Indeterminacy," *Law and Contemporary Problems* 39 (1975): 226.
18. *Barkley v. Barkley* (1980), 28 O.R. (2d) 136 at 136–141 (Prov. Ct.).
19. (1988), 18 R.F.L. (3d) 53, 22 R.F.L. (3d) 96 (Ont. C.A.).
20. (1990), 94 Sask. Rep. 316 (Q.B.).
21. (1989), 20 R.F.L. (3d) 368 (B.C.S.C.).

References

Anderson, M., et al., eds. *Family Matters: Sociology and Contemporary Canadian Families.* Toronto: Methuen, 1987.

Bala, N., et al. *Canadian Child Welfare Law: Children, Families and the State.* Toronto: Thompson, 1991.

Blumberg, A. "Cohabitation without Marriage: A Different Perspective." *U.C.L.A. Law Review* 28 (1981): 1125.

Conway, J. *The Canadian Family in Crisis.* Toronto: Lorimer, 1990.

Dekeseredy, W., and R. Hinch. *Woman Abuse: Sociological Perspectives.* Toronto: Thompson, 1991.

Divorce Act, R.S.C. 1985, c. 3.

Eichler, M. "The Limits of Family Law Reform, or the Privatization of Female and Child Poverty." *Canadian Family Law Quarterly* 7 (1990–91): 59.

Hamilton, R. "Women, Wives and Mothers." In *Reconstructing the Canadian Family: Feminist Perspectives,* edited by N. Mandell and A. Duffy. Toronto: Butterworths, 1988, Chapter 1.

Herman, J. "Are We Family? Lesbian Rights and Women's Liberation." *Osgoode Hall Law Journal* 28 (1990): 789.

Hovius, B. *Family Law: Cases, Notes and Materials.* 5th ed. Toronto: Carswell, 1998.

Hovius, B., and M. Youdan. *The Law of Family Property.* Toronto: Carswell, 1991.

Hughes, J., and L. Pask, eds. *National Themes in Family Law.* Toronto: Carswell, 1988.

Knetsch, J. "Some Economic Implications of Matrimonial Property Rules." *University of Toronto Law Journal* 34 (1984): 263.

Law Reform Commission of Canada. *Maintenance on Divorce: Working Paper 12.* Ottawa: Supply and Services, 1975.

Mandell, N., and A. Duffy, eds. *Reconstructing the Canadian Family: Feminist Perspectives.* Toronto: Butterworths, 1988.

Parr, J., ed. *Childhood and Family in Canadian History.* Toronto: McClelland & Stewart, 1982.

Rogerson, C. "The Causal Connection Test in Spousal Support Law." *Canadian Journal of Family Law* 8 (1989): 95.

Ryan, H. "Joint Custody in Canada: Time for a Second Look." *Reports on Family Law* (2d) 49 (1986): 119.

Ryder, B. "Equality Rights and Sexual Orientation: Confronting Heterosexual Family Privilege." *Canadian Journal of Family Law* 6 (1990): 39.

Smart, C. *The Ties That Bind: Law, Marriage and the Reproduction of Patriarchal Relations.* London, U.K.: Routledge and Kegan Paul, 1984.

Ziff, J. "Recent Developments in Marriage and Divorce." *Ottawa Law Review* 18 (1986): 121.

CHAPTER 9

ADMINISTRATIVE LAW: THE STATE AND ITS DUTY TO BE FAIR

The shift to regulatory governance has been wildly successful. In a word, it works. The complex modern state could not function without the many and varied administrative tribunals that people the legal landscape.

Tribunals provide specialized and technical resolutions in different situations, ensure greater innovation, flexibility and efficiency in the delivery of governmental programs and strategies, and provide an informal and rapid forum for public hearings, thereby minimizing time and costs related to litigation before ordinary courts.

As Justice Abella stated while she was sitting on the Ontario Court of Appeal:

> *Designed to be less cumbersome, less expensive, less formal and less delayed, these impartial decision-making bodies were to resolve disputes in their area of specialization more expeditiously and more accessibly, but no less effectively or credibly.*

In sum, without administrative tribunals, the rule of law in the modern regulatory state would falter and fail. Tribunals offer flexible, swift and relevant justice. In an age when access to justice is increasingly lacking, they help to fill the gap. And there is no going back.*

On the evening of November 13, 2000, Sukvir Singh Khosa, a citizen of India and a landed immigrant in Canada, drove his car at more than 100 kilometres per hour through a residential and commercial section of the city of Vancouver, causing the death of a female pedestrian. At his trial on a charge of criminal negligence causing death, the court concluded that he was street racing and convicted him. After appeal to the British Columbia Court of Appeal on the issue of sentence, Mr. Khosa was sentenced to house arrest of two years less one day, a driving ban, and community service.

The issue that arises in the context of administrative law is that of Mr. Khosa's deportation or "removal order" to India pursuant to his conviction, which was finally resolved by the Supreme Court in 2009. The Court's decision focuses on the role of judicial review of the decision of an administrative tribunal. Justice Binnie

---

*Remarks of the Right Honourable Beverley McLachlin, P.C. Chief Justice of Canada, 6th Annual Conference of the Council of Canadian Administrative Tribunals, Toronto, Ontario, May 27, 2013, titled: "Administrative Tribunals and the Courts: An Evolutionary Relationship." Reproduced with the permission of the Supreme Court of Canada, 2014.

noted the tribunal's initial views in writing the majority judgment for the Supreme Court[1]:

The majority of the Immigration Appeal Division recognized that its discretionary jurisdiction to grant "special relief" on humanitarian and compassionate grounds under s. 67(1)(c) of the IRPA should be exercised in light of the factors adopted in *Ribic v. Canada (Minister of Employment and Immigration)*, [1985] I.A.B.D. No. 4 (QL), and endorsed by this Court in *Chieu v. Canada (Minister of Citizenship and Immigration)*, 2002 SCC 3, [2002] 1 S.C.R. 84, at paras. 40, 41 and 90, namely:

(1) the seriousness of the offence leading to the removal order;

(2) the possibility of rehabilitation;

(3) the length of time spent, and the degree to which the individual facing removal is established, in Canada;

(4) the family and community support available to the individual facing removal;

(5) the family in Canada and the dislocation to the family that removal would cause; and

(6) the degree of hardship that would be caused to the individual facing removal to his country of nationality.

The majority considered that the last four Ribic factors were not particularly compelling for or against relief. As to the first two factors, the offence in question was "extremely serious" (para. 14) and the majority expressed particular concern over Khosa's refusal to accept without reservation the finding that he had been street racing. The Immigration Appeal Division majority considered that this refusal "reflects a lack of insight into his conduct" (para. 15). As to Khosa's prospects for rehabilitation, the majority decided that there was insufficient evidence upon which to make a finding one way or the other (paras. 15 and 23). However, even if Khosa had good prospects for rehabilitation, "balancing all the relevant factors,... the scale does not tip in [Khosa's] favour" (para. 23). Accordingly, "special relief" was denied.

The case was first appealed to the Federal Court, which upheld the judgment of the Immigration Appeal Division, and then to the Federal Court of Appeal, which overturned the removal order on the ground that the Appeal Division had acted unreasonably. Justice Decary wrote for the majority of the Court of Appeal: "It clearly appears from the transcripts of the hearing that the presiding member—who wrote the majority decision—and counsel for the Crown, had some kind of fixation with the fact that the offence was related to street racing, to such a point that the hearing, time and time again, was transformed into a quasi-criminal trial, if not into a new criminal trial."[2]

The majority of the Supreme Court of Canada restored the verdict of the Immigration Appeal Division—the administrative tribunal—noting that deference must be given to its role as a finder of fact unless the decision itself is unreasonable. In this instance, the majority argued, it was not unreasonable.

In terms of transparent and intelligible reasons, the majority considered each of the Ribic factors. It rightly observed that the factors are not exhaustive and that the weight to be attributed to them will vary from case to case (para. 12). The majority reviewed the evidence and decided that, in the circumstances of this case, most of the factors did not militate strongly for or against relief. Acknowledging the findings of the criminal courts on the seriousness of the offence and possibility of rehabilitation (the first and second of the Ribic factors), it found that the offence of which the respondent was convicted was serious and that the prospects of rehabilitation were difficult to assess (para. 23).

The weight to be given to the respondent's evidence of remorse and his prospects for rehabilitation depended on an assessment of his evidence in light of all the circumstances of the case. The IAD has a mandate different from that of the criminal courts. Khosa did not testify at his criminal trial, but he did before the IAD. The issue before the IAD was not the potential for rehabilitation for purposes of sentencing, but rather whether the prospects for rehabilitation were such that, alone or in combination with other factors, they warranted special relief from a valid removal order. The IAD was required to reach its own conclusions based on its own appreciation of the evidence. It did so.

As mentioned, the courts below recognized some merit in Khosa's complaint. Lutfy C.J. recognized that the majority "chose to place greater weight on his denial that he participated in a race than others might have" (para. 36). Décary J.A. described the majority's preoccupation with street racing as "some kind of fixation" (para. 18). My colleague Fish J. also decries the weight put on this factor by the majority (para. 141). However, as emphasized in Dunsmuir, "certain questions that come before administrative tribunals do not lend themselves to one specific, particular result. Instead, they may give rise to a number of possible, reasonable conclusions. Tribunals have a margin of appreciation within the range of acceptable and rational solutions" (para. 47). In light of the deference properly owed to the IAD under s. 67(1)(c) of the IRPA, I cannot, with respect, agree with my colleague Fish J. that the decision reached by the majority in this case to deny special discretionary relief against a valid removal order fell outside the range of reasonable outcomes.[3]

Administrative law is a form of public law. While it shares many of the characteristics of constitutional law, criminal law, and family law, it is nonetheless conceptually separate. It does not spring from the *Constitution Act,* the *Criminal Code,* or the *Divorce Act,* nor from any set of rules in statutory or regulatory form. There are statutes specific to certain realms of administrative law: labour relations, workers' compensation, parole, employment insurance, and radio-television communications, among others. But there is no overarching legislation that defines the essence of administrative law.

The heart of administrative law is—as can be seen in the *Khosa* case above—to be found in the competing views of the duty to act fairly in the practice of government, an onus that the state has placed upon itself both with common law and, more recently and significantly, with the *Canadian Charter of Rights and Freedoms* (the *Charter*). It is a duty that is also found within constitutional law. Most fundamentally, administrative law concerns the relationship between the state, broadly defined, and the individual citizen. Legal scholars Dussault and Borgeat have defined administrative law:

> Administrative law has been termed the "law of the public power in its relations with ordinary citizens," "the day-to-day public law," "the essential incarnation of public law outside of the constitutional sphere." It may be defined as the entire set of rules relating to the organization, operation, and control of the Administration.[4]

DELEGATION, INTERDELEGATION, AND THE POWERS ACCORDED WITHIN ADMINISTRATIVE LAW

The legal machinery that makes possible the construction of administrative law—the law relating to various boards, commissions, agencies, and tribunals—is typically referred to as **delegation**. Parliament, as the supreme authority in Canada, permits the federal government and provincial governments to delegate some legislative powers to these bodies. However, given the division of powers between federal and provincial governments (in sections 91 and 92 of the *British North America Act*), a province may not delegate its powers directly to the federal government; nor may the federal government delegate its powers directly to the provincial legislatures.

The federal government may, however, delegate its powers to a tribunal, board, commission, or agency created by a provincial legislature; similarly, provincial governments may delegate their powers to a body created by federal legislation. This process is known as **interdelegation**, and it is constitutionally permissible, with two provisos. The first is that not all authority in relation to a given jurisdiction is delegated to the "inferior" tribunal; the second is that there is no further delegation of decision-making power from the tribunal to another decision-making authority. Interdelegation, like any delegation of legislative power, serves a number of important social purposes. Jones and deVillars cite six:

(a) *The sheer magnitude of the business of government means that not everything can be dealt with by Parliament or a legislature.*

(b) *Much of governmental activity is technical in nature, and only broad principles should be contained in legislation.*

(c) *Delegating power to an administrator allows greater flexibility in applying broad statutory provisions to changing circumstances.*

(d) *It may not be possible to devise a general role to deal with all cases, which may be more conveniently determined in the discretion of a delegate.*

(e) *The need for rapid governmental action may require faster administrative response than can be accommodated by the necessity of legislative amendment.*

(f) *Innovation and experimentation in solving social problems may not be possible if legislation is required.*

(g) *Someone actually has to apply legislation, and that person has to have authority to do so.*[5]

With the governmental duty to act fairly now codified in various sections of the *Charter*, administrative law presents itself as both a relative and a derivative of constitutional law. Administrative law scholars Dussault and Borgeat note:

> Although they are both indispensable tools in analyzing the organization and operation of the Administration, constitutional law and administrative law may be distinguished from each other mainly by the fact that the former provides a skeleton of broad principles which the latter fleshes out. More concerned with the general structure of the State's bodies than with the operation of the Administration on a day-to-day basis, constitutional law seems to be more static when compared to administrative law, which has a more dynamic appearance.[6]

TYPES AND FUNCTIONS OF TRIBUNALS

The nature of the powers accorded within administrative law varies considerably, from the granting of a ministerial or executive authority to the granting of the power to direct public policy (i.e., make binding legal judgments) within the body's particular area of expertise. As recently as the 1970s, there were clear distinctions among types of **administrative tribunals**: the purely administrative tribunal, the administrative tribunal, the judicial or quasi-judicial tribunal, and the fully legislative tribunal. The provincial bodies that issue drivers' licences, for instance, are purely administrative tribunals; they have no discretionary authority beyond the provisions of the motor vehicle licensing statutes. By contrast, labour relations boards and municipal councils can exercise legislative powers. Such distinctions are, however, of limited use; they often overlap and fail to capture the essence of a given tribunal. Law professor Gerald Gall noted:

> [A] given tribunal may exercise different kinds of functions at different times. For example, a municipal council normally exercises a legislative function, but on occasion, a municipal council may be requested to render a decision which could substantially affect the appellant's rights. For this limited purpose, the municipal council will be exercising a quasi-judicial function.[7]

The key issue for an administrative tribunal is not its form, but its obligations to those subject to its findings and the extent to which its decisions are reviewable by a court—the applicability of **judicial review** to an administrative decision; this was the critical issue in *Khosa*, above. Such designations as administrative, judicial, or quasi-judicial are relevant only in that each one creates different expectations with respect to procedural rights and rights of appeal. Consider, for example, the decision of the Nova Scotia Supreme Court in *Thomas v. Mount Saint Vincent University*.

An application was made for *certiorari* to quash the decision of Mount Saint Vincent University to deny tenure to the plaintiff, Dr. Antoinette Thomas. [*Certiorari* is a Latin term that translates literally as "to be informed of." Such a writ, issued by a superior court to an inferior court, requires that court to produce a certified record of a specific case, so that the superior court can examine the record of events to determine whether there are any irregularities that would warrant reconsideration.]

The Facts

Antoinette Thomas is an educator with a doctorate in psychology. On July 1, 1980, she was appointed as an assistant professor in the Department of Education (Child Study) of the university under a two-year-term contract....

This contract was renewed as a probationary contract following a strong recommendation first from the Department of Education to the Committee on Appointment, Rank, Promotion and, Tenure (CARPT) and then a favourable recommendation from CARPT to the president....

In the fall of 1983, Dr. Thomas was again considered for reappointment and she was granted a further renewal, this time with a term contract of just one year, to end June 30, 1985. Although the contract was renewed, Dr. Pauline Jones, chairman of CARPT, when writing to Dr. Thomas in connection with the committee's recommendation for renewal, expressed some reservations about Dr. Thomas's performance:

The Committee has asked me to convey to you our concern over the fact that your contribution in terms of service to the Department is judged to be unsatisfactory, and we would have to be convinced of significant improvement in this area for any subsequent contract renewal. The Committee also feels that it must draw your attention to the need for improved productivity in the area of research and publication, and we would encourage you as well to maintain and improve wherever possible the level of your teaching effectiveness.

Dr. Margaret E. Fulton, president of the university, in approving the one-year contract, confirmed the concerns of the CARPT committee in a letter dated January 24, 1984:

After a review of your file and some discussion, I wish to inform you that I strongly endorse the committee's recommendations.

Dr. Thomas, in her fifth year at the university, was entitled as of right to be considered for tenure. In September, Dr. Patricia Canning, chairman of the Department of Child Study, initiated the process necessary for the consideration of tenure. She requested the fulltime members of her department to examine the files of Dr. Thomas and one other, who was also being considered, and submit their recommendation in writing to her.

In a memorandum dated October 1, 1984, Dr. Canning reported to CARPT that with the exception of one professor who had been employed for too short a time to know very much of Dr. Thomas's work and with the exception of Sister M. Young, who wrote directly to CARPT with a favourable recommendation, the whole of the department recommended nonrenewal of Dr. Thomas's contract. On the basis of these recommendations and her own evaluation, Dr. Canning recommended against the granting of tenure and against a renewal of Dr. Thomas's contract.

On January 31, 1985, Dr. Pauline Jones, chairman of CARPT, wrote to Dr. Thomas to advise her that "the motion to recommend the granting of tenure to you did not carry, and I have accordingly advised the President."

This letter was followed by a letter dated February 22, 1985, from the president, Dr. Fulton to Dr. Thomas, formally refusing tenure.[8]

At this point, Thomas exercised her right to appeal to the Senate Review Committee. A three-person Ad Hoc Appeal Committee was duly formed. It was composed of a representative appointed by Thomas, a representative appointed by the university president, and a third representative selected by the other two. This committee concluded that Thomas should be granted tenure.

Dr. Fulton refused to accept the recommendation of the Ad Hoc Appeal Committee because, as she said in her evidence given at this hearing, she had to weigh both the original recommendations to deny tenure to Dr. Thomas and the recommendation that came to her from the Appeal Committee to grant it. In her view, the latter recommendation was diluted in that it was not unanimous in all respects. Her decision, on balancing the recommendations, was to refuse tenure.

On June 26, 1985, Dr. Fulton wrote Dr. Thomas:

In accordance with faculty manual requirements, this is to inform you that I am unable to accept the decision of the Appeals Committee. You will not be granted tenure at Mount Saint Vincent University. As of July 1, 1985, you will no longer be an employee of the University. It would be appreciated if you would vacate your office by that date....

Does *certiorari* lie?

The threshold issue in this case is whether the refusal of tenure to Dr. Thomas by the president of Mount Saint Vincent University is amenable to *certiorari* proceedings so as to permit scrutiny by this Court.

My conclusion, after examining the various authorities cited to me, is that indeed such actions by a university, through its president, are subject to judicial review.

Mount Saint Vincent University is a creature of statute (see *Mount Saint Vincent Act*, 1966, above). It is a public university, open to everyone with the requisite academic qualifications, and with the enrolment not subject to religious restriction (see s. 22 of the Act).... [I]t is quite clear that Mount Saint Vincent has lost its former parochial and private status and has become a "public" institution. According to Dr. Fulton, up to 90 percent of its operating funds come from government....

The argument (of the university) is that since the Faculty Manual is not itself established by the legislation, but only authorized as regulations, it does not have the force of law so as to attract the remedy of *certiorari*.

I do not accept this argument. The Faculty Manual is no less law, whether statutory or delegated, because its establishment was discretionary rather than mandatory. Regulations or by-laws passed pursuant to an authorizing or empowering statute are just as "legal" as the statute itself....

Having reached the conclusion that *certiorari* is applicable, I must now determine whether this Court ought to intervene....

In the result, as we have seen, the Ad Hoc Appeal Committee recommended to the president that she overturn or overlook her earlier decision to refuse tenure to Dr. Thomas, and recommended that Dr. Thomas be granted tenure.

But this very elaborate and outwardly fair "appeal" process was in fact no appeal at all—because all the Ad Hoc Appeal Committee had power to do was to recommend to the very person from whom the appeal was taken that she grant tenure where she had earlier refused it. The committee was advisory only. It had no power to decide, as laid down in the Faculty Manual.

The effect of this whole elaborate process was that the president of Mount Saint Vincent University was sitting on appeal from her own decision. The Ad Hoc Appeal Committee was a mere cypher in the process—window dressing in a flawed procedure euphemistically referred to as an appeal.

The point here is not that Dr. Fulton was in fact biased when she considered again whether or not to grant tenure to Dr. Thomas. I am satisfied that she was not. But the point is rather, whether there was conveyed to others a reasonable apprehension of bias from the involvement of Dr. Fulton in the appeal process.... I conclude that there could not help but be a reasonable apprehension of bias in this situation on the part of a reasonable outside observer.

DEFECTS IN THE POWERS ACCORDED WITHIN ADMINISTRATIVE LAW

Thomas v. Mount Saint Vincent University raises two issues. The first concerns procedural fairness, in this case of the university's system of tenure and promotion. The second has to do with the circumstances in which an appeal can be launched through Canada's court system to remedy an apparent defect within a decision-making structure such as that of the university. Universities possess the power to make administrative decisions that have the impact of law, and there will always be varying degrees of procedural rigour attached to the range of decisions made by university administrators.

Do students have the right to appeal a final course grade to a Canadian court? Consider the case of Nalini Khan and the University of Ottawa Law School, decided by the Ontario Court of Appeal in 1997.[9] Ms. Khan claimed to have submitted four booklets in her Evidence exam, but only three were received by the instructor; she received a failing grade in the course. The majority of the Court held that a refusal on the part of the university to permit an oral hearing on the issue of whether Ms. Khan submitted the fourth booklet lacked procedural fairness:

I recognize that courts have at times shown great deference to the academic and disciplinary decision-making functions of universities. This deference is reflected in a reluctance to interfere by judicial review and in the application of a standard of "manifest unfairness" for reviewing procedural challenges. See, for example, *Paine v. University of Toronto et al.* (1981), 34 O.R. (2d) 770 (C.A.). To the extent that this deference recognizes the application of the adequate alternative remedy principle as in Harelkin, or the special expertise of university tribunals, it is unobjectionable. But I see no room for deference and no basis for a more stringent standard of judicial review when all internal university tribunals deny a student procedural fairness. If, as here, the procedures of the university committees do not conform to the requirements of fairness they should be reviewable. But even if deference is called for, in this case I hold that the proceedings of the Examinations Committee and of the Senate Committee were manifestly unfair. I would therefore grant Ms. Khan's application for judicial review and set aside the decisions of the Examinations Committee and the Senate Committee....

I would allow the appeal, set aside the order of the Divisional Court and quash the decisions of the Examinations Committee and the Senate Committee. I would refer Ms. Khan's appeal of her Evidence grade to the Examinations Committee for an oral hearing. I would award Ms. Khan her costs of this appeal, including the motion for leave to appeal, and of the judicial review application in the Divisional Court.

Consider, however, the logic of Justice Finlayson, dissenting from the majority:

Regarding the Senate Committee's proceeding, the appellant was given notice of the meeting, informed of the Faculty Committee's report, and she admits that she received written invitation to attend. She was given full opportunity to make written submissions on her own behalf, and she conceded that if given an oral hearing, she would have nothing further to add to those submissions. The Senate Committee reached its decision on the basis of all the evidence in the record, including the results of all the investigations noted above, the contents of the three examination booklets and the submissions of the appellant.

Finally, while counsel for the appellant is dismissive of the proceedings before the Senate Committee because in his submission the harm done before the Examinations Committee was irreparable, I endorse what was said by the Divisional Court from which this appeal lies:

[I]f there was any denial of natural justice in the proceedings before the Examinations Committee of the Faculty of Law, such defect was cured in the proceedings before the Senate Committee. The applicant was afforded an opportunity to appear before the Senate Committee and did not avail herself of that opportunity ... The policy of the Senate Committee to not permit students to appear and simply repeat orally their written submissions is not a defect amounting to a denial of natural justice. It does not prohibit an oral presentation to supplement and make complete the presentation of the student's view on the matter.

We disagree with the applicant's position that the credibility of the applicant was the pivotal concern in the matter before the Committees. She was not accused of dishonesty by the university administration. Rather, the applicant complained about a failure on the part of the university to properly assess her effort in completing the evidence examination....

The applicant did not discharge the burden on her of demonstrating on a balance of probabilities that the fourth examination booklet was handed in and had been mislaid.

It seems to me, with great respect to those who feel otherwise, that the appellant has succeeded in making a mountain out of a molehill. The notion that a student can dictate the level of review of her examination paper by making an allegation such as was made by the appellant here can lead only to mischief. The Committees in the case in appeal are criticized for not taking seriously an allegation that they did not consider to be determinative of what was before them. Instead of showing deference to these persons of experience that have the responsibility for maintaining academic standards within their faculty and university, they are criticized for not turning themselves inside out to affirmatively establish that the appellant was not telling the truth.

For all the reasons set out above, I would dismiss the appeal but in the circumstances, without costs.

When are judicial scrutiny and intervention appropriate? The simple answer is that when an administrative action is *ultra vires*—outside the legislative jurisdiction of the administration—it can be subject to judicial review. But how is a court or a student of law to determine whether a given administrative action is *ultra vires*? In fact, there is a range of grounds for making this determination: technicalities (failure to conform to enabling legislation), abuse of discretion, and violation of the principles of natural justice or procedural fairness. As previous cases such as *Khosa, Khan,* and *Thomas* make clear, the determination of procedural fairness in difficult cases is not an easy matter.

TECHNICAL DEFECTS

Technical defects may arise in various ways. If, for example, a municipal parks committee decided to spend some of its funds on building transition houses for battered women, the committee would clearly be operating outside its delegated jurisdiction; hence, its actions would be declared *ultra vires*. A more common example is the inappropriate delegation of some of its decision-making powers by an administrative agency. For example, in *Saumur v. City of Quebec,* which was discussed in Chapter 4, the City of Quebec's attempt to make the distribution of literature on the streets subject to permission from the chief of police was seen by the Supreme Court of Canada as an illegal delegation of authority to the police force, and hence was declared *ultra vires*.

Other *ultra vires* defects in the process of delegation can include failure to comply with the terms and conditions of appointment to a board, agency, commission, or tribunal; making a decision in the absence of a prescribed quorum; and appointing individuals to a board, agency, commission, or tribunal who do not meet mandated qualifications. Such technical defects may well include an abuse of discretionary authority or a violation of the duty to be fair, but they are defects in and of themselves, separate from the other grounds for making a determination of *ultra vires*.

ABUSE OF DISCRETION

Cases involving alleged abuse of discretion (or violation of the principles of procedural fairness, which will be addressed later) typically turn on the scope of judicial interference with an administrative agency. Consider the decisions of the Ontario Divisional Court and the Ontario Court of Appeal in *Re Sheehan and Criminal Injuries Compensation Board.*[10] As you read, ask yourself whether there was any abuse of the discretion granted the Criminal Injuries Compensation Board.

Holland, J.: This is an application for judicial review of a decision made by the Criminal Injuries Compensation Board, dated January 12, 1973, whereby two applications on behalf of Robert James Sheehan, hereinafter called Sheehan, were refused, A. Roy Wilmott Q.C. dissenting.

The first application arises out of an incident which occurred on January 2, 1970, while Sheehan was an inmate of Kingston Penitentiary, a federal penitentiary. He was assaulted and injured by a fellow prisoner.

The second application arises out of an incident which occurred on April 18, 1971, while Sheehan was an inmate of Kingston Penitentiary and occurred during the Kingston riot. Sheehan had been housed in protective custody and shortly after midnight on April 18, 1971, during the riot, he was forcibly removed, with other inmates, from a cell block, bound to a chair, and assaulted over a considerable period of time by fellow inmates. As a result of this latter series of assaults, Sheehan was most seriously injured....

In refusing the applications for compensation, the Board considered three circumstances:

(1) The fact that Sheehan, before the commission of the criminal assault above referred to, by which he suffered injury, had himself been guilty of criminal behaviour for which he had been convicted;

(2) The fact that the criminal assaults took place within the walls of Kingston Penitentiary, and at all relevant times Sheehan and his assailants were in the official and exclusive custody of another government, under conditions which were totally outside the power and jurisdiction of Ontario to deal with; and

(3) the fact that there was no evidence adduced before the Board to indicate that any application had been made to or proceedings taken on behalf of Sheehan against any other government department, ministry, or agency, to obtain compensation for damages.

The relevant legislation applicable to both of Sheehan's applications is the *Law Enforcement Compensation Act,* R.S.O., 1970, c. 237. The relevant sections … are as follows:

3. (1) Where any person is injured or killed by any act or omission of any other person occurring in or resulting directly from

(a) the commission of an offence against any statute of Canada or Ontario … the Board may, on application therefor and after a hearing, make an order in its discretion in accordance with this Act for the payment of compensation and the decision of the Board is final and conclusive for all purposes.…

5. In determining whether to make an order for compensation and the amount thereof, the Board may have regard to all such circumstances as it considers relevant, including behaviour of the victim that directly or indirectly contributed to his injury or death.…

7. (2) An order for compensation does not affect the right of any person to recover from any other person by civil proceedings lawful damages in respect of the injury or death, but, where the Board has granted an order, the Board is subrogated to all the rights of the person in whose favour the order is granted in respect of the injury or death to the extent of the amount awarded in the order.

If the three circumstances set out above, upon which the Board based its decision, are relevant, then any attack on such decision must fail. I will consider the relevance of each of the above circumstances in order.

It appears to me to be completely irrelevant that the victim, before the commission of the criminal assault giving rise to the claim, had himself been guilty of criminal behaviour for which he had been convicted. Counsel for the Board suggested that such was a proper consideration in view of the wording of s. 5, which includes as a proper consideration "any behaviour of the victim that directly or indirectly contributed to his injury.… " This surely must be restricted to relevant behaviour. If the victim is, for example, guilty of insulting behaviour that results in an assault, this would be a relevant consideration, but the fact that the victim was guilty of criminal behaviour unconnected with the incident in question to my mind cannot be considered to be relevant.

It is to be noted that the prison guard, on whose behalf an application for compensation had also been made, was not incarcerated by reason of his previous criminal behaviour and yet his application was also refused....

In this case in the assaults to Sheehan arising out of the riot, I think it can hardly be said that Sheehan contributed in any way to such assaults. He was forcibly removed from the cell block by other inmates and severely beaten, after having been tied to a chair. If compensation is to be refused in this case, I can hardly think of any circumstances that would warrant the Board in the future, if it follows its own decisions, allowing compensation to an inmate of a federal penitentiary. As such, the Board, notwithstanding its expression to the contrary, has disentitled inmates of federal penitentiaries, as a class to compensation under the Act.

In my view, the fact that Sheehan was an inmate of a federal institution or "an enclave situate within the Province of Ontario," as referred to by the Board, is not a proper consideration. If the legislature intended to exclude under the Act inmates of federal penitentiaries, it should have said so.

I now turn to the third circumstance considered by the Board and that is that there was no evidence to indicate that any application had been made by or on behalf of Sheehan to any other government department, ministry, or agency to obtain compensation for damages. Section 7(2) of the *Law Enforcement Compensation Act* provides that an order for compensation does not affect the right of any person to recover from any other person by civil proceedings lawful damages in respect of the injury and further provides that where the Board has granted an order, the Board is subrogated to the rights of the person in whose favour the order is granted, to the extent of the amount awarded in the order. No section imposes an obligation on an applicant to make an application or take any other proceedings against any other individual or authority....

For the above reasons, I have come to the conclusion that none of the three circumstances considered by the Board were relevant. The question remains whether this Court can, in view of the wording of s. 3(1) and (5) of the Act, set aside the dismissal of the application and direct that the matter be remitted to the Board for further consideration.

There is no obligation on the Board to award compensation. It could be argued that the payment is an *ex gratia* payment. Even so, the general intent of the Act is clear and that is to provide compensation to victims of crime. Claimants to *ex gratia* payments are entitled to have their claims considered on a proper basis: *Joy Oil Co. Ltd. v. The King* [1951] S.C.R. 624....

I conclude that the Court may properly review the decision of the Board in this case and that the matters considered by the Board were not relevant. In the circumstances, the decision of the Board will be quashed and the matter remitted to the Board for consideration.

Application granted.

However, Justice Kelly of the Ontario Court of Appeal had a different view of the matter, holding that the protection of an agency's discretionary authority is more important than subscription to the principles set out above.

Kelly, J.A.: In proceedings in the nature of judicial review, either under the Judicial Review Procedure Act, … or upon an application for one of the prerogative writs, the primary consideration is the nature of the jurisdiction of the body whose decision is sought to be brought under review. In this matter, the heart of the issue is this—has the Board, in refusing the application, done so within the proper limits of its discretionary function established by its parent statute, or has the Board, in ascribing its refusal to one or more of the circumstances above referred to, exceeded its statutory jurisdiction so as to bring its decision within the proper reach of judicial review?

The principal argument proffered in support of the contention that the Board had exceeded its jurisdiction and was accordingly subject to judicial review, was that the Board had escalated one or more of the circumstances above set out to the status of statutory conditions of eligibility and had thereby purported to vary the statute under which its authority was to be found. If the Board had said that the presence of any one or more of the factors would disentitle any applicant from receiving compensation, it might be arguable that it had exceeded its authority under the Act. But a clear-cut distinction must be drawn between the Board giving consideration to certain circumstances and the Board holding that a particular circumstance *ipso facto* disqualified an applicant from benefits under the Act….

With respect, I do not construe the Act as authorizing the Court to review the correctness of the Board's decision made within the scope of its authority. The Legislature has expressly assigned to the Board and not to the Courts the discretionary authority to grant or deny compensation.

Within the confines of its convening statute, the Board may, indeed must, perform this function and may do so free from judicial intervention, however a Court may view any particular exercise of its proper discretion.

In my opinion, the Divisional Court erred when it considered that its task was to determine if the said circumstances were relevant. In the light of the discretion vested in the Board to have regard to all circumstances which it considered relevant so long as it acted in good faith, the decisions of the Board as to what considerations are relevant are unchallengeable: see *C.N.R. et al. v. Canada Steamship Lines Ltd. et al.*, [1945] 3 D.L.R. 417, 420.

I would therefore allow the appeal with costs if demanded, set aside the order of the Divisional Court, and, in its place, substitute an order directing that the application for judicial review be dismissed, also with costs if demanded.

Appeal allowed.

The two decisions in *Re Sheehan* reveal contrasting points of view with respect to the scope of judicial review. The Ontario Court of Appeal decided against any interference with the board's decision to deny compensation, noting that section 3(1) gives the Ontario Criminal Injuries Compensation Board jurisdiction "to make an order *in its discretion* exercised in accordance with this Act for the payment of compensation." (A further appeal by Sheehan to the Supreme Court of Canada was denied.)

A question inevitably comes to mind. Have the courts, in granting such a range of discretion to an administrative agency, allowed that agency to incorporate irrelevant considerations in its decision-making processes? The decision in *Re Sheehan* appears to permit an unrelated criminal record to be used as a bar to compensation for a later criminal injury.

VIOLATION OF THE PRINCIPLES OF PROCEDURAL FAIRNESS

Allegations that an administrative agency has failed to follow principles of procedural fairness typically resemble allegations of abuse of discretion. Consider the following decision of the Ontario Court of Appeal in *Re Sawyer and Ontario Racing Commission*. The applicant, Sawyer, an owner of horses, had been suspended from racing for 10 years, after a hearing before the Ontario Racing Commission. The lawyer who represented the commission also wrote the decision. Sawyer claimed that this was a breach of the principles of **natural justice**.

Brooke, J.A.: In my opinion, the Commission misunderstood the function of counsel who presented the case against the appellant before them. He was variously described as counsel to the Commission, counsel for the Commission, and counsel for the Commission Administration. But there is no doubt that his role was to prosecute the case against the appellant and he was not present in a role comparable to that of a legal assessor to the Commission.... He was counsel for the appellant's adversary in proceedings to determine the appellant's guilt or innocence on the charge against him. It is basic that persons entrusted to judge or determine the rights of others must, for reasons arrived at independently, make that decision, whether it or the reasons be right or wrong. It was wrong for the Commission, who were the judges, to privately involve either party in the Commission's function once the case began and certainly after the case was left to them for ultimate disposition. To do so must amount to a denial of natural justice because it would not unreasonably raise a suspicion of bias in others, including the appellant, who were not present and later learned what transpired.

In *Re Bernstein and College of Physicians and Surgeons of Ontario* (1977), 76 D.L.R. (3d) 38, when the Discipline Committee of the College had arrived at a verdict that Dr. Bernstein was guilty of the offence charged, the chairman gave to counsel for the college who had prosecuted the case against the doctor a rough outline of the Committee's reasons for its decisions and requested him to prepare formal reasons for the Committee's approval. The original of the rough draft was not available for the Court's consideration. While the Court allowed the appeal because of a lack of sufficient credible evidence to uphold the conviction, of this issue O'Leary J., who delivered the judgement for the majority, said at 63–64:

In this particular case, Mr. Hunter, though asked by the Court for the same, was unable to locate the rough outline of the reasons for judgement sometimes prepared by the chairman.

In my view, it is an unusual and improper practice for counsel to write the reasons for the Discipline Committee, even if the chairman or some member of the Committee has drafted rough reasons to guide him. One who has stood trial before a disciplinary body is entitled to have that body's reasons for its decision and not the reasons the prosecutor composes for the decision. If the Committee has made an error in arriving at its conclusion, the one who has stood trial, in fairness, should learn of it.

In the case before us, the reasons for its decision were never made known by the Commission to anyone, including its counsel. I agree with O'Leary J. What he said is apt here. If it were otherwise, the accused's right of appeal or review would be illusory....

Counsel for the respondent contends that this Court should consider whether the conduct of the Commission has resulted in any prejudice to the appellant and in so doing, have regard to the following factors:

(1) that all of the relevant circumstances surrounding the preparation of the draft reasons for judgement had been disclosed in the affidavit;

(2) that counsel had played no part in the decision-making process of the respondent; and

(3) that the respondent adopted the draft reasons for judgement only after due consideration.

Further, counsel for the respondent contends that the ruling of the respondent ought to be examined apart from the reasons and in light of the record.

I have no doubt whatsoever that the affidavit made by counsel is a frank and accurate statement. However, I do not agree with the above submission. I think Mr. Laskin is right in his submission that justice cannot appear to have been done when the determination of how a case was decided depends, not upon the reasons over the signature of the real author, but rather upon the affidavit of a person who actually wrote the reasons and who now must explain how his thoughts were accepted after the decision of the tribunal. This is not good enough, for the appellant still has not been told by the tribunal why it found him guilty. Similarly, I do not agree that this Court should attempt to test the decision by considering the record. We should not retry the case or simply examine it to find if there is evidence which might support the judgment. This is not what is in issue here. What is in issue is that this man has not been dealt with according to the law.

Appeal allowed.[11]

JUDICIAL INTERVENTION AND THE PRINCIPLES OF NATURAL JUSTICE

The phrase "according to the law" in Justice Brooke's decision raises more questions than it answers. Given the scope of administrative discretion, allegations of bias and of failure to provide due process are central to any determination of what constitutes law. While many decisions can be resolved through the correction of technical defects and the application of precedents, other situations exist in which little or no guidance from precedent will be available. Because responsibility for directing policy has been delegated to a given administrative body, the courts are reluctant to intervene in such circumstances unless there has been a fundamental lack of fairness in the state's treatment of its citizens.

In *Thomas v. Mount Saint Vincent University,* the decision to intervene in the internal affairs of the university was based on the apprehension of bias in the university's decision to deny tenure to Dr. Thomas. In *Re Sheehan,* the Ontario Divisional Court held that Sheehan had been excluded from compensation for reasons that were irrelevant to the purpose of the act; in other words, that the board had exceeded its jurisdiction. The Ontario Court of Appeal reversed the decision, arguing that there was no lack of fairness and no excess of jurisdiction. In *Re Sawyer,* the Ontario Court of Appeal concluded that counsel's construction of the Racing Commission's decision failed to provide the appellant with due process.

In the late 1990s the Supreme Court of Canada elaborated on the notions of procedural fairness and apprehension of bias in *Baker v. Minister of Citizenship and Immigration.* In this case a Jamaican-born woman, Mavis Baker, was ordered deported from Canada after working in the country illegally for more than 10 years. Ms. Baker had four Canadian-born dependent children, and she applied for an exemption to deportation, citing humanitarian and compassionate considerations under section 114(2) of the *Immigration Act.* Her application noted that her departure was likely to have a very significant negative impact on her children.

A senior immigration officer replied to Ms. Baker by letter, indicating that there were insufficient humanitarian and compassionate grounds to warrant processing her application; no reasons were given for this decision—none were required by law. Counsel for Ms. Baker did, however, ask for the notes taken by the investigating immigration officer, notes that were relied upon by the senior officer in making his decision.

These notes were provided, and they revealed the following statements about Ms. Baker and her situation:

PC is unemployed—on welfare. No income shown—no assets. Has four Cdn. Born children—four others in Jamaica—HAS A TOTAL OF EIGHT CHILDREN.... There is nothing for her in Jamaica—hasn't been there in a long time—no longer close to her children there—no jobs there—she has no skills other than as a domestic—children would suffer—can't take them with her and can't leave them with anyone here.... Letter from Children's Aid—they say PC has been diagnosed as a paranoid schizophrenic—children would suffer if returned.... This case is a catastrophy [*sic*]. It is also an indictment of our "system" that the client came as a visitor in Aug. 81, was not ordered deported until Dec. '92 and in April '94 IS STILL HERE! ... The PC is a paranoid schizophrenic and on welfare. She has no qualifications other than as a domestic. She has FOUR CHILDREN IN JAMAICA AND ANOTHER FOUR BORN HERE. She will, of course, be a tremendous strain on our social welfare systems for (probably) the rest of her life. There are no H&C factors other than her FOUR CANADIAN-BORN CHILDREN. Do we let her stay because of that? I am of the opinion that Canada can no longer afford this type of generosity. However, because of the circumstances involved, there is a potential for adverse publicity. I recommend refusal but you may wish to clear this with someone at Region.

Justice L'Heureux-Dubé, in writing the judgment of the court, noted that the investigating officer had ignored a psychiatrist's letter suggesting that with consistent treatment, Ms. Baker was likely to be a contributing member of the community. Justice L'Heureux-Dubé wrote:

[T]he well-informed member of the community would perceive bias when reading (the investigating officer's) comments. His notes, and the manner in which they are written, do not disclose the existence of an open mind or a weighing of the particular circumstances of the case free from stereotypes.... His use of capitals to highlight the number of Ms. Baker's children may also suggest to a reader that this was a reason to deny her status. Reading his comments, I do not believe that a reasonable and well-informed member of the community would conclude that he had approached this case with the impartiality appropriate to a decision made by an immigration officer.[12]

The court held that there was a reasonable apprehension of bias and allowed Ms. Baker's appeal.

Several expressions are associated with these decisions: due process, excess of jurisdiction, **doctrine of fairness**, and natural justice. All flow from a common origin: common-law doctrine developed more than 400 years ago in judgments emanating from the British judiciary. Constitutional scholar Peter Hogg has noted:

Outside the realm of criminal law, the state and the individual usually come into conflict as the result of the exercise by officials of governmental powers over persons or private property. In Britain, common-law doctrine early developed that the King and his officials had no powers other than those granted by the law. With few exceptions, actions which infringe the liberty of the subject require the authority of a statute. This was settled in the great case of *Entick v. Carrington* (1765), in which it was held that neither a search warrant signed by a minister of the Crown, nor a claim of "state necessity" could justify Crown servants in entering the premises of the plaintiff and seizing his papers. The plaintiff's action in trespass against the Crown servants was successful, because they could not show that their actions were authorized by law.[13]

The concept of natural justice has developed over centuries of legal practice founded on the common law. There are two key principles of natural justice, expressed in Latin terminology: **audi alteram partem** and *nemo sibi esse judex vel suis jus dicere debet.*

Audi alteram partem means "hear the other side." *Black's Law Dictionary* expands on the definition: "hear the other side; hear both sides; no man should be condemned unheard."* The rule requires that parties to a dispute have a fair hearing, which includes being given notice of when and where the hearing is to be held, the opportunity to bring witnesses, and the chance to cross-examine the witnesses brought against them. It flows from claims that the legal process did not afford both sides the right to a fair hearing of their claims. This was essentially the argument in *Khan,* above, in relation to the need for an oral hearing.

Nemo sibi esse judex vel suis jus dicere debet, translated literally, means "no person should act as judge on his own behalf or speak the law for his own (ends)." The purpose of the **nemo judex** rule is to exclude bias or the appearance of bias from the proceedings of an administrative body. (The *Thomas* and *Re Sawyer* decisions hinged on an appearance of bias on the part of the decision makers—in the first, the university president, and in the second, the Ontario Racing Commission.) Both principles of natural justice date back to Greek and Roman law. Jones and deVillars note of *audi alteram partem:*

> The rule is an ancient one, known in Greek and even biblical times. It certainly made an appearance in English common law by the seventeenth century, and often appeared thereafter in cases having to do with restoration to offices. It extended to ecclesiastical matters, to societies and clubs, and later to protect members of trade unions from unfair expulsion. As administrative tribunals proliferated in the nineteenth and twentieth centuries, they were required to follow the same rules of fair procedure as their predecessors, the justices of the peace. The identity of the person who exercised the power was not decisive; rather, what mattered was the character of the power being exercised. If it affected a person's rights and interests, then the power had to be exercised in a fair manner.[14]

It is probably fair to suggest, therefore, that the basic principles now underlying administrative law have not changed in more than 2000 years. The judiciary has generally required that the state, in exercising powers over citizens and their commercial interests, treat those citizens and their interests fairly. During certain historical and political eras, this duty has been less strictly observed than at other times; but the basic philosophical thrust of the position has endured.

---

*Black's Law Dictionary. Found at: http://thelawdictionary.org/audi-alteram-partem/

The Doctrine of Fairness

During the late 1960s, the doctrine of fairness, fundamentally an extension of the rules of natural justice, was developed in both England and Canada. The last 50 years have seen increased judicial intervention in the interest of fairness or fair treatment. Evans et al. have noted:

> One good example of this trend is cases about prisoners, and their claims to hearings decisions about parole, discipline, transfers, and leaves. A lawyer from the 1960s could hardly believe that hearings for these decisions are now commonplace and that the fighting ground is whether hearings will be given for decisions about unescorted temporary absences. The reasons for this change are less clear. The thought that it is simply a response to the pervasiveness and immense complexity of modern government seems hopelessly vague; why, for example, would such a response have occurred at this time and not at almost any other time during the twentieth century? Is it useful to remember the controversy and protest during the 1960s?[15]

In a 1986 Ontario case, Justice Reid noted of the emerging doctrine of fairness:

> It is no longer necessary, as it was before the emergence of the doctrine of fairness, to find that rights were, or might be, affected. The old learning was that if rights were affected, the function of the tribunal was quasi-judicial and therefore subject to the rules of natural justice. It is sufficient now if interests only are affected.[16]

Consider the application of this doctrine to *Cardinal and Oswald v. Director of Kent Institution*. Cardinal and Oswald were inmates in British Columbia's Matsqui Penitentiary. They took a guard hostage at knifepoint and confined him for five hours. After the incident, they were charged with various criminal offences and transferred to the maximum security Kent Institution. The director of that institution placed them in segregation, officially known as administrative dissociation, and planned to keep them there until their criminal offences had been resolved by the courts. A prison Segregation Review Board recommended that the two men be released from segregation and placed in the general population of Kent Institution, but Cardinal and Oswald remained in administrative dissociation. They appealed to the courts, arguing that they had not been given a fair hearing by the director of Kent Institution. The Supreme Court of Canada brought down the following decision:

LeDain, J.: There can be no doubt, as was held by McEachern C.J.S.C. and the Court of Appeal, that the Director was under a duty of procedural fairness in exercising the authority conferred by s. 40 of the regulations with respect to administrative dissociation or segregation. This Court has affirmed that there is, as a general common-law principle, a duty of procedural fairness lying on every public authority making an administrative decision which is not of a legislative nature and which affects the rights, privileges, or interests of an individual....

The issue then is what did procedural fairness require of the Director in exercising his authority, pursuant to s. 40 of the Penitentiary Service Regulations, to continue the administrative dissociation or segregation of the appellants, despite the recommendation of the Board, if he was satisfied that it was necessary or desirable for the maintenance of good order and discipline in the institution. I agree with McEachern C.J.S.C. and Anderson J.A. that because of the serious effect of the Director's decision on the appellants, procedural fairness required that he inform them of the reasons for his intended decision and give them an opportunity, however informal, to make representations to him concerning these reasons and the general question whether it was necessary or desirable to continue their segregation for the maintenance of good order and discipline in the institution.

With great respect, I do not think it is an answer to the requirement of notice and hearing by the Director, as suggested by Macdonald, J.A., that the appellants knew, as a result of their appearance before the Segregation Review Board, why they had been placed in segregation. They were entitled to know why the Director did not intend to act in accordance with the recommendation of the Board and to have an opportunity before him to state their case for release into the general population of the institution. I do not think the Director was required to make an independent inquiry into the alleged involvement of the appellants in the hostage-taking incident. He could rely on the information he had received concerning the incident from the warden of Matsqui Institution and the personnel at regional headquarters. At the same time, he had a duty to hear and consider what the appellants had to say concerning their alleged involvement in the incident, as well as anything else that could be relevant to the question whether their release from segregation might introduce an unsettling element into the general inmate population and thus have an adverse effect on the maintenance of good order and discipline in the institution.

These were, in my opinion, the minimal or essential requirements of procedural fairness in the circumstances, and they are fully compatible with the concern that the process of prison administration, because of its special nature and exigencies, should not be unduly burdened or obstructed by the imposition of unreasonable or inappropriate procedural requirements. There is nothing to suggest that the requirement of notice and hearing by the Director, where he does not intend to act in accordance with a recommendation by the Segregation Review Board for the release of an inmate from segregation, would impose an undue burden on prison administration or create a risk to security.

There is the question, suggested by the reasons for judgement of Nemetz, C.J.B.C., whether the breach of the duty to act fairly in this case should be held not to have resulted in an excess or loss of jurisdiction and to have made the continuing segregation of the appellants unlawful because, having regard to the merits of the substantive issue, it did not result in a substantial injustice, or to use the words of Nemetz, C.J.B.C., was not of "sufficient substance." Both Nemetz C.J.B.C. and Macdonald J.A. considered the substantive issue of whether the appellants should be released from segregation and appeared to conclude that the Director's reasons for refusing to follow the recommendation of the Segregation Review Board were reasonable and fair. It is a possible implication of their approach that they were of the view that given the Director's reasons for refusing to follow the recommendation of the Board, a hearing by him of the appellants would not serve any useful purpose. Certainly, a failure to afford a fair hearing, which is the very essence of the duty to act fairly, can never of itself be regarded as not of "sufficient substance" unless it be because of its perceived effect on the result or, in other words, the actual prejudice caused by it. If this be a correct view of the implications of the approach of the majority of the British Columbia Court of Appeal to the issue of procedural fairness in this case, I find it necessary to affirm that the denial of a right to a fair hearing must always render a decision invalid, whether or not it may appear to a reviewing court that the hearing would likely have resulted in a different decision. The right to a fair hearing must be regarded as an independent, unqualified right which finds its essential justification in the sense of procedural justice which any person affected by an administrative decision is entitled to have. It is not for a court to deny that right and sense of justice on the basis of speculation as to what the result might have been had there been a hearing. Appeal allowed.[17]

The decision in *Cardinal and Oswald* is, in most important respects, consistent with the long-established rules of natural justice: the director of the prison must abide by the principle of *audi alteram partem*. What is singular about *Cardinal and Oswald* is that it expanded the rules of natural justice to include life behind the walls of Canada's penitentiaries.

More recently, consider the decision of the Supreme Court of Canada in 2005 in *May v. Ferndale Institution*. At issue in this case was the transfer of inmates from a minimum to medium security institution, based not on any conduct but on results obtained from a computerized reclassification scale. The majority of the court held that while the transfer of inmates to a different level of security, based on such a scale, might be appropriate, failure to disclose the scoring matrix to the inmates was a violation of procedural fairness:

Based on the evidence, we cannot accept the respondents' argument that the SRS was only a preliminary assessment tool. Although it is true that an individual assessment of each inmate's security classification is made subsequently to the SRS assessment, in our view, the SRS presumptively classifies inmates and constitutes an important aspect of the classification process.

Considering the nature of the scoring matrix and its role in the SRS, its nondisclosure constituted a major breach of the duty to disclose inherent in the requirement of procedural fairness. The appellants were deprived of information essential to understanding the computerized system which generated their scores. The appellants were not given the formula used to weigh the factors or the documents used for scoring questions and answers. The appellants knew what the factors were, but did not know how values were assigned to them or how those values factored into the generation of the final score.

How can there be a meaningful response to a reclassification decision without information explaining how the security rating is determined? As a matter of logic and common sense, the scoring tabulation and methodology associated with the SRS classification score should have been made available. The importance of making that information available stems from the fact that inmates may want to rebut the evidence relied upon for the calculation of the SRS score and security classification. This information may be critical in circumstances where a security classification depends on the weight attributed to one specific factor.

Hence, given the importance of the information contained in the scoring matrix, the presumptive validity of the score and its potential effect on the determination of security classification, it should have been disclosed. The respondents had a duty to do so under s. 27(1) of the CCRA.

In conclusion, the respondents failed to disclose all the relevant information or a summary of the information used in making the transfer decisions despite several requests by the appellants. The respondents concealed crucial information. In doing so, they violated their statutory duty. The transfer decisions were made improperly and, therefore, they are null and void for want of jurisdiction. It follows that the appellants were unlawfully deprived of their liberty.[18]

Consider, alternatively, the position of the three dissenting Justices of the Court:

...the relevant question is whether the non-disclosure of the scoring matrix deprived the appellants of their right to know the case they had to meet. Only if it did can we conclude that there has been a breach of the rules of procedural fairness. In my view, it did not. The appellants were advised that the SRS score formed part of the basis for the transfer recommendation. In the Assessment for Decision, they were provided with the list of relevant factors considered in computing the score. They were provided with the personal information that was relied upon in assessing each factor and it was open to them to dispute the accuracy of that information. They were provided with the reclassification score assigned to them. It is true, as contended, that without the scoring matrix, they could not check the accuracy of the total score. It is on that basis that I conclude that the scoring matrix should have been provided. Although the disclosure met the requirement under s. 27(1) of the CCRA that the prisoner be provided with "all the information to be considered in the taking of the decision or a summary of that information", detailed information beyond the summary was specifically requested in these cases and the respondents have not advanced any reason why it should not have been disclosed. However, I would not conclude that its non-disclosure resulted in a breach of procedural fairness in the context of these cases. The appellants had sufficient information to know the case they had to meet.[19]

NATURAL JUSTICE VERSUS FUNDAMENTAL JUSTICE: THE *CHARTER* AND ADMINISTRATIVE LAW

As mentioned at the outset of this chapter, a critical change in the structure of administrative law in Canada took place in 1982: the enactment of section 7 of the *Canadian Charter of Rights and Freedoms*.

> 7. *Everyone has the right to life, liberty and security of the person and the right not to be deprived thereof except in accordance with the principles of fundamental justice.*

The wording of this section has caused a great legal conundrum. Section 7 confers a right to be dealt with "in accordance with the principles of fundamental justice" rather than "in accordance with the principles of natural justice." Hogg has noted:

> The legislative history of s. 7 makes clear that the framers thought that "fundamental justice" meant natural justice, and were anxious to avoid judicial review that went beyond issues of procedure.... The trouble was that the phrase that was selected to replace due process was not "natural justice," which would certainly have been restricted to procedure, but "fundamental justice," a term that lacked any substantial body of defining case law."[20]

Since the passage of the *Charter*, Canadian courts have wrestled with the meaning to be accorded to the words "principles of fundamental justice." The courts have generally held that section 7 prohibits something more than procedural injustices.[21] Consider the commentary of the Federal Court of Appeal in *Re Howard and Presiding Officer of Inmate Disciplinary Court of Stony Mountain Institution*. Is this decision simply a logical extension of the principles of natural justice, or a more radical departure from existing common law, necessitated by the *Charter*?

Thurlow, C.J.: At the material time, the appellant was an inmate of Stony Mountain Institution serving a sentence of two years and four months. On December 31, 1982, he was involved in incidents with officers of the institution as a result of which five charges were laid against him under s. 39 of the Penitentiary Service Regulations. These were, possessing contraband, using indecent or disrespectful language to another person, an act calculated to prejudice discipline or good order of the institution, disobeying a lawful order of a penitentiary officer, and threatening to assault another person. The record does not disclose particulars of the charges other than that the first three occurred at 8:40 hours, the fourth at 9:00 hours, and the fifth at 9:20 hours, all on December 31, 1982. On January 6, 1983, the appellant appeared before a presiding officer and entered pleas of guilty to the charges of possessing contraband and disobeying a lawful order, and pleas of not guilty on the remaining three charges. Disposition of the charges to which he pleaded guilty was held in abeyance pending determination of the remaining three charges. Subsequently, charges of having contraband on January 4, 1983, and failing to obey a lawful order on January 20, 1983, were laid. To these the appellant pleaded not guilty. All the charges were categorized under the Commissioner's Directive No. 213 as "serious" or "flagrant" offences.

On February 3, 1983, by which time he had secured counsel, the appellant appeared before the presiding officer of the inmate disciplinary court who thereupon adjourned the hearing in order to obtain written submissions from counsel for the appellant and for the Department of Justice, on the request of the appellant to have counsel represent him at the hearing. The request was denied on April 11, 1983. The presiding officer held that s. 7 of the *Charter* does not create "a new wave of rights" and, as he was not persuaded that there were circumstances in the particular case which precluded the possibility of a fair hearing in the absence of counsel, he exercised his discretion and denied the request....

I come then to s. 7 of the *Charter* and whether it has the effect of affording an inmate in a disciplinary proceeding a right to counsel that is not subject to denial by the presiding officer on discretionary grounds.

What was said to be at stake in the disciplinary proceedings is the liberty and security of the inmate and his right not to be deprived of them except in accordance with the principles of fundamental justice. The inmate's liberty was said to be at stake because his earned remission was in jeopardy as was also the security of his person since solitary confinement—also referred to as dissociation—was one of the punishments to which he might be subjected. I accept this analysis so far as the appellant's liberty is involved and that, as I view it, is sufficient for present purposes. At the same time, it is to be noted that earned remission, which is a creation of the *Penitentiary Act,* has at all times been conditional in the sense that it has been subject to forfeiture in disciplinary proceedings of an administrative nature and thus has never had the quality of an absolute right to be set free on the completion of the unremitted portion of a sentence. To hold that an inmate's procedural rights have been increased by the enactment of s. 7 is accordingly to hold that its enactment has also enhanced the quality of the less than absolute right conferred by the *Penitentiary Act.*

In the course of their reasons, both the presiding officer and the learned trial judge referred to expression of judicial opinion in a number of reported cases supporting the view that at common law, a prison inmate had no absolute right to have counsel represent him in proceedings before a disciplinary tribunal, that the legal procedures established by law before the enactment of the *Charter* are procedures in accordance with the principles of fundamental justice, and that s. 7 of the *Charter* did not add to the rights of a person in the appellant's position. That may be a legitimate approach to the question. But it appears to me that in interpreting s. 7, and its meaning in the *Charter,* it is desirable to consider the wording of the provision in an effort to determine its ordinary meaning in its context.

The section is cast in broad terms. Its context is that of a constitutional charter. The *Charter* itself is part of the Constitution of Canada. These features suggest a broad interpretation. The extent of the *Charter*'s guarantee of the rights set out in s. 7 may be limited by s. 1, but that does not, as it seems to me, bear on how s. 7 itself should be interpreted or on the breadth of what it embraces. In the present case, no argument was presented on the effect of s. 1 on any right to counsel that may arise under s. 7.

Next, the subject matter of s. 7 is the right to life, liberty, and security of the person. These are matters of prime importance to everyone. Moreover, the fact that liberty and security of the person are lumped together with life itself shows that the importance of the right to them is in the same class with that of the right to life itself. The enjoyment of property is not included in the class as it is in ss. 1(a) and 2(e) of the Canadian *Bill of Rights*.

Further, while the argument in the present case focussed on the meaning and effect of the wording "in accordance with the principles of fundamental justice" as a guarantee of procedural standards, I would not rule out the possibility that the wording may also refer to or embrace substantive standards as well....

I am of the opinion that the enactment of s. 7 has not created any absolute right to counsel in all such proceedings. It is undoubtedly of the greatest importance to a person whose life, liberty, and security of the person are at stake to have the opportunity to present his case as fully and adequately as possible. The advantages of having the assistance of counsel for that purpose are not in doubt. But what is required is an opportunity to present the case adequately, and I do not think it can be affirmed that in no case can such an opportunity be afforded without also as part of it affording the right to representation by counsel at the hearing.

Once that position is reached, it appears to me that whether or not the person has a right to representation by counsel will depend on the circumstances of the particular case, its nature, its gravity, its complexity, the capacity of the inmate himself to understand the case and present his defence. The list is not exhaustive. And from this, it seems to me, it follows that whether or not an inmate's request for representation by counsel can lawfully be refused is not properly referred to as a matter of discretion, but is a matter of right where the circumstances are such that the opportunity to present the case adequately calls for representation by counsel....

This brings me to the question whether the present was a case in which the appellant's request could lawfully be refused. Its principal feature was that the whole of the appellant's 267 days of earned remission was in jeopardy. In my view, that alone suggests his need of counsel. Next, there is the lack of particulars of offences of which three are alleged to have occurred at the same instant.... Moreover, one of the three charges is that of an act calculated to prejudice discipline and good order, a notoriously vague and difficult charge for anyone to defend. These features, as well, suggest the need for counsel to protect the inmate.

There is not in the record anything that would indicate that the appellant suffered from physical or mental incapacity which would disable him from conducting his own defence as well as might be expected of an ordinary person without legal training. But he obviously felt the need for counsel because he obtained legal-aid assistance promptly. He must also have been able to persuade those who administer the legal-aid system of his need. Moreover, in a social system which recognizes the right of anyone to counsel in any of the ordinary courts of law for the defence of any charge, no matter how trivial the possible consequences may be, it seems to me to be incongruous to deny such a right to a person who, though not suffering from any physical or mental incapacity to defend himself, is faced with charges that may result in a loss of his liberty, qualified and fragile though it may have been, for some 267 days.

On the whole, I am of the opinion that the refusal of the appellant's request for counsel was a refusal of the opportunity to which he was entitled to adequately present his defence.... Appeal allowed.[22]

RECENT DEVELOPMENTS IN ADMINISTRATIVE LAW: WHAT IS THE JUDICIAL STANDARD OF REVIEW OF AN ADMINISTRATIVE DECISION?

It is often difficult to determine the extent or the amount of judicial review that is appropriate, with respect to the decision of an administrative tribunal. Two relatively recent Supreme Court decisions provide some guidance on this issue. Consider first this excerpt from *Dr. Q v. College of Physicians and Surgeons of B.C.*, decided by the Supreme Court in 2003:

McLachlin, C.J.: The relationship between Dr. Q and Ms. T began in early 1994 as a therapeutic one. Ms. T sought Dr. Q's help in treating her depression. Ms. T alleged that, at some point in the spring of 1995, the relationship became sexual and that this sexual relationship lasted for approximately 16 months. The case ultimately turned on an assessment of credibility. Dr. Q flatly denied Ms. T's allegations that they had been involved sexually. The Committee heard the oral evidence of both parties and considered corroborative evidence. In reaching its conclusion that sexual acts had occurred, the Committee stated that it accepted Ms. T's evidence and disbelieved that of Dr. Q (Report of the Inquiry Committee, January 5, 1998, p. 20).

Section 73 of the Act affords an appeal to the courts "on the merits" of the case. Dr. Q appealed to the British Columbia Supreme Court. On appeal, Koenigsberg J., in chambers, accepted that "[t]he task of the Committee was to determine the guilt or innocence of Dr. Q. based almost completely on the credibility of the witnesses" (para. 2). Koenigsberg J. posed the question before her as follows (at para. 4):

The issue is whether the evidence before the Committee objectively assessed meets the standard of clear and cogent evidence to support the finding that Dr. Q. was guilty.

She reviewed the evidence and disagreed with the Committee's findings as to credibility. As a result, Koenigsberg J. held that the evidence was not "sufficiently cogent" (para. 39) to make it safe to uphold the findings of the panel. She allowed the appeal and set aside the finding of infamous conduct.

The College appealed to the British Columbia Court of Appeal. The Court of Appeal reviewed Koenigsberg J.'s decision, felt that it could not reach the conclusion that she was "clearly wrong" (para. 30) and, therefore, dismissed the appeal....

Balancing these factors, I am satisfied that the appropriate standard of review is reasonableness *simpliciter*. The reviewing judge should have asked herself whether the Committee's assessment of credibility and application of the standard of proof to the evidence was unreasonable, in the sense of not being supported by any reasons that can bear somewhat probing examination (see *Ryan, supra,* at para. 46).

The reviewing judge did not adopt this analysis. Indeed, she made no reference at all to the pragmatic and functional approach. The effect of the reviewing judge's failure to conduct the usual administrative law analysis was essentially to proceed on what amounted to a correctness standard. One of the factors under the pragmatic and functional approach is whether the statute grants a right of appeal. But it is only one. The reviewing judge considered only this factor and, as a result, she applied too strict a standard. Specifically, she failed to address the need for deference in view of the purpose of the Act and the nature of the problem, credibility. A proper consideration of all the factors required by the pragmatic and functional approach would have yielded a standard of reasonableness *simpliciter*, not correctness. In effect, the reviewing judge erroneously instructed herself to review the Committee's findings of fact on a correctness basis.

The reviewing judge's analysis of the corroborative evidence confirms that she assessed the Committee's findings of credibility from the perspective of correctness, rather than reasonableness. For example, when addressing the Committee's reliance upon the discrepancy between Dr. Q's letter to the College and the number of times he had actually had lunch with Ms. T, the reviewing judge argued that "one explanation for Dr. Q.'s less than forthright description of his lunch relationship with Ms. T. is that the letter was written without dealing with specific allegations pursuant to legal advice" (para. 13). Yet when the standard of review is reasonableness, the reviewing judge's role is not to posit alternate interpretations of the evidence; rather, it is to determine whether the Committee's interpretation is unreasonable. When considering the Committee's conclusion that Ms. T's ability to describe distinct bodily markings suggested an intimate relationship between Ms. T and Dr. Q, the reviewing judge noted that Ms. T had some experience as a surgical nurse and asserted that, "[i]n my view, her description is no more vivid than one might expect from someone who has experience with surgical scars if such a scar had been described to her as Dr. Q testified he had done" (para. 20). With respect, when applying a standard of reasonableness *simpliciter*, the reviewing judge's view of the evidence is beside the point; rather, the reviewing judge should have asked whether the Committee's conclusion on this point had some basis in the evidence (see *Ryan, supra*). Finally, when assessing the Committee's finding that a letter sent by Dr. Q. to Ms. T supported the conclusion that a sexual relationship existed, the reviewing judge stated the following (at para. 25):

While there is no doubt that for many the wording of the letter is such as to raise a suspicion or question as to the nature of the relationship; nevertheless it is, in my view, not clear and cogent evidence corroborative of a sexual relationship as testified to by Ms. T.

If there is "no doubt" that the letter could be interpreted as evidence of a sexual relationship, such an interpretation cannot be unreasonable and, therefore, the reviewing judge's preferred view is irrelevant.

I conclude that the reviewing judge erred by applying too exacting a standard of review and substituting her own view of the evidence for that of the Committee.

C. The Role of the Court of Appeal

The Court of Appeal stated that "[t]he standard that we must apply in assessing the judgment of Madam Justice Koenigsberg is whether in her re-weighing of the evidence she was clearly wrong" (para. 25). This is not the appropriate test at the secondary appellate level. The role of the Court of Appeal was to determine whether the reviewing judge had chosen and applied the correct standard of review, and in the event she had not, to assess the administrative body's decision in light of the correct standard of review, reasonableness. At this stage in the analysis, the Court of Appeal is dealing with appellate review of a subordinate court, not judicial review of an administrative decision. As such, the normal rules of appellate review of lower courts as articulated in *Housen, supra,* apply. The question of the right standard to select and apply is one of law and, therefore, must be answered correctly by a reviewing judge. The Court of Appeal erred by affording deference where none was due.

The Court of Appeal should have corrected the reviewing judge's error, substituted the appropriate standard of administrative review, and assessed the Committee's decision on this basis. Judged on the proper standard of reasonableness, there was ample evidence to support the Committee's conclusions on credibility, burden of proof and application of the burden of proof to the factual findings. It follows that the decisions of the reviewing judge and the Court of Appeal should be set aside and the order of the College restored.[23]

What is particularly instructive about the Supreme Court's decision in this case is its focus on the standard of review to be applied by a reviewing judge. The judge's own view of the evidence is not relevant, provided that there is some basis within the testimony provided that would support the conclusion reached by the tribunal. If it is to be overturned, the decision of the tribunal would have to be unreasonable.

The logic of *Dr. Q v. College of Physicians and Surgeons of B.C.* is extended in the Supreme Court's decision in 2008 in *Dunsmuir v. New Brunswick.* In this case David Dunsmuir was hired by the Province of New Brunswick in 2002. His work was viewed as unsatisfactory and he received several written notices of various inadequacies. Finally, in 2004 he was told by his employer that his employment was being terminated, and that he would received several months of paid leave in order to help him find a new job. He filed a grievance against his dismissal and the issue ultimately arrived in the Supreme Court of Canada. The Supreme Court of Canada determined that his dismissal was appropriate, noting that where deference to an administrative decision maker is intended, the courts will review the decision on the basis of reasonableness. When no deference is intended, the administrative decision will be reviewed on the basis of correctness.

The Court: Having dealt with the nature of the standards of review, we now turn our attention to the method for selecting the appropriate standard in individual cases. As we will now demonstrate, questions of fact, discretion and policy as well as questions where the legal issues cannot be easily separated from the factual issues generally attract a standard of reasonableness while many legal issues attract a standard of correctness. Some legal issues, however, attract the more deferential standard of reasonableness.

The existence of a privative or preclusive clause gives rise to a strong indication of review pursuant to the reasonableness standard. This conclusion is appropriate because a privative clause is evidence of Parliament or a legislature's intent that an administrative decision maker be given greater deference and that interference by reviewing courts be minimized. This does not mean, however, that the presence of a privative clause is determinative. The rule of law requires that the constitutional role of superior courts be preserved and, as indicated above, neither Parliament nor any legislature can completely remove the courts' power to review the actions and decisions of administrative bodies. This power is constitutionally protected. Judicial review is necessary to ensure that the privative clause is read in its appropriate statutory context and that administrative bodies do not exceed their jurisdiction.

Where the question is one of fact, discretion or policy, deference will usually apply automatically (*Mossop,* at pp. 599–600; *Dr. Q,* at para. 29; *Suresh,* at paras. 29–30). We believe that the same standard must apply to the review of questions where the legal and factual issues are intertwined with and cannot be readily separated.

Guidance with regard to the questions that will be reviewed on a reasonableness standard can be found in the existing case law. Deference will usually result where a tribunal is interpreting its own statute or statutes closely connected to its function, with which it will have particular familiarity: *Canadian Broadcasting Corp. v. Canada (Labour Relations Board),* 1995 CanLII 148 (SCC), [1995] 1 S.C.R. 157, at para. 48; *Toronto (City) Board of Education v. O.S.S.T.F., District 15,* 1997 CanLII 378 (SCC), [1997] 1 S.C.R. 487, at para. 39. Deference may also be warranted where an administrative tribunal has developed particular expertise in the application of a general common law or civil law rule in relation to a specific statutory context: *Toronto (City) v. C.U.P.E.,* at para. 72. Adjudication in labour law remains a good example of the relevance of this approach. The case law has moved away considerably from the strict position evidenced in *McLeod v. Egan,* 1974 CanLII 12 (SCC), [1975] 1 S.C.R. 517, where it was held that an administrative decision maker will always risk having its interpretation of an external statute set aside upon judicial review.

A consideration of the following factors will lead to the conclusion that the decision maker should be given deference and a reasonableness test applied:

- A privative clause: this is a statutory direction from Parliament or a legislature indicating the need for deference.
- A discrete and special administrative regime in which the decision maker has special expertise (labour relations for instance).
- The nature of the question of law. A question of law that is of "central importance to the legal system ... and outside the ... specialized area of expertise" of the administrative decision maker will always attract a correctness standard

(*Toronto (City) v. C.U.P.E.*, at para. 62). On the other hand, a question of law that does not rise to this level may be compatible with a reasonableness standard where the two above factors so indicate.

If these factors, considered together, point to a standard of reasonableness, the decision maker's decision must be approached with deference in the sense of respect discussed earlier in these reasons. There is nothing unprincipled in the fact that some questions of law will be decided on the basis of reasonableness. It simply means giving the adjudicator's decision appropriate deference in deciding whether a decision should be upheld, bearing in mind the factors indicated....

In this case, the appellant was a contractual employee of the respondent in addition to being a public office holder. Section 20 of the *Civil Service Act* provided that, as a civil servant, he could only be dismissed in accordance with the ordinary rules of contract. In these circumstances it was unnecessary to consider any public law duty of procedural fairness. The respondent was fully within its rights to dismiss the appellant with pay in lieu of notice without affording him a hearing. The respondent dismissed the appellant with four months' pay in lieu of notice. The appellant was successful in increasing this amount to eight months. The appellant was protected by contract and was able to obtain contractual remedies in relation to his dismissal. By imposing procedural fairness requirements on the respondent over and above its contractual obligations and ordering the full "reinstatement" of the appellant, the adjudicator erred in his application of the duty of fairness and his decision was therefore correctly struck down by the Court of Queen's Bench.[24]

CONCLUSION: ADMINISTRATIVE LAW—A MIRROR TO THE STATE

Since the 1970s the scope of administrative law, like the scope of government, has expanded considerably. More specifically, since 1982, the *Charter* has given a constitutional character to the state's commitment to act fairly in dealing with its citizens, notably those charged with criminal offences or deprived of liberty. Administrative law decisions are required of marketing boards, human rights commissions, labour relations boards, workers' compensation tribunals, children's aid societies, welfare agencies, parole boards, and government ministries from National Revenue to Education. Administrative law is, for better or worse, the most accessible and most pervasive symbol of the fairness of the state in dealing with its citizens. The task for the next decade will be little different from the task of the past century: to give life to the state's obligations to treat its constituents fairly and reasonably.

WEB LINKS

Bora Laskin Law Library, University of Toronto
http://www.law-lib.utoronto.ca/resources/topic/admin.htm
The resources site at the University of Toronto's Bora Laskin Law Library provides information on administrative law as well as on other areas of law.

CanLII: Canadian Legal Information Institute
http://www.canlii.org
CanLII is a non-profit organization managed by the Federation of Law Societies of Canada; its goal is to make Canadian law accessible for free on the Internet.

The Supreme Court of Canada
http://scc-csc.lexum.com/scc-csc/en/nav.do
At the Supreme Court of Canada site maintained by Lexum, find a list of law terms linked to SCC cases.

QUESTIONS FOR DISCUSSION

1. Is the Supreme Court's decision in *Dr. Q* compelling? Should the criticism of the initial reviewing judge have been allowed to stand?
2. Is the majority's logic in *May v. Ferndale* compelling? How far should disclosure extend, in order to satisfy procedural fairness? Discuss.
3. Should Mr. Khosa have been subject to a removal order, as mandated by the Supreme Court of Canada? How should courts weigh the relevant variables of concern? How much deference should be given to the administrative tribunal? Discuss.

FURTHER READING

Dussault, R., and L. Borgeat. *Administrative Law: A Treatise.* 2nd ed. 5 vol. Toronto: Carswell, 1988.

> This is an English-language edition of a classic and exhaustive five-volume text on the subject of administrative law in Canada. The authors cover the role of law in the administration (volume one), personal and financial management in public administration (volume two), management of the Crown domain and government information in public administration (volume three), judicial review of the legality of administrative action (volume four), and Crown liability (volume five).

Jones, D.P., and A.S. deVillars. *Principles of Administrative Law*. 5th ed. Toronto: Carswell, 2009.

>This text provides the reader with a good statement of the key principles of administrative law. It offers a useful conceptual framework for understanding the basic building blocks within this realm of law. Both authors practise administrative law in Alberta.

McCallum, S.K. *Canadian Journal of Administrative Law and Practice*. Toronto: Carswell, 2013.

>This journal is published three times each year. It contains current articles, case comments, practice notes, and book reviews from the realm of administrative law in Canada. It is an excellent source of current information about developments within the field of administrative law, providing a forum for discussion of issues and the critical roles of boards, commissions, and tribunals within this sphere.

NOTES

1. *Canada v. Khosa*, 2009 S.C.C. 12 [2009] 1 S.C.R. 339.
2. *Canada v. Khosa* (para. 18).
3. *Canada v. Khosa*.
4. R. Dussault and L. Borgeat, *Administrative Law: A Treatise*, vol. 1 (Toronto: Carswell, 1985), 12.
5. D.P. Jones and A.S. deVillars, *Principles of Administrative Law* (Toronto: Carswell, 1985), Pg. 58. Reproduced by permission of Carswell, a division of Thomson Reuters Canada Limited.
6. Dussault and Borgeat, *Administrative Law*, 13.
7. G. Gall, *The Canadian Legal System*, 3rd ed. (Toronto: Carswell, 1990), 356.
8. *Thomas v. Mount Saint Vincent University* (1986), 28 D.L.R. (4th) 230 at 246 (N.S.S.C.). See also *Khan v. University of Ottawa*, (1997), 148 D.L.R. (4th) 577.
9. *Khan v. University of Ottawa*.
10. *Re Sheehan and Criminal Injuries Compensation Board* (1973), 37 D.L.R. (3d) 336 at 337–43 (Ont. Div. Ct.), rev'd (1975), 52 D.L.R. (3d) 728 (Ont. C.A.).
11. *Re Sawyer and Ontario Racing Commission* (1979), 99 D.L.R. (3d) 561 at 564–6 (Ont. C.A.).
12. *Baker v. Minister of Citizenship and Immigration*, [1999] 2 S.C.R. 813 at 850–1.
13. P.W. Hogg, *Constitutional Law of Canada*, 3rd ed. (Toronto: Carswell, 1992), 768.
14. Jones and deVillars, *Principles of Administrative Law*, 3rd ed. (Toronto: Carswell, 1999), 197.
15. J.M. Evans, H.N. Janisch, D.J. Mullan, and R.C.B. Risk, *Administrative Law: Cases, Text and Materials* (Toronto: Emond Montgomery, 1989), 70.

16. *Re Collins and Pension Commission of Ontario* (1986), 31 D.L.R. (4th) 86 at 101 (Ont. Div. Ct.).
17. *Cardinal and Oswald v. Director of Kent Institution,* [1985] 2 S.C.R. 643 at 653–61.
18. *May v. Ferndale Institution,* [2005] 3 S.C.R. 809, 2005 S.C.C. 82.
19. Ibid.
20. Hogg, *Constitutional Law of Canada*, 1032–3.
21. See, for example, the Supreme Court of Canada's decision in *Re B.C. Motor Vehicle Act,* [1985] 2 S.C.R. 486.
22. *Re Howard and Presiding Officer of Inmate Disciplinary Court of Stony Mountain Institution* (1985), 19 D.L.R. (4th) 502 at 507–21 (F.C.A.).
23. *Dr. Q. v. College of Physicians and Surgeons of British Columbia,* 2003 SCC 19 (CanLII); 223 D.L.R. (4th) 599; 1 S.C.R. 226.
24. *Dunsmuir v. New Brunswick,* 2008 S.C.C. 9 (CanLII) 1 S.C.R. 190. Found at: http://scc-csc.lexum.com/scc-csc/scc-csc/en/item/2408/index.do

References

Arthurs, H.W. "Jonah and the Whale: The Appearance, Disappearance and Reappearance of Administrative Law." *University of Toronto Law Journal* 30 (1980): 225.

Chayes, A. "The Role of the Judge in Public Law Litigation." *Harvard Law Review* 79 (1976): 1281.

Dussault, R., and L. Borgeat. *Administrative Law: A Treatise.* 2nd ed. Vol. 1. Toronto: Carswell, 1988.

Evans, J.M., H.N. Janisch, D.J. Mullan, and R.C.B. Risk. *Administrative Law: Cases, Text and Materials.* Toronto: Emond Montgomery, 1989.

Gall, G. *The Canadian Legal System.* 3rd ed. Toronto: Carswell, 1990, Chapter 12.

Jones, D.P., and A.S. deVillars. *Principles of Administrative Law.* 5th ed. Toronto: Carswell, 2009.

Kernaghan, K. "Canadian Public Administration: Progress and Prospects." *Canadian Public Administration* 25 (1982): 444.

Mullan, D.J. *Administrative Law,* Irwin Law, Toronto, 2001.

———. "The Federal Court Act: A Misguided Attempt at Administrative Law Reform?" *University of Toronto Law Journal* 23 (1973): 14.

Thomas, P.G. "Administrative Law Reform: Legal versus Political Controls on Administrative Discretion." *Canadian Public Administration* 27 (1984): 120.

Wade, H.W.R. "Crossroads in Administrative Law." *Current Legal Problems* 21 (1968): 75.

Willis, J. "Canadian Administrative Law in Retrospect." *University of Toronto Law Journal* 24 (1974): 225.

———. "Three Approaches to Administrative Law: The Juridical, the Conceptual, and the Functional." *University of Toronto Law Journal* 1 (1935): 53.

CHAPTER 10

CRIMINAL LAW: *MENS REA, ACTUS REUS,* AND CHANGING DEFINITIONS OF CRIME

The mood and temper of the public in regard to the treatment of crime and criminals is one of the most unfailing tests of any country. A calm, dispassionate recognition of the rights of the accused and even of the convicted criminal,... the treatment of crime and the criminal mark and measure the stored-up strength of a nation, and are the sign and proof of the living virtue within it.

(Winston Churchill, public speech, 1910)

Friends, let's never forget, this is the one party that believes those who do the crime should do the time and that the rights of victims and law-abiding citizens are more important than the "rights" of criminals.

(Prime Minister Stephen Harper, 2013)

THE INTENT OF THE CRIMINAL LAW AND THE DEFINITION OF CRIME

Criminal law is probably the most widely discussed and debated of the many forms of Canadian law, as the two quotes above aptly illustrate. We all have opinions about the operation of the criminal justice system: it is, by turns, too lenient and too harsh; too intrusive and not intrusive enough; too little and too much concerned with individual rights.

We must always remind ourselves that the criminal law is the most coercive and intrusive form of public law. The task of those who create, enforce, and administer it is to ask continually about the circumstances in which this force should be used. As Winston Churchill observed, the state of a civilized society can be divined from the manner in which it responds to its criminals.

The purpose of the criminal law is to punish certain acts that have been declared in law to be threats to the established social order. Crime can be conceptualized as falling into one of three categories: offences against persons; offences against property; and offences considered to be evil in themselves, irrespective of whether harm befalls another person or the property of another person. Examples of the first category of crime are straightforward enough: culpable homicide, sexual assault, robbery, assault, attempted murder, and the like. Crimes against property are also easily determined: theft, fraud, income tax evasion, insider trading, forgery, and so on. Offences considered to be punishable irrespective of their immediate impact on others include soliciting for prostitution, pornography, the use and distribution of certain drugs, and certain gaming activities.

In pre-state societies, no criminal law existed as such. Killings and other serious assaults prompted myriad reactions: revenge executions, compensation from one tribe or clan to another, and conciliation between individuals or collectives. In Canada, no criminal code existed until as late as 1892, when the federal government adopted the British reform code written by Sir James Fitzjames Stephen. Despite its designation, this code was not really reformist, since it did not originate in a fresh reconstruction of principles and practice. As Mewett and Manning noted,

> The *Criminal Code* of 1892 was only ... the collecting into one more or less comprehensive statute of a multitude of existing provisions and common-law doctrines with some elimination of inconsistencies and tidying up of anomalies. But no attempt was made to find a rational basis for the criminal law or to formulate a new Code on that basis. The essential substance of the law was merely adopted as it stood.[1]

Criminal law, unlike tort law, is concerned with public wrongs. The state or the collective has determined that certain kinds of conduct must be responded to with various penalties, both to deter those who might be inclined to engage in these activities and to express community outrage and/or concern about a particular act. The historical distinction between criminal and tort law creates an inevitable tension. A citizen's notion of justice is likely to be compensation for an inflicted harm, but the criminal law makes the state's interest in **conviction** and punishment the objective of prosecution. For victims of crime, the criminal law is typically less personal and less emotionally satisfying than the compensatory imperative of tort. The victim receives no tangible benefit from the penalty imposed, be it a suspended sentence, discharge, fine, probation order, community service order, or imprisonment.

Another way of expressing the intent of the criminal law is to say that it defines what the state regards as intolerable deviance. Over time, the definitions of deviance and the associated penalties have changed markedly, particularly for crimes defined as evil in themselves, the victimless offences listed earlier.

While most legal scholars and the Canadian public agree that the designation of crimes against persons and property can be morally justified, debate continues about the appropriateness of using the criminal law to control such matters as the commercialization of sex, the public-health risks involved in the use and distribution of certain drugs, and the potential economic exploitation involved in certain forms of gambling. But debate also continues about what constitutes crimes against persons and property. Sociologists Herman and Julia Schwendinger have examined the moral criteria employed in defining crime:

> [T]he definition of crime should openly face the moral issues.... Traditionally, these issues have been inadequately represented by such unanalyzed terms as "social injury," "antisocial act," or "public wrongs." But how does one confront the problem of explicating "social injury" or "public wrongs"? Is this done by reference to the functional imperatives of social institutions or by the historically determined rights of individuals? ... Isn't it time to raise serious questions about the assumptions underlying the definitions of the field of criminology, when a man who steals a paltry sum can be called a criminal while agents of the state can, with impunity, legally reward men who destroy food so that price levels can be maintained, while a sizable portion of the population suffers from malnutrition.[2]

A more cautious assessment of the problem of defining what constitutes crime has been advanced by sociologist Steven Box:

> Deviant behaviour is nothing less or more than it has always been: rule breaking. It is behaviour which is proscribed by those who have the institutionalized power, and occasionally the consensual authority, to create rules; it is behaviour which places its perpetrator at risk of being punished by those who have the institutionalized power, and occasionally the consensual authority, to do something to those who do not keep to the rules.[3]

MENS REA AND ACTUS REUS: PREREQUISITES FOR CONVICTION

The definitions of crime fluctuate with changes in the social, political, and economic order. But the basic conceptual elements of a crime remain, at least in theory, consistent over time. The concepts of *mens rea* and **actus reus** (introduced in Chapter 7) have their origins in the development of the criminal law of England. In order to be convicted of a criminal offence, an individual must have committed an *actus reus*, an evil act, and must simultaneously possess *mens rea*, an evil mind or intention. It is only the coincidence of *mens rea* and *actus reus* that can lead to criminal conviction.

In many contexts, the connection between the two concepts is straightforward. Take the theft of a chocolate bar. The *actus reus* is the taking of the bar from a store without giving payment; the *mens rea* is the intention to do so. However, if a person were forced at gunpoint to steal the bar or were two years old, there would clearly be no intention to commit the offence. If, in another example, the police were to discover marijuana in a person's luggage, they could fairly presume *actus reus*—commission of the act of possession of marijuana. But if the possessor had no knowledge of the presence of the marijuana, and the court believed this to be true, there would be no *mens rea*—no intent to possess the illegal drug.

How does one find a coincidence of *mens rea* and *actus reus* in the commission of the offence of murder? Consider the following excerpt from the Supreme Court of Canada's judgment in *R. v. Cooper*. The Newfoundland Court of Appeal had allowed an appeal by the accused from his conviction for second degree murder; the Crown was appealing that ruling.

Cory, J.: At issue, on this appeal, is the nature of the intent required to found a conviction for murder pursuant to s. 212(a)(ii) of the *Criminal Code*, R.S.C. 1970, c. C-34 (now R.S.C. 1985, c. C-46, s. 229(a)(ii)).

[Section 229(a)(ii) is part of section 229(a), one of three legal definitions of murder. Section 229(a)(ii) reads:

Culpable homicide is murder

    (a) where the person who causes the death of a human being

        (i)   means to cause his death, or

        (ii) means to cause him bodily harm that he knows is likely to cause his death, and is reckless whether death ensues or not.]

Factual Background

The respondent Lyndon Cooper and the deceased Deborah Careen lived in Labrador City, Newfoundland. At one time, they had been friends and lovers. On January 30, 1988, they met at a gathering place known as the K-Bar in Labrador City. Although by this time the respondent was living with somebody else, they spent the evening together at the bar. There is no doubt that they consumed a considerable amount of alcohol. Eventually, Cooper, the deceased, and a mutual friend left the bar in a taxi. After they dropped off the friend, they continued in the cab to the residence of another of Cooper's friends, where he borrowed a Jeep. Cooper then drove the deceased to the secluded parking lot of a power station.

At the parking lot, the respondent testified that he and the deceased engaged in some form of consensual sexual activity. He said that they began to argue at one point and that the deceased struck him. At this he became angry. He hit the deceased and grabbed her by the throat with both hands and shook her. He stated that this occurred in the front seat of the Jeep. He then said that he could recall nothing else until he woke in the back seat and found the body of the deceased beside him. He had no recollection of causing her death. He pushed her body out of the Jeep and drove away. Later, during the drive to his home, he found one of her shoes in the vehicle and threw it out the window into the snow.

The expert evidence established that the deceased had in fact been struck twice. However, these blows could not have killed her. Rather, death was caused by "a classic pattern of one-handed manual strangulation." That same evidence confirmed that death by strangulation can occur as quickly as 30 seconds after contact with the throat and that a drunken victim is likely to die from asphyxiation more quickly than a sober one. Nonetheless, the presence of petechial hemorrhages on the neck of the deceased and the finding that the hyoid bone in her throat was not fractured suggested to the expert that death occurred rather more slowly, probably after two minutes of pressure.

The position of the defence was that the respondent was so drunk that he blacked out shortly after he started shaking her with both hands. Thus, it was said that the respondent did not have (i) the required intent to commit murder, or (ii) alternatively, did not foresee that holding someone by the neck was likely to cause death....

What degree of concurrency is required between the wrongful act and the requisite *mens rea*?

There can be no doubt that under the classical approach to criminal law, it is the intent of the accused that makes the wrongful act illegal. It is that intent which brings the accused within the sphere of blameworthiness and justifies the penalty or punishment which is imposed upon him for the infraction of the criminal law. The essential aspect of *mens rea* and the absolute necessity that it be present in the case of murder was emphasized by Lamer, J. (as he then was) in *R. v. Vaillancourt* (1987), 39 C.C.C. (3d) 118.... At p. 133 he stated: "it may well be that, as a general rule, the principles of fundamental justice require proof of a subjective *mens rea* with respect to the prohibited act, in order to avoid punishing the "morally innocent"....

However, not only must the guilty mind, intent or *mens rea* be present, it must also be concurrent with the impugned act. Professor D. Stuart has referred to this as "the simultaneous principle": see *Canadian Criminal Law 2nd. ed.* (1987), p. 305. This principle has been stressed in a number of cases. For example, in *R. v. Droste* (1979), 49 C.C.C. (2d) 52, 18 C.R. (3d) 64 (Ont. C.A.), the accused had intended to murder his wife by pouring gasoline over the interior of the car and setting fire to it while she was within it. Before he could light the gasoline, the car crashed into a bridge and ignited prematurely. As a result, both his children were killed rather than his wife. He was charged with their murder and convicted. On appeal, Arnup, J.A., speaking for the Court of Appeal in directing a new trial, stated at pp. 53–54:

... the trial Judge did not instruct the jury of the necessity of the Crown showing that at the time of the occurrence at the bridge, the appellant, intending to kill his wife, had done an act with that intention, and in the course of doing so, his children were killed. In short, he did not tell them that the mens rea and the actus reus must be concurrent. [Emphasis added.]

... There is, then, the classic rule that at some point, the *actus reus* and the *mens rea* or intent must coincide. Further, I would agree with the conclusion of James J. that an act *(actus reus)* which may be innocent or no more than careless at the outset, can become criminal at a later stage when the accused acquires knowledge of the nature of the act and still refuses to change his course of action....

Yet, with respect, I do not think that it is always necessary that the requisite *mens rea* (the guilty mind, intent, or awareness) should continue throughout the commission of the wrongful act. There is no question that in order to obtain a conviction, the Crown must demonstrate that the accused intended to cause bodily harm that he knew was ultimately so dangerous and serious that it was likely to result in the death of the victim. But that intent need not persist throughout the entire act of strangulation. When Cooper testified that he seized the victim by the neck, it was open to the jury to infer that by those actions, he intended to cause her bodily harm that he knew that was likely to cause her death. Since breathing is essential to life, it would be reasonable to infer the accused knew that strangulation was likely to result in death. I would stress that the jury was, of course, not required to make such an inference but, on the evidence presented, it was open to them to do so.

Did the accused possess such a mental state after he started strangling the victim? Her death occurred between 30 seconds and two minutes after he grabbed her by the neck. It could be reasonably inferred by the jury, that when the accused grabbed the victim by the neck and shook her, that there was, at that moment, the necessary coincidence of the wrongful act of strangulation and the requisite intent to do bodily harm that the accused knew was likely to cause her death. Cooper was aware of these acts before he "blacked out." Thus, although the jury was under no compulsion to do so, it was nonetheless open to them to infer that he knew that he was causing bodily harm and knew that it was so dangerous to the victim that it was likely to cause her death. It was sufficient that the intent and the act of strangulation coincided at some point. It was not necessary that the requisite intent continue throughout the entire two minutes required to cause the death of the victim....

In the result, I would set aside the order of the Court of Appeal directing a new trial and restore the conviction.

Appeal allowed; conviction restored....

Lamer, C.J.C. (dissenting): It is crucial to a correct charge under s. 212(a)(ii) that the jury understand that there must be intention to cause bodily harm which the accused knows is likely to cause death. Intention to cause bodily harm, without knowledge that such is likely to cause death, is not sufficient. Given the position of the defence in this case, a clear understanding of this aspect was essential to a fair trial....

I do not raise this point to question whether the accused here intended to cause bodily harm. That was conceded in the argument before us. I raise it rather to emphasize that the intention to cause bodily harm by no means leads inexorably to the conclusion that the accused knew that the bodily harm was likely to cause death. It is, of course, this second aspect which is essential to a finding of guilt of murder under s. 212(a)(ii). Particularly with respect to an action such as grabbing by the neck, there may be a point at the outset when there is no intention to cause death and no knowledge that the action is likely to cause death. But there comes a point in time when the wrongful conduct becomes likely to cause death. It is, in my view, at that moment or thereafter, that the accused must have a conscious awareness of the likelihood of death. This awareness need not, however, continue until death ensues.

Cooper intended to choke the deceased and cause her bodily harm. Under s. 212(a)(i), it was open to the jury to infer from his conduct and on all of the evidence that in doing so, he intended to kill her. To be found guilty under s. 212(a)(ii), however, he must have been aware of the fact that he persisted in choking her long enough for it to become likely that death would ensue.

This instruction, given the particular facts of this case and the nature of the defence presented by the accused, had to be given. Additionally, the jury should have been instructed to consider the evidence of drunkenness in relation to this awareness. In my respectful view, upon a reading of the whole charge, this was not done adequately.

I would dismiss the appeal.[4]

The differing judgments of Justice Cory and former chief justice Lamer raise questions about the *mens rea* required to substantiate a conviction for murder. Justice Cory argues that "it could be reasonably inferred by the jury that ... there was ... the necessary coincidence of the wrongful act of strangulation and the requisite intent to do bodily harm that the accused knew was likely to cause her death." Justice Lamer argues, on the contrary, that it is not clear that Cooper was "aware of the fact that he persisted in choking her long enough for it to become likely that death would ensue." The difference between the two positions hinges on the inferences that one is willing to draw with respect to intention. Justice Lamer asserts that any conviction for murder requires proof of subjective knowledge of the likelihood of death; it is not sufficient to base criminal conviction under section 229(a)(ii) upon an inference of knowledge of likelihood of death, in the absence of supporting evidence.

The question whether criminal conviction for murder should be premised upon **objective** or **subjective intention** is one that will continue to be debated within criminal law. In essence, the distinction is between what a reasonable person would be expected to intend and what the accused actually did intend. The American jurist Oliver Wendell Holmes set out the following proposition in 1863:

> If the known present state of things is such that the act done will very certainly cause death, and the probability is a matter of common knowledge, one who does the act, knowing the present state of things, is guilty of murder, and the law will not inquire whether he did actually foresee the consequences or not. The test of foresight is not what this very criminal foresaw, but what a man of reasonable prudence would have foreseen.[5]

But consider the comments of Justice Dickson in R. v. *City of Sault Ste. Marie,* in direct opposition to Holmes's sentiments:

> Where the offence is criminal, the Crown must establish a mental element, namely, that the accused who committed the prohibited act did so intentionally or recklessly, with knowledge of the facts constituting the offence, or with wilful blindness toward them. Mere negligence is excluded from the concept of the mental element required for conviction. Within the context of a criminal prosecution, a person who fails to make such enquiries as a reasonable and prudent person would make, or who fails to know facts he should have known, is innocent in the eyes of the law.[6]

There are many criminal offences for which the requisite *mens rea* is a subjective intention to commit the given offence, but is founded on "recklessness" or "advertent negligence" rather than a direct intent. Consider the following excerpt from the Supreme Court's decision in *R. v. Hundal,* a case concerned with the criminal offence of dangerous driving causing death:

Cory, J.: At issue on this appeal is whether there is a subjective element in the requisite *mens rea* which must be established by the Crown in order to prove the offence of dangerous driving....

Factual Background

The accident occurred at about 3:40 in the afternoon in downtown Vancouver. The streets were wet at the time, a situation not uncommon to that city. The downtown traffic was heavy. The appellant was driving his dump truck eastbound on Nelson Street, a four-lane road, approaching its intersection with Cambie Street. At the time, his truck was overloaded. It exceeded by 1160 kilograms the maximum gross weight permitted for the vehicle. He was travelling in the passing lane for eastbound traffic. The deceased was travelling southbound on Cambie Street. He had stopped for a red light at the intersection with Nelson Street. When the light turned green, the deceased proceeded into the intersection through a crosswalk, continued south across the two lanes for westbound traffic on Nelson Street, and reached the passing lane for eastbound traffic. At that moment, his car was struck on the right side by the dump truck, killing him instantly.

The appellant stated that when he approached the intersection of Nelson and Cambie Streets, he observed that the light had turned amber. He thought that he could not stop in time, so he simply honked his horn and continued through the intersection when the impact occurred. Several witnesses observed the collision. They testified that the appellant's truck entered the intersection after the Nelson Street traffic light had turned red. It was estimated that at least one second had passed between the end of the amber light and the time when the dump truck first entered the intersection. A Vancouver police officer gave evidence that the red light for Nelson at this intersection is preceded by a three-second amber light and there is a further one-half-second delay before the Cambie light turned green. One witness observed that the deceased's vehicle had travelled almost the entire width of the intersection before it was struck by the truck. Another witness, Mr. Mumford, had been travelling close to the appellant's truck through some 12 intersections. He testified that on an earlier occasion, the appellant went through an intersection as the light turned red. He estimated the speed of the truck at the time of the collision was between 50 and 60 km/h....

The relevant portions of s. 233 read as follows:

233. (1) Every one commits an offence who operates
(a) a motor vehicle on a street, road, highway, or other public place in a manner that is dangerous to the public, having regard to all the circumstances, including the nature, condition,

and use of such place and the amount of traffic that at the time is or might reasonably be expected to be on such place; ... (4) Every one who commits an offence under subsection (1) and thereby causes the death of any other person is guilty of an indictable offence and is liable to imprisonment for a term not exceeding fourteen years....

The appellant contends that the prison sentence which may be imposed for a breach of s. 233 (now s. 249) makes it evident that an accused cannot be convicted without proof beyond a reasonable doubt of a subjective mental element of an intention to drive dangerously. Certainly every crime requires proof of an act or failure to act, coupled with an element of fault which is termed the mens rea. This court has made it clear that s. 7 of the Canadian Charter of Rights and Freedoms prohibits the imposition of imprisonment in the absence of proof of that element of fault....

Depending on the provisions of the particular section and the context in which it appears, the constitutional requirement of *mens rea* may be satisfied in different ways. The offence can require proof of a positive state of mind such as intent, recklessness or wilful blindness. Alternatively, the *mens rea* or element of fault can be satisfied by proof of negligence whereby the conduct of the accused is measured on the basis of an objective standard without establishing the subjective mental state of the particular accused. In the appropriate context, negligence can be an acceptable basis of liability which meets the fault requirement of s. 7 of the *Charter*....

[T]he wording of the section itself which refers to the operation of a motor vehicle "in a manner that is dangerous to the public, having regard to all the circumstances" suggests that an objective standard is required. The "manner of driving" can only be compared to a standard of reasonable conduct. That standard can be readily judged and assessed by all who would be members of juries.

Thus, it is clear that the basis of liability for dangerous driving is negligence. The question to be asked is not what the accused subjectively intended but rather whether, viewed objectively, the accused exercised the appropriate standard of care. It is not overly difficult to determine when a driver has fallen markedly below the acceptable standard of care. There can be no doubt that the concept of negligence is well understood and readily recognized by most Canadians. Negligent driving can be thought of as a continuum that progresses, or regresses, from momentary lack of attention, giving rise to civil responsibility through careless driving under a provincial *Highway Traffic Act* to dangerous driving under the *Criminal Code*....

The trial judge carefully examined the circumstances of the accident. He took into account the busy downtown traffic, the weather conditions, and the mechanical condition of the accused's vehicle. He concluded, in my view very properly, that the appellant's manner of driving represented a gross departure from the standard of a reasonably prudent driver. No explanation was offered by the accused that could excuse his conduct. There is no reason for interfering with the trial judge's finding of fact and application of the law.

In the result, the appeal must be dismissed.[7]

It is fair to conclude from Justice Cory's reasoning that the very nature of *mens rea* changes as one moves from offence to offence.

Once we leave the realms of subjective intention, recklessness, or wilful blindness, we move into the territories of **strict and absolute liability offences**. Strict liability offences are public welfare or regulatory offences requiring no proof of intention and rarely raising the issue of the liberty of the accused. The prosecutor must prove an objective intent, but an element of reverse onus applies to the accused: the accused must prove that he or she had no intent to commit the crime or, alternatively, that he or she exercised due diligence or had a reasonable belief in the legitimacy of his or her conduct, based on a mistake of fact. For example, the hunting of a particular species out of season, contrary to the *Migratory Birds Convention*, would likely be considered a strict liability offence.

An absolute liability offence is an offence for which intent is irrelevant; the prosecutor need prove only that the person in question committed the offence. Certain parking infractions may be constructed as absolute liability offences, though it may well be that, at least in certain circumstances, courts would hold such an approach to be contrary to the presumption of innocence guaranteed by the *Charter*.[8]

MENS REA AND PARTIES TO AN OFFENCE

One final issue with regard to *mens rea* should be discussed: parties to an offence. Under section 21 of the *Criminal Code*, parties to an offence may be held as criminally responsible as the person or persons who actually commit the crime.

> 21. *(1) Every one is a party to an offence who*
>
>   (a) *actually commits it,*
>
>   (b) *does or omits to do anything for the purpose of aiding any person to commit it;*
>   *or*
>
>   (c) *abets any person in committing it.*
>
> *(2) Where two or more persons form an intention in common to carry out an unlawful purpose and to assist each other therein and any one of them, in carrying out the common purpose, commits an offence, each of them who knew or ought to have known that the commission of the offence would be a probable consequence of carrying out the common purpose is a party to that offence.*

In most circumstances, the meaning of this section of the *Code* can be readily understood. If a person provides a gun for the purpose of a crime, drives the getaway car, or keeps a lookout for the police, that person will be held to be as guilty of the crime as the person who pulls the trigger or robs the bank.

What of the following instance, however? Stan is walking down the street and sees his friend Fred beating Jim, whom Stan knows and doesn't particularly like. If he simply walks by and allows Fred to continue the beating, is he a party to the offence? What if he smiles at Fred? What if he shouts encouragement to him? What if Stan volunteers to hold Jim down? In short, at what point does Stan violate section 21 of the *Code* by doing or omitting to do anything for the purpose of aiding another person to commit an offence? Mewett and Manning provide a framework, if not a definitive answer, for this conundrum:

> Where a person is actually present when the crime is committed by the actor, whether his mere presence will amount to aiding or abetting depends upon the circumstances but, as a general proposition, some act of aiding or abetting must occur over and above mere presence.... In the case of *Coney,* the accused were present at an illegal prize fight and were charged with aiding and abetting a battery. The court held that the mere presence of persons at a prize fight, unexplained, is not in itself conclusive proof of the intent to encourage the fight, but where the accused bet on the fight or shouted encouragement to the fighters, then that would amount to aiding and abetting. Thus, while mere voluntary presence, in itself, does not amount to aiding or abetting, presence together with some form of participation might.[9]

DEFENCES TO AND MITIGATIONS OF CRIMINAL OFFENCES

There are many circumstances in which people charged with criminal offences will be able to escape responsibility, or some degree of responsibility, for their crime. For example, they may have inflicted harm in self-defence; they may have been enticed by the police to commit a crime (usually related to illegal drugs or prostitution); they may have been forced at gunpoint to help rob a bank; they may have been mistaken about a woman's consent to sexual relations; or they may have been too intoxicated or too emotionally or mentally disturbed to understand or appreciate the alleged offence.

These "excuses" for crime are highly controversial and are often criticized for supporting unjust societal assumptions. Is it reasonable, for example, that the voluntary consumption of alcohol should diminish an accused's responsibility for the offence of murder? How does that affect your judgment of the *Cooper* case, above? Is it reasonable for a man who sexually assaults a woman to argue that he was mistaken about the woman's consent—that in his world, women "like it rough"? In these contexts—murder and sexual assault—the state of the criminal law often reflects the values of a culture that forgives men their preconceptions and, at least tacitly, lends support to excessive use of alcohol.

In the pages that follow, we look at two specific kinds of defence to a criminal charge—drunkenness and mistake of fact. These are only two of many possible **defences or mitigations of criminal responsibility**. There are many other ways in which a person may defend himself or herself against a criminal charge. It may be possible, first, to negate *mens rea* or *actus reus*—to establish that the accused did not have the "evil intent" to commit the crime in question, or that he did not commit the "evil act" in question. For example, if an illegal substance is found in the accused's apartment, but the accused establishes that he had no knowledge of the presence of this illegal substance, this will negate *mens rea*—he had no evil intent to possess the prohibited substance. Similarly, if it is established that the accused attacked a victim after she was already dead, there can be no *actus reus* for homicide—no "evil act" of killing another human being.

As noted above, there are also a number of justifications for the commission of crimes: acting under duress, necessity, defence of the person, provocation, defence of property, and entrapment. If an accused is attacked on the street by a man wielding a baseball bat and defends himself, assaulting his attacker in the process, the person attacked will typically be able to claim self-defence, provided that his response was reasonable given its circumstances and the nature of the threat posed by the initial attack.

Section 17 of the *Criminal Code* sets out a justification for the commission of crime under duress:

> 17. *A person who commits an offence under compulsion by threats of immediate death or bodily harm from a person who is present when the offence is committed is excused for committing the offence if the person believes that the threats will be carried out and if the person is not a party to a conspiracy or association whereby the person is subject to compulsion, but this section does not apply where the offence that is committed is high treason or treason, murder, piracy, attempted murder, sexual assault, sexual assault with a weapon, threats to a third party or causing bodily harm, aggravated sexual assault, forcible abduction, hostage taking, robbery, assault with a weapon or causing bodily harm, aggravated assault, unlawfully causing bodily harm, arson, or an offence under sections 280 to 283 (abduction and detention of young persons).*

In other words, in order for an accused to claim duress as a defence to a criminal charge, the threat must be immediate, the person making the threat must be present when the offence is committed, the accused must believe that the threats will be carried out, and the person threatened must not be part of a criminal conspiracy. Finally, in most circumstances, Canadian courts have held that duress cannot apply as a defence where serious offences involving personal violence have been committed by an accused. The defence of necessity is somewhat similar to the defence of duress. The distinction is clearly explained by Mewett and Manning in their text on criminal law:

> There may arise the situation where a person is confronted with the choice of two evils. If he is faced with threats of death or grievous bodily harm if he does not commit an offence, he may have the defence of compulsion. Necessity may arise when he has a free choice between one thing and another and chooses the one that amounts to a criminal offence. A starving man may have to choose between starvation and stealing a loaf of bread; a man whose wife is in labour may have to choose between exceeding the speed limit or have his wife give birth in his car.[10]

In the case of *Morgentaler v. R.*,[11] a crime (as it then was) of procuring the miscarriage of a woman through the surgical intervention of abortion, the accused argued that his behaviour was necessary to protect the mental and/or physical health of the woman in question.

The defence of entrapment typically varies in instances of consensual crime. The police often intervene in the underground economy of drugs or prostitution, posing as interested purchasers of the services in question. The argument in some of these circumstances is that, had it not been for the actions of the police in requesting drugs or sex from the accused, the crime would not have been committed. In other words, normally law-abiding accused were "entrapped" by the actions of the police. Canadian courts have generally not permitted entrapment as a defence. Only in circumstances where police conduct amounts to an abuse of process—where conduct, in the words of section 24(2) of the *Charter,* "would bring the administration of justice into disrepute"— can this defence be successfully raised. In other words, it is not technically accurate to think of entrapment as a defence to a criminal charge. Rather, the court is asked to balance the value of illegally obtained evidence with the tendency of police conduct in obtaining that evidence to "bring the administration of justice into disrepute." If the tendency of the conduct to bring our system of justice into disrepute is greater than the value of the evidence obtained, the evidence will be excluded. If not, regardless of whether entrapment has taken place, the evidence will be admitted.

Finally, the *Charter* itself, as in the case of entrapment, can produce a range of potential "defences" to criminal charges, particularly in relation to sections 2 to 7 and section 15: for example, the right to freedom of expression; the right to life, liberty, and security of the person; the right to be tried within a reasonable time; the right to equality before the law; and so on.

THE DEFENCE OF DRUNKENNESS

Consider the following excerpt from the judgment of the Alberta Court of Appeal in the case of *R. v. Point*; the case makes clear that intoxication must be extreme in order to qualify as a defence to a criminal charge:

Fraser, C.J.A. (for the Court): The defence appeals Deborah Point's conviction for the second degree murder of Audrey Trudeau. The primary ground of appeal is that the trial judge erred in the application of the "air of reality" test and as a result, wrongly declined to charge the jury on manslaughter, despite the request of both the Crown and the defence to do so. The defence contends that the trial judge ought to have left the lesser charge of manslaughter with the jury on the basis that Point may have been so impaired by alcohol that she lacked the necessary intent required for murder.

Whether the defence of intoxication should be left with a jury is a question of law and is therefore subject to review on a standard of correctness: *R. v. Cinous* 2 S.C.R. 3, (2002) 162 C.C.C. (3d) 129 at 157 (S.C.C.).

In considering whether a defence should be put to a jury, the threshold determination for the trial judge is whether it has an air of reality. Supreme Court of Canada decisions, including, most recently, *R. v. Cinous, supra* at 169, have made it clear that there are two components to the air of reality test:

The question is whether there is (1) evidence (2) upon which a properly instructed jury acting reasonably could acquit if it believed the evidence to be true.

The second part of this question requires the trial judge to determine whether the evidence relied upon is reasonably capable of supporting the inferences required to acquit the accused. The forensic evidence here revealed that the victim died from 15 crushing blows to the back of the head caused by either an axe or a hatchet or similar chopping weapon. All these blows were inflicted while she was alive. (Evidence of Dr. Alakija at A.B. 1420, 1459, 1436, and 1428.) This is the context in which the claimed defence of intoxication must be considered.

What then is the evidence of intoxication? Two Crown witnesses testified that on the night of the murder, Point had been drinking. One, Jeanne Revoy, stated that she saw Point for about two hours and that she was "drinking the whole time that [Ms. Revoy] was there," with "the bartender frequenting the table quite often" and "a lot of liquor buying and drinking" (at A.B. 1250). She testified that Point seemed to be "a little bit" under the influence of alcohol and that she "continued to drink ... heavily" during the time that Revoy was at the bar (at A.B. 1251). Heather Humphrey testified that Point was "drinking, what appeared to be fairly heavily" and was "well on her way" to "getting drunk" (at A.B. 1259). both witnesses described Point's pacing back and forth, apparently agitated. They also testified that Point threw her keys in the air and caught them repeatedly with a punching motion (at A.B. 1242–3, 1254–5). Point herself denied drinking heavily on the night in question and testified that she was not "a heavy drinker" (at A.b. 2276). Indeed, the most Point would say is: "I may have had a couple of drinks" (at A.b. 2276).

This is the extent of the evidence on intoxication. In our view, the conclusion of the trial judge that this evidence, if believed, could not reasonably raise a reasonable doubt, is correct. The trial judge heard extensive submissions from both the Crown and defence on this issue, carefully considered all the evidence and applicable law, as she was required to do, applied the correct test and determined that in these circumstances, there was no air of reality to a defence of intoxication. We agree.

The core issue is whether the evidence here, if believed, could reasonably support the inference that Point was too drunk to know that 15 forceful blows to the back of the victim's head with an axe or hatchet would likely cause serious bodily harm or death. The evidence on the degree of Point's alleged intoxication is minimal. Since neither Crown witness was cross-examined on the extent of Point's consumption of alcohol and since Point herself denied drinking heavily, there is no evidence as to how many drinks she consumed and over what period of time. Nor is there any evidence as to what Revoy meant when she testified that Point was "drinking heavily" or seemed to be "a little bit" under the influence of alcohol. Similarly, there is no evidence of what Humphrey meant when she testified that Point was "well on her way to getting drunk." Evidence of drinking is not, without more, evidence of intoxication and certainly not the degree of intoxication necessary to raise a reasonable doubt on the primary or secondary intent required for murder.

Nor was there any evidence of Point's physical or mental impairment. The nature, extent and force of the blows Point inflicted speak to physical co-ordination on her part and purposive action. The suggestion that she might not have known what the consequences were of her wielding an axe or hatchet in such a brutal manner because of drunkenness lacks any air of reality. There is nothing in the evidence of what happened when Trudeau was killed that would detract from this conclusion. Point never claimed that when she hit Trudeau with the axe she did not know or foresee that her actions would result in Trudeau's death. Instead, her defence was that she did not kill her.

In the result, there is nothing on the facts of this case that would lend an air of reality to the defence that Point lacked the necessary *mens rea* for the offence of murder because intoxication prevented her from knowing or foreseeing that the blows to Trudeau's head with an axe or hatchet were likely to cause death. This was the trial judge's conclusion and in our view, she did not err in failing to leave the defence of drunkenness vitiating the specific intent for murder with the jury....

Finally, we are satisfied that on the issue of intent, the trial judge's charge, read as a whole, left this issue with the jury as required: *R. v. Cooper,* 1993 CanLII 147 (S.C.C.), [1993] 1 S.C.R. 146; *R. v. Evans,* 1993 CanLII 102 (S.C.C.), [1993] 2 S.C.R. 629.

Thus, in the result, the appeal must be dismissed.[12]

The *Point* case indicates that, while drunkenness continues to be a defence to a criminal charge (in order to reduce a conviction for murder to a conviction for manslaughter), such a claim can be established only in relatively restricted circumstances—those circumstances in which an "air of reality" exists. But should we go further? Should drunkenness ultimately be irrelevant to the determination of guilt and have potential applicability only to the sentence to be imposed?

The answer to this question was at least partially decided by the Supreme Court of Canada in the 1994 case of *Daviault v. R.*[13] In this case a 65-year-old woman who was confined to a wheelchair invited Mr. Daviault to her home for a drink. He brought with him a 40-ounce bottle of brandy. The complainant had a drink and fell asleep. When she awoke during the night to go to the bathroom, Mr. Daviault appeared, threw her on the bed, and sexually assaulted her. He had consumed seven or eight beers before arriving at the woman's home and drank the entire 40-ounce bottle of brandy between 6 p.m. and the assault some nine hours later. Mr. Daviault remembered nothing of the assault, having experienced an alcoholic blackout. Testimony at trial by the accused and by a pharmacologist supported the view that Mr. Daviault had lost contact with reality, his brain temporarily dissociated from normal functioning.

The Court held that Mr. Daviault's conviction could not stand, and ordered a new trial. The majority argued that even though voluntary intoxication may be reprehensible, it does not follow that its consequences in every conceivable situation are voluntary or predictable. Accordingly, if on rare occasions the accused can establish on a balance of probabilities that he was so intoxicated as to be in a state akin to automatism or insanity, he should not be held to have the *mens rea* necessary for criminal conviction. Further, the Court argued that a conviction of the accused in such circumstances would offend the presumption of innocence, and could not be saved by section 1 of the *Charter*.

There was, perhaps predictably, a negative public reaction to the Court's decision in *Daviault*. In response to much criticism of the Court's ruling, the federal government enacted section 33.1 of the *Criminal Code*, which states, in effect, that self-induced intoxication is no longer a defence to a criminal charge of "assault or any other interference or threat of interference by a person with the bodily integrity of another person." Drunkenness can, however, serve to reduce a charge of murder to one of manslaughter, as the *Point* case and many others indicate. For the Supreme Court's most recent pronouncement on drunkenness as a defence, see the 2011 case of *R. v. Bouchard-Lebrun*.[14] The facts in this case are summarized by Justice LeBel:

The relevant facts of this case are not in dispute. For the purposes of this appeal, it will suffice to mention that the appellant, Tommy Bouchard-Lebrun, and a long-time acquaintance of his, Yohann Schmouth, had smoked marijuana and taken amphetamines during the day on October 23, 2005. In the evening, they decided to go to Amqui so the appellant could visit his parents. They took the bus from Rivière-du-Loup, where the appellant lived, to the last stop in Mont-Joli. They were still intoxicated when they got on the bus.

When they arrived in Mont-Joli during the night on October 24, the appellant and his friend decided to hitchhike to Amqui. At about 1:30 a.m., Gilles Tremblay, an old acquaintance of the appellant's family, picked them up in his car. At that time, no signs of intoxication were apparent from the appellant's behaviour. At trial, Mr. Tremblay stated that he had not noticed anything unusual about the appellant at any time during the car trip. His statements confirmed Mr. Schmouth's testimony that the appellant was [TRANSLATION] "OK" again when they were around Val-Brillant, a municipality about 15 kilometres from Amqui. Therefore, it seems that the drugs taken by the appellant during the day on October 23 had ceased to have effect before he arrived in Amqui with Mr. Schmouth.

In Amqui, the two young men purchased ecstasy pills of a type known as "*poire bleue*", which they took during the night on October 24. During the hours that followed, the appellant and Mr. Schmouth decided to go and beat up Dany Lévesque, who was known as "Pee-Wee", for the real or imagined reason that he wore an [TRANSLATION] "upside-down cross" around his neck. Around 5:00 a.m., the appellant and Mr. Schmouth illegally entered the building where Mr. Lévesque lived. Roger Dumas, who lived on the second floor of the building, was woken up by noise coming from the ground floor and went down to Mr. Lévesque's apartment to find out what was going on. The two occupants of the building met in the stairs and realized that the appellant and Mr. Schmouth were there, and the latter two then brutally attacked Mr. Lévesque by punching and kicking him many times.

Mr. Dumas saw that Mr. Lévesque could not defend himself against his two attackers and tried to intervene. The appellant grabbed him and threw him violently down the stairs. Mr. Dumas lay on the floor at the bottom of the stairs. The appellant went down to where he was and stomped on his head. The assault left Mr. Dumas disabled, and he will have to spend the rest of his life in a hospital.

At the time of the assault, the appellant was highly intoxicated because of the effects of the "*poire bleue*" pill he had taken a few hours earlier. In addition to the "normal" symptoms of intoxication resulting from the use of that drug, the highly toxic pill had produced a striking and, according to the appellant, unanticipated effect on him, as it caused a complete dissociation between the appellant's subjective perceptions and the objective reality. To put it bluntly, he was

[TRANSLATION] "on another planet". Two witnesses at the trial stated that he [TRANSLATION] "started acting weird" and was "completely out of it" after taking the *poire bleue* pill.

Justice LeBel goes on to conclude of this defence of intoxication:

Finally, after considering all the circumstances of this case, I am satisfied that there is no valid reason to initiate the special procedure provided for in Part XX.1 of the *Criminal Code*. An accused whose mental condition at the material time can be attributed exclusively to a state of temporary self-induced intoxication and who poses no threat to others is not suffering from a "mental disorder" for the purposes of s.16 *Cr. C.* The scheme of Part XX.1 applies only if the accused actually suffered from a disease of the mind at the material time. It is not intended to apply to accused persons whose temporary madness was induced artificially by a state of intoxication.

In this context, I conclude that the appellant was not suffering from a "mental disorder" for the purposes of s. 16 *Cr. C.* at the time he committed the assault. He has failed to rebut the presumption that his toxic psychosis was a "self-induced stat[e] caused by alcohol or drugs" in accordance with the definition in *Cooper*. A malfunctioning of the mind that results *exclusively* from self-induced intoxication cannot be considered a disease of the mind in the legal sense, since it is not a product of the individual's inherent psychological makeup. This is true even though medical science may tend to consider such conditions to be diseases of the mind. In circumstances like those of the case at bar, toxic psychosis seems to be nothing more than a symptom, albeit an extreme one, of the accused person's state of self-induced intoxication. Such a state cannot justify exempting an accused from criminal responsibility under s. 16 *Cr. C.*

THE DEFENCE OF MISTAKE OF FACT

It is impossible in an introductory text to detail the law relating to all the defences to and mitigations of criminal charges: intoxication, insanity, self-defence, duress, entrapment, and mistake. Consider, however, the ambit of the defence of mistake of fact. If a man has an honest but mistaken belief that a woman has consented to sexual activity, should this preclude a conviction for sexual assault? What can you conclude from the following excerpts of facts in *Pappajohn v. R.*[15] and *Sansregret v. R.*[16]—should either accused be able to avail himself of the defence of honest but mistaken belief in consent, with the *mens rea* of the crime negated by this belief? First consider the case of *Pappajohn v. R.*:

McIntyre J.: The complainant was a real estate saleswoman employed by a well-known and well-established real estate firm in Vancouver. She was successful in her work. The appellant is a businessman who was anxious to sell his home in Vancouver, and he had listed it for sale with the real estate firm with which the complainant was associated. She was to be responsible for the matter on her firm's behalf. On August 4, 1976, at about 1:00 p.m., she met the appellant by appointment at a downtown restaurant for lunch. The purpose of the meeting was to discuss the house sale. The lunch lasted until about 4:00 or 4:30 p.m. During this time, a good deal of liquor was consumed by both parties. The occasion became convivial, the proprietor of the restaurant and his wife joined the party, and estimates of the amount of alcohol consumed varied in retrospect, as one would expect. It does seem clear, however, that while each of the parties concerned had a substantial amount to drink, each seemed capable of functioning normally.

At about 4:00 p.m. or shortly thereafter, they left the restaurant. The appellant drove the complainant's car while she sat in the front passenger seat. They went to the appellant's house, the one which was listed for sale, to further consider questions arising in that connection. Up to the time of arrival at the home, at about 4:30 or 5:00 p.m., there is no significant variation in their accounts of events. From the moment of arrival, however, there is a complete divergence. She related a story of rape completely against her will and over her protests and struggles. He spoke of an amorous interlude involving no more than a bit of coy objection on her part and several acts of intercourse with her consent. Whatever occurred in the house, there is no doubt that at about 7:30 p.m., the complainant ran out of the house naked, with a man's bow tie around her neck and her hands tightly tied behind her back with a bathrobe sash. She arrived at the door of a house nearby and demanded entry and protection. The occupant of the house, a priest, admitted her. She was in an upset state and exhibited great fear and emotional stress. The police were called, and these proceedings followed....

Dickson, J.: There is circumstantial evidence supportive of a plea of belief in consent: (1) Her necklace and car keys were found in the living room. (2) She confirmed his testimony that her blouse was neatly hung in the clothes closet. (3) Other items of folded clothing were found at the foot of the bed. (4) None of her clothes were damaged in the slightest way. (5) She was in the house for a number of hours. (6) By her version, when she entered the house, the appellant said he was going to break her. She made no attempt to leave. (7) She did not leave while he undressed. (8) There was no evidence of struggle. (9) She suffered no physical injuries, aside from three scratches....

Now consider the Supreme Court of Canada's decision in *R. v. Sansregret*:

McIntyre, J.: The appellant, a man in his early 20s and the complainant, a woman of 31 years, had lived together in the complainant's house for about a year before the events of October 15, 1982. Their relationship had been one of contention and discord with violence on the part of the appellant: "slappings" or "roughing up" in his description, "blows" in hers. The appellant had left the house for short periods and in September 1982, the complainant decided to end the affair. She told the appellant to leave and he did.

On September 23, 1982, some days after his dismissal, the appellant broke into the house at about 4:30 a.m. He was "raging" at her and furious because of his expulsion. He terrorized her with a filelike instrument with which he was armed. She was fearful of what might occur, and in order to calm him down, she held out some hope of a reconciliation and they had intercourse. A report was made to the police of this incident, the complainant asserting she had been raped, but no proceedings were taken. The appellant's probation officer became involved and there was evidence that he had asked the complainant not to press the matter, presumably because it would interfere with the appellant's probation.

On October 15, 1982, again at about 4:30 a.m., the appellant broke into the complainant's house through a basement window. She was alone, and awakened by the entry, she seized the bedroom telephone in an effort to call the police. The appellant picked up a butcher knife in the kitchen and came into the bedroom. He was furious and violent. He accused her of having another boyfriend; pulled the cord of the telephone out of the jack and threw it into the living room; threatened her with the knife and ordered her to take off her nightdress and made her stand in the kitchen doorway, naked save for a jacket over her shoulders, so he could be sure where she was while he repaired the window to conceal his entry from the police, should they arrive. He struck her on the mouth with sufficient force to draw blood, and on three occasions rammed the knife blade into the wall with great force, once very close to her. He told her that if the police came, he would put the knife through her, and added that if he had found her with a boyfriend, he would have killed them both. At one point, he tied her hands behind her back with a scarf. The complainant said she was in fear for her life and sanity.

By about 5:30 a.m., after an hour of such behaviour by the appellant, she tried to calm him down. She pretended that there was some hope of a reconciliation if the appellant would settle down and get a job. This had the desired effect. He calmed down and after some conversation, he joined her on the bed and they had intercourse. The complainant swore that her consent to the intercourse was solely for the purpose of calming him down, to protect herself from further violence. This, she said, was something she had learned from earlier experience with him. In her evidence she said:

I didn't consent at any time.

I was very afraid. My whole body was trembling. I was sure I would have a nervous breakdown. I came very, very close to losing my mind. All I knew was I had to keep this man calm or he would kill me.

At about 6:45 a.m., after further conversation with the appellant, she got dressed and prepared to leave for work. She had a business appointment at 8:00 a.m. She drove the appellant to a location which he chose, and in the course of the journey, he returned her keys and some money that he had taken from her purse upon his arrival in the early morning. Upon dropping him off, she drove immediately to her mother's home, where she made a complaint of rape. The police were called and the appellant was arrested that evening.

In both *Pappajohn* and *Sansregret*, the Canadian judiciary was divided about the defence of mistaken belief in consent. In *Pappajohn*, Supreme Court Justice Dickson concluded, "It does not follow that, by simply disbelieving the appellant on consent, in fact, the jury thereby found that there was no belief in consent and that the appellant could not reasonably have believed in consent."[17] In other words, the appellant may not have been believed by the jury, but the jury may have been mistaken. And in *Sansregret*, the trial judge concluded:

> [H]is honest belief finds support in the testimony of the complainant. She knows him and, in her opinion, notwithstanding all the objective facts to the contrary, he did believe that everything was back to normal between them by the time of the sexual encounter. His subsequent behaviour as well attests to that fact.
>
> I do not like the conclusion which this leads me to. There was no real consent. There was submission as a result of a very real and justifiable fear. No one in his right mind could have believed that the complainant's dramatic about-face stemmed from anything other than fear. But the accused did. He saw what he wanted to see, heard what he wanted to hear, believed what he wanted to believe.

Both cases were resolved in the Supreme Court of Canada, and in both instances the accused was convicted. The defence of honest mistake of fact remains as a legal possibility, but it seems clear that it is not to be a purely subjective test of the accused's intention; wholly unreasonable beliefs, however honestly held, are not likely to be viewed as negating the *mens rea* required for conviction.

In 1992, partially in response to cases such as *Daviault*, *Pappajohn*, and *Sansregret*, the federal government enacted the following definitions of consent with respect to sexual assault:

Meaning of "consent"

273.1(1) Subject to subsection (2) and subsection 265(3), "consent" means, for the purposes of sections 271, 272 and 273, the voluntary agreement of the complainant to engage in the sexual activity in question.

Where no consent obtained

273.1(2) No consent is obtained, for the purpose of sections 271, 272 and 273, where

    (a) the agreement is expressed by the words or conduct of a person other than the complainant;

    (b) the complainant is incapable of consenting to the activity;

    (c) the accused induces the complainant to engage in the activity by abusing a position of trust, power or authority;

    (d) the complainant expresses, by words or conduct, a lack of agreement to engage in the activity; or

    (e) the complainant, having consented to engage in sexual activity, expresses, by words or conduct, a lack of agreement to continue to engage in the activity.

273.1(3) Nothing in subsection (2) shall be construed as limiting the circumstances in which no consent is obtained.

Where belief in consent not a defence

273.2 It is not a defence to a charge under section 271, 272 or 273 that the accused
believed that the complainant consented to the activity that forms the subject-matter of
the charge, where

    (a) the accused's belief arose from the accused's

        (i) self-induced intoxication, or

        (ii) recklessness or wilful blindness; or

    (b) the accused did not take reasonable steps, in the circumstances known to the
        accused at the time, to ascertain that the complainant was consenting.

One of the more intriguing decisions of the Supreme Court of Canada with respect to mistake of fact is to be found in the 1999 case of *R. v. Ewanchuk.*[18] Steve Ewanchuk was a man in his late thirties, living in Edmonton, looking for staff to work at his retail booths in several shopping malls in the city. The complainant was a 17-year-old woman who was looking for work. At Ewanchuk's suggestion, her job interview took place in his trailer, where he stored the custom wood products that he was selling. Ewanchuk was quite friendly with the young woman, touching her hand, arms, and shoulder as he spoke. He asked her to give him a massage, as he was feeling tense. She agreed, but later told the court that she was made uneasy by his request. He then began massaging her, bringing his hands up close to her breasts. She pushed her elbows in between his arms and said "No."

The accused stopped immediately, but later asked the young woman to turn and face him. He began massaging her feet, and his touching progressed up to her inner thigh and pelvic area. She was uncomfortable, but worried that he might become violent. He began to lay himself against her and grind his pelvic area into hers. He asked her to put her arms around him, but she did not. After about a minute of this pelvic grinding, she asked him to stop, which he again did.

Ewanchuk then reached over to hug the complainant, and once again, continued his pelvic grinding. He also moved his hand inside her shorts for a brief time and, while on top of her, fumbled with his shorts and took out his penis. Once again, she asked him to stop, and once again he did, saying something to the effect of, "It's okay. See, I'm a nice guy. I stopped."

The accused then got up, opened his wallet, and gave the complainant a $100 bill, saying that it was for the massage, and asking her not to tell anyone about it. Shortly after receiving the money, she said that she had to go; she left the trailer, walked home, and called the police. At trial, Ewanchuk was acquitted by the trial judge on the basis of "implied consent."[19] More specifically, the judge could not be convinced beyond a reasonable doubt of a lack of consent.

When the case was reviewed by the Supreme Court of Canada, however, Ewanchuk's actions were seen as sexual assaults. As the Court noted,

> [T]he accused relies on the fact that he momentarily stopped his advances each time the complainant said No as evidence of his good intentions. This demonstrates that he understood the complainant's Nos to mean precisely that.... The

> trial record conclusively establishes that the accused's persistent and increasingly
> serious advances constituted a sexual assault for which he had no defence.

This is a reasonable inference. Ewanchuk's first attempt to engage in a physical relationship did not amount to sexual assault, but his persistence in the face of opposition, and his eventual offering of a $100 bill, point to his knowledge that he was engaging in sexual advances that were not wanted.

As Osgoode Hall criminal law professor Alan Young has noted, 20 years ago Ewanchuk would have been labelled a male pig, but never have been convicted of a crime because of the lack of resistance by the complainant—"her passivity would have been taken as a sign of consent." According to Young, Ewanchuk's conviction was probably justified, considering the combination of the age difference, the location of the activity, his persistence, and his indifference to her requests.[20] But consider the precedent set by the language of the Supreme Court of Canada in *Ewanchuk*:

> If the trier of fact accepts the complainant's testimony that she did not consent, no
> matter how strongly her conduct may contradict that claim, the absence of consent
> is established.... There is no defense of implied consent to sexual assault in Canada
> ... the complainant's fear need not be reasonable, nor must it be communicated to
> the accused in order for consent to be vitiated.

The bottom line, as Young notes, is that "convictions will be obtained even if women do not express or manifest their fears, and even if women do not express or manifest a lack of consent. Criminality is established once the complainant testified that she subjectively and internally felt that way."[21]

The Supreme Court went even further, however, requiring consent to be communicated by the complainant, in order to avoid criminal conviction:

> ... the evidence must show that he believed that the complainant communicated
> consent to engage in the sexual activity in question. A belief by the accused that
> the complainant, in her own mind, wanted him to touch her, but did not express
> that desire, is not a defence. The accused's speculation as to what was going on in
> the complainant's mind provides no defence.[22]

The Supreme Court's commentary in *Ewanchuk*, independent of the appropriateness of its decision, raises significant questions about the meaning of consent and the ambit of the defence of mistake of fact in such circumstances.

More recently, in March of 2014 the Supreme Court, following Ewanchuk, considered *R. v. Hutchinson,* where a complainant had agreed to sexual activity with her partner, but insisted that he use a condom in order to prevent pregnancy. He had poked holes in the condom, unknown to her, and she became pregnant. The Supreme Court concluded that this was a sexual assault, employing the following logic at one point in their decision:

> At its core, this case concerns the right recognized in *R. v. Ewanchuk*, 1999 CanLII 711
> (SCC), [1999] 1 S.C.R. 330, to determine how sexual activity will take place. Society's com-
> mitment to protecting a person's autonomy and dignity requires that individuals have the

right to determine *who* touches their body, and *how* the touching will occur. This protection underlies the definition of consent set out in s. 273.1(1) as "the voluntary agreement of the complainant to engage in the sexual activity in question". Consent to the "sexual activity in question" necessarily means the complainant's voluntary agreement both to engage in touching of a sexual nature and to the manner in which that touching is carried out. The starting point for the analysis of consent under the *actus reus* of sexual assault is s. 273.1(1). When a complainant does not voluntarily agree to the sexual activity which occurred, consent does not exist within the meaning of s. 273.1(1), and the inquiry for the purposes of the *actus reus* of sexual assault is complete. If there is *no* consent *ab initio*, it is pointless to inquire whether there was fraud under s. 265(3)(*c*) which would have vitiated the complainant's consent. In other words, without voluntary agreement as to the "how"—the manner in which the sexual activity in question occurred—there is no consent within the meaning of s. 273.1(1).

Unlike under s. 265(3)(*c*), which requires both a dishonest act *and* a deprivation, consent under s. 273.1(1) has never required an analysis of the risks or consequences caused by unwanted sexual touching. It is the unwanted nature of non-consensual sexual activity that violates the complainant's sexual integrity and gives rise to culpability under the criminal law, not just the risk of further harm that the sexual touching may create. Requiring an analysis of the risks or consequences of non-consensual touching by applying s. 265(3)(*c*) whenever deception is later discovered, adds a barrier to the simple ability to demonstrate whether the activity which occurred was agreed to *when it occurred*. It thereby undermines the values of personal autonomy and physical integrity sought to be protected by making sexual assault an offence.

It does not follow that because a condom is a form of birth control, it is not also part of the sexual activity. Removing the use of a condom from the meaning of sexual activity in s. 273.1(1) because the condom may have been intended for contraceptive purposes, means that an individual has no right to require the use of a condom during intercourse where pregnancy is not at issue. All individuals must have an equal right to determine how they are touched, regardless of gender, sexual orientation, reproductive capacity, or the type of sexual activity they choose to engage in. By any definition, when someone uses a condom, it is part of the sexual activity. It is therefore part of what is—or is not—consented to. When individuals agree to sexual activity with a condom, they mean an intact condom. They are not merely agreeing to a sexual activity, they are agreeing to how it should take place. That is what s. 273.1(1) was intended to protect.

SELF-DEFENCE: *R. V. LAVALLEE*

A clear defence to a criminal charge of assault and to other offences against persons is to be found in self-defence—the concept that the assault, or, in some circumstances, even the homicide, cannot be labelled a culpable act as the individual in question was only defending him or herself (in the case of a homicide, from a potentially lethal attack). Section 34 of the *Criminal Code*[23] states:

> 34. (1) *Every one who is unlawfully assaulted without having provoked the assault is justified in repelling force by force if the force he uses is not intended to cause death or grievous bodily harm and is no more than is necessary to enable him to defend himself.*
>
> (2) *Every one who is unlawfully assaulted and who causes death or grievous bodily harm in repelling the assault is justified if*
>
> > (a) *he causes it under reasonable apprehension of death or grievous bodily harm from the violence with which the assault was originally made or with which the assailant pursues his purposes; and*
> >
> > (b) *he believes, on reasonable grounds, that he cannot otherwise preserve himself from death or grievous bodily harm.*

Consider the ambit of this defence in the 1990 decision of the Supreme Court in *R. v. Lavallee.*[24] Lyn Lavallee had been living with Kevin Rust for three to four years. From all accounts it was a highly dysfunctional and violent relationship. Rust beat Lavallee regularly, and had threatened to kill her. She had pointed a gun at Rust on at least two occasions and threatened to kill him if he ever touched her again.

One summer night in August 1986 Lavallee shot Rust in the back of the head as he was leaving her bedroom. She made the following statement to the police:

> He grabbed me by the arm right there. There's a bruise on my face also where he slapped me. He didn't slap me right then, first he yelled at me, then he pushed me and I pushed him back and he hit me twice on the right-hand side of my head. I was scared. All I thought about was all the other times he used to beat me, I was scared. I was shaking as usual. The rest is a blank, all I remember is he gave me the gun and a shot was fired through my screen. This is all so fast. And then the guns were in another room and he loaded it the second shot and gave it to me. And I was going to shoot myself. I pointed it to myself, I was so upset. OK, and then he went and I was sitting on the bed and he started going like this with his finger (Lavallee made a shaking motion with her index finger) and said something like "You're my old lady and you do as you're told" or something like that. He said, "Wait till everybody leaves, you'll get it then," and he said something to the effect of "Either you kill me or I'll get you," that was what it was. He kind of smiled and then he turned around. I shot him but I aimed out. I thought I aimed above him and a piece of his head went that way.

The arresting officer told the court that en route to the police station Lavallee had said "He said if I didn't kill him first he would kill me. I hope he lives. I really love him."

The Supreme Court of Canada concluded that Lyn Lavallee was not guilty of any criminal offence—that her actions in shooting Kevin Rust amounted to self-defence. The decision has met with mixed reviews. Many women's groups have praised the judgment as an important step forward, a long-overdue expansion of the concept of self-defence through recognition that a battered woman does not need to be in immediate danger of being killed to have a reasonable fear of lethal attack. Others have been sharply critical, suggesting that her actions are highly relevant to the sentence to be imposed, but not to the issue of her guilt of the crime of manslaughter. The issue of the ambit of self-defence is particularly difficult to calculate, particularly in cases where there has been a lengthy history of physical abuse. A reasonable conception of danger may vary significantly from one individual to the next.

SENTENCING: DOES THE PUNISHMENT FIT THE CRIME?

The **sentencing** of those convicted of criminal offences is of great interest to Canadians. Discussions about crime in the House of Commons typically centre on the penalties thought to be appropriate for certain kinds of crimes. As discussed in earlier chapters, the *Criminal Code* sets out three categories of criminal offences: summary offences, indictable offences, and **hybrid offences**. A maximum penalty for **summary conviction offences** is stated in s. 787(1) of the *Code*:

> 787. (1) Unless otherwise provided by law, everyone who is convicted of an offence punishable on summary conviction is liable to a fine of not more than five thousand dollars or to a term of imprisonment not exceeding six months or to both.

The *Criminal Code* sets punishments for indictable offences according to the nature of the prohibited conduct. A conviction for the indictable offence of first degree murder, for example, carries an automatic term of life imprisonment without parole eligibility for 25 years; conviction for the indictable offence of sexual assault with a weapon carries a term of up to 14 years' imprisonment. All stated punishments are a maximum, unless otherwise indicated.

Sentencing attempts to accomplish a range of potentially complementary purposes: general deterrence, specific deterrence, community denunciation, and rehabilitation. When a court adopts the principle of general deterrence, it imposes a sentence in order to deter the general public from committing the specific crime. Specific deterrence is deterrence particular to the individual offender; the court attempts to find a penalty that is sufficient to deter that offender. Community denunciation, although often conceptualized as state vengeance, can also be understood and appreciated for its educative purpose and impact. As the Ontario Court of Appeal noted in *R. v. Ramdass*, social denunciation can fairly be linked to the possibility of a general deterrent effect:

> The sentence by emphasizing community disapproval of an act and branding it as reprehensible has a moral or educative effect and thereby affects the attitude of the public. One then hopes that a person with an attitude thus conditioned to regard conduct as reprehensible will not likely commit such an act.[25]

The sentencing goal of rehabilitation is somewhat more elusive, focusing society's response on the offender rather than on the act committed by the offender. The rise of rehabilitation as a sentencing strategy reflects a belief in the science of corrections. Legislators and the judiciary now share—with social scientists, psychiatrists, and administrators—the responsibility for the control of criminals. As Clayton Ruby noted in his book *Sentencing,* the promise has been hollow. Often individual liberty is imperiled by claims to knowledge and therapeutic effectiveness that we do not possess and by failure to candidly concede what we do not know. At times, it is the practitioners of the behavioural sciences who are guilty of these faults; but more often, legislators, lawyers, and public foolishly assume an expertise and an efficacy that simply [do] not exist.[26]

Ruby went on to discuss the factors considered most important in arriving at an appropriate sentence for a specific crime. He set out 10 such factors:

1. the degree of premeditation involved;
2. the circumstances surrounding the actual commission of the offence; i.e., the manner in which it was committed, the amount of violence involved, the employment of an offensive weapon, and the degree of active participation by each offender;
3. the gravity of the crime committed, in regard to which the maximum punishment provided by statute is an indication;
4. the attitude of the offender after the commission of the crime, as this serves to indicate the degree of criminality involved and throws some light on the character of the participant;
5. the previous criminal record, if any, of the offender;
6. the age, mode of life, character, and personality of the offender;
7. any recommendation of the trial judge, any presentence or probation official's report, or any mitigating or other circumstances properly brought to the attention of [the] Court;
8. incidence of crime in jurisdiction;
9. sentences customarily imposed for the same or similar offences;
10. mercy.[27]

How these factors are to be interpreted is largely a matter of ideology, with individual judges espousing social and political choices, albeit within the framework of existing statute and case law. Consider *R. v. Horon,* for example.

Stevenson, J.A.: The Crown seeks to appeal the sentence (a fine, probation, a community service order, and a two-year driving prohibition) imposed upon the accused for impaired driving causing bodily harm.

The issue we must address is the approach to be taken in imposing a sentence for this consequence-related crime.

The accused, respondent, had been drinking at a party. The evidence is that he was in a depressed state and an alcoholic. One witness testified she urged the accused not to drive because of his condition. He drove moving to the wrong side of the road. An oncoming vehicle took evasive action and the accused then turned toward the right side of the road, resulting in a head-on collision. The oncoming driver suffered a fractured wrist and lacerations to the head and knee. The accused was convicted after a trial....

Parliament has laid to rest any argument about the irrelevancy of the consequences. The wrong is to take control of a motor vehicle when ability is impaired by alcohol. The punishment will reflect the consequences. It will also reflect any other aggravating factors which exacerbate the wrong, such as undertaking that control when the accused has been warned of the risks attendant upon driving in the impaired condition, or the degree of impairment (which may be evidenced by the driving pattern)....

A number of appellate authorities deal with punishment for impaired driving causing injury or death.... In *R. v. Gutoski,* January 4, 1990, the Manitoba Court of Appeal ... expressed the view that a sentence of imprisonment is normally required in such cases. They also noted that since the gravamen of the offence is driving while impaired, excuses for the drinking do not excuse the criminal conduct of driving afterwards. I agree with that proposition and add that, once the offence is found, drink-induced inability to comprehend the extent of the impairment or the possible consequences will not be a mitigating circumstance. The Court there imposed a sentence of six months' imprisonment where young children suffered moderately severe injuries as a result of the accused's impaired driving....

I have already outlined the circumstances of this case. The driving pattern was "not bad." Fortunately, the injuries were not serious. What then are the aggravating and mitigating factors applicable to this accused?

In aggravation there was ... "a serious, significant level of impairment." There is evidence he was cautioned not to drive. There is an old record of impaired driving.

In mitigation, the judge notes the accused to be a fine upstanding citizen except for the drinking problems. He showed remorse and a desire to rehabilitate himself, manifested by a prompt entry into a treatment program which he has followed. There is considerable evidence of rehabilitation and we note that some of his family are dependent upon his ability to continue working. Rehabilitation, reducing the risk of reoffending is relevant, but cannot overwhelm a deterrent sentence. It all lies in the mouth of an accused to plead the hardship his action brings to others.

Nonetheless, undue hardship may be a ground for tempering an otherwise appropriate sentence. The judge also cites the special circumstances that led the accused into alcoholism and into drinking on this occasion. Having regard to the gravamen of this offence, namely operating a motor vehicle when impaired, these special circumstances cannot mitigate.

In my view, a jail sentence is necessary in this case. Having regard to the factors I have discussed, the ends of justice would be served by a two-month sentence. The probation and prohibition order remain. The accused may elect to serve this sentence intermittently and may apply through the registrar to any member of the Court to fix reporting times. He will be governed by the probation order when not serving the sentence.

The community service order and fine are vacated.[28]

Sentencing an accused convicted of a criminal offence is a judicial exercise that relies upon a complex matrix of relevant concerns. Offence and offender are placed against the backdrop of existing precedents and are further constrained, to some degree at least, by the mood of legislators and the public, as expressed within a specific historical context. In *Horon,* the judge notes that the accused is a father with dependants and "a fine upstanding citizen"; these are factors that mitigate his punishment. One might ask, however, why men without children who cannot claim to be "fine upstanding citizens" should be treated more harshly for the crime of impaired driving causing bodily harm.

RESTORATIVE JUSTICE: A FRAMEWORK FOR THE FUTURE?

Restorative justice is defined in the following manner by the Centre for Restorative Justice at Simon Fraser University:

> Restorative Justice is an old idea with a new name. Its roots can be found in Aboriginal healing traditions and the non-retaliatory responses to violence endorsed by many faith communities.
>
> It represents a return of the simple wisdom of viewing conflict as an opportunity for a community to learn and grow. It operates on the premise that conflict, even criminal conflict, inflicts harm, and therefore individuals must accept responsibility for repairing that harm. Communities are empowered to choose their response to conflict. Victims, offenders and communities actively participate in devising mutually beneficial solutions, and implementing those solutions. Conflicts are resolved in a way that restores harmony in the community members' relationships, and allows people to continue to live together in a safer, healthy environment.[29]

Restorative justice means many different things to many different people, and many organizations claim to be practitioners of restorative justice: police agencies, community groups, victims' groups, and so on. As a consequence, some have suggested that there needs to be a universal standardized approach to restorative justice. In the excerpt that follows, Toronto lawyer Jonathan Rudin points out the shortcomings of such an approach—that it would essentially contradict the value of restorative justice itself.[30]

> The first rationale—that everyone should be treated the same when coming before the courts—suffers from two problems. The first is that it compares an idealized version of the justice system with the practical realities of restorative justice programs. A better comparison would be with the actual reality of justice as it is practised on the ground as compared to the actual practice of restorative justice.
>
> On this basis, the argument collapses at the outset. Despite the fact that criminal law is the same across the country, there is no uniformity in sentencing today. Within provinces there is great discrepancy in the way certain offences are handled. In some cases those discrepancies emerge when comparing even neighbouring judicial districts. More broadly, for example, crime tends to be treated with longer jail sentences in smaller communities than in big cities. Offences that might result in suspended sentences, discharges or terms of probation in a city such as

Vancouver, regularly result in jail sentences in smaller towns. This problem is even more pronounced when the sentencing practices are examined on a province by province basis. It is clear when looking at such figures that some provinces are, for example, more likely to use jail as a sanction than other provinces.

The second problem with this argument is that it advocates a model of equality that is at odds with the prevailing view of equality held by the courts. The idea that equality is achieved by making sure everyone receives a similar sentence for a similar crime is an argument for formal equality - equality of treatment. Increasingly in Canada, particularly with the introduction of the Charter of Rights and Freedoms in 1982, Canada has moved to a vision of substantive equality - the focus is on equality of outcome. Sometimes we must treat people differently in order to achieve the same result. If the result we wish to achieve through the sentencing process is to deter offenders form committing offences and keeping communities safe, then we must recognize that there are many ways to accomplish this goal within the sentencing process. The Supreme Court of Canada has explicitly recommended that courts adopt a more restorative, and thus a more individualized, approach to sentencing.

The bureaucratic impetus for standardization, although understandable, has two regrettable and related difficulties. The first is that by centralizing what can be funded, the amounts of funds available, and often the types of offences amenable to restorative justice programs, local creativity and responsiveness is choked off and the scope for restorative justice programs is pushed to the lowest common denominator.

Restorative justice programs develop in response to local needs and as the result of collaboration among a variety of actors at the local level. These creative and innovative responses then form the basis for more communities wishing to undertake such projects. Ironically, this growth then spurs the need for "standards," thus choking off the very factors that made the programs such a success in the beginning.

In some ways, this situation is an extension of the classic historic debate between core and periphery which has played itself out in many ways in Canadian history. The difficulty with centralizing power and regulating local processes is that the responses lose their ability to actually respond to local needs. When restorative justice programs begin to resemble cookie cutter solutions, they lose their ability to respond to local needs and thus their effectiveness is compromised.*

Finally, we should consider the relevance of restorative justice for the future of sentencing. To date, our courts in Canada and in most other Western jurisdictions have been dominated by a rationale of either punishment or enforced treatment. In the sentencing circles that have recently emerged among Canada's Aboriginal peoples we see an alternative model, one that stresses restorative justice, consensus, and the building of community in response to the offender's crime. Consider the following excerpt from *Canadian Criminology*. Could this kind of approach find an appeal

---

*Jonathan Rudin, "Pushing Back – A Response to the Drive for the Standardization of Restorative Justice Programs in Canada," Paper presented at the 6th International Conference on Restorative Justice, Vancouver, 2003.

that extends beyond Canada's Aboriginal community, albeit with perhaps different modalities than sentencing circles but with an emphasis on restorative justice for the offender, the victim, and the community?

One of the more innovative approaches to sentencing is "circle sentencing," which is being practised by territorial and provincial judges in the Yukon Territory and in several provinces. In circle sentencing, all of the participants in the case—the judge, prosecutor, defence lawyer, victim, offender, and community residents—sit in a circular arrangement and discuss all facets of the case. The circle, which represents a radical departure from the formal courtroom decorum, is designed to break down the formality of the court process and to provide a forum for the disposition of cases that is based on healing, consensus building, and returning to communities the responsibility for resolving conflicts.

The discussions surrounding the case centre not only on the offender and his or her behaviour, but also on the needs of the victims and the community. Community sentencing is an attempt to empower communities and to provide a mechanism for residents, aboriginal and nonaboriginal alike, to become directly involved in the delivery of justice services.

In cases adjudicated in sentencing circles, the judge sets an upper limit on the sentence that may be imposed. Participants in the circle informally discuss the offender and his or her circumstances. When the discussion has concluded, a consensus on the most appropriate sentence is reached, and this is the disposition that is imposed on the offender. Circle sentencing not only empowers the community but also expands the information base from which sentencing decisions are made. In addition to considering the facts of the case and the circumstance of the offender, the discussions in sentencing circles often include a dialogue on problems that exist in the community and how these can be addressed and resolved.[31]

An amendment to the *Criminal Code* in 1995 codified the purpose and principles of sentencing in Canada.

Purpose

718. The fundamental purpose of sentencing is to contribute, along with crime prevention initiatives, to respect for the law and the maintenance of a just, peaceful and safe society by imposing just sanctions that have one or more of the following objectives:

    (a) to denounce unlawful conduct;

    (b) to deter the offender and other persons from committing offences;

    (c) to separate offenders from society, where necessary;

    (d) to assist in rehabilitating offenders;

    (e) to provide reparations for harm done to victims or to the community; and

    (f) to promote a sense of responsibility in offenders, and acknowledgment of the harm done to victims and to the community.

This section simply sets out the objectives of the sentencing process, as developed within the common law. A more controversial sentencing principle emerged, however, in the same amendment to the *Criminal Code*. Section 718.2(e) states: "A court that imposes a sentence shall also take into consideration the following principles: (e) all available sanctions other than imprisonment that are reasonable in the circumstances should be considered for all offenders, with particular attention to the circumstances of Aboriginal offenders."

This principle was more clearly set out in the Supreme Court of Canada's decision in *R. v. Gladue.*[32] In this case the Supreme Court made it very clear that sentencing judges must take into account the unique circumstances of Aboriginal peoples in sentencing—that the kind of sentence appropriate for an Aboriginal person may well be quite different from the kind of sentence appropriate for a non-Aboriginal person, whether he or she is living on or off a reserve. This decision has, perhaps understandably, provoked a significant amount of discussion, with both Aboriginal and non-Aboriginal support and criticism. Some argue that the decision is a politically correct justification of inequality, while others argue that *Gladue* represents an important first step toward recognizing the distinct nature of First Nations peoples and their long-standing overrepresentation within Canada's criminal justice system.

Consider the recent decision of the Ontario Court of Appeal in *R. v. Peters.*[33] Justice Blair set out the facts of the case:

The respondent and the victim were acquaintances. They had an earlier altercation but had temporarily reconciled their differences until they found themselves together, along with the victim's boyfriend, at a bar on March 8, 2008. Ms. Peters, the respondent, had been drinking and during the conversation took offence at something the victim said. She pushed the victim. The scuffle escalated and the boyfriend intervened to attempt to separate the pair. While he was doing so, the respondent lunged past him and swung the beer bottle she was holding at the victim's head, breaking the bottle with the blow. She then followed through with her swing in a downward motion with the broken bottle, causing two lacerations to the victim's face that required 21 stitches to close.

Nearly a year after the incident, the victim was still experiencing continuing pain in her left eye and face, headaches, left eyelid muscle spasms, and facial asymmetry. The scars remain visible and may require plastic surgery.

The respondent pled guilty to aggravated assault after the preliminary hearing and after the complainant had testified at that hearing. At the sentencing hearing, the Crown sought a custodial sentence of 12 to 18 months. The defence suggested a suspended sentence followed by two years probation. A conditional sentence was not open to the sentencing judge because the amendments to the *Criminal Code*, R.S.C. 1985, c. C-46, in 2007 prohibit the granting of such a sentence where a serious persona injury offence—of which aggravated assault is an example—has been committed.

After considering all of the various factors involved and in particular, the Gladue report, the sentencing judge imposed a suspended three-year sentence with a lengthy series of probationary terms during that period. The Crown now seeks to appeal that sentence.

Justice Blair went on to dismiss the appeal by the Crown, quoting from former Chief Justice Antonio Lamer,

A sentencing judge ... enjoys a position of advantage over an appellate judge in being able to directly assess the sentencing submissions of both the Crown and the offender. A sentencing judge also possesses the unique qualifications of experience and judgment from having served on the front lines of our criminal justice system. Perhaps most importantly, the sentencing judge will normally preside near or within the community which has suffered the consequences of the offender's crime. As such, the sentencing judge will have a strong sense of the particular blend of sentencing goals that will be "just and appropriate" for the protection of that community. The determination of a just and appropriate sentence is a delicate art which attempts to balance carefully the societal goals of sentencing against the moral blameworthiness of the offender and the circumstances of the offence, while at all times taking into account the needs and current conditions of and in the community. The discretion of a sentencing judge should thus not be interfered with lightly.

Justice Blair concluded in *Peters*:

I am not persuaded that the sentence imposed was manifestly unfit. In her factum, Ms. Papadopoulos submits that "[a]n offender, irrespective of descent, who violently swings a beer bottle at a female victim's head, resulting in two serious gashes, ongoing pain, and facial scarring requiring surgery must serve a custodial sentence." Respectfully, while such a result may often be the case, to say that an offender in such circumstances—particularly an aboriginal offender—must serve a custodial sentence is to state the sentiment too strongly, and is inconsistent with the Gladue jurisprudence and, indeed, the jurisprudence respecting sentencing generally.

The Crown relied on this Court's recent decision in *R. v. Chickekoo*, 2008 ONCA 488 (CanLII), 2008 ONCA 488, a case with some similarities to this case. There, this Court upheld an 18 month sentence plus two years probation for an aboriginal female who broke a beer bottle over a victim's head, leaving the victim permanently disfigured. There are distinctions between the cases, however. In Chickekoo, the injuries were more severe and the appellant's adult criminal record was more pronounced. In any event, the two cases provide an example of how sentencing judges can arrive at different decisions in the proper exercise of their sentencing discretion, depending upon the nuances of the circumstances. I am not persuaded that the decision in Chickekoo leads to the conclusion that the decision of the sentencing judge here was manifestly unfit.

Consider, alternatively, the contrary view, expressed by Justice Watt in dissent:

With respect to the views of my colleagues, I am satisfied that the reasons of the sentencing judge reveal misapprehensions of relevant evidence (compliance with prior probation orders and the number of prior convictions or findings of guilt) and errors in principle (failure to give effect to the predominant principles of denunciation, deterrence, promotion of responsibility and acknowledgement of harm) and resulted in the imposition of a sentence for a serious and violent offence that is manifestly unfit.

In the result, I would grant leave to appeal, allow the appeal, set aside the sentence imposed at trial and in its place substitute a sentence of imprisonment for 12 months to be followed by a period of probation for three years on the same terms as those imposed by the sentencing judge. The term of imprisonment that I would impose is circumscribed by the position of Crown counsel on appeal and should not be taken as dispositive of the lowest end of the appropriate range of sentence for aggravated assault in circumstances such as these.

CONCLUSION: THE CRIMINAL LAW AS A BAROMETER OF CULTURE

The criminal law, like all forms of law, is, for better or worse, a barometer of the culture in which we live. In closing, we should recall a point made at the outset of this chapter: the task of those who create, enforce, and administer this law is to continually question the circumstances in which such force should be used. To paraphrase Churchill, how we define and respond to our criminals will tell us a lot about ourselves.

WEB LINKS

International Centre for Criminal Law Reform and Criminal Justice Policy
http://icclr.law.ubc.ca/
This website has an excellent publications page that provides access to documents on issues of criminal law.

Criminal Lawyers' Association
http://www.criminallawyers.ca/
This is the website for the Criminal Lawyers' Association, an organization of criminal lawyers in Canada. It provides direct links to most national and many international sites of interest to criminal lawyers, including links to relevant statutes, to Supreme Court decisions, journals, and to other associations of criminal lawyers.

Criminal Code of Canada
http://laws.justice.gc.ca/en/C-46/index.html
The text of the *Criminal Code* is available online from the Department of Justice.

QUESTIONS FOR DISCUSSION

1. Should restorative justice become a much more important part of our responses to crime within our communities, and if so, how? Is the majority or the dissenting position in the *Peters* case more compelling? Does the decision suggest that there is a lack of equality in sentencing? Discuss.
2. Self-induced intoxication remains as a defence, despite section 33.1 of the *Code*. Describe the ambit of the defence after *Bouchard-Lebrun* and discuss its value in current criminal law and procedure.
3. Do you agree or disagree with Churchill's observation that the strength of a civilization is to be seen in the way it responds to crime? Why?

FURTHER READING

Gold, A.D. *The Practitioner's Criminal Code, 2014 Edition.* Toronto: Lexis-Nexis, 2014.
   This annotated code, prepared as a hardcover edition and ebook, is an extremely useful source of information about the changing content of Canada's *Criminal Code*. The annotations allow the student to understand, at least in a cursory manner, the changes to law over time.
Stuart, D., R. Delisle, and S. Coughlan. *Learning Canadian Criminal Law.* 12th ed. Toronto: Carswell, 2012.
   This text provides an introduction to the criminal law in Canada, covering the subject matter in a compelling manner. The text is exhaustive and its emphasis on purposes of the law, elements of a crime, defences, and recent key judicial decisions provides students with the essential building blocks of criminal law.
Verdun-Jones, S. *Criminal Law in Canada: Cases, Questions, and the Code.* 5th ed. Toronto: Nelson Thomson Learning, 2010.
   This text presents a very useful combination of general principles of the criminal law and an analysis of specific cases. The book's 12 chapters cover subjective and objective liability in the *mens rea* of crime, the *actus reus* elements of a criminal offence, causation, regulatory offences, modes of participation in crime, mental disorder as a defence to crime, and, more generally, defences to criminal charges. An excellent source of information for an informed lay reader.

NOTES

1. A.W. Mewett and M. Manning, *Criminal Law* (Toronto: Butterworths, 1978), 11.
2. H. Schwendinger and J. Schwendinger, "Defenders of Order or Guardians of Human Rights?" in *Critical Criminology*, edited by I. Taylor, P. Walton, and J. Young (London, U.K.: Routledge and Kegan Paul, 1975), 132–7.
3. S. Box, *Deviance, Reality and Society*, 2nd ed. (London, U.K.: Holt, Rinehart and Winston, 1981), 97.
4. *R. v. Cooper*, (1980) 1 S.C.R. 1149.
5. O.W. Holmes [1863], cited in D. Stuart and R. Delisle, *Learning Canadian Criminal Law* (Toronto: Carswell, 1986), 254–5.
6. Cited in Stuart and Delisle, *Learning Canadian Criminal Law*, 255.
7. *R. v. Hundal*, [1993] 79 C.C.C. (3d) 97 at 99–109 (S.C.C.). (Reproduced with permission of Canada Law Book, through the Canadian Copyright Licensing Agency [CANCOPY].)
8. See *Reference re: Section 94 (2) of the Motor Vehicle Act (B.C.)* (1986), 147 D.L.R. (3d) 539.
9. Mewett and Manning, *Criminal Law*, 43.
10. Ibid., 302.
11. (1975), 20 C.C.C. (2d) 449 (S.C.C.).
12. *R. v. Point*, 2003 ABCA 113.
13. [1994] 93 C.C.C. (3d) 21 (S.C.C.).
14. *R. v. Bouchard-Lebrun*, 2011 S.C.C. 58 [2011] 3 S.C.R. 575.
15. [1980] 2 S.C.R. 120.
16. [1985] 1 S.C.R. 570.
17. *Pappajohn v. R.*, [1980] 2 S.C.R. 120.
18. 131 C.C.C. (3d) 481. (1999).
19. 131 C.C.C. (3d) 494. (1999).
20. A. Young, *Justice Defiled* (Toronto: Key Porter Books, 2003), 73.
21. Ibid.
22. This section on the Ewanchuk case is taken from Neil Boyd, *Big Sister: How Extreme Feminism Has Betrayed the Fight for Sexual Equality* (Vancouver: Greystone, 2004), 177–9. See also *R. v. Hutchinson*, 2014 SCC 19.
23. R.S., 1985, c. C-46, s. 34; 1992, c. 1, s. 60(F).
24. 55 C.C.C. (3d) 97 (S.C.C.).
25. *R. v. Ramdass* (1983), 2 C.C.C. (3d) 247 at 249 (Ont. C.A.).
26. C.C. Ruby, *Sentencing*, 3rd ed. (Toronto: Butterworths, 1987), Pg. 15.
27. Ibid., 21–2.
28. *R. v. Horon* (1990), 58 C.C.C. (3d) 418 at 420–3. (Reproduced with permission of Canada Law Book, through the Canadian Copyright Licensing Agency [CANCOPY].)

29. The Centre for Restorative Justice. Found at: http://www.sfu.ca/crj/.
30. Jonathan Rudin, "Pushing Back—A Response to the Drive for the Standardization of Restorative Justice Programs in Canada," Paper presented at the 6th International Conference on Restorative Justice, Vancouver, 2003.
31. M.A. Jackson and C.T. Griffiths, eds., *Canadian Criminology; Perspectives on Crime and Criminality,* 2nd ed. (Toronto: Harcourt Brace, 1995), 396. (Reprinted with permission of Nelson Thomson Learning, a division of ThomsonLearning.)
32. [1999] 1 S.C.R. 688.
33. *R. v. Peters,* 2010 ONCA 30 (CanLII) (see http://www.canlii.org/en/on/onca/doc/2010/2010onca30/2010onca30html).

References

Boyd, N. *Big Sister: How Extreme Feminism Has Betrayed the Fight for Sexual Equality.* Vancouver: Greystone, 2004.

———. *High Society: Legal and Illegal Drugs in Canada.* Toronto: Key Porter, 1991.

———. *The Last Dance: Murder in Canada.* Scarborough: Prentice-Hall, 1988.

Boyle, C.M. *Sexual Assault.* Toronto: Carswell, 1984.

Grosman, B., ed. *New Directions in Sentencing.* Toronto: Butterworths, 1980.

Healy, P. "*R. v. Bernard:* Difficulties with Voluntary Intoxication." *McGill Law Journal* 35 (1990): 610.

Jackson, M.A., and C.T. Griffiths. *Canadian Criminology: Perspectives on Crime and Criminality.* 2nd ed. Toronto: Harcourt Brace, 1995.

Law Reform Commission of Canada. *Recodifying Criminal Law: Working Paper 31.* Ottawa: Law Reform Commission of Canada, 1988.

Mewett, A.W. *An Introduction to the Criminal Process in Canada.* Toronto: Carswell, 1987.

Osborne, J. "Rape Law Reform: The New Cosmetic for Canadian Women." *Women and Politics* 4 (1984): 49.

Packer, H. *Limits of the Criminal Sanction.* Stanford: Stanford University Press, 1968.

Ruby, C.C. *Sentencing.* 5th ed. Toronto: Butterworths, 1999.

Schur, E. *Victimless Crimes.* Englewood Cliffs, NJ: Prentice-Hall, 1974.

Stuart, D., R. Delisle, and S. Coughlan. *Learning Canadian Criminal Law.* 11th ed. Toronto: Carswell, 2009.

Verdun-Jones, S. *Criminal Law in Canada, Cases, Questions and the Code.* 4th ed. Toronto: Nelson Thomson, 2006.

Williams, G. *The Mental Element in Crime.* Jerusalem: Magnes Press, 1965.

Zimring, F., and G. Hawkins. *Deterrence.* Chicago: University of Chicago Press, 1974.

APPENDIX

Canadian Charter of Rights and Freedoms
Part 1—Schedule B of the Constitution Act, 1982

Whereas Canada is founded upon principles that recognize the supremacy of God and the rule of law:

Guarantee of Rights and Freedoms

1. The *Canadian Charter of Rights and Freedoms* guarantees the rights and freedoms set out in it subject only to such reasonable limits prescribed by law as can be demonstrably justified in a free and democratic society.

Fundamental Freedoms

2. Everyone has the following fundamental freedoms:
   - (a) freedom of conscience and religion;
   - (b) freedom of thought, belief, opinion and expression, including freedom of the press and other media of communication;
   - (c) freedom of peaceful assembly; and
   - (d) freedom of association.

Democratic Rights

3. Every citizen of Canada has the right to vote in an election of members of the House of Commons or of a legislative assembly and to be qualified for membership therein.

4. (1) No House of Commons and no legislative assembly shall continue for longer than five years from the date fixed for the return of the writs at a general election of its members.

   (2) In time of real or apprehended war, invasion or insurrection, a House of Commons may be continued by Parliament and a legislative assembly may be continued by the legislature beyond five years if such continuation is not opposed by the votes of more than one-third of the members of the House of Commons or the legislative assembly, as the case may be.

5. There shall be a sitting of Parliament and of each legislature at least once every twelve months.

Mobility Rights

6. (1) Every citizen of Canada has the right to enter, remain in and leave Canada.
   (2) Every citizen of Canada and every person who has the status of a permanent resident of Canada has the right
      (a) to move to and take up residence in any province; and
      (b) to pursue the gaining of a livelihood in any province.
   (3) The rights specified in subsection (2) are subject to
      (a) any laws or practices of general application in force in a province other than those that discriminate among persons primarily on the basis of province of present or previous residence; and
      (b) any laws providing for reasonable residency requirements as a qualification for the receipt of publicly provided social services.
   (4) Subsections (2) and (3) do not preclude any law, program or activity that has as its object the amelioration in a province of conditions of individuals in that province who are socially or economically disadvantaged if the rate of employment in that province is below the rate of employment in Canada.

Legal Rights

7. Everyone has the right to life, liberty and security of the person and the right not to be deprived thereof except in accordance with the principles of fundamental justice.
8. Everyone has the right to be secure against unreasonable search or seizure.
9. Everyone has the right not to be arbitrarily detained or imprisoned.
10. Everyone has the right on arrest or detention
      (a) to be informed promptly of the reasons therefor;
      (b) to retain and instruct counsel without delay and to be informed of that right; and
      (c) to have the validity of the detention determined by way of *habeas corpus* and to be released if the detention is not lawful.
11. Any person charged with an offence has the right
      (a) to be informed without unreasonable delay of the specific offence;
      (b) to be tried within a reasonable time;
      (c) not to be compelled to be a witness in proceedings against that person in respect of the offence;
      (d) to be presumed innocent until proven guilty according to law in a fair and public hearing by an independent and impartial tribunal;
      (e) not to be denied reasonable bail without just cause;
      (f) except in the case of an offence under military law tried before a military tribunal, to the benefit of trial by jury where the maximum punishment for the offence is imprisonment for five years or a more severe punishment;
      (g) not to be found guilty on account of any act or omission unless, at the time of the act or omission, it constituted an offence under Canadian or international law or was criminal according to the general principles of law recognized by the community of nations;

(h)   if finally acquitted of the offence, not to be tried for it again and, if finally found guilty and punished for the offence, not to be tried or punished for it again; and

(i)   if found guilty of the offence and if the punishment for the offence has been varied between the time of commission and the time of sentencing, to the benefit of the lesser punishment.

12.   Everyone has the right not to be subjected to any cruel and unusual treatment or punishment.

13.   A witness who testifies in any proceedings has the right not to have any incriminating evidence so given used to incriminate that witness in any other proceedings, except in a prosecution for perjury or for the giving of contradictory evidence.

14.   A party or witness in any proceedings who does not understand or speak the language in which the proceedings are conducted or who is deaf has the right to the assistance of an interpreter.

Equality Rights

15.   (1)   Every individual is equal before and under the law and has the right to the equal protection and equal benefit of the law without discrimination and, in particular, without discrimination based on race, national or ethnic origin, colour, religion, sex, age or mental or physical disability.

        (2)   Subsection (1) does not preclude any law, program or activity that has as its object the amelioration of conditions of disadvantaged individuals or groups including those that are disadvantaged because of race, national or ethnic origin, colour, religion, sex, age or mental or physical disability.

Official Languages of Canada

16.   (1)   English and French are the official languages of Canada and have equality of status and equal rights and privileges as to their use in all institutions of the Parliament and government of Canada.

        (2)   English and French are the official languages of New Brunswick and have equality of status and equal rights and privileges as to their use in all institutions of the legislature and government of New Brunswick.

        (3)   Nothing in this Charter limits the authority of Parliament or a legislature to advance the equality of status or use of English and French.

17.   (1)   Everyone has the right to use English or French in any debates and other proceedings of Parliament.

        (2)   Everyone has the right to use English or French in any debates and other proceedings of the legislature of New Brunswick.

18.   (1)   The statutes, records and journals of Parliament shall be printed and published in English and French and both language versions are equally authoritative.

        (2)   The statutes, records and journals of the legislature of New Brunswick shall be printed and published in English and French and both language versions are equally authoritative.

19. (1) Either English or French may be used by any person in, or in any pleading in or process issuing from, any court established by Parliament.

(2) Either English or French may be used by any person in, or in any pleading in or process issuing from, any court of New Brunswick.

20. (1) Any member of the public in Canada has the right to communicate with, and to receive available services from, any head or central office of an institution of the Parliament or government of Canada in English or French, and has the same right with respect to any other office of any such institution where

(a) there is a significant demand for communications with and services from that office in such language; or

(b) due to the nature of the office, it is reasonable that communications with and services from that office be available in both English and French.

(2) Any member of the public in New Brunswick has the right to communicate with, and to receive available services from, any office of an institution of the legislature or government of New Brunswick in English or French.

21. Nothing in sections 16 to 20 abrogates or derogates from any right, privilege or obligation with respect to the English and French languages, or either of them, that exists or is continued by virtue of any other provision of the Constitution of Canada.

22. Nothing in sections 16 to 20 abrogates or derogates from any legal or customary right or privilege acquired or enjoyed either before or after the coming into force of this Charter with respect to any language that is not English or French.

Minority Language Educational Rights

23. (1) Citizens of Canada

(a) whose first language learned and still understood is that of the English or French linguistic minority population of the province in which they reside, or

(b) who have received their primary school instruction in Canada in English or French and reside in a province where the language in which they received that instruction is the language of the English or French linguistic minority population of the province, have the right to have their children receive primary and secondary school instruction in that language in that province.

(2) Citizens of Canada of whom any child has received or is receiving primary or secondary school instruction in English or French in Canada, have the right to have all their children receive primary and secondary school instruction in the same language.

(3) The right of citizens of Canada under subsections (1) and (2) to have their children receive primary and secondary school instruction in the language of the English or French linguistic minority population of a province

(a) applies wherever in the province the number of children of citizens who have such a right is sufficient to warrant the provision to them out of public funds of minority language instruction; and

(b) includes, where the number of those children so warrants, the right to have them receive that instruction in minority language educational facilities provided out of public funds.

Enforcement

24. (1) Anyone whose rights or freedoms, as guaranteed by this Charter, have been infringed or denied may apply to a court of competent jurisdiction to obtain such remedy as the court considers appropriate and just in the circumstances.

(2) Where, in proceedings under subsection (1), a court concludes that evidence was obtained in a manner that infringed or denied any rights or freedoms guaranteed by this Charter, the evidence shall be excluded if it is established that, having regard to all the circumstances, the admission of it in the proceedings would bring the administration of justice into disrepute.

General

25. The guarantee in this Charter of certain rights and freedoms shall not be construed so as to abrogate or derogate from any Aboriginal, treaty or other rights or freedoms that pertain to the Aboriginal peoples of Canada including

(a) any rights or freedoms that have been recognized by the Royal Proclamation of October 7, 1763; and

(b) any rights or freedoms that now exist by way of land claims agreements or may be so acquired.

26. The guarantee in this Charter of certain rights and freedoms shall not be construed as denying the existence of any other rights or freedoms that exist in Canada.

27. This Charter shall be interpreted in a manner consistent with the preservation and enhancement of the multicultural heritage of Canadians.

28. Notwithstanding anything in this Charter, the rights and freedoms referred to in it are guaranteed equally to male and female persons.

29. Nothing in this Charter abrogates or derogates from any rights or privileges guaranteed by or under the Constitution of Canada in respect of denominational, separate or dissentient schools.

30. A reference in this Charter to a province or to the legislative assembly or legislature of a province shall be deemed to include a reference to the Yukon Territory and the Northwest Territories, or to the appropriate legislative authority thereof, as the case may be.

31. Nothing in this Charter extends the legislative powers of any body or authority.

Application of Charter

32. (1) This Charter applies

(a) to the Parliament and government of Canada in respect of all matters within the authority of Parliament including all matters relating to the Yukon Territory and Northwest Territories; and

(b)   to the legislature and government of each province in respect of all matters within the authority of the legislature of each province.

(2)   Notwithstanding subsection (1), section 15 shall not have effect until three years after this section comes into force.

33.   (1)   Parliament or the legislature of a province may expressly declare in an Act of Parliament or of the legislature, as the case may be, that the Act or a provision thereof shall operate notwithstanding a provision included in section 2 or sections 7 to 15 of this Charter.

(2)   An Act or a provision of an Act in respect of which a declaration made under this section is in effect shall have such operation as it would have but for the provision of this Charter referred to in the declaration.

(3)   A declaration made under subsection (1) shall cease to have effect five years after it comes into force or on such earlier date as may be specified in the declaration.

(4)   Parliament or a legislature of a province may re-enact a declaration made under subsection (1).

(5)   Subsection (3) applies in respect of a re-enactment made under subsection (4).

Citation

34.   This Part may be cited as the Canadian Charter of Rights and Freedoms.

GLOSSARY

access Considered an "incident of custody" and means that a non-custodial parent may have visiting or contact rights with the child. (p. 261)

actus reus Literally "the evil act," a key component of conviction for any criminal offence. For an individual to be convicted of a crime, *actus reus* and *mens rea* must coincide at the time of the offence. Without a coincidence of an evil act and an evil intent, there can be no conviction for crime. (p. 303)

administrative law A form of public law that obligates the state to act fairly in the practice of government. The law, which applies to decisions of the bureaucracy and of government-appointed tribunals, implies a responsibility to deliver services in an equitable manner. (p. 269)

administrative tribunals Bodies empowered by government to make decisions that range from purely non-discretionary decisions, such as applying the regulations or definitions of a particular statute, to quasi-judicial decisions, such as determining questions of fact or law. (p. 271)

adversarial system This system suggests that "the truth" is most likely to emerge from strong advocacy for opposing points of view. The adversarial system places its confidence in the counsel who appear before the court, in contrast to an *inquisitorial system* (see below in this glossary). (p. 147)

amending formula Sections of the *Constitution Act, 1982* that allow for changes to that legislation. At present in Canada, three sections allow for the

Constitution to be changed: sections 38, 41, and 43. (p. 100)

anarchist perspective on law Perspective that emphasizes the role of an oppressive and intrusive state as central to understanding social life. Anarchists typically endorse a non-state-based communitarian ethic, whereas libertarians view the rights of the individual as more deserving of support than the rights of the community. (p. 19)

articling An LL.B. graduate's period of learning in a legal setting and further series of tests referred to as Bar Admissions. Only upon successful completion of these criteria can a person be "called to the bar" of a province, and practise law. (p. 173)

audi alteram partem Latin maxim that means, literally, "hear the other side." This rule requires that parties to a dispute have a fair hearing, which includes notice of when and where the hearing is to be held, the opportunity to bring witnesses, and the right to cross-examine the witnesses brought by the opposing litigant. (p. 285)

bicameral Parliament A legislative body consisting of two houses that jointly enact laws for a country. In Canada, the bicameral Parliament is composed of the elected House of Commons and the appointed Senate. (p. 99)

books of authority Authoritative texts or commentaries on the meaning and development of specific forms of law and their applicable principles. (p. 54)

British North America Act, 1867 British statute that created Canada by politically joining Upper and Lower Canada (now Quebec and Ontario) with Nova Scotia and New Brunswick, and granted constitutional powers to the duly elected representatives of the Canadian people. It is Canada's original and defining source of law and sets out in sections 91 and 92 the respective powers of federal and provincial governments (see below in this glossary). In 1982, it was renamed the *Constitution Act, 1867.* (pp. 98)

Canadian Bill of Rights Arguably the precursor to the *Canadian Charter of Rights and Freedoms*, the Canadian *Bill of Rights* was a federal statute without the status of a constitutional document. The *Bill* was occasionally used to strike down legislation that offended its principles, but in other judgments it was said to be only a guide to be used by legislators in the construction of statutes. (p. 115)

Canadian Charter of Rights and Freedoms An entrenched charter of rights and freedoms that requires Canada's courts to strike down all federal, provincial, or municipal legislation that fails to conform to the *Charter*'s specific provisions. (p. 98)

Canadian Judicial Council Created by Parliament in 1971, its statutory mandate is to set out the *Judges Act*, which states that the council is established to "promote efficiency and uniformity, and to improve the quality of judicial service" in Canada's federally appointed courts. The council, which has 39 members and is chaired by the chief justice of Canada, is responsible for the disciplinary measures concerning all federally appointed judges. (p. 191)

case law Judicially constructed law—that is, law that is established by decisions in specific court cases, with the decisions of the Supreme Court of Canada established as final case law. (p. 54)

Charlottetown Accord An attempt to bring Quebec into the constitutional fold after the province refused to sign the *Constitution Act, 1982.* The accord was put to a referendum of the people of Canada in 1992, but rejected by both Quebec and the rest of the country. (p. 108)

child custody The determination of which parent is best prepared to have custody of a child or children is made in accordance with the admittedly vague standard of "the best interests of the child." (p. 240)

child support The obligation of a parent to contribute to the best of his or her financial ability to the care and costs of raising his or her children. Under federal law, child support is usually determined by applying a quantum from a table set out in the Federal Child Support Guidelines. (p. 240)

common-law relations A statutorily defined term that means a relationship between two people who, although not legally married to each other continuously, cohabited in a marriage-like relationship for at least three years, or if there is a child of the relationship by birth or adoption, cohabited in a marriage-like relationship of some permanence. (p. 237)

conflict resolution Also known as alternative dispute resolution, this new model for deciding disputes has been developed by communities and the legal profession as an option to the court process. Most common forms are mediation, a form of negotiated settlement between the disputing parties, and arbitration, which has a non-judicial officer determine how the issue in dispute between the parties should be resolved. (p. 153)

consent A defence to allegations that an intentional tort has been committed; can also be used as a defence in criminal law. (p. 210)

Constitution Act, 1982 A constitutional enactment, in 1982, that gave life to the Canadian Constitution as a legal creation of Canada itself. In addition to incorporating the *British North America Act, 1867*, the act also brought into existence both the entrenched *Canadian Charter of Rights and Freedoms* and various amending formulas to enable further change to the governance of the country. (p. 98)

Constitution Act of 1791 The British statute that divided Canada into Upper and Lower Canada. At the Canadians' request it also created legislative and executive governments in Canada, although these were both answerable to Britain. (p. 32)

constitutional law The rules that define and interpret the powers of federal and provincial governments and, as a consequence, establish the rights and responsibilities of citizens. (p. 98)

contributory negligence A partial defence for a defendant in a negligence action when it can be shown that the plaintiff was partially responsible for the harm suffered. (p. 217)

Controlled Drugs and Substances Act Legislation passed in 1997 as an update and relatively minor revision of the former *Narcotic Control Act*. (p. 54)

conviction In a criminal law context refers to the determination by a court that a person is responsible for or "guilty" of the crime that he or she has been accused of. (p. 302)

Criminal Code The federal statute, first enacted in 1892, which sets out most public crimes (such as assault, murder, and criminal negligence) and their penalties. (p. 203)

custom A source of law that derives from the practices and patterns of behaviour through which society has come to order itself. Sometimes referred to in Canada as "convention." (p. 47)

defences or mitigations of criminal responsibility Used by the accused to demonstrate that they were not criminally responsible for the crime that they committed, or that they had diminished responsibility. (p. 311)

defendant The person against whom a private law proceeding has been brought as well as the term used for the person who is charged in criminal law. (p. 210)

delegation In the context of administrative law, the term for the transfer by federal Parliament and provincial legislatures of some of their legislative duties to non-elected government officials. (p. 270)

dialectical materialism The doctrine or theory of history espoused by Marxism. In ancient Greek "dialectic" means dialogue or conversation, thus the doctrine of dialectical materialism holds that history progresses in stages that are based solely on the supremacy of different economic classes: feudalism replaced aristocracy, capitalism replaced feudalism, and socialism or communism will replace capitalism. (p. 13)

divorce A petition under federal jurisdiction for the dissolution of a marriage; since 1985, granted on the basis of living separate and apart for one year, or on the basis of adultery, mental or physical cruelty, alcoholism, or incarceration. (p. 238)

doctrine of fairness An extension of the principle of natural justice, which requires administrative tribunals to act with both substantive and procedural fairness to all parties. (p. 284)

domestic law The law of a single nation-state, which is different from the domestic laws of other nations and also from international law. (p. 34)

ejusdem generis **and** *noscitur a sociis* Although theoretically separate, these two Latin maxims essentially make the same point: the meaning of an ambiguous word or phrase within a statute is to be inferred from the context in which it appears. (p. 75)

ex turpi causa, non oritur actio Latin for "an action does not occur (or arise) for a base (or illegal) cause." (p. 217)

expressio unius est exclusio alterius Latin maxim requiring that the express mention of one class of subjects necessarily excludes another class of subjects. If a statute specifies that x is to be the subject of the statute, y is necessarily excluded from the ambit of this law. (p. 72)

Federal Court of Canada Composed of the Federal Court: Trial Division and the Federal Court: Appeal Division. The Trial Division has original jurisdiction in most cases where relief is claimed against the Crown as well as exclusive jurisdiction for judicial review of most decisions of federal boards, commissions, or other tribunals. The court's jurisdiction also includes interprovincial and federal–provincial disputes, intellectual property proceedings, admiralty matters, immigration proceedings, matters pertaining to the *Charter*, citizenship appeals, and appeals under certain federal statutes. The Appeal Division hears appeals from the Trial Division. (p. 146)

feminist theory of law A theory that places the subjugation of women and denial of the equality of women as central foci of centuries of lawmaking. This perspective views the oppression of women as the unexamined bedrock of the legal process. (p. 16)

feudalism The political and economic system of England that granted the aristocracy nobility and land in exchange for the labour and military service of serfs or vassals on the land. In France and New France, this system was referred to as the seigneurial system, whereby the aristocracy were called "seigneurs" and the serfs, "censitaires." (p. 32)

golden rule The rule of statutory interpretation that softens the impact of the plain meaning rule, requiring that although the ordinary sense of words is to be adhered to, that ordinary sense may be modified if it necessarily leads to an absurdity or incongruity within the statute. (p. 73)

Hansard The official report of the proceedings of Parliament. (p. 52)

hybrid offences Crimes in the *Criminal Code* for which the Crown attorney may decide (elect) whether to proceed by summary conviction or indictment. In determining whether to proceed by indictment, the Crown will assess the nature of the crime and the facts that are evident before the trial. (p. 325)

indictable offences Those crimes in the *Criminal Code* that are considered to be very serious and that carry substantial penalties. (p. 143)

injustice A word that refers to a situation in which the law or the legal system treats someone or something unfairly. The opposite of *justice* (see below in this glossary). (p. 5)

inquisitorial system A legal system that places its confidence in the judge or arbitrator, who is required to ask relevant questions in an effort to determine "the truth" of the matter. (p. 147)

intentional tort Torts that occur as a result of a wrongdoer intentionally (or apparently intentionally) harming another either physically or mentally. These include the torts of assault, trespass, and defamation, to name a few. (p. 202)

interdelegation A constitutionally permitted process whereby the federal government may delegate its powers to a provincially appointed tribunal, commission, or board; or the provincial government may transfer some of its powers to a federally appointed commission, board, or tribunal provided that not all the delegating authorities are transferred and that the receiving commission, tribunal, or board does not transfer the powers to any other body. (p. 270)

international law A form of law mediated by international institutions such as the United Nations. The law attempts to provide governance and accommodation of nations in relation to global treaties, conventions, and customs. It is usually enforceable through the use of international suasion, not through traditional judicial remedies. (p. 34)

intra vires Latin for "within the power of"; used as the antithesis of *ultra vires* (see below in this glossary). (p. 105)

judicial review The process whereby a court considers whether decisions of administrative tribunals were properly made or *ultra vires* the jurisdiction of the tribunal. Judicial review is not the same as an appeal, which refers to a court of higher jurisdiction rehearing a legal proceeding from a lower court. Administrative decisions can be judicially reviewed for a limited number of reasons, including abuse of discretion, violation of the principles of natural justice or procedural fairness, or failure to conform to the technicalities of the empowering legislation. (p. 271)

jury A panel of one's "peers" that is responsible for fact finding or determining the truth or falseness of facts in evidence at a trial. In Canada, the jury is mostly used in criminal proceedings and is not expected to make determinations on the law, a matter left to the trial judge. (p. 147)

justice A term derived from the Roman term for law, *justicia*, which means "to give each man his due." In modern terms it has come to represent an idea of legal fairness. It is often used to reflect the personal or societal understanding of the upholding of rights and the punishment of wrongs, when undertaken by the law. (p. 5)

laissez-faire capitalism Doctrine that the free market functions to the greatest good when left unfettered and unregulated by government. Some authors give different definitions based on notions of justice and human nature. (p. 14)

law schools The term used to refer to Faculties of Law at specific universities. Students gain admission to these institutions after completing an undergraduate degree, or a portion thereof, from a recognized university; one cannot attend directly from secondary school. Some universities now offer a law major in an Arts or Social Science bachelor's degree. (p. 173)

law societies Provincial associations (which can be subsets of the Canadian Bar

Association) that license lawyers to practise in each province in Canada. Licences are granted after a period of articling and successful completion of Bar Admission examinations. (p. 173)

legal realism An approach to law that takes account not only of doctrinal developments, but also the social, political, and economic bases of specific law. It is an empirically based system of analysis that arguably has its roots in positivism. (p. 12)

lex iniusta non est lex Latin for "an unjust law is no law at all," the principal tenet of the natural law perspective. (p. 9)

liability What the court decides in a private law action. In this situation, the court assesses fault and decides whether damages are awarded. Liability differs from a "finding of guilt," which is the determination that a judge must make before a wrongdoer can be convicted in criminal law. (p. 208)

limitations clause Section 1 of the *Canadian Charter of Rights and Freedoms* is often referred to as the "limitations" clause because it states that not all the rights guaranteed within the *Charter* are absolute, but are rather subject to "reasonable limits prescribed by law"—limits that "can be demonstrably justified in a free and democratic society." (p. 118)

LL.B. degree Bachelor of Laws degree granted from a law school in recognition that its holder has completed a university-mandated legal education. This degree alone does not entitle the holder to practise law in Canada. (p. 177)

LSAT (Law School Admission Test) An aptitude test developed in the United States as a means of determining suitability for legal education and the practice of law. Often criticized for its cultural ethnocentricity and its lack of useful performance indicators, the LSAT remains a requirement for admission to Canada's law schools. (p. 173)

Magna Carta A document attributed to King John of England in 1215 wherein he legally specified that royal powers were not absolute, ceding some power to his barons to change some of his decisions. It is seen as the first movement of English monarchism toward democracy. (p. 31)

marriage The legal definition of marriage currently applies only to state-registered heterosexual unions, though there remains considerable debate both within and outside the homosexual community as to whether same-sex marriages ought to be considered the legal equivalent of heterosexual marriages. See also the definition of spouse. (p. 238)

Marxism The theory that espouses the notion that law is created from an irreconcilable conflict between labour and capital. The theory is based upon a view of social life that emphasizes the guiding role of material circumstances, and the inherently contradictory nature of economic inequality. (p. 13)

Meech Lake Accord Part of a multi-pronged attempt to bring Quebec into the constitutional fold, after the province's refusal to sign the *Constitution Act, 1982*. The Meech Lake Accord foundered in the Manitoba legislature. (p. 108)

mens rea Latin for "evil mind," the intent to commit the act complained of. In order for an individual to be found guilty of a crime, he or she must have an "evil mind." (p. 56)

natural justice The written and unwritten rules and procedures to be followed by any person charged with the duty of adjudicating disputes. The chief rules are a duty to act fairly, to act in good faith, and to act impartially or without bias. (p. 281)

natural law A theory that has its roots in Judeo-Christian conceptions of social life. This theory holds that law and morality must be synonymous. (p. 9)

negligence A person or legal entity will be found to be negligent when his, her, or its conduct falls below the standard expected of the reasonable person in the specific circumstances in question, and when damages are incurred as a result of this negligence. (p. 202)

nemo judex This abbreviation of a Latin maxim means, literally, that no person should act as judge on his own behalf. In other words, the apprehension of bias on the part of the decision maker must be excluded from all decision making within an administrative tribunal, board, committee, or commission. (p. 285)

noscitur a sociis See *ejusdem generis*. (p. 75)

notwithstanding clause Section 33 of the *Canadian Charter of Rights and Freedoms*, which allows a legislature to enact laws that specifically "override" the rights and freedoms in the *Charter* by stating that the legislation will operate even though it could or does infringe constitutional rights. (p. 134)

nulla poena sine lege According to *The Concept of Law* by H.L.A. Hart, "there shall be no penalty without a valid law." (p. 9)

Oakes **case** A rule of Canadian constitutional interpretation first established by the Supreme Court of Canada in *R. v. Oakes* (1986). It applies to the use of the limitations clause and requires that the court apply a two-part test of central importance and proportionality before allowing a validly enacted federal or provincial statute to infringe on a right or freedom set out in the *Charter*. (p. 119)

objective intention An element of *mens rea* that is applied in certain cases and determines whether a reasonable person would have expected a criminal deed to flow from the defendant's actions. (p. 307)

parent Can be a mother, father, or person who has treated a child as if the child were his or her own. All parents have a legal responsibility to provide support for their children. (p. 240)

parliamentary supremacy The doctrine that Parliament is the supreme lawmaker and no person or body (including the courts) has the legal right to override or set aside the laws enacted by Parliament. (p. 116)

patriation A term used to refer to a country's assuming complete control of its own constitution. In Canada, as long as constitutional amendments were made by Britain, the Constitution was not patriated. The *Constitution Act, 1982* patriated the Constitution by creating an "amending formula" that allowed the Canadian legislatures the right and the responsibility to make changes to our constitutional documents. (p. 99)

plain meaning rule The rule of statutory interpretation that dictates that an ambiguous section of a statute is to be read in accordance with its literal meaning, even if a literal reading appears to lead to an incongruous result. (p. 73)

plaintiff A person who has been harmed by the actions of another and commences a lawsuit to redress the wrong, usually by seeking an award of damages. (p. 203)

positivism The theory that law can be understood as a valid set of rules whose content is to be determined through a logical system of precedents, rather than through the application of moral considerations. (p. 7)

precedent "A judgment or decision of a court of law cited as an authority for deciding a similar set of facts; a case [that] serves as an authority for the legal principle embodied in its decision" (*Osborn's Concise Law Dictionary*). (p. 86)

private law An area of law that responds to matters that are primarily of private interest; a type of law that, at least in theory, regulates not so much the interests of the collective, but primarily various economic relations among individuals and their legal creations. (p. 35)

procedural law Sets out the process, formalities, or mechanisms for enforcing the law. Also referred to as *lex fori,* which means the law of the forum or court in which a case is tried. (p. 34)

provincial court The first stop in the hierarchy of Canada's court system. The trial courts of the province have four divisions: criminal, youth, small claims, and family; 90 percent of all criminal offences are heard in provincial court, criminal division. (p. 142)

public law An area of law that is primarily concerned with the public interest and the regulation of matters of collective rather than individual interest. (p. 35)

punitive damages Damages that are awarded in tort beyond what is necessary to compensate an individual or a legal entity for losses sustained and for pain and suffering. The purpose of punitive damages is to deter the conduct in question, thus bringing a public law objective to the realm of private law. (p. 204)

Quebec Act Statute passed by the British Parliament in 1774 that provided for, among other things, the right of Roman Catholics to participate in government and the use of the French language in civil law. (p. 32)

reasonable person A fictional character who exists in private law (primarily tort) and who decides whether explanations offered by the wrongdoer are rational. (p. 203)

restorative justice Models of dispute resolution, such as sentencing circles, that can apply to Aboriginal populations and are said to more accurately reflect the participants' interpretations of justice than those imposed through the British-based Canadian legal system. (pp. 162, 328)

Royal Proclamation of 1763 The Treaty of Paris, signed in 1763, ended the Seven Years' War between the French (and its allies) and the British (and its allies). The British acquired most of the French empire in North America, including Canada. Attempting to resolve the growing dissatisfaction of the First Nations people living in Canada, the British issued the Royal Proclamation, which specified conditions of British contact with Aboriginals; set out political, legal, and religious rights of the French in Quebec; and promised democratically elected institutions for English Canadians. (p. 32)

rule in Heydon's case The rule that states that the intention of a statute is to be derived from an understanding of the "mischief" that the law aims to correct—the "defect" in the common law that existed prior to the implementation of the statute. This rule is often referred to as the "mischief rule." (p. 73)

sections 91 and 92, *British North America Act, 1867* The two sections of Canada's Constitution that define the areas of jurisdiction where the provinces can enact laws (s. 92) and where the federal Parliament can enact laws (s. 91). Section 91 of the act also reserves a residual right to the federal government to enact laws that deal with Canada's "Peace, Order, and Good Government." (p. 98)

sentencing The task of imposing a penalty for a crime. The purposes of sentencing are set out in section 718 of the *Criminal Code*—denouncing unlawful conduct, deterring the offender and others, separating offenders from society where necessary, assisting in rehabilitation, providing reparation for harm done to victims, and promoting a sense of responsibility within offenders, and acknowledgement of the harm done by their actions. (p. 325)

separation A term used in both federal law and provincial law referring to the period after a couple determines that they will no longer live together as partners. Separation is usually followed up with a "separation agreement," which is a document signed by both parties to the separation outlining how the couple intend to resolve the issues arising from their marriage, such as custody, support, and division of assets. If the separating parties cannot reach an agreement, they may apply to a court to resolve the outstanding legal issues arising on separation. (p. 240)

social contract A term usually attributed to Jean-Jacques Rousseau, who in 1762 wrote *Social Contract or Political Right,* in which he states, "The problem is to find a form of association which will defend and protect with the whole common force the person and goods of each associate, and in which each, while uniting himself with all, may still obey himself alone, and remain as free as before." This is the fundamental problem for which the social contract is said to provide the solution. (p. 8)

sovereign The supreme authority in an independent political society. It is now considered to mean the absolute lawmaker. In Canada, the sovereign now refers to the legislative sovereign—Parliament, which can make or unmake any law, subject only to the limitations that Parliament has placed on itself, such as those emanating from the Constitution or the judiciary. (p. 7, 8)

spousal support The provision of support for a spouse in the event of marriage breakdown. Support is to be granted in specific circumstances, depending upon a mix of factors including the economic consequences of the dissolution of the marriage and the efforts made by each spouse to become economically self-sufficient. (p. 240)

spouse As a result of the passage of Bill C-38, a spouse may be one of a man and a woman who are married to each other, or a couple of the same sex. In July 2005 Canada passed this legislation, which provides for the equality of heterosexual and homosexual men and women within civil unions, although religious organizations can continue to bar homosexual men and women from marriage within their churches, synagogues, or mosques. (p. 239)

Star Chamber Derives its title from the Court of Star Chamber, which from 1487 to 1640 sat *in camera* (privately) and handed down legal and often arbitrary decisions that were not open to scrutiny by the public. (p. 148)

stare decisis Latin for "to stand by decided things." The term refers to the development of case law within the context of a legal hierarchy. (p. 86)

statute law Law that is enacted by duly elected legislatures, whether federal or provincial. (p. 37)

strict and absolute liability offences Offences that arise from the breach of regulatory or public welfare statutes and that do not typically lead to incarceration; nor is intent a necessary element of the offence. The fact that the action occurred is evidence that the offence was committed. Usually in these situations, the onus is on the defendant to prove that he or she was not the cause of the offence. (p. 310)

subjective intention An element of *mens rea* that asks the question whether the defendant expected that a criminal deed would result from his or her actions. (p. 307)

substantive law The actual law, as opposed to adjectival or procedural law. Substantive laws set out specific penalties for specific kinds of conduct by the public that is prohibited by statute. (p. 34)

suffragette A woman in Britain, Canada, or the United States in the early twentieth century who was a member of a group that demanded voting rights for women and who increased awareness of the matter with a series of public protests. The suffragette Emily Davidson threw herself under the king's horse at the Derby in 1913 to draw attention to the campaign. (p. 16)

summary conviction offences Crimes specified in the *Criminal Code* that are considered to be less serious than others and that carry a maximum sentence of a fine of no more than $2000 or six months' incarceration. (p. 325)

superior courts of the province There are two divisions within the superior courts of the provinces: the Trial Division, which hears the most significant of criminal and civil cases, and the Appeal Division, which hears all appeals prior to possible consideration by the Supreme Court of Canada. (p. 142)

Supreme Court of Canada The court of last resort in our country since 1949; the Supreme Court has nine justices and hears appeals in relation to significant criminal and civil cases, and references regarding constitutional matters. (p. 142)

tort A private wrong (as opposed to a crime, which is a public wrong punishable by the state). Torts can only be pursued as a private matter by or against another individual, corporation, or arm of government. (p. 201, 224)

ultra vires Latin for "beyond the power." Used in constitutional interpretation when a court strikes down or declares invalid legislation that has been enacted outside a legislature's constitutional authority or jurisdiction. (p. 105)

INDEX